Restoring Climate Stability
By Managing Ecological Disorder

A Non-Equilibrium Thermodynamic Approach
To Climate Change

Written By:
Daniel Arthur Young

Carbon Resources Research
PO Box 99
Hyde Park, VT 05655

Phone: (802) 888-4675
Cell: (802) 730-6899
dyoung6820@comcast.net

Library of Congress Control Number: 2017916642
CreateSpace Independent Publishing Platform, North Charleston, SC

I dedicate this book to my grandsons Jos and Luc Boswell who helped me greatly with conceptual matters and with computer technology during its production.

Contents

Table of Contents

Table of Contents (Continued)

PART THREE
ENTROPY AND ORDER

PART FOUR
PHYSICAL MANIFESTATIONS OF ENTROPY

Table of Contents (Continued)

PART FIVE

ENERGY INDUCED ORDERING

PART SIX

THE BIOSPHERE

Table of Contents (Continued)

Table of Contents (Continued)

PART NINE
BIOCHAR – A TOOL

PART TEN
CONCLUSIONS

List of Illustrations

List of Illustrations (Continued)

List of Illustrations (Continued)

Author's Introductory Comment

Our Closed Planetary System

There is nothing more fundamental to thermodynamics, and therefore to science and all of human experience, than the fact that order emerges out of chaos when energy flows through a constrained environment. This is why a heat engine can produce work and why your refrigerator can get cold. The order produced is quantitatively related to the energy flow and to the characteristics of constraints on the environment. Complex systems are the result of extensive ordering of system contents due to prolonged, continuous energy flow.

A thermodynamically closed system, one whose boundaries pass energy but not matter, like the surface of the earth, rejects disorder, becoming more and more ordered, complex and functional all the time. In short, disorder dissipates, order sustains and organizes. This is the basis for evolution on certain planetary bodies, and it is the root of all technological progress.

Life precipitates naturally and spontaneously in such a system. Like a morning mist on the meadow, the opacity of randomness disperses revealing the clarity of order as soon as energy flow is established through the system. If the energy flow is impeded in any way, the order diminishes, reverting to randomness and disorder again. Carbon dioxide in our atmosphere impedes the flow of energy through our system, allowing it to revert to disorder and dissipate, letting randomness retake the system.

Author's Introductory Comment

Our new imperative is to encourage and enhance energy flow and the accumulation of order in our planetary system. Reducing carbon dioxide levels in our atmosphere will free up the path of energy flow, allowing the system to continue to produce the order necessary for biological proliferation and evolution to continue. But to maintain the order in the system it is necessary to preserve and protect the order that has already been established.

Nature requires an order balance. Through the process of photosynthesis, nature creates persistent order, but our appetite for consumption of nature's products drains the order out of the system. When we attempt to consume nature's order faster than nature creates it, the system cannot keep up with demand, and it breaks down.

We consume nature's order to the maximum extent, and at the maximum rate, we can. Our unlimited consumption of nature's ordered products leaves a system severely deprived of order, and the build-up of thermal opacity in our atmosphere leaves it unable to reorganize itself.

We must preserve the order that nature creates if we are to ensure the habitability of the earth. Unfortunately our culture has been determined to do just the opposite, to consume nature's order as fast as we can without regard for the consequences. Disorder has both material and thermal consequences. You cannot disorganize what nature has put together without altering its thermal parameters. This book discusses some of the reasons why this is so.

Preface

A Search for Lost Worlds, of the Past and Future

Preface Summary

Energy flows constantly and consistently through all systems on the surface of the earth. If more energy flows into the system than flows out, the system accumulates energy and becomes warmer and more disordered. If more energy flows out of the system than flows in, the system depletes its energy reserve and becomes cooler and more ordered. A balanced system in which energy discharge and energy input are the same remains at a constant temperature.

Entropy, disorder, is intimately related to energy. It flows through systems in much the same way. If more entropy flows in than flows out the system accumulates entropy and becomes disordered. If more entropy flows out than flows in, system entropy content is depleted and the system becomes ordered.

Entropy content includes incoming entropy and also entropy created within the system by processes going on there. One can tell a great deal about the projected order and complexity of a system by analyzing incoming and outgoing entropy flows.

The biosphere, the total biomass content of the earth, is a measure of the order of the planet. Living matter is the most ordered state of matter we know, and its existence is an indication of a high entropy discharge rate. The Preface introduces some of these ideas and provides a starting point from which to approach the book

A Search for Lost Worlds, of the Past and Future

I grew up in a small town in southwest Connecticut. It was a relatively rural landscape, but it was within commuting distance of New York City, and it was being "discovered" as a haven, an ideal place to escape to, to own a home and raise a family. It was in the 1940's just after the end of World War II. The country was on the verge of recovery and Wilton was ripe for economic expansion.

The land in southwestern Connecticut was rich in natural resources. The hills were blanketed with a heavy carpet of mixed oak-hickory and beech-maple forested ecosystems[1]. Natural biomass was so thick it was in the way.

The first activity necessary to improve the value of a parcel of real estate was to clear it of unwanted biomass so that the land could be used for other purposes. Whether it was to be used for farmland, for public buildings, for commercial purposes, or for private homes, the natural biomass had to go.

In the post-war recovery and subsequent economic boom years, the town did grow, and the new American middle class took to the life style provided by Wilton in droves. To quote from Robert H. Russell, author of the book, "Wilton Connecticut – Three Centuries of People, Places and Progress"[2] about the period from 1945 to 1970:

> *Over ten thousand people came to Wilton in this twenty five year period and the population increased from 3,200 to 13,572. Over 2,750 houses, 7 schools, three school additions and 160 new roads were built.*

The population of Wilton in 2010 was 18,062. The rural community I had known, so rich in functional biomass had been replaced by homes, lawns, streets, commercial buildings, industries and all the other accouterments of society. What happened to all the rich stores of functional biomass?

My father was a landscape nurseryman. I always thought he was returning, in some small sense, the value taken from the land when first it had been coveted by its early inhabitants and "improved" for their own purposes.

While the plantings he created were selected for their beauty and function, they were not usually native varieties and therefore not as hardy, nor as functional in the environment, as the original plants they replaced. Their extent was restricted to suit the human sense of proportion and purpose, a mere minor fraction of the density and continuity of the original biomass.

I always thought the original decimation of the biomass had taken some major value from the land that we owed back. Things could only be made right again, in my view, by returning the function that we had removed in that original clearing of the land.

It always fascinated me to ponder how such obvious impediments to value the way things were could be missed so dearly for their obvious value in their absence later on. In the words of Joni Mitchel's, "Big Yellow Taxi", it was clearly a case of "Pave paradise, put in a parking lot". This book is a search for the values that we sacrificed in our search for economic well-being. I remain convinced that we decimated a major asset when we destroyed our stores of biomass.

Ancient philosophers intuitively realized that the order of the world had emerged out of chaos. They understood that the world that fathered them was not always as ordered and complex as the world of their experience. Though they didn't know why or how this came about, they wondered deeply about it and inquired in their hearts and minds what nature could tell them about this creative ordering process.

Robin Wall Kimmerer is the Director of the Center for Native Peoples and the Environment in Syracuse, NY. She is also Professor of Environmental and Forest Biology at the State University of New York College of Environmental Science and Biology there. She has written a book about the relationships between indigenous wisdom and scientific knowledge that she calls "Braiding Sweetgrass"[3].

In Her book, Dr. Kimmerer refers to ancient tribal beliefs in the "*dual powers of destruction and creation that shape the world*". This dynamic tension between chaos and order is rooted in mythology and creation stories in many cultures around the world including the themes of "God vs. the devil" in Christianity, Judaism and Islam.

Scientists, too, recognize the significance of the deteriorating effect of disorder on systems in the natural world. Josiah Willard Gibbs, in 1873, devised a method for evaluating the potential for change in a physical system. His famous equation for determining this potential, called the Gibbs free energy, is as follows:

$$\Delta G = \Delta H - T\Delta S$$

In this equation ΔG represents the change in Gibbs Free Energy, the potential for change, which always decreases to a minimum in spontaneous processes in the natural world. ΔH represents the change in energy content (specifically enthalpy content) of the system, a term that enhances the potential for order in the system. T is the temperature of the system. And ΔS is the change in entropy content of the system, a term that describes the rise of disorder in natural systems.

The Gibbs free energy concept supports the intuitive wisdom of tribal insight and myth. The mathematical precision of the sciences gives exactness, expansion and clarity to the indigenous wisdom of ancient peoples as well as to the mythology of religion. All reach the same conclusion: the inexorable imposition of disorder on natural systems must be counteracted by the input of energy to sustain the potential for constructive change.

As long as the energy term (ΔH) is greater than the entropy term (TΔS) the reacting system proceeds to develop in the direction of increasing order, growth and proliferation of natural systems. When the two terms are equal, ΔG equals zero and no processes at all can proceed. This condition is called equilibrium. All change ceases under equilibrium conditions. When the entropy term (TΔS) becomes greater than the energy term (ΔH) chemical processes will proceed to deteriorate in the direction of chaos, and so natural systems decline.

Accumulation of entropy in a system is a very serious problem. Natural processes become sluggish, slow down, stop and even reverse direction under excessively entropic conditions. Entropy escalation causes dissolution and deterioration of existing order. The only way to maintain a healthy operating condition in natural systems is to assure that the entropy created by natural processes is freely discharged from the system.

Ancient peoples knew that energy had to be provided to keep a system ordered, productive, and growing. People of the spirit looked on the system with wonder and awe. Religious teachings held that God was the driving force that made ordered conditions emerge. Now scientists are able to add to these points of view by quantifying the effects of entropy discharges.

The insights of the ancients endured, and they are central to our scientific understandings in the present. The creative power of energy in natural systems continues to be appreciated. The success of the scientific method of rational thought in unlocking the secrets of naturally ordered systems has been unprecedented.

But there are exceptions. We regularly find misinterpretations of scientific data and theories that lead to errors in our understanding of the universe. Charles Darwin's "random mutations", it turns out, are not random at all, leading to a much more complex and interesting understanding of evolution than Darwin had in mind. Isaac Newton's Law of Universal Gravitation is at variance with some observations of planetary orbits in ways that are better described by Einstein's concept of curved space-time.

Often whole realms of understanding are repudiated by new discoveries that give rise to new understandings of natural phenomena. One such advancement occurred in the science of thermodynamics in the latter half of the twentieth century. The Second Law of thermodynamics says that any and every spontaneous natural process results in an increase in the entropy (disorder) content of the universe. This law was formulated by the French scientist Sadi Carnot in 1824. A corollary to this law is that any system from which entropy cannot escape, any isolated system, will experience an increase in entropy content or disorder every time a spontaneous process occurs in the system. The entropy content of such a system proceeds toward an extreme, a maximally disordered state, in which no more change can occur. This condition is called equilibrium or heat death.

Since the universe is the sum of all such systems, and since it is considered thermodynamically isolated, it has been assumed that entropy would inexorably increase everywhere in the universe and that disorder would increase everywhere as well. Every system would therefore become progressively more disordered. This form of the Second Law was thought to be inviolable. Any observations that violated this principle were invalidated simply by the fact that they were at variance with the accepted authority.

But these theorists vastly underestimated the transport properties of entropy. In non-isolated systems entropy can escape from the system leaving an ordered system behind. This order may be manifested in the material contents of the system and locked within the system creating a system that becomes progressively more ordered. Such systems are called closed systems because they lock in order in complicated material configurations.

Order may also be manifested as dynamic ordered patterns of energy that can be extracted from the system as work. Among such systems are the heat engines studied by the pioneers in thermodynamics. They are open systems, that can pass both matter and energy flows . Such systems tend to maintain a constant internal entropy level in a flow-through condition known as "steady state".

Entropy disperses rapidly from closed systems leaving order behind. Systems whose boundaries readily release entropy to dissipate into the vastness of the outer reaches of the universe are likely to become very ordered. Ordered systems are likely to become complex, and complex systems are likely to become functional in ways that might never have been dreamed about in simple systems.

Researchers have shown that the idea that entropy maximizes everywhere the world is incorrect. Systems exist whose boundaries reject entropy faster than it can be accumulated leading to the natural emergence of ordered systems. Others have observed that the universe is not fixed, but ever-expanding leading to the dispersion of existing entropy into newly created space and the diminishing of entropy concentrations.

Erwin Schrodinger showed in 1944 that biological membranes could reject entropy becoming very ordered inside[4]. Ilya Prigogine showed (1980) that in order for biological systems to reject entropy they had to develop extensive surface areas that he called "dissipative surfaces" through which to disperse it[5]. Edwin Hubble showed that starlight was "red shifted" because the stars were receding from each other, an indication that the universe was expanding.[6]

All of these discoveries fly in the face of the idea that the entropy content of every system is always rising. Thermodynamic scientists are reconsidering the idea that systems must become more disordered. Only systems that retain the entropy they produce become disordered. Systems that reject enough entropy may become very ordered.

This idea is beautifully expressed in a recent book by the historian and journalist, Peter Watson called "Convergence: The Idea at the Heart of Science"[7]. At the beginning of the second part of the book he says:

> *The conservation of energy and evolution by natural selection set the scene for this book. However, they embody a contradiction. The thermodynamicists said plainly that the world was running down, its useful energy leaking out, that organization was being lost, that "entropy tends to a maximum". But evolution showed that biological systems at least were running up, becoming more - not less – complex and organized.*

Complexity scientists, like Stuart Kauffman'[8] Terrance Deacon[9] and Geoffrey West[10], have shown that ordered systems interact in a super-linear fashion providing disproportionately more means to interact in autocatalytic progression. This allows complex molecules to acquire the ability to function in far more diverse ways than simpler systems do.

My personal view is that order blooms under these conditions, functional processes proliferate and life arises naturally and spontaneously.

Preface

Entropy must be selectively removed from a system in order to produce an ordered system. Order must be retained. A large diffusion coefficient is a natural characteristic of highly entropic materials leading them to be naturally extracted from any system boundary that will allow them to pass. Ordered materials naturally have a low diffusion coefficient and are less likely to disseminate away from the system. Extraction of the entropic materials leaves the ordered ones behind.

I hope in this book to establish a basis for understanding the spontaneous and autocatalytic rise of order in the earth's biosphere and the need to preserve that order to stabilize the climate.

In addition to damaging our planet's ability to discharge entropy, by increasing the carbon dioxide concentration in the atmosphere, we also have converted our reservoir of biological order into disorder by consumptively decimating the biosphere, increasing the entropy content needing to be discharged.

Destroying existing order by converting it into entropy, and diminishing the ability to reject disorder are two ways to elevate the entropic state of any system, including the earth. In an elevated entropy state, disorder prevails. Highly evolved, complex systems, such as living ecosystems, cannot sustain under these circumstances. Converting order into disorder, complexity into simplicity, has thermal consequences. When done on a worldwide scale, the climate warms.

This book is about how the climate is affected by the biosphere. It took several years of studying how the biosphere will be affected by changes in the climate to reach an understanding that the causal relationships also operate the other way around. This insight leads me to analyze the implications of non-equilibrium thermodynamics on the kinetics of climate change and on the distribution of climate and temperature patterns on the surface of the earth.

The book is written from the point of view of a chemical engineer with a Master's Degree in Environmental Science. It would be presumptuous of me to present it as established, peer reviewed science, but the urgency of the climate change problem and its existential implications for life on Planet Earth have motivated me to put my ideas into written form for distribution as soon as possible. The reader should check the analysis against other sources and use his own judgment in assessing the validity of the conclusions.

The work is intended for people with a college level education in a science-related discipline. I have used mathematical equations in a few places to illustrate relationships, but otherwise no training or expertise in mathematics is necessary.

The major message of the book is that loss of global biomass is a major factor responsible for climate change. Several examples cite where destruction of biomass has coincided with warming of the climate, locally, regionally and globally. Reasons for this phenomenon are suggested, and theoretical mechanisms are discussed.

One primary finding of the book is that order and complexity are not miracles; they are "the natural order of things". The phrase "natural order of things" is not a cliché, it is a description of the way things really are, they are ordered; they are not random.

This is not in conflict with the Second Law of thermodynamics, in fact, the Second Law predicts it. Dispersion of order through entropy production is a vector function; consistently increasing as time goes on. But time's arrow has a spatial dimension as well. Entropy increases in the direction of energy flow. For any system it has an entry point and an exit point. At the entry point the entropy increases and the system becomes disorganized. At the exit point the entropy decreases and the system becomes orderly. Entropy exits along with energy flowing from a system leaving order behind in its wake.

> Entropy, time's arrow, has a spatial component as well. It always increases in the direction of energy flow, leaving depleted entropy stores behind in its wake. This depleted entropy content is manifested as various kinds of order in the system.

Energy flowing through a thermodynamic system produces order, not chaos. Entropy generated in the process is rejected from the system with the waste heat. The process that rejects entropy leaves an ordered system behind.

Preface

It is not enough to know that entropy always increases in any thermodynamic process. It is necessary to understand that entropy, like any fluid medium, flows along a potential gradient. As it does so it may produce ripples, eddies, waves, troughs and patterns of any flow system in steady state. It also leaves low entropy ordered conditions in the areas through which it passed.

A system in steady state flow seeks to maximize entropy production, not entropy content. Ejecting more entropy than the system can create accomplishes this. As a system rejects entropy, it leaves order behind, a state of affairs that can lead to very ordered systems.

Entropy maximizes in thermodynamically isolated systems because they are the terminus of flow; they are regions of space through which neither matter nor energy flows. But an isolated system is a figment of the imagination, an abstraction generated to make a point. No real system is truly isolated. Non-isolated systems naturally project their entropy outward and become ordered. This principle is fully consistent with, and predicted by, the Second Law of thermodynamics and it is discussed by many of the top physicists of our time[11, 12, 13]. Some systems can be closed to the extent that some of the order they produce is retained and accumulates within them. Others are open enough to discharge all of the order they generate, and not accumulate it.

Entropy is disorder or uniformity, lack of identity. When a system is high in entropy it has little recognizable content, no identifiable objects. Everything is dispersed, diffused and uniformly spread out. Order is the reverse of entropy, character, distinction, differentiation, "a place for everything and everything in its place". Complexity is order compounded - higher levels of order overlying simpler, more basic, ordered relationships.

The difference between an ordered system and a disordered system lies in the properties of the system boundaries that enable them to pass certain types of disorder and retain certain types of order. An ordered system that undergoes a

The difference between an ordered system and a disordered system lies in the properties of its boundaries that enable the passage of certain types of disorder and retention of certain types of order.

change in its boundary properties such that it can no longer discharge its disorder but begins to retain it within its boundaries becomes less ordered by virtue of the fact that it can no longer discharge its disorder.

That's why carbon dioxide in the atmosphere is destructive to the order of the earth. It prevents the escape of entropy (disorder) to outer space, retaining it on earth, and preventing the development of more complex ordered systems.

Life is a complex, ordered system, and retention of entropy is threatening to its very existence. Life emerged taking advantage of the differentials in the non-equilibrium environment of a cooling earth from which energy was being extracted. It adapted to changing conditions, and it modified the environment to maintain the continuity of its out-of-equilibrium status. It continues to complexify in order to utilize ever-diminishing differentials.

As this process continues, more and more energy must flow through the system to generate enough order to maintain the complexity of living species as they already exist, so less and less energy is available to advance the quality and complexity of the biosphere through the process of evolution.

Although energy is plentiful, it has its limits. The quality or usefulness of energy is reduced by decreasing its temperature, a process that decreases its density, increasing its entropy content. In order to decrease the entropy content of a system you must withdraw some of its entropy. A system border must be able to pass entropy in order to maintain internal order. Passing entropy involves discharging energy or high entropy matter from the system, usually in the form of heat or disordered waste materials.

Discharging entropy from the earth involves crossing the atmospheric boundary. But as the atmospheric discharge pathway becomes more and more clogged with carbon dioxide and other greenhouse gases, an entropy back-up occurs, damaging ordered systems and diminishing the rate of evolution.

When the concentration of greenhouse gases in the atmosphere increases, disorder can no longer discharge freely into space, but must accumulate on the surface of the earth. Accumulation of disorder on the surface of the earth is destructive to the order that exists there, the biomass reservoir.

Another major message of the book is the importance of complexity to higher order biological functions. Biomass is the resilient structure of low entropy complexity in the ecosystems on the earth's surface. Life is a complex process, and as such it is dependent upon low entropy complexity such as biomass in the environment.

There is only one species that has developed the ability to control the complexity relationships in the environment. That

> Mankind has developed the ability to control the order and complexity relationships in his environment.

species is mankind, the toolmaker, and the energy consumer. If we allow our activity to degrade the permeability of our atmospheric boundaries increasing the disorder of the surface of the earth, our environment will no longer be able to build and support complex biological systems. As this process proceeds we will sacrifice the progress made by evolution and turn the evolutionary clock back to times of lesser complexity development.

In less than 200 years we have reduced the biomass content of the earth by more than 40%. And that's on top of a reduction of nearly 10% in the previous 10,000 years. This behavior has completely undone the orderly build-up of resilient biomass structure that took place over the 10,000 years following the last glacial maximum (see Figure 2) on page 35.

Not unpredictably, the surface of the globe is now warming, just as it did the last time the biomass reached this critical level. The last biological minimum heralded the end of an ice age and the recovery of the biomass. The current warming trend is not leading us in the direction of a similar recovery. A biological minimum, a glacial

> The last time the global biomass reserve was reduced to its present level the globe warmed, pushing back glaciers and allowing the biomass to expand again, restoring the complexity of the global biomass reserve.

minimum and a thermal acceleration are all occurring at the same time.

These occurrences are all indicative of a single fundamental condition, a rise in the entropy content on the surface of the earth.

The demise of the biomass has interrupted the photosynthetic process that produces order out of the solar energy that impinges on the earth's surface. As predicted by the Second Law, the existing order degrades into entropy. Without the continuous replacement of this order the reservoir of order declines as disorder increases.

The boundary conditions that retain order while allowing the disorder to escape the system are essential to keeping the earth from becoming disordered. When the atmosphere becomes too clogged with carbon dioxide it cannot continue to reject disorder. The disorder in the environment begins to rise at the expense of the existing order making it more and more difficult to maintain the complexity in living systems.

The only way to restore health to the biosphere is to re-establish the biomass reservoir that constrains energy flow and enables differentials to persist in the environment. Some projects have been remarkably successful in modifying the climate on a regional level. Successful projects should be carefully examined to assess the costs and benefits that accrue to the environment, ecosystems, human life and the economy.

I owe a great deal of gratitude to a number of individuals who have encouraged me with helpful ideas and insights into the consequences of the ideas I was discovering. First, I owe special thanks to Dr. John Todd, President of Todd Ecological Design, founder of Ocean Arks International and Distinguished Professor Emeritus at the University of Vermont's School of Natural Resources. John has mentored me through telephone and email communications and has been largely responsible for broadening my focus from biochar issues to include ecological influences on the climate.

I also owe a great deal of thanks to Dr. Richard Perritt, Executive Director of the North Carolina Farm Center For Innovation and Sustainability, and Assistant Professor at North Carolina State University, for discussing relevant factors affecting the effectiveness of biochar in agricultural applications.

Preface

I also owe thanks to Dr. Len Bull, Professor Emeritus at North Carolina State University, Chair of the Vermont Agricultural Development Board, and Senior Core Advisor to the World Heritage Animal Genetic Resources Institute. Len advised me on the use of biochar in agricultural applications in Vermont.

I also owe a debt of gratitude to Dr. Steve Shepard, publisher of books and papers on biological matters, and to my grandsons Jos and Luc Boswell for their ideas and discussions on biology, astrophysics and computer usage and, most especially to my wife, Carol Skiff Young, for allowing me the freedom to pursue the studies required to produce the book.

With the help of these people I directed my research into the thermodynamics of ecological processes. My conclusions are of interest to scientists, consultants and policy makers as well as the interested casual reader. I hope a wide range of people uses the book.

Preface References

[1] Wharton, E. H. et al: "The Forests of Connecticut": United States Department of Agriculture Forest Service, Newton Square, PA

[2] Russell, Robert H.: "Wilton, Connecticut – Three Centuries of People Places and Progress": Connecticut Historical Society.

[3] Kemmerer, Robin Wall: "Braiding Sweetgrass": Milkweed Editions, Minneapolis, Minnesota; Copyright 2013.

[4] Schrodinger, Erwin: "What is Life", Cambridge University Press, Cambridge, UK, Copyright 1967.

[5] Prigogine, Ilya: "From Being to Becoming – Time and Complexity in the Physical Sciences" W. H. Freeman Company, San Francisco, Copyright 1980.

[6] Christianson, Gale E.: "Edwin Hubble: Mariner of the Nebulae": The University of Chicago Press, Chicago, Ill., Copyright 1995.

[7] Watson, Peter: "Convergence: The Idea at the Heart of Science": Simon and Schuster, New York, NY; Copyright 2016

[8] Kauffman, Stewart, A.: "Origins of Order – Self Organization and Slection in Evolution", Oxford University Press, NY, NY, Copyright 1993.

[9] Deacon, Terrance W.: "Incomplete Nature - How Mind Emerged From Matter", W>W>Norton & Company, LTD, London, UK, Copyright 2013.

[10] West, Goeffrey, "SCALE: The Universal Laws of Growth, Innovation, Sustainability, and the Pace of Life in Organisms, Cities, Economies, and Companies": Penguin Press, New York, NY; Copyright 2017.

[11] Chaisson, Eric: "Cosmic Dawn – The Origins of Matter and Life", Universe.com, Inc, Lincoln NE, Copyright 1981.

[12] Schwartzman, David: "Life, Temperature and the Earth – The Self-Organizing Biosphere": Columbia University Press, NY, NY, Copyright 2002.

[13] Spier, Fred:" Big History and the Future of Humanity": John Wiley and Sons, West Sussex, UK: Copyright 2015.

Part One

Introduction, New Ideas and Summary

Chapter One

Introduction - The Background of the Book

Chapter Summary

Global warming can be related to world biomass reserves which act to resist convective energy flows across the surface of the earth. The flow of energy from the tropics to the poles determines temperature distributions around the globe and provides order, character and definition to the climate system. Biomass removal allows the atmosphere to mix more freely, distributing tropical warmth more evenly and reducing the thermal differences between the Tropics and the Poles. Biomass proliferation restores the differentials enhancing the cooling of the Polar Regions and restoring order and character to the climate. This is an example of order created by the flow of energy across surface resistances, and it is a general principle supported by the Second Law of thermodynamics.

These relationships impressed themselves on people long before the emergence of scientific thought. This chapter will attempt to pursue the history of these ideas before mathematics and thermodynamics made them a quantitative science.

Order and energy are interrelated. Order occurs as a result of energy flow, and energy only flows along differences in potential. Order is additive. The greater the amount of energy that flows through a system, the more ordered the system may become. This chapter introduces the reader to the concepts of energy flows, global biomass accumulation and that warming can be attributed to the state of system ordering as well as its energy content.

These concepts apply to art and poetry as well as hard science. To function as a reservoir of information, a system must be organized with structures defining its contents. Even such an obscure concept as "intellectual space" needs the structure associated with concepts and ideas in order to be functional.

The system in which we live, including the earth's biosphere, is structured by the resiliency of its biomass which constrains energy flows and provides continuity of function and processes.

This chapter addresses the broad concepts of order, structure and creativity; and how they affect the climate and the biosphere.

Energy and Creativity: Since long before history was written, people have congregated around their campfires and pondered with wonder and awe at the mysterious motion of the dancing flames. Without further evidence, it is indeed mysterious how destroying the structure of the fuel creates an event as dynamic and ephemeral as the energy in the fire.

The first lesson of fire is that it destroys the structures that God has made. The second lesson is that it creates something else in its place, something dynamic and ethereal, short-lived and fleeting, but warm.

The destructiveness of fire demands respect. Its warmth and utility make it fascinating and desirable. The dichotomy between destructiveness and utility was always a source of wonder for ancient peoples.

The dynamic nature of the flames and the comfort and utility that emerged from the process gave a hint to the observer that there was something creative about the flow of energy induced by the fire.

The Book of Genesis discusses this matter in its words written, presumably by Moses, nearly a thousand years before Christ.

> *"And the earth was without form and void*
> *And darkness was upon the face of the deep*
> *And the spirit of God moved*
> *Upon the face of the waters"*

The idea that energy, as embodied in "the spirit of God" could be a creative force is as old as humanity. Equally important is the fact that it moved. Stationary energy is not constructive, but when it flows it becomes creative of variety of form and structure.

The ancients sensed these relationships, and they were drawn to appreciate and understand them. Whether it drew them to socialize around their campfires or to worship the creative power of their God in religious appreciation, energy flow affected the lives of ancient men as it does today.

Climate Change: This book is about the creative power of energy flow; how it works and the effects it has on our lives. It is a book about climate change. What it is. What makes it happen? What we can do about it.

My purpose in writing the book is to try to expose the root causes of the climate change phenomenon to make it more understandable and predictable. Current thinking asserts that global warming is caused by excessive amounts of CO_2 in the atmosphere. This explanation has a lot of scientific backing and rationale to support it. However, as I see the problem it is significantly more complicated. I view the accumulation of CO_2 in the atmosphere as a proxy indicator for a deeper thermodynamic causal condition. At the same time that we are overloading the atmosphere with CO_2 we are also devastating the world's ecosystems leading to a significant drop in biodiversity and a reduction the amount of carbon in the earth's biosphere. Because of this, the ecosystem services provided by the biosphere are declining as well. Ecosystem services are numerous, and they include a significant cooling and stabilizing effect on the earth's surface, the atmosphere and the climate.

> The accumulation of CO_2 in the atmosphere is a proxy indicator for a deeper thermodynamic causal condition, the rise of entropy in the environment.

Accelerated carbon dioxide accumulation in the atmosphere warms and destabilizes the surface of the planet, but proliferation of biomass has a recognized cooling and stabilizing effect as well.

Still more important is a significant change in the mechanisms of heat transfer that distribute solar thermal energy across the surface of the globe. Surface resistance to flow, like the flickering flames of the ancient's campfires, creates the thermal gradients and temperature differentials across the surface of the earth, that distribute weather patterns and climate gradients to the far flung corners of the globe.

Chapter One
Introduction

When we destroy the reservoir of biomass on the earth, decreasing its cooling effect and eliminating this resistance to energy flow, and we flood the atmosphere with CO_2 at the same time, we compound the effects of both activities on the planet.

> When we destroy the reservoir of biomass on the earth, and flood the atmosphere with CO_2 at the same time, we compound the effects of both activities on the planet.

It is easy to assert that the earth gets warmer because more heat is added at some times than others, or that one chemical or another blocks the escape of energy from the surface of the earth, causing it to overheat. The cause and effect rationale of these explanations is easy to understand, and the logic of it is hard to refute.

But my view of these phenomena is a little different. Global warming can just as well be caused by a redistribution of the temperature patterns produced by radiation already impacting the planet, without adding any more heat or discharging any less as current theory would suggest. It may not be an energy balance phenomenon at all, but a change in heat transfer regimes caused by encroachment of entropy, making the existing ordered systems unstable and causing it to switch to a whole new order of transfer kinetics.

Climate change can be caused by a breakdown of the constraints inherent in the environmental systems that normally impose order on energy flows and the climate. A disordered earth would equilibrate to an average temperature of about 60°F[1, 2] across its entire surface and support no ice at all (see discussions of equilibrium earth temperatures later in the book).

This is quite a different scenario from the current idea that warming is produced by increased solar energy impacting the earth or decreased extraction of waste heat through radiation to the vastness of space.

All of these causes may work in concert to create the effects that we have been seeing. Some of them may be interdependent, or they may be different expressions of the same thing, but it is important to understand that these different mechanisms are all responsible for the effects we are experiencing.

I feel a need to start with the very most basic ideas and apply them to the facts at hand to see if I can't get a model that predicts recent weather events better than the models that have been advanced before. So I start with the laws of thermodynamics that govern heat and mass transfer phenomena. I consider the effects of entropy, that devilish concept of disorder that increases in all processes, eventually dissipating all order and robbing all function from the universe.

Constraints to Entropy Increase: As I worked on this puzzle, I discovered that the onslaught of entropy is constrained by natural inherent resistances that restrict the world from degenerating into complete chaos. When energy flows across these resistances it creates differences in potential that counteract entropy creation and that persist as long as the energy flow and the associated constraint continue. Flow is critical. Differences in potential are maintained only so long as flow persists.

An example of such a constraint is the resistor system shown in the electrical diagram in Figure 1 (next page). A voltage differential, ΔE, applied across the terminals induces an electric current to flow through the resistor. As long as the flow of current across the resistor remains constant the voltage differential is constant. But as soon as the flow changes, the differential changes. If the flow diminishes to zero, no more voltage differential will exist. The absence of flow makes the electrical potential uniform at all points in the circuit. This is analogous to the maximum entropy condition, or uniformity, in a thermodynamic system.

If a system is thermodynamically isolated by a boundary, shown here as a heavy line, the energy source, such as a battery, runs down and the flow through the resistor eventually stops. When this happens, the electrical potential no longer exists. The system reaches equilibrium.

If the circuitry is extended through the boundary, so that energy can flow through the system from an outside source such as perhaps a solar energy collector, the flow can continue indefinitely as long as the external energy source persists. Under these conditions the system is stable and energy differentials persist as long as the outside source continues to provide energy flow.

With the circuitry extended through the boundary, the system becomes a thermodynamically closed system, no longer an isolated one. Matter is still unable to enter or leave the system, but energy can freely flow through the circuit. The heat generated by the resistor will radiate from the walls of the system. If the system boundary were permeable or penetrated so that matter could flow through it as well, the system would then become a thermodynamically open system.

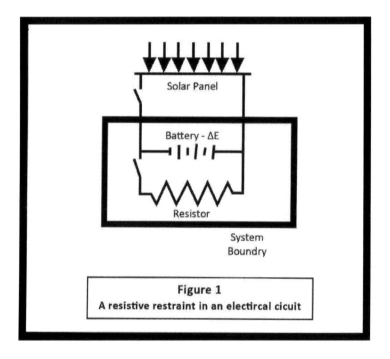

Solar Panel

Battery - ΔE

Resistor

System
Boundry

Figure 1
A resistive restraint in an electircal cicuit

In an isolated system, as soon as the flow slows down or stops; all differentials depreciate - entropy, uniformity, and chaos take over and the system is no longer functional. That's why entropy always maximizes in isolated thermodynamic systems. There is no flow in an isolated system, so entropy inevitably takes over. But in more open systems where flow persists across a wide variety of resistances, differentials are maintained and order sustains itself.

> Resistances create differentials proportional to the energy flow.

Even the earliest thermodynamic scientists knew that entropy didn't maximize in an open system. An open system is a flow-through system that discharges as much entropy as it generates and sometimes more. Entropy flows out of the system as fast, or faster, than it is generated, so it can never accumulate or achieve a maximum. When the rate of entropy discharge from an open system is equal to the sum of the entropy generated by processes going on within the system plus the entropy flowing into it from outside, a constant entropy level is maintained within the system called "steady state".

A steady state is defined as a condition wherein flow persists through all parts of the system continuously so that nothing accumulates or depletes within the system. The steady state maintains a continuous entropy flow out of the system, keeping the entropy level within the flow-through system constant at a level that is less than (more ordered than) that which would be achieved at equilibrium. In this state of "constant entropy level" order neither increases nor decreases within the system.

Some open systems are heat engines. They act like an entropy separator. They split the input energy into two streams, one with high entropy (waste heat), and the other with low entropy (work). In an open system at steady state both energy streams are discharged from the system so the internal entropy of the system remains constant.

The ordered energy discharge from an engine is organized so that it can provide useful work while the disordered energy discharge appears as waste heat. The waste heat dissipates into the atmosphere increasing disorder and adding to the entropy burden of the universe, but not accumulating within the system.

The ordered energy discharge from an engine also dissipates into entropy once it escapes into the outside world. This satisfies the Second Law of thermodynamics, which stipulates that the entropy of the universe is always increasing. But the increase in entropy is limited to the world outside the system. The heat engine achieves a decrease in entropy, an increase in order, in a localized space for a limited amount of time. The entropy of the universe external to the system always increases.

This was the state-of-the-art of classical thermodynamics in the 1800's when scientists and engineers were trying to explain the operation of crude energy conversion systems such as the early steam engines. It was a great tool for understanding how energy could be manipulated to achieve useful work for the benefit of man.

But the early thermodynamic scientists didn't get it quite right about what happens in a closed system like a biological cell or the planet earth. Modern scientists don't have it thoroughly nailed down yet either.

A closed system allows energy to pass through the system boundaries, but does not allow matter to pass. Since matter cannot enter or leave the system, it is considered closed. Energy, however, can pass freely through a closed system.

Order that is imposed on matter trapped in a closed system is confined within the system.

Like the open system, the closed system is an entropy separator. The high entropy stream is discharged as waste heat as in the open system. But the extraction of waste heat imposes low entropy order on the matter that remains contained within the system. Since the definition of a closed system is one that cannot pass matter, the order, once it is imposed on the matter, is trapped within the system, accumulating and becoming more and more organized. As more and more disorder is extracted from

As more and more disorder is extracted from the already ordered contents of a closed system, higher levels of order (more complex forms) appear. When all the retained matter has reached a certain level of organization, portions of it undergo transitions to higher states of order. By this means complexity emerges the already ordered contents of a closed system higher levels of order (more complex forms) appear.

The more energy that passes through the closed system, the more organization accumulates in the matter it contains. The matter retained in the system becomes more and more organized as more energy and related disorder traverse across the boundary out of the system. When all the retained matter has reached a certain order level, portions of it undergo transitions toward higher states of order. Higher states of order include such things as increased molecular size, condensation phase changes, complexity, functionality, and eventually responsiveness and life. These characteristics are emergent properties that appear as disorder is extracted from closed systems.

So I want to start this book with an analysis of the constraints that keep entropy at bay and make matter functional. Then I want to consider the details of the thermodynamic laws that give matter the potential for order, functionality and responsiveness.

We will consider how order is initiated by energy flow and how it compounds itself to create complexity and functionality. Then we can consider how order arises in simple, non-living systems and even more so in complex living systems. Finally we can consider the growth and maintenance of the biosphere.

> Order is initiated by energy flow, and it compounds itself to create complexity and functionality, eventually becoming self-organizing and "alive".

Armed with an understanding of how entropy runs the universe on the micro-scale, we can embark on our effort to determine how it works on an environmental landscape scale and a planetary scale as well. Then we can consider how we might harness the power of naturally generated constraints to prevent the disorganization, warming and instability of our climate, and we can discuss some examples of projects already underway.

We will discuss how the principles we used apply to charcoal and how charcoal may be used to stimulate a greener, more vibrant, planet. In the process we will consider how to make biochar efficiently and effectively and how to use it to maximum effect.

In this book we consider the science of climate change and relate it to the fundamental principles of thermodynamics. We will view global warming as a form of entropy excursion caused by the removal of biological order from the surface of the earth.

Global warming is a form of entropy excursion caused by removal of accumulated biological structures from the surface of the earth.

Biological structures compose vast stores of resilient complexity and order generated by the flow of heat from the surface of the earth through radiation of low temperature (long wavelength) energy into the ever expanding energy sink of outer space to maintain the heat balance of our planet and to discharge entropy along with it. Flowing heat carries entropy with it, entropy that increases as the heat dissipates and cools.

Discharging entropy leaves order behind. Just as removal of heat (and its associated entropy) from a refrigerator causes water to freeze in the ice cube trays, entropy escaping from the earth causes matter to coagulate into complex forms. Living complexity is an emergent property of matter

Discharging entropy leaves order behind. Just as removal of heat from a refrigerator causes water to freeze in the ice cube trays, entropy escaping the earth causes matter to coagulate into complex forms. Living complexity is an emergent property of matter that appears as internal order proliferates when energy escapes from a closed system.

that appears as internal order proliferates when energy escapes from a closed system.

Complex solid structures constrain the processes that generate entropy and have a moderating effect on the approach to equilibrium. Equilibrium is a terminal condition and therefore the most constraining of all states. Once you are in it, you can't get out without some outside intervention. In a state of true equilibrium, no differentials of any kind can exist, so no activity of any kind can take place. It is truly a "heat death" as described by the early thermodynamic scientists.

In the lack of any differences, activity, change, and even time are ultimately eliminated. The advance of natural systems toward equilibrium takes place as rapidly as system constraints will allow. [3] In the absence of constraints, equilibrium occurs rapidly, irregularly, discontinuously and often destructively. A system must therefore be buffered by constraints to modulate the advance toward equilibrium if any continuous process, particularly life, is to proliferate or even continue to exist.

In the blinding flash that was the Big Bang, constraints couldn't exist, and so the universe expanded with blinding speed. But as the universe expanded and cooled, energy, matter and their associated properties precipitated from the primordial mixture, giving rise to the constraint patterns that give the universe its character today.

There is evidence in scientific theory that after the first 10^{-37} seconds of cosmic existence the universe grew exponentially reaching expansion rates faster than the speed of light. In these most early moments, when the universe was about the size of a grapefruit, photons were non-existent, and matter had not yet precipitated from the quark-gluon plasma. Expansion speeds were not yet limited by the speed of light because this form of energy had not yet precipitated from the cosmic mix, and so the constraints associated with it were not yet relevant.

But just as water and then ice precipitate from steam as it cools, ordered forms precipitate from cooling mixtures. The behavior of a system is predicated on its physical form, and it becomes more predictable and less random as the system cools to more moderate temperatures.

> Just as water, and then ice, precipitate from steam as it cools, ordered forms precipitate from cooling systems.

On earth, some of the necessary system constraints are provided by solid structures. Some structures are geological; some are the products of living things. Still other types of constraints are provided by the properties of matter that determine the things it will do as described by the laws of physics or the rules of chemical interactions as described by the Periodic Table of the Elements.

Without constraints, the energy differentials of the earth disperse rapidly, driving the energy of the tropics toward the poles, a process perceived as warming over most of the earth. Destruction of the phytomass (the total amount of living plant material) in our biosphere eliminates the biological constraints and removes structure and order from our planet, and as a consequence, removes continuity and predictability from our climate.

Throughout the remainder of this book I will attempt to explain why this is so. But first I'd like to comment on the process that led me to write the book and the priorities that led me to persist in the studies that were necessary to uncover the relationships that have emerged from its writing.

I began with an interest in how to improve the efficiency of energy extraction from fuels by taking advantage of gasification processes that could create fuel gases from solid fuels including biomass and coal.

Extraction of energy from biomass is destructive in two ways. It releases carbon dioxide into the atmosphere increasing the atmospheric entropy content and resisting the passage of that entropy from the earth, and it destroys the biomass, removing its constraining influence from the biosphere and eliminating its cooling, stabilizing effect on the atmosphere, while reducing the ability of ecosystems to recover.

The journalist, Roger Drouin, reporting from the Yale School of Forestry and Environmental Studies, has written a story entitled, "Wood Pellets, Green Energy or New Source of CO_2 Emissions"[4]. In it he quotes Debbie Hammel, the Director of Land Markets Initiative of the National Resources Defense Council as follows:

> It would be a mistake for the EPA to give biomass energy producers a free pass on carbon accountability. Cutting down and burning

trees for energy is a step in the wrong direction for the climate and our forests.

Burning wood, for example, emits slightly more CO_2 per kilowatt of energy produced than burning coal does. And it also depletes active, reproducing biomass. The constraints to equilibrium provided by the biosphere prevent thermodynamic uniformity from overtaking the planet and destroying the complex living systems that abound.

Dr. Michael Williams, emeritus professor of geology and the environment at the University of Oxford and Fellow of Oriel College has written a book about the biomass removal problem. The book is called "Deforesting the Earth – From Prehistory to Global Crisis"[5]. I quote Dr. Williams as follows:

> *"In the annals of deforestation, the experience of medieval Europe must be accorded a prominent place for what happened in Europe itself and for what happened subsequently in the world. Whereas about four-fifths of the land surface of temperate western and central Europe had been covered with forests and swamps in about AD 500, possibly only half, or less, of that amount remained 800 years later."*

With all due respect for the concept that the carbon in wood is "current" while the carbon in coal is "fossil", the world must do without the services provided by the biomass while it regrows, and the carbon dioxide from both has exactly the same effect on our atmosphere.

The carbon in biomass, because it regrows, is considered "renewable". Acres of forest can be removed and turned into fuel-wood, and they will be replaced in some portion of a century. Meanwhile the biosphere is required to operate without the environmental services that the forest provides while more forests must be removed for more fuel-wood. Removal of biomass is one of the more damaging environmental insults perpetrated on the biosphere by mankind.

The Industrial Revolution emerged using biomass fuels. But as the requirements for fuel increased, the British Isles, and then the European

Continent, ran out of accessible forests that could continue to provide fuel.

The switch to coal saved western civilization from running out of biomass, its first biomass crisis.

> The Industrial Revolution emerged using biomass fuels. But as the requirements for fuel increased, the British Isles, and then the European Continent, ran out of accessible forests that could continue to provide fuel. The switch to coal saved Western Civilization from its first biomass crisis.

It was primarily an issue of supply and demand. Neither the population nor the technology was advanced enough to cause an environmental crisis. But the advent of fossil fuels saved us from the first biomass crisis. It is astonishing to contemplate that some people advocate going back to biomass fuels to relieve demand for fossil fuels today.

Today's biomass crisis is far more extreme than the crisis of the late 1700's to early 1800's. Today's world has about half the biomass that existed before the discovery of the Americas. China's civilization collapsed from loss of biomass before that.

The effect of collapsing civilizations on the climate of the Earth is discussed in a recent book by Dr. Richard John Aspinall titled, "Geography of Climate Change"[6]. The collapse of civilizations along the Amazon River caused by decimation of human populations through disease during the 16th century is assessed with the following conclusion:

> *"We contend that by 1500 AD the global imprint of human land use on the carbon cycle was sufficient to produce measurable atmospheric warming, and that the decrease in atmospheric CO_2 from 1500 to 1750 (AD) was in part caused by carbon sequestration in the lowland tropical forests of the Americas."*

My own contention is that the direct conversion of biomass to CO_2 may be the least effect of biomass loss on climate change. The effect of biomass on global heat transfer mechanisms, thermodynamic system closure, and atmospheric weathering of calcium and magnesium silicate rocks, may be far more important.

Dr. Vaclav Smil, a prolific writer of books and papers on the subject of environmental energetics, and Professor Emeritus at the University of Manitoba, has written a book called "Harvesting the Biosphere – What We Have taken From Nature"[7]. He presents data on the biomass content of the Earth from the time of the last glaciation. Although they are sparse and imprecise, the data can be plotted to give the graph shown in Figure 2 (Page 35).

The illustration shows that the total biomass carbon content of the biosphere during the height of the Wisconsin Glaciation of 20,000 years ago was slightly over 500 gigatons of carbon (500 billion tons). This is less than half of the biomass that existed on Earth during the interglacial period when the earth began to cool. Glacial scouring and an inhospitable climate had removed the missing biomass. But as the climate warmed, biomass recovered in areas left bare by ice removal. The process continued as glaciers retreated and biomass moved north. Figure 2 shows that biomass recovery reached a maximum of around 1000 gigatons of carbon by the glacial minimum about 10,000 years ago.

At this point another biomass removal cycle began. But advancing Ice sheets did not drive this new biomass cycle. Instead human consumption of biomass was the imperative that drove the cycle.

At first, tool making, construction and agriculture were the motivations for biomass removal. Then use of biomass for fuel became prominent. By the time of the Industrial Revolution the biomass content of the world was in freefall.

Today estimates of the biomass content of the world put the total in the range of 500 – 600 gigatons of carbon, a biomass level eerily reminiscent of the 500 gigatons that existed when the globe warmed at the end of the last glacial period and stimulated a recovery of the biomass.

Is this coincidental or causal? Does a global biomass level around 500-600 gigatons cause warming of the surface of the earth? If so, Why? These questions may be answered by analyzing the thermodynamics of global heat transfer mechanisms in ecological systems.

The importance of biomass to global surface temperatures is obvious on the micro scale where biomass creates recognizable microclimates all the time. What then is the effect of biospheric biomass on the macroclimate? Can we find processes in chemistry, physics, thermodynamics, geology, biology and related sciences that confirm our observations that biomass and climate are directly related?

All the more concerning is the fact that biomass is being sold as a renewable fuel, a means to a solution of the global warming problem. Commercial enterprises and respected scientists are advocating that

> If the earth warms when biomass is removed, conversion of biomass to fuels, and then to additional energy, will exacerbate our global warming problems.

biomass carbon recovers itself naturally, and thus gets replaced leaving a carbon footprint of zero and this is considered a justification for unrestrained biomass destruction to replace fossil fuels. But if the Earth warms when biomass is removed, conversion of biomass to fuels will exacerbate our global warming problems.

This is illustrated by the fact that biomass was our original energy source. Its destructive removal for fuels was ruinous to the environment and depleted the resource. Fossil fuels saved the day then. Is it not totally inappropriate to consider biofuels renewable now?

The assumption of biomass renewability and "zero carbon foot-print" ignores the dynamics of thermodynamic ecosystem responses to biomass removal. In fact, the setback to gross primary productivity caused by biomass removal is often more damaging to ecosystem continuity than fossil fuel combustion. Increasing concentrations of carbon dioxide in the

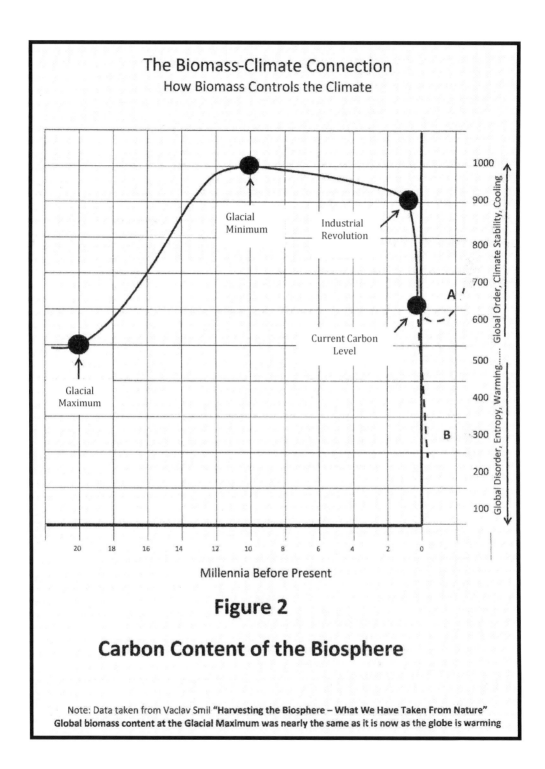

Figure 2

Carbon Content of the Biosphere

Note: Data taken from Vaclav Smil **"Harvesting the Biosphere – What We Have Taken From Nature"**
Global biomass content at the Glacial Maximum was nearly the same as it is now as the globe is warming

atmosphere are known to stimulate photosynthetic plant growth and ecosystem recovery.

The assumption of biomass renewability and "zero carbon foot-print" ignores the dynamics of thermodynamic ecosystem responses to biomass removal. In fact, the setback to gross primary productivity caused by biomass removal is often more damaging to ecosystem continuity than fossil fuel combustion ever was.

The rise of fossil fuels was motivated in part by the fact that fossil fuel burning caused less environmental destruction. Biomass combustion was unable to provide the necessary energy to run the Industrial Revolution without excessive destruction of the environment. Fossil fuels were introduced to solve the problems caused by biomass depletion due to biofuel use.

It is a dilemma to think that we could save the environment from destruction by returning to practices that were too environmentally destructive the last time we used them. Still, it is true that restricting ourselves to using "current" carbon will prevent carbon build up due to the use of "fossil" fuels. The question is, is there enough biomass, and is the trade-off worth it?

My research led me to the conclusion that the answer to both of these questions is a resounding, "No". To understand why I took this position let us look at quantitative amounts of carbon in the atmosphere, the biosphere, the oceans and the geosphere; and the carbon fluxes that cycle back and forth between these reserves when the cycle is in balance. It is clear that natural carbon fluxes are massive compared to the carbon released by fossil fuels. But the natural carbon fluxes are cyclic and do not affect the average composition of the various reservoirs. Carbon dioxide from fossil fuels adds a small but steady stream to the atmosphere increasing the carbon dioxide levels in the atmosphere from which it gets distributed to the other reservoirs.

All the carbon dioxide released by burning all types of fossil fuels together amounts to only 6% of the natural, biological carbon dioxide flux. Put another way, increasing the growth rate of the biosphere by 6% would absorb all of the carbon dioxide produced by burning fossil fuels. But since the biosphere's carbon dioxide flux is cyclical, all the carbon dioxide absorbed is returned to the atmosphere

> All the carbon dioxide released by burning fossil fuels amounts to only 6% of the natural, biological carbon dioxide flux.

by the process of decay. Carbon cycles through the biomass reservoir but it is not permanently removed from the atmosphere by the process of photosynthesis.

If living biomass were to reproduce itself at a rate proportional to its mass, an annual increase in the mass of the biosphere of 6% would achieve a balance with the present rate of fossil fuel burning. A decrease in the mass of the biosphere compounds the problem.

Alternatively, something could be done to interrupt the decay cycle keeping the absorbed carbon out of the atmosphere.

It was at this point in my research that I discovered biochar. Biochar is an agricultural soil supplement that has been demonstrated to increase agricultural productivity by factors from a few percentage points to hundreds of percent. It is the product of partial gasification of biomass. The gas driven off in the gasification process carries about two thirds of the heat of combustion of the biomass, heat that can be recovered and converted into electricity or used for space heating or other productive processes.

Biochar is the remnants of biomass structures preserved in elemental carbon. Energy has been extracted from biomass without destroying the complexity of its structure. Elemental carbon, it turns out, is resistant to environmental degradation and decay and its structure persists in the soil for hundreds to thousands of years.

Chapter One
Introduction

Biochar interacts with mineral nutrients, organic molecules, biological macromolecules, and soil microbes. In short, biochar is not living, but it is

> Biochar is the remnants of biomass structures. It is biological complexity preserved in elemental carbon. Energy has been extracted from biomass without destroying the complexity of its structure.

functional in the support of living processes and things. When biochar is used as a soil additive it boosts biomass productivity while storing carbon in the soil. This achieves the basic goals of increasing biosphere growth while reducing decay rates, the two requirements that will promote offsetting carbon dioxide production from fossil fuel combustion.

Much work is being done these days in some of our top universities to demonstrate that biochar is capable of increasing yields in agricultural applications. This work is very important because the success of using biochar in either agricultural or environmental applications depends not only on its ability to sequester carbon through increased biomass production, but also on its ability to prevent the return of carbon to the atmosphere through decay.

Environmental biomass yields can be manipulated in many ways. Since the dawn of agriculture, productivity has depended on the destruction of ecosystems to make way for agricultural activities. Since the Industrial Revolution woodland ecosystems have been decimated for the production of biomass fuels. Sedentary and social lifestyles depend upon large areas dedicated to buildings, transportation networks and energy infrastructure.

The total demand for biomass to serve these functions has reduced world biomass by nearly 50%. Since new biomass comes from existing biomass, global biomass production has been reduced by nearly 50% also, and photosynthetic carbon dioxide removal from the atmosphere has been reduced by 50% as well. A sure way to increase the biomass yield of the biosphere and the CO_2 removal from the atmosphere is to replace the missing biomass.

Since new biomass is produced at a rate proportional to existing biomass, and existing biomass has been reduced by 50%, then global biomass production has been reduced by 50% as well. A sure way to increase the biomass yield of the biosphere is to replace the missing biomass.

Biomass replacement projects include afforestation of arid lands, reclamation of mined areas, recovery of degraded agricultural lands and other conservation practices. In some cases cessation of activities is all that is necessary to allow the natural progression toward a climax community to re-establish itself. In other cases an ecosystem must be reconstructed in an area that has been destroyed or damaged beyond the limits of its resiliency. In still other circumstances, an ecosystem must be constructed in an area where none has ever existed. In any case, an area must be made productive of biomass.

Large projects are being undertaken with varying degrees of success in the United States, Canada, Brazil, Israel, China, Australia, and across the entire African Sahel among other places. Nearly every continent of the world has areas where forests that have been destroyed are being rebuilt.

The ability of ecosystems to recover from damage is extraordinary. The new ecosystem is never exactly like the old one, but biomass yields increase, watersheds recover, habitats emerge and become occupied. Sometimes new species arise and adapt themselves to the new conditions.

This restorative process is dependent upon re-establishing healthy soils. The process of building healthy soils involves arresting erosion, building water-holding capacity, establishing nutrient adsorption and retention and establishing biomass populations. With few exceptions, all of these critical functions are provided and enhanced by biochar addition.

Chapter One
Introduction

The Poetic Connection: Language is a set of constraints on sounds that restrict them to specific meanings so that different individuals can communicate ideas between themselves. An alphabet is a set of constraints on specific symbols that restrict them to specific sounds so that a verbal language can be written down. When such constraint systems are applied to shapes and sounds they can suddenly convey information. An alphabet gives permanence to ideas expressed in language.

The importance of constraining shapes to meanings related to verbal sounds was recognized by a silversmith of the Cherokee Nation named Sequoyah after he witnessed the advantages of communicating in this way from the Europeans who had invaded his country. Starting in about 1809 Sequoya devised a written alphabet for the Cherokee Nation known as the Cherokee Syllabary.

> Just as constraints on physical systems allow them to be functional and to contain information, constraints on sounds that confine them to specific meanings allow them to portray information. Language is a set of constraints on sounds that restrict them to specific meanings so that different individuals can communicate ideas between themselves. An alphabet is a set of constraints on specific symbols that restrict them to specific sounds so that a verbal language can be written down. When such constraint systems are applied to shapes and sounds, they can suddenly convey information. An alphabet gives permanence to the ideas expressed in language.

The Cherokee peoples, having seen no other examples of written language, were suspicious of organized communication at first, but as the advantages became obvious the practice spread, and in 1825, the Syllabary became the official adopted written language of the Cherokee people. The literacy of the Cherokee people grew rapidly and soon surpassed that of the surrounding European-American settlers.

The resiliency and sophistication of the Cherokee people is demonstrated by this easy adaptation to written language and an invading culture. It is ironic that within 15 years American President Andrew Jackson adopted an Indian Removal Policy that forced the Cherokee Nation to give up all its lands east of the Mississippi River and to migrate to a restricted area in present day Oklahoma. The move had devastating effects on the Indian culture and life-style and was known as the "Trail of Tears".

Personally, I think there was a great deal of jealousy involved among the American invaders seeing their own culture so easily surpassed by the "savages" they had conquered. Nothing is so damaging to a person's self-esteem than to see the folks he has classified as "inferior savages" outdo him intellectually.

Still, it is the power of constraints to make a language of sounds and provide meaning to shapes. Extra layers of complexity can be added to such systems by adding layers of organization and construction on top of the basic language. Specific systems of rhythm and rhyming make language poetic. Special feelings and meanings emerge as written messages are expressed in poetic form.

As a young man I learned to love poetry. Constraint systems can be added to sounds to create music in the same way. The constraining of elements to specify meaning and interaction is a universal property. The elements of constraint systems that give meaning to symbols apply to all natural phenomena – and spiritual phenomena as well.

In an even more abstract framework, Harvey Cox, professor of theology at Harvard Divinity School, has written a book on moral theology called, "When Jesus Came to Harvard – Making Moral Choices Today"[8]. In this spiritual paradigm, Cox makes arguments that are exactly parallel to the story of Sequoya in the literary world and to my viewpoint in the physical world.

Cox's third chapter, *A World Full of Stories,* describes how "intellectual space" is filled with stories. These stories make up the structure of the space that give it relevance, consistency and functionality. Without the stories, the space is vacant, dysfunctional and, entropic.

Chapter One
Introduction

In Cox's view the stories don't have to be true to be relevant, experience will tell us whether or not the stories are true. They can be dead wrong and make a point equally well. They

> Stories make up the structure of intellectual space that gives it relevance, consistency and functionality. Without the stories, the space is vacant, dysfunctional and entropic.

define our intellectual space, our values, and our basis for behavior. We have a huge accumulated reserve of fictional literature that serves this function.

In this abstract framework Cox is expressing exactly the same thing that makes structure so important in language, in physical systems and in our literary systems. Systems, abstract or otherwise, can't function without the orientation provided by constraints and other structures within them.

> Abstract or otherwise, systems cannot function without the orientation provided by the constraints and other structures within them.

This understanding was very interesting to me because it seemed to be a universal quality pervading through spirituality, art, poetry and hard science. Truths that persist over such a wide range of paradigms hold a special place in my philosophy.

At each crossroad in the writing of this book, I have tried to establish a point of view as a part of a structural framework for moving on to the next subject matter. Sometimes the rationale is based upon recognized scientific principles, and sometimes the rational is quite personal based on my own experience. Sometimes the rationale is controversial or even contrarian in the light of more conventional views in these areas of study. I have had to summon up the courage of my convictions as I chose the direction of my rationale, hoping that it would be most understandable and productive. In most cases, I relied on my own understanding of the issues to provide the reader with the best and most rational understanding that I could. In other cases, I relied on the advice of great thinkers from the past, often literary and scientific giants who pondered similar ideas in different contexts.

Great ideas stand out in contrast to the rest. They glisten like gold in a prospector's pan. William Shakespeare caught the essence of this contrast in his play, *The Merchant of Venice*. Two wanderers, Portia and Nerissa, are groping through the woods on a dark night guided by a candle glowing in a distant window. Portia says,

> How far that little candle throws its beams
> So shines a good deed in a weary world.

As a candle glowing in the distance in the dark, good ideas guide our explorations through the maze of scientific data. Good ideas are precious! It takes work to understand the meaning of them. Researching several sources uncovers different interpretations. In the end, one is left to his own instincts and resources to judge the best meaning of the observed data.

In Shakespeare's play, *Hamlet*, Polonius, a counselor to King Claudius, advises his son, Laertes:

> *This above all: to thine own self be true,*
> *And it shall follow, as the night the day,*
> *Thou canst not then be false to any man.*

Being true to my own insights has produced a novel document. It has introduced biases, to be sure, and I want to acknowledge those biases at the beginning. I hope that it has also introduced new ways of looking at the data, and perhaps better correlations between observations and theory. I offer this book as my contribution to the understanding of reality as revealed through scientific observation.

Some guidelines for research can be expressed in great poetry. The Vermont Poet Laureate, Robert Frost, examines the dynamics of decision making in his poem, "The Road Less Traveled". He also writes about the consequences of directing his path in this way:

Chapter One
Introduction

Two roads diverged in a yellow wood
And, sorry I could not travel both
And be one traveler, long I stood
And looked down one as far as I could
To where it bent in the undergrowth;
Then took the other as just as fair
And having perhaps the better claim
For being grassy and wanting wear
Though as for that the passing there
Had worn them really about the same
And both that morning equally lay
In leaves no step had trodden black.
I kept the first for another day
Though, knowing how way leads on to way
I doubted if I should ever come back...

At such a crossroad the theoretical scientist must examine his options carefully just as Frost does, "*Looking down one as far as he could to where it bent in the undergrowth*". The scientist must, like Frost, evaluate the potential for each choice to accurately represent the truth about his subject. In the end, his choice is personal and gives the conclusions his own point of view.

Unlike Frost, the scientist cannot just:

Keep the first for another day
Knowing how way leads on to way
Doubting if he should ever come back

The scientist must constantly return to the crossroad in the light of the most current observations and re-evaluate the road he took. His approach to all new problems in the future will always be affected by the conclusions he drew from problems in the past. Frost ends his poem with the lines:

And I shall be saying this with a sigh
 Somewhere ages and ages hence.
 Two roads diverged in a wood and I
 Took the one less traveled by
 And that has made all the difference.

The final understanding of the subject will depend on the decisions made at each crossroad in the development of the theory, and it is worth re-evaluating those decisions repeatedly to see if the unchosen road will produce different insights. I hope I have chosen wisely so that I may present the most understandable and accurate explanations to my readers.

Frost chooses "The Road Less Traveled" maximizing his opportunity to examine new viewpoints and savor new experiences. Like him, I tend to lust for a new point of view less established in the annals of science to maximize the potential for generating new insights. Still, I find it important to see "around the bend" at each juncture to assure myself of a balanced perspective before I proceed.

Works of poetry can often express some beautiful insights into the practice of science. Frost's poetry encompasses a wisdom way beyond his knowledge of his subject matter. In his poem, "West Running Brook", he captures the essence of non-equilibrium thermodynamics and quasi-stability as well as linked energy flows in biological energetics, and the rise of order and complexity in the face of increasing entropy, and while he cannot express it with mathematical precision, he presents it with intuitive insight and poetic awareness. Without knowing exactly, but with depth of understanding, he applies these principles to his poetic

> "West Running Brook" captures the essence of non- equilibrium thermodynamics and quasi stability as well as linked energy flows in biological energetics and the rise of order and complexity in the face of increasing entropy.

observations of an eddy in "West Running Brook" in the following lines:

Chapter One
Introduction

...That wave's been standing off this jut of shore
The black stream catching on a sunken rock,
Flung backward on itself in one white wave, And
the white water rode the black forever,
Not gaining, but not losing, like a bird...
White feathers from the struggle of whose breast
Flecked the dark stream and flecked the darker pool
Below the point, and were at last driven wrinkled
In a white scarf against the far shore alders.
That wave's been standing off this jut of shore
Ever since rivers were made in heaven....
...See how the brook
In that white wave runs counter to itself.
It is from that in water we were from
Long, long before we were from any creature
Here we, in our impatience of the steps
Get back to the beginnings
The stream of everything that runs away
Some say existence, like a Pirouot
And Pirouette, forever in one place
Stands still and dances, but it runs away
It seriously, sadly, runs away
To fill the abyss' void with emptiness
It flows beside us in this water brook.
Save by some strange resistance in itself
Not just a swerving, but a throwing back
As if regret were in it and were sacred
It has this throwing backward on itself
So that the fall of most of it is always
Raising up a little, sending up a little.
Our life runs down in sending up the clock
The brook runs down in sending up our life
The sun runs down in sending up the brook
And there is something sending up the sun
It is this backwards motion towards the source
Against the stream that most we see ourselves in
The tribute of the current to the source
It is from this in nature we are from
It is most us.

In this beautiful poem the West Running Brook symbolizes the flow systems that overcome resistances to reach steady state and maintain quasi-stability in nature. As long as the flow persists within the necessary limits, the system is stable and the wave persists *"off the jut of shore."*

> Flow systems overcome resistances to reach steady state and maintain quasi-stability in nature. As long as the flow persists within necessary limits, the system is stable and the wave persists off the jut of shore.

> *Like a pirouot*
> *And pirouette forever in one place*
> *Stands still and dances, but it runs away*
> *It seriously, sadly, runs away...*

The wave is an eddy, a reaction of the flow to a constraint on the bottom of the stream, a bit of order, a contrariness created by the conversion of energy into order.

The persistent running down of the components is the inevitable formation of entropy, and the linkages that send up each of the components represent the flow of energy through chemical reactions that dictate the generation of biological systems.

> *The sun runs down in sending up the brook*
> *The brook runs down in sending up our life*

The contrariness that results in the persistence of order in the face of the dominant downhill flow, Frost sees as *"Most us"*, the pinnacle of complexity. He regards us as *"A tribute to the source"*, that initial flash of energy so long ago.

I witnessed this *"tribute to the source"* in migratory salmon at the Hiram M. Chittenden Locks that maintain the level of water in Lake Union and Lake Washington in the Seattle area twenty-five feet above the level of Puget Sound. The locks that lift shipping traffic from Puget Sound to Lake Union hug the north shore of the Lake Washington Ship Canal. Snuggled against the south shore is a fish ladder that allows the passage of migratory fish up and down the watershed. The concrete pools that salmon must traverse to complete their life cycles are equipped with glass panels so that the public can view the passage of migrating fish.

My visit was in the Fall so that I couldn't see the glut of mature fish that migrate upstream in Spring and Summer to spawn in the headwaters. But there were occasional small fish progressing down the fish ladder on their way out to sea.

What caught my eye about these migrating fish was they were all facing upstream as the current carried them downward toward the ocean. This flew in the face of my concept of fish migration, which I had conceived as a valiant effort on the part of the little fish to free itself from the confines of its upland home and to battle its way downstream directed toward its ultimate aim and goal, the sea. But these fish did not seem to have any intention to reach the sea. Instead, they seemed to be swimming upstream.

The Ranger on duty explained that salmon are genetically programmed to swim against the current, upstream as it were,

> The immature fish find virtue in going against the flow. They develop their individuality and "self" as they battle the flow.

even as the river current carries them to the ocean. These salmon fry were swimming upstream allowing the river to take them, tail first, downstream. They migrate all the way down the river.... backwards!

When the fry reach brackish water they develop into smolts, the next stage of their life cycle, in which they develop silvery scales, stronger swimming abilities and better directional orientation. In this stage, they are able to be more self-directed in their new environment.

As fry, these immature fish persistently buck the system. They find virtue in going against the flow as they maintain themselves and develop the swimming skills they will need as adults when they return. They develop their individuality and "self" as they battle the flow. But, like the baby Moses set adrift, they are at the mercy of the river in their pursuit of the future.

Frost expresses this phenomenon in the lines:

It is this backwards motion towards the source
Against the stream that most we see ourselves in,
The tribute of the current to the source.
It is from this in nature we are from
It is most us.

I find it is important for me to keep my thoughts swimming upstream in just this manner. It is important to me that I pursue "the road less traveled" lest that I should find myself:

Saying this with a sigh
Somewhere ages and ages hence
Two roads diverged in a wood and I
Took the one less traveled by

Only to find that it is the wrong road.

The English poet Alexander Pope, writing in the early 16th century, produced his poem "An Essay on Criticism", a long rambling philosophical essay on the consequences of judging things. In it he points out that science is an endless adventure. We are warned that we should not start on the adventure unless we are in it for the long haul and that we should not make decisions lightly and based on too little information lest we be led to erroneous conclusions. Instead, we must examine all roads at every juncture and keep our perspective on the rest of science as we make our decisions. Pope says:

A little learning is a dangerous thing;
Drink deep or taste not the Pierian Spring:
There shallow draughts intoxicate the brain,
But drinking largely, sobers us again,
Fired at first with what the muse imparts,
In fearless youth we tempt the heights of Arts;
While from the bounded limits of our mind
Short views we take, nor see the lengths behind,
But, more advanced, behold with strange surprise
New distant scenes of endless science rise!
So pleased at first the towering Alps we try,
Mount o'er the vales and seem to tread the sky;
The eternal snows appear already past,

Chapter One
Introduction

And the first clouds and mountains seem the last;
But those attained we tremble to survey
The growing labors of the lengthened way;
The increasing prospect tires our wandering eyes,
Hills peep o'er hills, and Alps on Alps arise.

Pope is cautioning us about making quick, unwarranted judgments about scientific relationships. It is in the nature of the scientific endeavor that each discovery raises more questions than it provides answers, and our objectivity in addressing current problems is affected by the decisions we made in the past. The studious learner needs to be aware that his decision of the moment will bias his objectivity in the future. Like Frost, Pope would have us "*Look down each path as far as we could to where it bent in the undergrowth*" before we embark on our journey.

> It is in the nature of the scientific endeavor that each discovery raises more questions than it provides answers, and our objectivity in addressing current problems is affected by the decisions we made in the past.

Still, it is important that we embark. Robert Browning, an English poet of the nineteenth century wrote a poem he calls "Andrea Del Sarto, (Called the Faultless Painter)". He assesses Del Sarto's work as technically perfect but lacking in spiritual quality. Browning's famous conclusion:

Ah, but a man's reach should exceed his grasp
Or what's a heaven for.

Browning encourages us to reach into unknown areas where our skills are imperfect. Clearly, he feels that that is where progress is made. This book is my contribution to such a body of knowledge.

The great contemporary entomologist and theoretical biologist E.O. Wilson weighs in on the pursuit of new paths in scientific theory as follows:

*Scientific theories are a product of the imagination –
informed imagination. They reach beyond their grasp to
predict the existence of previously unexpected phenomena.*

In doing the research for this book, I encountered a plethora of "unexpected phenomena". It has been very rewarding to glimpse a world unconflicted by some of my past assumptions, and to experience the expanse of the Alps that extend in front of me.

Dr. Wilson has encountered great success in spreading scientific understanding to new areas of biology and to the social sciences as well, where these guiding principles were previously unknown.

Therefore, it is from great minds such as these that I gain the courage to express my own understanding of scientific current events. I do not pretend to be of the caliber of E.O. Wilson or Robert Frost, but I recognize the value of using tried and true ideas in new areas of application, and I understand the hazards of doing so. I hope I have been successful in applying fundamental physical principles to ecological situations, and in spreading fundamental understanding to complex biological, environmental and geological processes.

Chapter One References

[1] Center for Science Education: "Calculating Planetary Energy Balance and Temperature": University Corporation for Atmospheric Research, Boulder, CO; Copyright 2015, UCAR

[2]: Liou, Kuo-Nan: "An Introduction to Atmospheric Radiation": Academic Press, Inc, New Yourk, NY: Copyright 1980

[3] Swenson, Rod: "Emergence and the Principle of Maximum Entropy Production": Multi-level System Meeting, 32 Theory, Evolution and Non-equilibrium Thermodynamics: Proceedings of the 32nd Annual Meeting of the International Society for General Systems Research.

[4] Roger Drouin: "Wood Pellets: Gr een Energy or New Source of CO_2 Emissions": Yale Environment 360, Yale School of Forestry and Environmental Studies, November 1, 2016

[5] Williams, Michael: "Deforesting the Earth – From Prehistory to Global Crisis"; University of Chicago Press, Chicago, Ill. Copyright 2006

[6] Aspinall, Richard John: "Geography of Climate Change"; Routledge Press; NY, NY; Copyright 2012

[7] Smil, Vaclav: "Harvesting the Biosphere – What We Have Taken From Nature", MIT Press, Cambridge, Ma, Copyright 2013

[8] Cox, Harvey: "When Jesus Came to Harvard: Making Moral Choices Today" Mariner Books; Copyright 2004.

Chapter Two

Explanation of New Ideas

Chapter Summary

Matter, energy and space itself are structured in ways that define the way they behave. Forms and properties and states of being function predictably, defining the behavior of systems. When system properties change, whole new classes of behavior are seen which limit the production of entropy by a system.

Order is the inevitable result when energy flows through this kind of constraint system. When energy flows from a region of high temperature to a region of low temperature, it drags disorder with it, and it depletes the supply of disorder behind it. It orders the system.

Order may accumulate to very high levels within a closed system. The property that results from precipitation of new levels of order is called complexity.

As solar energy flows over the surface of the earth, order is created, and complexity emerges in the form of biomass. This process of producing order by energy flow is called autocatakinesis by the world's complexity scientists.

The system has to keep up with the constant generation of entropy by natural processes. It does this by allowing entropy to escape through its boundaries. If the system boundary conditions start to move toward isolation, increasing the resistance to the passage of entropy, the entropy content of the system will increase, and the complexity and order in the system will decrease, driving the system toward equilibrium or "heat death".

Decreased order and complexity of our biosphere is manifested in diminished biomass, already at its lowest level since the last Ice Age. This chapter discusses these ideas and how they might lead to an anticipated climate catastrophe.

Chapter Two
New Ideas

New Concepts: This book is a result of a great deal of study in Biology, Physics, Chemistry, Geology, Ecology and other related areas. It has taken ideas from many different disciplines and attempted to formulate a consistent rationale to explain observations in the real world. In the course of this work I have come up with some concepts that are truly my own. I make no claim to being the first person to develop these ideas, but they are different from the usual explanations in popular and professional scientific literature, and they are critical to the understanding of the subject matter at hand, so I want to identify them at the beginning of the book for the reader to consider and to judge according to his own experience and understanding.

Some of the conclusions may be intuitively obvious while others may seem counter-intuitive. Hopefully, the concepts that are combined in new and novel ways will produce a consistent rationale that will provide a constructive approach to understanding the origin and persistence of our biosphere and they can then be used to develop a strategy to enable it to continue to expand in the face of the existential threats it faces today.

Because these ideas are new to me, and different and possibly controversial, even contrarian, I want to draw attention to them in advance so that when the reader encounters them in the arguments in the book he or she will recognize them as new and seek the necessary confirmation from other sources in the literature to satisfy any concerns about possible inconsistencies.

Concept #1 – Systems: The word "system" is often used in discussions about thermodynamic concepts. A system is just a portion of the universe that is clearly defined so as to be the focus of one's attention. In its simplest form it consists of two parts, a boundary and its contents. Both parts have characteristics that affect the performance of the whole system.

The science of thermodynamics is based on the study of the behavior of matter and energy in systems and the effect that flow has on the system. Classical thermodynamics recognizes three different types of systems, isolated, open and closed.

Isolated Systems: If a system is completely isolated from the rest of the universe, neither matter nor energy can enter into or escape from the system. The only option is for system contents to interact with each other within the system until all differentials are resolved and no more potential exists for further interaction. This condition is called equilibrium or heat death. It is a maximally exhausted condition in which no more potential for change exists and hence no further change can take place.

Open Systems: If the boundaries of a system are completely open to flow of both matter and energy, it is called an open system. Rather than being isolated, open systems are always interacting with the outside universe. Matter and energy are continuously flowing through these systems.

Open systems do not exhaust themselves by approaching equilibrium as isolated systems do. Instead they seek a condition of continuous, steady state flow in which they are not exhausted and uniform but ordered, graded and active. This is very different from the state of equilibrium or maximum disorder in isolated systems. It is actually a state of maximum order instead. Ordered systems will seek a level of maximum order consistent with the flows of matter and energy, the characteristics of the materials involved and the other constraints that define the system.

Entropy: Another quantity, related to energy but not the same, is called entropy. Entropy content is related to disorder and so it is often called disorder. Entropy, or disorder, can enter or leave the system along with the flows of matter and energy. Entropy is also generated by each and every process going on in the system. Entropy entering the system with the energy can be transferred to the matter in the system and/or vice versa. The overall constraint on entropy flow is that it must balance over the entire system. That is the entropy flowing out of the system must equal the entropy flowing into the system plus the entropy being generated by processes within the system.

The condition of equilibrium in isolated systems is completely different from the condition of steady state in open systems. Equilibrium is a condition of uniformity and stagnation. Steady state is a condition of diversity, activity and flow.

Open systems maintain a constant entropy level within the system by discharging entropy with the flows of matter and energy discharged from the system. An entropy balance is thereby achieved, and the entropy content of the system is kept constant at a level of order and activity determined by the flow balance.

Closed Systems: Some systems are open to the flow of energy but closed to the flow of matter. Because of their closure to matter flow they are called closed systems. Such systems must retain any ordered conditions that are associated with the matter it contains. The discharge of entropic disorder with the flow of energy from the system leaves a potential for order behind .The system imposes this order on the matter retained in the system. Since the system is closed to the passage of matter this order cannot escape from the system, and it accumulates within the system. Systems that are closed in this way tend to accumulate order, becoming more and more ordered, organized and complex as time goes on.

Selectively Closed Systems: Some systems, including most biological systems are partially closed or selectively closed. Such systems include those whose boundaries are semi-permeable membranes as found in plant root systems which lead to osmosis and osmotic pressure in plant tissues. Boundaries that are semi or selectively permeable almost always are selective for high entropy materials allowing them to pass into and out of a system while preventing the passage of lower entropy, more ordered materials.

A boundary that allows entropic materials to pass while preventing ordered materials from escaping will tend to maximize the presence of ordered matter in the system. This is especially true if the system has a functional metabolism that generates ordered products from disordered materials within its boundaries.

Systems that become naturally ordered and complex are those that are selectively or partially closed, and can release their entropy as disordered materials and energy into the environment while retaining ordered, complex matter within.

Quality Factors vs. Quantity Factors: It is remarkable how the character of system contents is affected by flows of matter and energy. The following are a few examples.

- If the system boundary will allow more energy to enter a system than can leave the system, an energy surplus will accumulate in the system, and so the system will become warmer.
- If the system boundary will allow more matter to enter than leave, a matter surplus will accumulate, and so the system will become fuller.
- The reverse is also true, if the more energy or matter escapes the system than enters it, the system will become cooler or emptier.

The passage of matter into and out of the system generally affects the quantity of matter in the system. The passage of energy into and out of the system generally affects the quality or characteristics of the matter, but not so much the quantity. Energy entering the system makes the material contents warmer. Energy leaving the system makes the material contents cooler.

In a very similar manner, when entropy passes into the system it makes the material contents more disordered, and when entropy leaves it makes the material contents more ordered. The region surrounding the entry point of entropy is becoming more disordered because of the incoming entropy, while the region surrounding the discharge point is becoming more ordered because of the discharging entropy.

Entropy Transfer: The contents of a system interact with each other while they remain within the system. These interactions determine, and are determined by, the flows of energy and materials across the boundary. This particular fact is somewhat counter-intuitive, and it requires an understanding of the transfer properties of entropy.

Entropy is a property inversely related to the state of order in the system, and so it is described as disorder. Actually it is a function of energy and material distribution in the system. If entropy enters the system from outside, the entropy content of the system goes up, and so the system becomes more disordered. If entropy leaves, the system entropy content goes down, and so the system becomes more ordered.

Only in the middle of the twentieth century did scientists begin to realize that entropy was mobile to the extent that systems could release entropy and become ordered, or retain entropy and become disordered. Ordered systems that continue to discharge entropy proceed toward ever increasing levels of organization. Living systems were realized to be systems that had boundaries that would release enough entropy to become ordered and even highly complex.

The state of complexity in a system can be determined by evaluating the amount of entropy entering a system and comparing it with the amount of entropy leaving the system. Systems that release more entropy than they receive and/or produce can become very complex.

Living systems have cellular structures that are surrounded by semi-permeable, and selectively permeable, membranes that discharge entropy according to the laws of physics, and in particular the Second Law of thermodynamics, faster than they accumulate it, and they therefore become very ordered and complex.

The Tank Analogy: A system may be regarded as analogous to a tank. The boundary of the system is like the tank walls. The interior of the tank is like the system contents.

If a tank has no inlet or outlet and is heavily insulated, it is analogous to an isolated system. Matter and energy cannot penetrate the walls and so they cannot affect the contents of the tank. The only process going on in the tank is the diffusion of its contents, gradually increasing the uniformity of the mixture by depleting any gradients that might exist. Such an isolated tank will eventually become completely mixed or uniform, a condition of maximum entropy.

If an inlet and an outlet are added to the tank, it becomes possible to add and remove materials to and from the system. If more matter flows in than flows out the tank accumulates matter (fills up). When more matter flows out than flows in the tank depletes its matter content (empties out).The amount of matter in the tank at any given time is a function of the balance of flows entering and leaving the tank.

If the insulation is removed from the tank it becomes possible for energy to enter and leave the tank as well. The tank may absorb energy from a higher temperature source at one end and discharge the energy to a lower temperature sink at the other end. The tank boundaries allow energy to flow through the system as well as matter. The system is now called an open system since it will pass both matter and energy and it will display the characteristics of other open systems.

If the inlet and outlet of the tank are fitted with valves that can be shut off to eliminate the flow of matter through the system, the tank can be made into a closed system, one that will allow heat flow but will not allow matter to flow.

The balance of matter flowing into and out of a tank determines the amount of matter accumulating within the tank at any given time. Similarly, the balance of energy flowing into and out of the tank determines the amount of energy accumulating within the tank at any given time. Within the tank, energy interacts with the matter making it warmer or cooler as thermodynamic relationships dictate. The material contents of the tank are not quantitatively changed by the energy flow, but the thermal quality (temperature) of the material may be changed a great deal by the addition of energy.

In a closed system the energy entering the system increases the temperature of the matter within the system. The energy that is absorbed by the matter in the system is trapped within the system since the system is closed with respect to the passage of matter. Once the energy is associated with the matter, it cannot be removed from the tank without cooling the matter back to its original temperature.

It is not necessarily intuitive but it is very significant that the passage of energy into and out of a system drastically alters the quality of its material contents. As energy is accumulated within the tank the material contents become warmer and warmer, and since they are materials they cannot leave, but must stay within the system including their energy content.

In an open system through which both matter and energy can flow the system stays in balance by discharging matter at a temperature different from that it had when it came in. In a closed system, since the matter cannot be discharged, it must absorb energy until it is too hot to absorb any more heat at the inlet temperature. Then the system balances because it discharges energy at the same temperature it had when it came in.

So energy flowing through a closed system changes the character, but not the quantity of the matter the system contains. There are other quantities that flow through systems, one of which is called entropy. Entropy is related to molecular disorder, and so it is often referred to as disorder. As you may know from a casual understanding of thermodynamics, entropy has the peculiar characteristic that it always increases in any process that ever takes place. This has led to the perception that the universe is becoming more and more disordered, simpler and more uniform all the time.

But just as energy flowing through a system changes the energy level of the matter it contains, so also entropy flowing through a system changes the entropy level of the matter it contains. In general as energy leaves a system it carries more disorder with it than it had when it came in. This leads to an excess discharge of disorder in closed systems. When a system discharges more entropy than it takes in from incoming energy plus whatever entropy it generates within itself, the entropy level within the system diminishes and the system becomes more ordered with time.

This process is, in fact, the way evolution occurs. If the entropy balance for a system is positive the system trends toward uniformity and exhaustion, or heat death. If the entropy balance is negative the system proceeds toward order, complexity, functionality and life.

As will be discussed in later chapters, the earth is a closed system that discharges many times more entropy than it takes in. This entropy deficit results in a steadily increasing state of order on the earth's surface and a planet with a rich diversity of living ecosystems.

This has nothing to do with biology or life force. It has to do with the ability of system boundaries to pass entropy and the ability of system contents to respond to differentials in entropy driving forces. We will discuss the tendency for systems to become ordered, more organized, complex and ultimately functional in later chapters. This is a fascinating property of matter in thermodynamically closed systems. Understanding this process goes a long way toward explaining the appearance of order, complexity, self-replication, life and complex social and economic systems under certain thermodynamic circumstances.

Concept #2 - Constraints: The next concept is the idea that matter must be constrained against entropy formation in order to remain functional. Most people are familiar with the concept of entropy formation, the idea that in the absence of energy flow matter will diffuse into a maximally uniform condition at which point no further change is possible.

In a maximally entropic condition matter and energy are completely dysfunctional, but if their interactions are adequately constrained they

> In an entropic condition matter and energy are completely dysfunctional, but if their interactions are adequately constrained, they become predictable and functional.

become predictable and functional. Like the constraints on sounds and symbols in the Syllabary of Sequoyah, constraints on matter and energy give them predictability and functionality.

A bottle of perfume left uncorked in a room will diffuse continuously into the air until the whole room is scented with sweet ambrosia. The diffusion will continue until the concentration in the entire room is as high as that in the bottle. When this happens the perfume will diffuse back into the bottle as fast as it is diffusing out, so no more change in concentration will occur. This is the condition of equilibrium or maximum entropy for the system. Even though the molecules continue to move, no further net movement of perfume out of the bottle will occur.

Chapter Two
New Ideas

Now if we heat the bottle, more perfume evaporates increasing the concentration in the room. If we chill the walls of the room condensate will form on them drawing perfume from the air in the room. The whole system has now been made into a flow-through system, and perfume is flowing from the bottle through the air in the room and concentrating on the walls. By our manipulations we have made the room into a flow-through system for energy, and the perfume is concentrating on the walls of the room. The concentrated perfume on the walls is purer, at a lower entropy state, than it was when it was in the bottle. By instigating a flow of energy we have made our room into a lower entropy state, more organized than it was before the energy was induced to flow. As long as we continue to supply energy to the perfume bottle and to remove it at the walls, the system continues to produce more order, concentrating perfume on the walls. In this case, the bottle and the walls of the room are some of the constraints that define the system and require it to continuously produce order as long as energy flows.

It is clear that entropy content is a measure of dysfunctionality. The energy discharge at the walls is functioning to concentrate the perfume. As soon as the energy ceases to flow, the perfume will stop concentrating and begin to diffuse randomly once again. In order for matter to remain organized and functional, it has to have energy flowing, and it has to have constraints that oppose the rise of entropy and establish persistent differentials throughout the system.

In order for matter to remain organized and functional, it has to have energy flowing, and it has to have constraints that oppose the rise of entropy and establish persistent differentials throughout the system.

The air gap, the bottle and the walls in the room provide physical

Constraints provide resistance and direction to energy flows which establish differences in potential that enable activities and allow processes to persist in the system.

constraints in the system. The nature of the perfume and the air through which it flows provide chemical constraints. Constraints provide resistance and direction to energy flows, which establish differences in potential as is the case in the analogy to the resistor in Figure 1. The combined effect of constraints and energy flows establishes quasi-stable variations in potential that enable activities and allow processes to persist in the system.

In this book, we define our system as the biosphere, the surface of the earth, and our energy flow as a response to the vast temperature differential

> The properties of matter determine how it will interact with itself and other matter. Structures of various kinds provide additional constraints.

between the sun, at 5600°K and the emptiness of outer space, at 2.6°K. Structures of various kinds, physical, chemical, biological, geological and otherwise provide a complex series of constraints. The properties of matter provide additional constraints that determine how it will interact with itself and other matter.

Constraints are related to probabilities and randomness. In an entropic system there is a high degree of randomness i.e. the probability of every state of the system is the same.

Matter however, is not random. It has properties that make it react to energy flows in very specific ways (and not in other ways). These

> Matter has properties that make it react to energy flows in very specific, non-random ways.

properties constrain the behavior of matter to specific non-random functions. Constraints may take the form of properties of materials that favor some system states over others. They also may take the form of structures that direct or contain materials so that some states are required while others are precluded.

Anything that predicts the behavior of a system precludes it from doing something else. It is a constraint on equiprobability or randomness. A determinant of how a system will behave is a constraint on alternative behaviors.

At any rate, in order for a system to have definition and substance, it must be constrained to prevent it from diffusing away into nothingness and complete non-functionality. Science is the understanding of constraints that control the activity of the world and prevent the take-over of entropy

> In order for a system to have definition and substance, it must be constrained to prevent it from diffusing away into nothingness and complete non-functionality.

and randomness. The constraints we talk about constrain entropy and randomness, and they enable active functionality. This idea will be developed further in subsequent sections of the book.

Concept #3: Origin and Accumulation of Order: The next idea that I found to be novel and perhaps controversial is that order is a natural result of energy flow through a thermodynamic system.

It is a well-known fact that in every process in the known universe entropy or disorder increases. This fact is known as the Second Law of thermodynamics. In an isolated thermodynamic system through which neither matter nor energy can flow, disorder inevitably maximizes.[1]

But this concept has been abused by over application to other types of systems. Any system through which heat flows necessarily discharges more entropy than it takes in. Sometimes it discharges more entropy than the sum of the entropy it takes in plus the entropy it creates by the processes it contains. The net loss of entropy necessarily leaves diminished entropy levels behind. The entropy deficit is manifested by an increase in order within the system.

> Any system through which heat flows necessarily discharges more entropy than it takes in. Sometimes it discharges more entropy than the sum of the entropy it takes in plus the entropy it creates by the processes it contains. The net loss of entropy necessarily leaves diminished entropy levels behind. The entropy deficit is manifested by an increase in order within the system

In a thermodynamically closed system at steady state, bounded by a border that retains matter but passes energy, more entropy is discharged with the heat flowing out of the system than is brought in with the energy flowing into the system, sometimes more than is created by processes within the system as well. The order thus left behind is imposed on the matter in the system and thus retained within the system. Order accumulates in the matter within the system as entropy discharges with the energy stream.

In a thermodynamically open system where both matter and energy can freely enter and leave, entropy discharge orders matter as in the closed system. But the ordered matter escapes the system just as the energy does and dissipates in the external environment. This kind of a system cannot accumulate order. It takes a special degree of retention or closure for a system to accumulate order.

> In a thermodynamically open system, where both matter and energy can freely enter and leave, the ordered matter escapes the system just as the energy does and dissipates in the environment. This kind of system cannot accumulate order.

Recent studies in Astrophysics, Biology and Sociology indicate that complex systems process energy faster than simple ones and that the rate of energy processing is a direct indication of the complexity of a system. (See the discussion of work by Dr. Eric Caisson[2] at Harvard University in Chapter Thirty).

Concept #4: Complexity and Emergence: Complexity is seen as a type of order achieved when organized matter is retained in a thermodynamic system and is subjected to continued ordering from further entropy discharge. This situation leads to a compounding of order in a limited

> Complexity is a higher level of order that occurs when entropy discharge imposes additional ordering on matter in which lower states of order are already filled.

amount of matter. Complexity is order compounded. It is a higher level of order that occurs when entropy discharge imposes additional order on matter in which lower states of order are already filled.

New states of order occur commonly as phase changes. When water vapor diminishes its entropy load beyond the minimum required of an ethereal vapor, a new state of order emerges. The new state is the liquid phase. Water molecules transition to the liquid phase as they give up entropy and take up more ordered and predictable positions with respect to each other.

When all the molecules have converted to the liquid state, the liquid can lose more entropy by cooling still further, and when it reaches the minimum entropy required to maintain the liquid state a new state of order emerges called a solid.

Entropy shuttles from place to place as new states of order are formed. Those reactions that produce lower states of entropy are generally called condensation reactions. Carbon chemistry is full of examples of diverse reactions that produce low entropy products by consuming energy.

Emergence is an imposition of relationships on consciousness or perception. At small sample sizes (or focused observation levels) relationships may not be perceptible, but they emerge as greater numbers of samples (and more widespread observations) are considered.

As Alexander Pope puts it:

> From the bounded limits of our mind
> Short views we take, nor see the length behind,
> But more advanced, behold with strange surprise
> New distant scenes of endless science rise!
> So pleased at first the towering Alps we try,
> Mount o're the vales and seem to tread the sky;
> The eternal snows appear already past,
> And the first clouds and mountains seem the last;
> But these attained we tremble to survey
> The growing labors of the lengthened way;
> The increasing prospect tires our wandering eyes,
> Hills peep o'er hills, and Alps on Alps arise!

Pope sees perception as a function of position. The complexity of what we can perceive depends on the vantage point from which we observe. Functional complexity of living systems emerges to our senses as we focus in on details.

Living complexity is an emergent property of compounded ordering in biological macromolecules. Its functionality increases to the point of self-sustainability, at which point we consider it "alive".[3, 4]

Concept #5: Global Equilibration: Global order relates to the mass of the biosphere. Biomass is the most complex, ordered assemblage of materials on the face of the earth. It is a source of structure that constrains entropy generation and maintains differentials in the climate system. Differentials in the climate system keep the poles cold and the tropics hot. Under these conditions, glaciers tend to grow at higher latitudes and elevations and warm climates are restricted to equatorial regions.

> Biomass is a source of complex structure that constrains entropy generation and maintains differentials in the climate system. Differentials in the climate system keep the poles cold and the tropics hot.

Nevertheless, the growth of glaciers is destructive to biomass. The destruction of biomass destroys the system of constraints and allows disorder to expand across the surface of the earth. At low biomass levels, climate zones become unstable and tend to equilibrate allowing heat from the tropical zones to spread to higher latitudes. When this happens most of the world experiences warming, and glaciers are not be supported, even at the poles.

> Expansion of biomass into higher latitudes provides a resistance to convective heat transfer so that global equilibration starts to decline again and climate zone differentials begin to regrow.

Chapter Two
New Ideas

Under these conditions, biomass expands into higher latitudes. Expansion of biomass into higher latitudes provides a resistance to convective heat transfer so that global equilibration starts to decline again and climate zone differentials begin to grow. As biological resistance to convective heat transfer grows, the poles begin to cool again and glaciers form again in higher latitudes.

In this scenario, cycles of glaciation are seen as entropy cycles driven by the energy from the sun. The earth is an entropy oscillator cycling back and forth between states of high entropy and states of low entropy with a periodicity determined by phase changes in glacial ice, convective heat transfer rates and biomass growth rates (and other things as well).

> Cycles of glaciation are entropy cycles driven by the flow of energy from the Sun.

Maximum entropy, or equilibrium is never attained, only oscillations back and forth between higher and lower entropy states. Schneider and Kay (referenced in endnote 4 above) comment as follows:

> *We see that the earth-climate system, as well as other dissipative systems, do not reach a static equilibrium state because they are open thermodynamic systems constantly receiving a supply of external energy (i.e. from the sun) which drives them and maintains them in a non-equilibrium organized state.*

Previously the glaciation cycles have been explained by variations of insolation caused by a complicated coincidence of orbital variations (Milankovitch Cycles), wobbles of the axis of the earth, and sunspot activity. These factors are explained very well in a book called "Ice Ages: Solving the Mystery"[5] by John Imbrie, Professor of Oceanography at Brown University and Katherine Palmer Imbrie, Editorial Assistant at the Boston Museum of Science. The analysis that I propose in this book explains the cycles of the Ice Ages without relying on increased insolation to explain the warming trends. No Milankovitch Cycles, sun spot activity, orbital variability or changes in albedo are necessary. The book does not attempt to deny or ignore Milankovitch Cycles, but only to demonstrate that they are unnecessary while acknowledging that they may function in addition to thermodynamic entropy cycles.

Concept #5: Biomass Shortage. We live in a biomass-depleted age. The earth contains about 610 gigatons of biomass carbon. Not since the last Ice Age when ice sheets eradicated biomass from large portions of the earth has the totality of biomass been so low. It should be noted that when the reservoir of biomass approached 500 gigatons, a distinct warming trend

> Not since the last Ice Age when ice sheets eradicated biomass from large portions of the earth has the totality of biomass been so low

occurred, and the Ice Age came to an end (See Figure 2 on page 35).

During the interglacial period, when the surface of the earth was more differentiated, a healthy crop of biomass extended across the temperate climate zone, and the carbon content of the biomass reached more than 1000 gigatons. The relentless consumption of biomass by humankind has reduced the biomass of the planet to its present level. Now, at 610 gigatons, a distinct warming trend is again in process. A review of the history of the biomass content of the earth depicted in Figure 2 on page 35 might be helpful at this point.

Concept #6: Space Density Reduction. In 1929, Edwin Hubble discovered that all heavenly objects were receding from us with velocities that increased with their distance. The celebrated Hubble's Law explains this phenomenon and attributes it to the fact that we live in a Universe that has been expanding since the Big Bang.

The creation of new space as the Universe expands can be reconciled with the Conservation of Matter and Energy (The First Law of thermodynamics) only by accepting the fact that the material and energy density of the Universe must be continuously

> The adiabatic expansion of the Universe cools its contents and causes precipitation of new forms of order including the precipitation of new forms of ordered matter out of the disordered background energy. This process increases the orderly constraints on entropy production

declining. New space becomes occupied only by the flow of existing matter and energy into the newly created space. The First Law of thermodynamics, the conservation of matter and energy, says that no new matter and energy are created along with the creation of new space.

The adiabatic expansion of the Universe cools its contents and causes precipitation of new forms of order including the precipitation of new forms of ordered matter out of the disordered background energy. This process increases the orderly constraints on entropy production in the universe. It also allows the total entropy of the universe to increase (according to the Second Law of thermodynamics) without ever increasing the concentration or density of entropy in space. In fact, the density of entropy in the universe seems to be diminishing even as the total entropy is increasing.

All of the above-described concepts will be utilized to analyze the establishment, persistence and behavior of complexity on earth.

> The density of entropy in the Universe seems to be diminishing even as the total entropy is increasing.

Other interesting ideas are introduced, but those described above are particularly interesting, basic to the discussion and somewhat controversial in today's scientific context. They should be thoroughly understood and confirmed by anyone seeking to understand the behavior of order, complexity and climate change.

Chapter Two References

[1] Ben-Naim, Arieh: <u>Entropy and the Second Law: Interpretation and Misss- Interpretationsss</u>: World Scientific Publishing Company, Hackensack, NJ: Copyright 2012

[2] Chaisson, Eric: <u>"Cosmic Evolution – The Rise Of Complexity In Nature"</u>, Harvard University Press, Cambridge, MA, Copyright 2001

[3] Gregersen, Niels Henrik: "<u>From Complexity to Life: On the emergence of Life and Meaning</u>": Oxford University Press, New York, NY: Copyright 2003

[4] Schneider, Eric, D., Kay, James, J.: "<u>Life as a Manifestation of the Second Law of Thermodynamics</u>": Mathematical and Computer Modelling, Vol 19, No.6-8, pp25-48

[5] Imbrie, John and Imbrie Katherine Palmer: <u>"Ice Ages – Solving the Mystery"</u>, Enslow Publishers, Short Hills, NJ, Copyright 1979

Chapter Three

Summary of the Book

Chapter Summary

The inevitable increase of entropy by system processes, the changing boundary conditions of systems and the tendency for systems to discharge more entropy than they take in can lead to an instability or oscillation in entropy conditions in the biosphere. When order increases, biomass proliferates, climate differentiates and the earth becomes variable and organized. When order decreases, biomass recedes, climate becomes more erratic and mixed and the earth becomes less variable, more uniform; less differentiated. These entropy cycles can be mitigated by increasing the resilience and permanence of complexity in the biosphere and by taking steps to ensure order-producing energy flows on earth.

In addition to reducing the carbon dioxide in the atmosphere which improves the extraction of both energy and entropy from the earth, it is important to maintain the mass and complexity of the biomass in order to keep the climate of the earth within the limits necessary for advanced life.

In this chapter, we will lay the framework for the more detailed arguments that follow.

Chapter Three
Summary

This chapter will summarize the basic rationale underlying the book. It will give the reader an understanding of the relevance of the subject matter without getting lost in the details of the analysis. If the reader is motivated to go further he can move into the more complex material in subsequent chapters. Others can skip the details and go directly to the conclusions section (Part Ten).

Randomness and Constraints: The universe is a system rich in potential for interactions between its components. So rich, in fact, that if they were interacting randomly, that is, if all interactions had equal probability, no accumulation of order could occur and complete randomness would prevail. Science is quite clear that under those circumstances order and complexity in any form are infinitely improbable. Order, structure and complexity diffuse into disorder and uniformity. Bulk functional behavior is impossible under these circumstances.

> If all the matter in the Universe were interacting randomly, no accumulation of order could occur, and complete randomness would prevail. Science is quite clear that under those circumstances order and complexity in any form are infinitely improbable. Bulk functional behavior is impossible under these circumstances.

Fortunately, time, space, matter, energy and systems in general are not random, they are structured. Their structures constrain and direct their interactions in ways that guide and enable all processes. The relative probabilities of different kinds of interactions are determined by these constraints. Elimination of large numbers of interactions by constraints increases the probability of the remaining interactions, so constraints are the factor that enables and defines the functionality of every system.

> Time, space, matter, energy and systems in general are not random. Constraints direct their interactions in ways that guide and enable all processes.

Far from limiting the things that systems can do, constraints free a system from the bounds of equal and infinite improbability so that functionality

Constraints free a system from the bounds of infinite improbability so that functionality is enabled.

is enabled. Like the constraints on sounds that made up the Cherokee language and the constraints on symbols that made up Sequoya's Syllabary, constraints define, rather than reduce, the functionality of the system. They constrain entropy, and enable bulk activity.

Types of Systems: The fundamentals of thermodynamic science define the properties of three kinds of systems, isolated, closed and open systems[1]; and the differences between them. Entropy inevitably

Isolated systems maximize disorder. Closed systems allow order to accumulate in their internal matter. Open systems lose their ordered materials and cannot accumulate any order in either their materials or their energy.

accumulates to a maximum in an isolated system, but order is created by the escape of entropy (disorder) from closed and open systems. A system that is too open loses matter as fast as it can manifest order, so no order accumulates in such a system. The accumulation of order is a property of a special degree of closure in a system.

Figure 3 (see next page) is a rendition of the three types of thermodynamic systems and the way each behaves with matter and thermal energy. They are differentiated by the properties of their boundaries. The boundaries of an isolated system are perfectly impervious to both matter and energy. Those of a closed system will freely pass energy, but not matter. And the boundaries of an open system will freely pass both matter and energy.

Figure 3
Three Types of Thermodynamic Systems

Isolated System

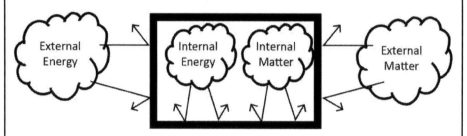

Matter and Energy Cannot Cross System Boundary

Closed System

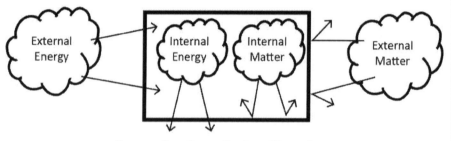

Energy Can Cross System Boundary
Matter Cannot Cross System Boundary

OpenSystem

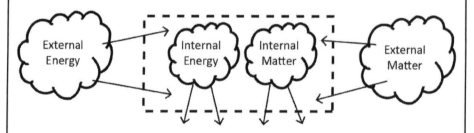

Matter & Energy Can Cross System Boundary

Open, closed, and isolated systems are recognized as mere conceptual idealizations that offer a framework for understanding the emergent effects of constraints within a system. Constraints are variously resistant to the passage of energy and matter, and this leads to differences in temperature, pressure, concentration and physical state as energy and/or matter traverse the array of constraints within a system.

Differentials are persistent and quasi-stable, like the wave in Robert Frost's "West Running brook" as long as the flow of energy and/or matter continues within the required limits for stability. This imposes a quality of order on any matter enclosed in the system.

It may be observed that a closed system is rather special in that it differentiates between matter and energy. Energy may pass through the system, but matter is retained. If incoming energy enters the system in a concentrated, low entropy state, and outgoing energy leaves the system in a more dispersed, high entropy state, there is a tendency for entropy to be carried out of the system faster than it is being brought in, leaving order behind within the system.

Energy Flow and Order: Order, complexity and responsiveness accumulate in this hypothetical closed system as long as the flow of energy persists[2]. But if energy through-put is diminished, the characteristics of the system trend toward a state resembling isolation, so entropy rises, order, complexity and responsiveness deteriorate to a low level again. The system becomes inert, un-responsive and dead when energy flow falls below that which is required to maintain the necessary order level in the system. Isolated systems that allow no passage of matter or energy always trend toward this thoroughly dysfunctional condition[3].

This is what happens on the surface of the earth when carbon dioxide impedes the passage of entropy into outer space. Entropy at the surface rises. Ordered responsive complexity deteriorates. The earth becomes inert and unresponsive as complexity simplifies and the more complex species become extinct. The situation approaches the classical "heat death".

On the other hand, as we have just discussed, a system that is too open loses its ability to accumulate order and become complex because it passes its materials and the order they have acquired out into the Universe where they no longer affect the system. The escaping materials carry their imposed order with them as they leave the system so no order can accumulate. The ability to accumulate order is purely related to the characteristic boundary conditions that affect the openness of the system, a fact consistent with the prevalence of semi-permeable cell membranes in biological systems.

Energy from the sun escaping the earth as long wave radiation into outer space draws a lot of entropy with it, ordering the matter that is left behind (see Figure 18 and Figure 23 in Chapter Six). The process is not designed, as some people insist, nor is it random as proposed by Darwinian theorists. The process is directed - toward complexity and functionality on the surface of the earth - by the thermodynamic discharge of entropy into outer space, a universal, and expanding, sink for disorder. Discharging entropy leaves order behind it in the systems in its wake.

Our technological advances in energy consumption and use have not depleted our carbon, or our energy. The amounts of these things are constant as stated in the First Law of thermodynamics. What we have depleted is the order of the system, the system constraints that make the carbon and the energy functional. The high entropy state of carbon dioxide and of dispersed energy saps the utility of these resources. The

> What we have depleted is the order of the earth, the constraints that make the carbon and the energy functional.

only way to restore utility to them is to restore their order, which can only be done by increasing the photosynthetic activity that builds constraints and order back into the system.

The primary driver of order on earth is the sun, and it operates through the biosphere. When the biosphere expands the planet becomes ordered and functional, and climate differentials increase. When the biosphere contracts the planet becomes entropic, or dysfunctional, causing climate differentials to decrease. Since the Tropics are the area where the most solar energy impinges on the earth they are the warmest part of the globe. Energy spreads to other areas by convective heat flow across the surface. More energy also radiates back out into outer space from the

When the biosphere expands the planet becomes ordered and functional, and climate differentials increase. When the biosphere contracts the planet becomes entropic, or dysfunctional, causing climate differentials to decrease.

tropics than from any other part of the globe.

These heat flows determine the climate conditions in most areas of the world. They are characterized by the spreading out of tropical conditions across the globe, a process experienced in most areas as warming.

Entropy Oscillations: When constraints from biomass proliferate on earth, resistance to convective flows and energy transfer increases and temperature differentials between latitudes also increase. High and persistent differentials between climate zones reflect the imposition of order and a low entropy condition. Diversity and biomass emerge as low entropy products of this condition, offering resistance to convective heat transfer confining impinging solar energy to the Tropics and allowing the temperature of the poles to decline.

Cooling of the poles allows the persistence and accumulation of ice and snow and the formation of glaciers. Glaciers accumulate in the high arctic during times of low entropy conditions, when temperature differentials are at their peak and the arctic is cold. They accumulate to such an extent that they cause ice to form and flow from higher elevations and across the landscape from areas of greater accumulation to areas of lesser accumulation. They scour the land surface and uproot and destroy established biomass as they advance, eliminating the resistance to convective heat transfer as they move. These terraforming masses of ice occur with cyclic regularity.

Chapter Three
Summary

When enough biomass has been destroyed and the constraints to convective heat transfer have been adequately removed, tropical heat is once more allowed to expand into temperate zones. This melts back the glaciers and allows biomass to retake the surface of the earth, increasing the resistance to convective flow again and re-establishing the energy differentials that characterize the climate.

In this scenario the earth behaves like an entropy oscillator powered by the flow of energy from the sun flowing over the surface of the earth and discharging into outer space. The system swings back and forth through entropy maxima and minima with a variable periodicity determined by the constraints inherent in melting ice sheets and convective heat transfer rates.

> The earth behaves like an entropy oscillator powered by the flow of energy from the sun flowing over the surface of the earth and discharging into outer space. The system swings back and forth through entropy maxima and minima with a variable periodicity determined by the constraints inherent in melting ice sheets and convective heat transfer rates.

Biomass and Climate: The present cycle of order has been interrupted during the last millennium. An alternative destructive force has intercepted the biomass recovering from the last glacial maximum. Instead of glaciers destroying the biomass, mankind, the tool-making animal, is wiping out nature's bounty.[4]

The biomass level in the biosphere has been reduced to a level not seen since the last glacial maximum, 20,000 years ago (see Figure 2), and climatic entropy is once again on the march. Heat is escaping from the tropics to the

> The biomass level in the biosphere has been reduced to a level not seen since the last glacial maximum, 20,000 years ago and climatic entropy is once again on the march.

temperate regions and to the poles, causing them to warm. But this time the biomass has not been a victim of glacial ice scouring the surface of the earth. This time the biomass has succumbed to land clearing for agriculture, for buildings, for impervious surface cover and for energy infrastructure. Warming of the temperate and arctic zones has left few continental glaciers or ice sheets to melt, providing space for recovering biomass. More likely deserts will expand, the few remaining mountain glaciers will melt, sea levels will rise, land areas will shrink and weather characteristics will become increasingly convective and violent as economic activity increases and biomass destruction proceeds at an ever increasing rate.

In many places the environment has been degraded to such an extent that biomass cannot recover by itself without human intervention. Replacement of biomass to stabilize the climate must be given our highest priority.

In many places the environment has been degraded to such an extent that biomass cannot recover by itself without human intervention. Replacement of biomass to stabilize the climate must be given our highest priority.

Biomass and soils contain three times more carbon than there is in the atmosphere.[5] The amount of carbon absorbed from the atmosphere through photosynthesis in green plants could return atmospheric carbon dioxide concentration to pre-industrial levels within two years if it were kept out of the atmosphere and not returned through decomposition.

If the amount of carbon stored in the biosphere were increased by 10%, it could remove all the excess carbon dioxide from the atmosphere. This would reverse the accumulation of carbon dioxide in the oceans, drawing it out into the atmosphere, and initiating a trend toward natural ocean pH levels that would begin to reduce ocean acidification immediately and return it to steady state over a period of a few thousand years.

Changing to policies and practices that encourage biomass proliferation rather than biomass destruction could accomplish this objective in less than a decade. Two case studies are discussed in this book where huge amounts of biomass are being created that are noticeably improving environmental conditions and correcting the carbon balance of the earth. These projects are also producing regional economic prosperity and political stability as they are reducing regional poverty levels.

One of these projects, the Restoration of the Loess Plateau in Northeast China (also called the Three North Shelter Belt Development Program) has included the creation of 18 million hectares of new forests by planting tens of billions of trees.

The second project, in an earlier stage of development, is the Great Green Wall of the African Sahel, a nine-mile wide wall of forest stretching 4,300 miles across the African Continent. The completed project will cover 24 million acres with forest and will impede or prevent the southward expansion of the Sahara Desert.

The biomass replacement in the Loess Plateau project alone could have a significant mitigating effect on global warming and climate stability. Smaller projects are underway in many countries on every continent.

Replacement of biomass in the biosphere is a low-tech way to replace what we have taken from nature that has destroyed the constraints on the climate and unleashed the entropy dragon. This can be done by improving horticultural and forest management practices and by taking stewardship of our natural biomass resources.

> Replacement of biomass in the biosphere is a low-tech way to replace what we have taken from nature that has destroyed the constraints on the climate and unleashed the entropy dragon.

Biochar: Biochar, or charred biomass, (charcoal) is one tool out of many that may be used for achieving these ends.[6] Biochar enhances plant growth in some circumstances by large percentages. Biochar is resistant to decay and stays in the soil for hundreds to thousands of years increasing the carbon content of the soil and decreasing the carbon content of the atmosphere. Making biochar releases copious quantities of recoverable heat that can be used to offset energy presently generated by fossil fuels.

> Biochar supercharges the photosynthetic process that removes carbon from the atmosphere and stores it as biomass in the environment.

Biochar supercharges the photosynthetic process that removes carbon dioxide from the atmosphere and stores it as biomass in the environment. It provides a store of non-decaying carbon in the soil, reducing the proportion of soil carbon that returns to the atmosphere. Energy generated during biochar making can be recovered at higher efficiency than energy generated by combustion of solid fuels.

The production and use of biochar in agriculture and in the environment packs a triple bonus punch, so it is a source of great excitement among agricultural and environmental scientists. This book is about how global warming is affected by the transfer of energy across the surface of the globe and how the use of biochar may stimulate the biosphere and correct climate instability by restoring order to the climate system.

Chapter Three
Summary

Chapter Three References

[1] Valsaraj, Kalliat, T: "Elements of Environmental Engineering-Thermodynamics and Kinetics": CRC Press, Baton Rouge, Fla., Copyright 1995

[2] Schneider, Eric, D, & Sagan, Dorion: "Into the Cool: Energy Flow, Thermodynamics and Life": University of Chicago Press, Chicago, Ill.: Copyright 2005

[3] Strogatz, Stephen, H.: "Sync: How Order Emerges From Chaos in the Universe, Nature and Daily Life': Hyperion Books, New York, NY: Copyright 2003

[4] Smil, Vaclav: "Harvesting the Biosphere – What We Have taken From Nature" MIT Press, Cambridge, Mass. Copyright 2013

[5] Goreau, Thomas J., and Larson, Ronal W.: "Geotherapy: Innovative Methods of Soil Fertility Restoration, Carbon Sequestration and Reversing CO_2 Increase": CRC Press, Taylor and Francis Group, Boca Raton, Fla.: Copyright 2015

[6] Bates, Albert: "The Biochar Solution, Carbon Farming and Climate Change": New Society Publishers, Gabriola Island, B.C., Canada, Copyright 2010

Part Two

Basic Concepts

Chapter Four

Constraints and Functionality

Chapter Summary

Functionality is a bulk property of a system. Randomness is a molecular scale property. In order for useful functionality to emerge from a system molecular properties must be constrained to work in unison. As more and more molecular interactions are constrained to work in unison utility emerges from the system.

A system in equilibrium is minimally constrained, and so it has no utility or functionality. As constraints are added to the system promoting bulk activity the properties of utility and functionality emerge.

The utility and functionality of a system are totally dependent on the ability of the molecular sub-units to work together in an organized fashion. Randomness is the arch-enemy of utility and functionality.

When the randomness of the world increases, order disintegrates and function ceases. When constraints proliferate and energy flow stabilizes, the world becomes functional and its utility increases.

In this chapter, we will describe these relationships and develop an understanding of how and why they work that way.

Chapter Four
Constraints and Functionality

It is important to understand that complexity represents a degree of constraint. A system is functional only if it is constrained. No system can undergo any macroscopic change unless it has energy flow and constraints. In this chapter, we will try to make the reasons for this clear.

Any system that is totally isolated from the rest of the world will undergo diffusion caused by thermal agitation that will eventually smooth out all variability within the system and leave it completely uniform to the maximum extent allowed by the system constraints. Physical scientists also call this condition of maximum uniformity maximum entropy or equilibrium.

The property of uniformity means that no part of the system is different from any other. In this state there are no differences in potential to drive any change, and so no bulk activity of any kind will take place within the system. When all differentials have equilibrated in this way the system is said to have experienced a "heat death".

When all differentials have equilibrated the system is said to have experienced a "heat death"

One of the things that make entropy so deadly is that every condition or state has an equal probability of occurring. In a universe of nearly infinite numbers of states, the probability of any particular state occurring is nearly zero. So the probability of the system taking on any definable configuration is virtually non-existent.

Fortunately, matter has properties that define the states a system is capable of taking. Once the system is defined, the fatal improbability of assuming a recognizable configuration is removed. The system definition reduces the probability of impossible states to zero and leaves the system with a manageable number of relatively highly probable states.

Matter has properties that define the states a system is capable of taking. Once the system is defined, the fatal improbability of assuming a recognizable configuration is removed.

The properties of matter restrain the system from assuming all those states that are impossible and define the states that are possible. They even define the probabilities of most states. The system once defined is constrained away from states that are improbable and toward more probable states.

A system is constrained into functional status by defining its properties. It is also constrained by defining its boundaries and their types of permeability.

> A system is constrained into functional status by defining its properties. It is also constrained by defining its boundaries and their types of permeability.

We will address some of these issues in our discussion of thermodynamics.

Generally, systems of interest are not very entropic, or random, or without direction. They have shape and boundaries and structure and properties that cause them to be functional and interesting. Most interesting systems can increase their entropy by a lot and still be functional and far from their maximum entropy.

It is an intuitive reaction to think that a system that is constrained is prevented from occupying some states and therefore cannot do as much as an unconstrained system can. In fact, exactly the opposite is true! By eliminating many entropic configurations and by defining the possible configurations, constraints relieve the system of the deadly randomness that saps all utility.

> Constraints relieve the system of the deadly randomness that saps all utility.

There is no tool that can perform every job. Until you define what the job is, it is impossible to design a tool for it. Once freed of the need to do everything, a system can be functional within its range of utility. This is why constraints on sounds are necessary to make a language, constraints on symbols are necessary to make an alphabet like Sequoya's Syllabary and constraints on molecular interactions are necessary to form an ordered universe.

Figure 4 illustrates how order, complexity and functionality emerge when constraints are applied to thermodynamic systems. Entropy, randomness and dysfunctionality are all characteristic of unconstrained systems.

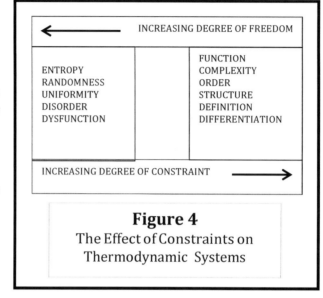

INCREASING DEGREE OF FREEDOM		
ENTROPY RANDOMNESS UNIFORMITY DISORDER DYSFUNCTION		FUNCTION COMPLEXITY ORDER STRUCTURE DEFINITION DIFFERENTIATION

INCREASING DEGREE OF CONSTRAINT

Figure 4
The Effect of Constraints on
Thermodynamic Systems

The constraints we are talking about constrain entropy formation, not system function. The universal tendency to increase entropy needs to be constrained in order to enable systems to provide utility and functionality.

The act of constraining a system allows it to be functional in ways that could never be realized without the constraints, just as it is impossible to play a game until some rules are decided upon. Rules constrain the set of possible moves to those that shape the aspect of the game.

Like the stories in Harvey Cox's intellectual space, constraints provide a structure. Until a system is ordered by constraints there is no way to define it except that a disordered system is simply uniform. No part of the system is any different from any other part. Within such a system there is no way to find any condition different from the average condition that exists everywhere.

A uniform system has no differentials, no variability in its conditions. Under these circumstances there is no potential for change other than absolute infinitesimal chance. There are no gradients to resolve, no driving forces to respond to.

This is the condition of maximum entropy that scientists call equilibrium. When a state of equilibrium is reached in a system, no further change will take place. No processes can occur. The system is essentially "dead". It has expended all its differentials. This is the fate of every system that is isolated from interactions with the rest of the world. Figure 5 illustrates such a system and lists some of its properties.

> When a state of equilibrium is reached in a system, no further change will take place. No processes can occur. The system is essentially "dead". It has expended all its differentials.

Neither matter nor energy can penetrate the boundaries of this system nor affect the behavior of its contents.[1]

It is a worthwhile mental exercise to consider what would happen if an isolated system could be perturbed in such a way as to induce a differential in its internal conditions. Of course, the definition of an isolated system precludes this possibility, but the exercise is worthwhile anyway.

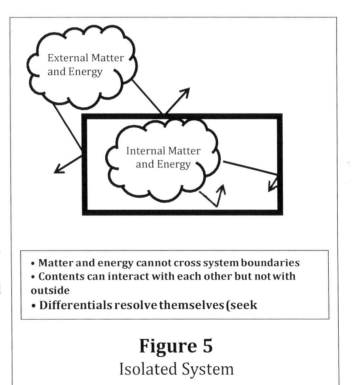

- Matter and energy cannot cross system boundaries
- Contents can interact with each other but not with outside
- Differentials resolve themselves (seek

Figure 5
Isolated System

Such an exercise leads to the condition illustrated in Figure 6. Once perturbed, the process of diffusion would induce a flow across the differential until the system equilibrates once again. The system rapidly returns to the original state of

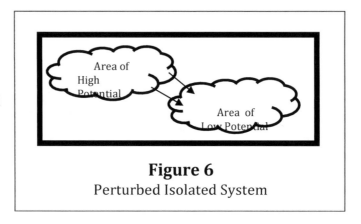

Figure 6
Perturbed Isolated System

uniformity or equilibrium otherwise known as maximum entropy.

This behavior is characteristic of isolated systems, systems in which the boundaries are completely impervious to matter and energy. Classical thermodynamics does not deal with structures, barriers or boundaries that exist within the system, like the one shown in Figure 7, only the boundaries of the system itself. Internal structures or barriers may delay or prevent the return to equilibrium.

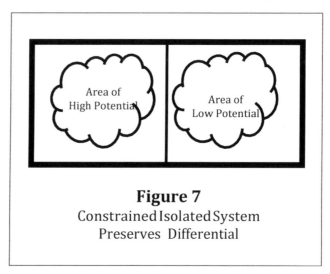

Figure 7
Constrained Isolated System
Preserves Differential

The way to prevent or delay the take-over by entropy involves restraining the system by the insertion of a barrier or constraint that restricts the flow that is necessary to return it to equilibrium. Such a constrained system is illustrated in Figure 7. The barrier obstructs the reorientation of the system back to the entropic or uniform state. If such a barrier is absolutely impermeable, the system will stay out of equilibrium as two independent isolated systems forever. The result is two systems, each at equilibrium, under different conditions.

If the barrier is not absolute, but permeable instead, the two systems will continue to interact with each other through the constraint until they eventually reach the same equilibrium condition. This kind of barrier is shown in Figure 8. The permeable barrier has introduced a time function by delaying the approach to equilibrium. The systems still equilibrate with each other, but they do so slowly over an extended period of time.

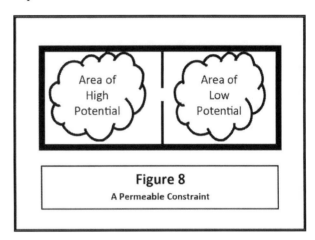

Figure 8

A Permeable Constraint

Like the resistor shown in Figure 1, this type of barrier allows a system to maintain different conditions in its different parts as long as flow persists through the system, specifically across the barrier. It also allows the system to equilibrate slowly if flow through the system stops. This kind of barrier offers continuity to the system in the face of varying flows and differentials.

Any barrier or structure that divides an isolated system changes the system in one fundamental and important way. Without the barrier there was no difference in conditions throughout the system. There was no hope of change since no different conditions existed. As soon as the barrier is inserted, a system is created with a second set of conditions. The barrier has made the difference between a system that has no potential for differentials or any hope of change at all, i.e. the condition known as maximum entropy; and a system that has two different sets of conditions to choose from.

The system has been elevated from one in which there is no variation to one in which the concept of choice has meaning. Anything existing within the system that has the ability to make a choice now has choices to be made. The system and the entity within it have been elevated to the status of being able to make a choice, and it is the barrier or constraint that has made the difference.

The barrier that has restricted the ability of the system to flow and to resolve or eliminate differences has endowed the system with the ability to maintain differences and variations. Multiple internal barriers will further restrict flow rates and delay attainment of equilibrium. Figure 9 shows the effect of several barriers. Whole networks of structures within a system give it the ability to maintain many different and highly variable conditions as it reacts to variable energy flows.

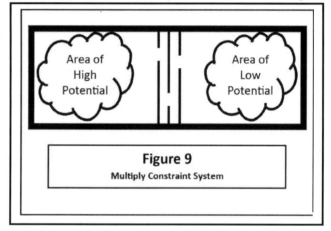

Figure 9

Multiply Constraint System

The potential on the left side of Figure 9 gradually diminishes in successive compartments as it works its way down to the low potential area. Whole networks of structures within a system give it the ability to maintain many different and highly variable conditions, and flows of many different rates and kinds.

No barriers are absolute, they are permeable or semipermeable. Flows that are proportional to the differential but inversely proportional to resistance will establish themselves across each barrier, and if the system is a fully isolated one, it will proceed to advance slowly toward the equilibrium state or heat "death" in every area of the system. Only if energy and/or matter are allowed to enter the system from some outside point of higher potential and to leave the system to some area of lower potential will it maintain the differentials necessary for life.

Matter and/or energy flow must continue across the barriers and/or structures inside a system (such as cell walls and organelle membranes) until it discharges at an area of reduced potential. The very nature of the flow will maintain differences in potential across barriers as long as the flow persists.

This combination of flow plus resistance (barriers) insures continuous variability of conditions in nature. The system represented by the surface of the earth and its contents is "liberated" from the crushing uniformity of entropy that characterizes most planets and other heavenly bodies and delivered into the world of variability of options and potentials by the resistances to flow processes offered by the structures within it and by the flux of energy passing through it from the sun to the vastness of space.

This is the basis for the idea that nature is "liberated" by "constraints". Biological constraints have a way of reproducing themselves in the form of biomass. Under the right conditions they proliferate into living matrices of elaborate complexity. Life emerges and evolves under these conditions.

> Under the right conditions biological constraints proliferate into living matrices of elaborate complexity. Life emerges and evolves under these conditions.

Diffusion: Diffusion is the bulk flow of materials under the influence of a concentration differential. The concentration differential is a driving force and the constraint is a property of the material called the diffusion coefficient. The relationship between flow and potential differences is discussed in great detail and mathematical precision by Professor Park S. Nobel of the Department of Ecology and Environmental Biology at the University of California at Los Angeles in his book "Physicochemical and Environmental Plant Physiology"[2]. Dr. Nobel explains how, in a world of diffused energy, any differential represents a driving force and how physical properties of materials represent constraints to flows. Material and energy transfer occur in response to the driving forces and are resisted by the constraints. Different physical properties and energy potentials define how matter responds to differentials.

Chapter Four
Constraints and Functionality

Fick's First Law, for example, describes the diffusion of chemical components.

$$J = -D \, \frac{dc}{dx}$$

Where: J is the material flow or flux

    D   Is the diffusion coefficient (a physical property/constraint

    $\dfrac{dc}{dx}$ Is the concentration differential (a driving force)

The diffusion coefficient, D, is a function of particle mobility. For example, large, heavy molecules have more inertia than smaller, lighter ones and so they will not respond to collisions with other molecules as readily. Hence, larger, more massive and more complex molecules are less mobile and have smaller diffusion coefficients. From this it is clear that larger, more massive and more ordered molecules are more resistant to diffusion than smaller, more entropic molecules are. Entropic molecules diffuse away into space and leave the more ordered and massive molecules behind.

Diffusion is a special case of the general tendency for matter and energy to flow toward a state of lower chemical potential. Concentrated solutions have higher chemical potential than more dilute solutions so matter tends to disperse or flow from a region of higher concentration/potential energy state to a lower one.

The idea that a concentration differential represents a driving force is not necessarily an intuitive one. It is not easy to relate to the idea that material flux can be induced by a concentration differential just as it is by a pressure differential. Yet, this is indeed the case. Material flux is induced from a high concentration to a low concentration just as flow is induced from a high pressure to a low pressure or from a high elevation to a low elevation. In all cases material and energy flow down a potential gradient toward a minimum value, which is achieved at equilibrium when the differential is fully depleted.

In biological systems, the energy potential is measured by something called the Gibbs free energy, which is the energy available from a process during which the temperature and pressure remain constant. Usually the pressure and temperature of biological reactions are atmospheric pressure, at 14.7 psia, and normal body temperature at 98.6 °F. Alternatively, room temperature may be used as a basis.

The relationships between solute concentration and chemical potential in an ideal solution are quite complicated and are based on the ideal gas laws formulated by the British chemist Robert Boyle, French scientist, Jacques Charles, and the French physicist Gay Lussac in the 17th and 18th centuries. They are defined by the following equation:

$$\mu = \mu^* + RT \ln c$$

Where: μ is the chemical potential of the solute
μ^* is the chemical potential of pure solute
R is the perfect gas constant
T is the absolute temperature
ln c is the natural log of the solute concentration

Hence, in diffusing from areas of high concentration to areas of low concentration the solute molecules are flowing down a potential energy gradient. Several other kinds of potential energy gradients exist in nature. For example, the "force" of gravity creates a potential energy gradient between two masses. The attraction between two opposite electrical charges creates a potential gradient between two electrically charged ions. Dr. Nobel defines the overall chemical potential of a solution as the sum of the individual potentials of all the dissolved chemicals, and he represents it with the equation:

$$\mu = \mu^* + RT \ln c + \bar{V}P + zFE + mgh$$

Where: $\mu, \mu^*, R, T and c$ are all as defined above
V-is the change in volume per mol of chemical
P is the absolute pressure
z is the charge on the ion

Chapter Four
Constraints and Functionality

F is Faraday's constant
E is the electrical potential
m is the mass of the molecule
g is the gravitational constant
h is the height above a baseline

In this equation, the term RT ln c. represents the chemical potential due to concentration, the ⊽P term represents the potential due to volume change at constant pressure, the zFE term represents potential due to electrical interactions, and the mgh term represents potential due to elevation changes in the gravitational field.

This equation describes how energy and matter flow in all biological processes. Dr. Nobel describes it as *"one of the most elegant relations in all of biology"*. It describes the constraints that define how each chemical species responds to the various gradients encountered in biological systems.

Chemical and physical processes interact spontaneously in such a manner as to minimize the total chemical potential or Gibbs free energy. Some potentials may increase at the expense of others, as Frost would say, "The sun runs down in sending up the brook", but the equilibrium state is reached when the sum of all the potentials is minimized at which point all flows of energy and matter cease, a state which is known as "heat death". Even Frost's "West Running Brook" equilibrates as its flow stops and dissipates when it reaches the sea.

Chemical and physical processes interact spontaneously in such a manner as to minimize the total chemical potential or Gibbs free energy. Some potentials may increase at the expense of others, but the equilibrium state is reached when the sum of all the potentials is minimized at which point all flows of energy and matter cease, a state which is known as equilibrium, or "heat death".

The equilibrium state is the final state of all thermodynamically isolated systems in which no matter or energy can enter or leave the system. However, when systems are more open, as in the case of a closed system (one that can take in and discharge energy but not matter) or an open system (one that can take in and discharge both matter and energy), the equilibrium state is never reached.

> When systems are more open the equilibrium state is never reached. Flows enter the system from areas of higher potential and leave the system to areas of lower potential. Such systems operate under more ordered conditions of lower entropy called "steady state".

Flows enter the system from areas of high potential (low entropy) outside and leave the system to areas of lower potential (higher entropy) outside. Such systems operate in a more ordered condition of lower entropy called "steady state" flow.

These flows are resisted by material constraints, and in overcoming the constraints they produce potential differences. This kind of differentiation is contrary to the uniformity that is required by equilibrium, or entropy. So, unless a system is isolated, or immersed in an environment in equilibrium, it can never attain equilibrium itself.

The photosynthetic production of biomass produces an array of structures throughout the biosphere that offer containment and continuity to natural processes. The variability and restrictions provided by biomass offer continuity of flow and natural associations without which the

> Biomass constitutes an array of structures throughout the biosphere that offer containment, differentiation and continuity to natural processes. The constraints provided by biomass offer continuity of flow and natural associations without which the conditions suitable for life, including climate conditions, will quickly deteriorate through increasing entropy into those unsuitable for life.

conditions suitable for life, including stable climate conditions, will quickly deteriorate through increasing entropy to those unsuitable for life.

Dr. Geoffrey Poole works for Montana State University and the Montana Institute on Ecosystems developing constraint based ecological modeling techniques. The constraints that Dr. Poole models control river and floodplain ecosystems across spatial scales from stream reaches to river networks.

In their paper, "A Generalized Optimization Model of Microbially Driven Aquatic Biogeochemistry Based on Thermodynamic, Kinetic and Stoichiometric Ecological Theory", Dr. Poole, et al, describe some of the physical and chemical constraints that cause ecological differentiation.[3]

Advanced thinkers in the fields of biochemistry and biophysics are developing an understanding of the role of constraints and restrictions on the way materials behave. This understanding offers us insights into the processes that originate and proliferate living systems. Two statements by leading scientists in the field of life sciences illustrate this new level of understanding how physical processes respond to constraints.

Donald T. Haynie, director of the Bionanosystems Engineering Laboratory and Research Professor of Biochemistry and Biophysics at Central Michigan University, has recently authored a book on biological thermodynamics[4]. In describing the First Law of thermodynamics he says:

> *The First Law tells us with breathtaking generality that a boundary on the possible is a basic characteristic of our universe.*

What Dr. Haynie calls a "boundary on the possible" is the constraint system that leads to the functionality of matter. By his statement Dr. Haynie is telling us that the basic properties of matter act as inherent constraints on how materials interact and behave. Matter is not random. It follows the rules and reflects the basic order of the universe. The science of thermodynamics is an expression of some of the rules that constrain the activities of the universe.

Dr. Terrence W. Deacon, Professor of Biological Anthropology and Neuroscience and Chair of Anthropology at the University of California, Berkeley, has written a book called "Incomplete Nature – How Mind Emerged From Matter"[5]. Toward the end of his book, Dr. Deacon reaches the conclusion:

> *The subtitle of this book is slightly misleading. Mind didn't exactly emerge from matter, but from constraints on matter.*

Both of these scientists are realizing that the way space is constrained and the inherent properties of the materials it contains, determine the functionality of the system it comprises. The properties of energy, matter and space are a manifestation of the constraints that are inherent in nature. Solid structures form additional constraints that are external to matter itself. With the proper constraints and a flow of energy, a system organizes, becomes ordered and functional. Without the constraints, or without flow, a system disorganizes, becomes disordered and non-functional.

There is hard evidence that the relationship between energy flow and constraints determines exactly how much order and complexity a system can maintain against the natural tendency to disorganize. Dr. Eric Chaisson, Professor of Astro-Physics at Harvard University, has developed a field of study he calls "Cosmic Evolution" that describes the energy flow density that will produce and maintain a specific amount of order. The order in the system increases as the energy flow density is increased.

Dr. Chaisson describes this relationship in detail in his recent book, *Cosmic Evolution – The Rise of Complexity in Nature*[6]. The conclusion of his work is that the complexity of a system can be quantified by identifying the mass density of energy flowing through it. By this means, Dr. Chaisson defines the relationship between energy flow through a system, system size and system complexity.

Excessive Differentials: Resiliency of constraints is important as well. Energy differentials can be destructive. Constraints can be overwhelmed. Order can be destroyed. The force of gravity acting on its huge mass, for example, can overwhelm a star. As its nuclear fuel runs out it collapses and then explodes in a supernova obliterating its ordered state. A biological cell is kept in turgor by osmosis. If the balance of chemical concentrations becomes unfavorable the cell can collapse (by wilting) or explode (rupturing) from excursions of osmotic pressure.

> Energy differentials can be destructive. Constraints can be overwhelmed. Order can be destroyed.

It is important for stability that differentials remain within the structural strength parameters of their constraining systems. Abrasion must be limited to values that can be tolerated by emerging ordered systems. If incipient order is ruptured or eroded away, the procession toward complexity is thwarted.

The cellular nature of biological systems is a response to these facts. Entropy discharged from a system can simply diffuse back in, and order once established can be carried out, unless a semi-permeable barrier like a cell wall encloses the system. Once entropy is discharged from a cell, the cell wall functions to contain the order that is left behind and to keep the entropy from diffusing back in. This allows order and functionality to concentrate, accumulate and compound itself within the boundaries of the cell wall.

Many natural systems develop excessive differentials that, if allowed to resolve themselves unconstrained, would be destructive to ordered patterns. By segmenting itself into tiny individual structures, living systems distribute these differentials and the forces and stresses they produce over a network of interconnected structures that, together, can sustain the imposition of large stresses that could not be tolerated individually.

Information and Constraints on Probability: Like the constraints on sounds in languages and the constraints on symbols in an alphabet and the constraints on intellectual space from stories, constraints on probability allow physical systems to carry information.

To gain further insight into the nature of constraints we can make use of concepts from information science. How do you quantify information? One way is to consider the amount of information in a binary decision, a decision that can exhibit only two states; yes or no, on or off, heads or tails, up or down. If the two states are equally probable, a 50% probability of each outcome, as in a coin toss, there is no way to predict in advance which state the system will come to. In this case one can only wait for the process to finish (the coin to be tossed) and observe the final state (heads or tails). Since there was no way to predict the outcome in the beginning our observation of the final state carries the maximum amount of information.

If the coin had been weighted so that the two outcomes were not equiprobable, say a 75% chance of heads and 25% chance of tails, you would have an advance indication of the probability of the outcome. The information you would gain from observing that the flip came out heads is considerably less because you expected it to be heads in the first place. Observing the results of the flip would only confirm or refute your suspicion.

The more you already know about the probability of the outcome of a binary decision, the less information is revealed by

> The more you already know about the probability of the outcome of a binary decision, the less information is revealed by the actual observation.

the actual observation. This results in an information vs. probability curve like the one shown in Figure 10 (next Page).

The information revealed by the process is maximized when the process is totally random so that both final states are equally probable.

In a case where the outcome is already known in advance the information revealed by the process is zero since you already knew the outcome.

This system of quantifying information can be elaborated to apply to almost any system, and it is very useful since all modern computers and other information technologies are based on binary information systems. The amount of information contained in a binary choice between two

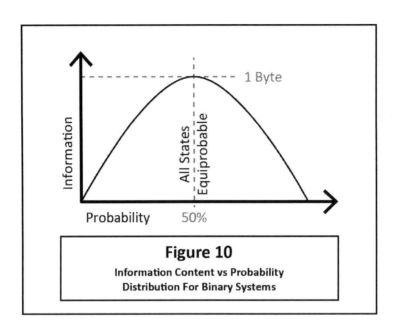

Figure 10
Information Content vs Probability
Distribution For Binary Systems

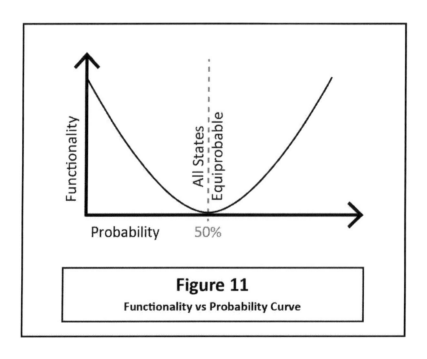

Figure 11
Functionality vs Probability Curve

equally probable states is called one byte, and it is the standard measurement for information systems.

The Functionality Curve: To understand the effect of system parameters or constraints on functionality one needs to consider a reflected curve, the one shown as a line on Figure 11.

The curve in Figure 11 indicates the amount of information that is known about the system in advance of the operation (coin flip) and before the observation. If the two states are totally random and, therefore equiprobable, it is impossible to make any prediction about the outcome. The information known in advance is therefore zero. If the outcome is known before the operation begins the information previously known is one byte. The

> If the two states are totally random, and therefore equiprobable, it is impossible to make any prediction about the outcome.

information known at any other probability distribution is defined by the curve represented by the Figure 10.

Having established the ideas in Figures 10 & 11 I want to consider what it takes to have a system that is in any way functional. To function is, by definition, to behave in a predictable way. Predictable behavior is by definition, not random, but following some kind of rule. A curve of functionality on a binary decision chart would look something like Figure 11. A random system in

> To function is, by definition, to behave in a predictable way. Predictable behavior is by definition, not random, but following some kind of rule.

which every interaction has an equal probability has zero functionality. A system that is behaving, not randomly, but according to some predetermined probability has increasing functionality.

In order to be functional a system's behavior must be governed by unequal probabilities, not random chance. This is why the constraints encountered in natural systems

> In order to be functional a system's behavior must be governed by unequal probabilities, not random chance.

make the universe function rather than diffusing into nothingness.

For a system consisting of one binary choice the functionality curve may look like the curve in Figure 11. But for a system of many parallel choices with varying probabilities the functionality curve may have an unexpected shape. The important thing to take from this analysis is that functionality depends on a departure from randomness, unequal probabilities of various outcome states.

A system in which every state and every interaction is equally probable may provide the most information when an observation is finally made, but it is completely unpredictable and therefore totally non-functional. On the other hand, a system in which some states and interactions are far more probable than others can't help but be functional.

This, then, is inherent in the definition of a constraint. A constraint is anything that changes the probability function of a system away from equiprobability or randomness, which is entirely dysfunctional, and toward order and variability which enables function.

Constraints may be properties of materials. A carbon atom, for instance, is not equally likely to interact with a hydrogen atom as it is with an oxygen atom. The probabilities are governed by concentration, temperature, pressure and chemical properties among other things. Any attempt to predict the results of such interactions by assuming randomness or equal probabilities is doomed to failure. This explains the utter failure of attempts to defend or refute evolution by assuming that it may be the result of random molecular interactions.

Constraints may also be imposed by solid structures within a system. A solid material makes a better container than a semi-permeable membrane. Constraints define a system and predict its functionality. Science is the study of constraint systems and predicting the functionalities that emerge.

Constraints define a system and predict its functionality. Science is the study of constraint systems and predicting the functionalities that emerge.

The point of all this is that entropy (randomness) must be constrained in order for functionality to emerge. The more that is known about the constraints that define a system, the more predictable its functionality will be.

In conclusion it may be stated that scientists may very well assume randomness as a first approximation in the absence of other information, sometimes with remarkable success. Early chemists, for example, like Robert Boyle and Jacque Charles studied the properties of gases and formulated laws predicated on the idea that gas molecules moved with random motion. This representation proved to be very accurate, and the behavior of gases is still predicted based on Charles and Boyles Laws. The assumption of randomness is very close to correct in describing the motion of "ideal" gas molecules. Almost from the beginning, however, it was recognized that size and complexity were properties that caused deviation from the "Ideal Gas Laws".

Charles Darwin, for lack of any better information, chose to assume that genetic information was subject to random mutations as it passed from generation to generation. This assumption led to a body of science that very closely described the observations that were available in Darwin's day.

Modern technologies in the study of genetics and ecology are far more sophisticated, and they are able to detect differences between Darwin's data and modern day observations. It is now clear that mutations are not at all random, but constrained to follow the laws of chemistry and physics. Modern modeling techniques take advantage of ecosystem constraints to accurately determine effects from ecosystem changing patterns.[7] This observation leads to significantly different conclusions that are discussed later in the thermodynamics section of the book.

Chapter Four References

[1] Valsaraj, Kalliat T.: "Elements of Environmental Engineering: Thermodynamics and Kinetics": CRC Press, Lewis Publishers, Boca Raton, Fla.: Copyright 1995.

[2] Nobel, Park: "Physicochemical and Environmental Plant Physiology", Academic Pres, Inc. San Diego, CA. Copyright 1991

[3] Payne, R.A., A.M. Helton, G.C. Poole, C. Izureta, A.J. Burgin and F.S. Bernhardt: "A Generalized Optimization Model of Microbially Driven Aquatic Biogeochemistry Based on Thermodynamic, Kinetic and Stoichiometric Ecological Theory"; Ecological Modelling, 279: 1-18

[4] Haynie, Donald T.: "Biological Thermodynamics"' Cambridge University Press, Copyright 2008

[5] Deacon, Terrance W.: "Incomplete Nature - How Mind Emerged From Matter", W>W>Norton & Company, LTD, London, UK, Copyright 2013

[6] Chaisson, Eric: "Cosmic Dawn – The Origins of Matter and Life", Universe.com, Inc, Lincoln NE, Copyright 1981

[7] Xiao, Xiao, O'Dwyer, James P. and White, Ethan, P.: "Comparing-Process Based and Constraint-Based Approaches For Modelling Macroecological Patterns": Ecology, Volume 97 Issue 5, May 27 2016 pages 1228 – 1238

Chapter Five

The Laws of Thermodynamics

Chapter Summary

Since the beginning of scientific thought, people have been fascinated by the proliferation of order and structure in biological systems. The science of thermodynamics, specifically the Second Law, was thought to define the limits of such complexity, and to demonstrate the impossibility of emerging complexity in physical systems.

Careful analysis of the definition of entropy and its properties and flow characteristics reveals how it does not maximize in thermodynamically closed systems. In fact, exactly the opposite is the case. Entropy proliferates as heat flows from a closed system, but it does so on the downstream side of the system boundary, that is, in the greater universe. As it does so it leaves an entropy deficit behind.

In fact, the faster a system produces entropy, the more it is directed toward the outside universe, leaving more ordered contents within the system.

In this chapter we will attempt to clarify the mechanics of these processes and how they work.

Chapter Five
The Laws of Thermodynamics

There is a widespread impression that the laws of thermodynamics require that matter and energy disperse and that order deteriorates into disorder everywhere without exception. This idea is based on the study of isolated systems as shown in Figures 3 & 5, and it has been used to explain a wide range of observations in scientific circles and in every-day life. As a concept it has been very successful at explaining the degrading of ordered systems in many applications. Engineered systems were demonstrated to follow this principle, and the emergence of order in biology was thought of as an unknowable mystery, a miracle of proportions unapproachable by scientific theory.

But this is a concept that has been abused by over application. There is precedent within the laws of thermodynamics to explain the emergence of order. Order precipitates in gross physical ways in engineered systems as well as in more subtle ways in living systems. The aim of this chapter is to understand the cause of the rise of order in natural and unnatural systems, so bear with me as I review some of the concepts from the centuries-old study of thermodynamics.

> There is precedent within the laws of thermodynamics to explain the emergence of order. Order precipitates in gross physical ways in engineered systems as well as in more subtle ways in living systems.

First Law of Thermodynamics – Conservation of Matter and Energy... The philosophers of ancient Greece sensed the importance of thermodynamic principles. Epicurus (343BC – 230BC) said that *"The sum total of things was always such as it is now, and such it will forever remain"*. In these words he inadvertently stated the First Law of thermodynamics.

The First Law of thermodynamics states that matter and energy can neither be created nor destroyed. This seemingly simplistic observation is the basis for a wide range of analytical techniques including mass and energy balances.

Isolated Systems... Early attempts to analyze matter and energy interactions were simplified by conceptually isolating the system under consideration so that no extraneous matter or energy could enter or leave the system and affect the accuracy of the results (see Figure 12). This is an example of the scientific practice of reductionism, the

Figure 12

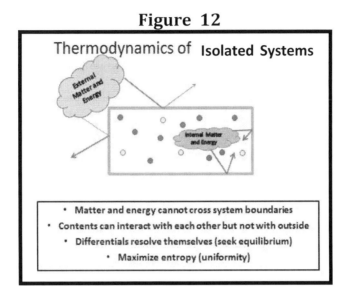

elimination of extraneous effects by focusing on smaller and smaller systems and constraining the system to the point where no other processes can interfere. Adding this kind of constraint makes it possible to understand the functional dynamics of the system in isolation from the environment.

In an isolated system where neither matter nor energy may enter or leave the system, the First Law states that the matter and energy content in the system cannot change. Though the contents may interact chemically or physically, the total mass and energy content of the system is constant.

Thermal agitation within an isolated system causes its contents to equilibrate, differentials to resolve themselves, and disorder or entropy to maximize. Isolated systems tend to progress toward a condition of maximum uniformity, equilibrium or disorder. How uniform the final condition will be is determined by constraints inherent in the system including the physical and chemical properties of its contents and its structural organization.

Chapter Five
The Laws of Thermodynamics

Open Systems... The concept of an isolated system is an abstraction. All real systems interact with their environment in ways that absorb and emit mass and energy through their boundaries. The need to study systems where matter and energy can enter or leave the system has led to the concept of an open system. An open system is depicted in Figure 13.

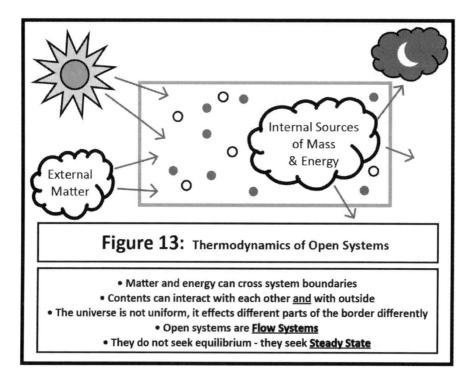

Figure 13: Thermodynamics of Open Systems

- Matter and energy can cross system boundaries
- Contents can interact with each other _and_ with outside
- The universe is not uniform, it effects different parts of the border differently
- Open systems are **Flow Systems**
- They do not seek equilibrium - they seek **Steady State**

For open systems an axiomatic extension of the first law is that matter and energy fluxes will balance over the system. Accumulation in the system will occur at a rate equal to the difference between the matter and energy entering a system minus the matter and energy leaving the system. This assurance allows us to do a great deal of analysis of processes that would not have been possible if this had not been the case. For example, if we know the input to a process and we know what the process is we can predict the quantity, composition and condition of the product materials. Alternatively, if we know the input and output of a process we can tell a great deal about what's happening within the process. Process engineers in the design and analysis of all industrial, civil, physical and chemical systems use these techniques.

Biological systems comply with the first law as well. Everything we know about metabolism, for instance, starts with a basic first law analysis of the life process.

Since the universe is not uniform, it affects different parts of an open system boundary differently. Matter and energy enter at some places and leave at others. The system becomes a flow system. It no longer seeks equilibrium, but rather seeks steady state, a condition of constant, continuous flow and maximum entropy production rate, but not maximum entropy content. In fact, "maximum entropy production rate" implies less than "maximum entropy content". Non-isolated systems necessarily seek and maintain order levels greater than maximum entropy content.

> Flow systems do not seek maximum entropy as isolated systems do. Rather, they seek steady state, a condition of constant, continuous flow and maximum entropy production rate, but not maximum entropy content. In fact, maximum entropy production rate implies less than maximum entropy content, a more ordered condition.

Steady state is a quasi-stable condition. It maintains differentials that are stable and persist as long as the flows continue. When inputs and outputs change, conditions within the system change in response.

Closed Systems: Energy is more difficult to contain than matter is because it can propagate by conduction through most materials that would contain matter. Because of this it is well to recognize that systems may exist that would contain matter rather well but would not present much of a barrier to the passage of energy. This kind of system is called a "closed system". The matter contained in such a system is constant, but the energy content of the system may change as a result of the fact that energy can pass right through the boundary.

Chapter Five
The Laws of Thermodynamics

Most systems that appear to be isolated are actually closed systems. For instance, if the entire earth is taken as a system it will be noted that little or no exchange of matter occurs between it and surrounding areas. However, energy pours continuously on the surface of the planet from the sun, our nearest star, and energy radiates continuously from the surface of the earth into the vastness of outer space. A system of this sort, one that is closed to the exchange of matter, but is subject to a constant energy flux is considered a closed system.

> Energy pours continuously on the surface of the earth, and energy radiates continuously from the surface into outer space. Yet virtually no matter transfer takes place. A system of this sort, one that is closed to the exchange of matter but subject to energy flux is considered a closed system.

Constrained Systems: As mentioned before, no boundary is an absolute barrier to the passage of matter or energy. Leakage or permeability is a property of all obstructions. A boundary is therefore not a complete barrier to the passage of matter and energy, but a resistance to it, like the resistor depicted in Figure 1 or the constraints discussed in Chapter 4. The resistance to flow offered by a barrier determines the time it takes for something to pass through, and therefore the time it takes for the system to approach equilibrium. The difference between isolated, open and closed systems is therefore based on the resistance of their boundaries to flows of matter and energy and not to any fundamental difference in the nature of the systems. I find this understanding helpful to the analysis of non-equilibrium thermodynamic systems.

> The difference between isolated, open and closed systems is therefore based on the resistance of their boundaries to flows of matter and energy and not to any fundamental difference in the nature of the systems.

Second Law of Thermodynamics – the Entropy Law... Aristotle, (384BC – 322BC) claimed that, "Nature abhors a vacuum". And he was right! He had hit upon an example of the Second Law of thermodynamics.

The Second Law of thermodynamics takes Aristotle's insight to a much broader and more general, over-arching view, claiming that "Nature abhors a differential of any kind". Aristotle's observation about a vacuum was a special case of the more general Second Law.

The Second Law says that for any process in an isolated system entropy (uniformity) always increases until it reaches a maximum called equilibrium under the specified conditions. Another way to say this is "differentials resolve themselves." Systems tend toward uniformity. Unless energy is added, anything in nature flows from areas where it is plentiful to areas where it is lacking. This applies to matter, to energy, even to order and to information. The ultimate result of diffusion is the even distribution of matter and energy throughout space; complete uniformity or equilibrium.

Thermal entropy, however, is neither matter nor energy. Entropy is a function of energy content and temperature. It is a measure of disorder and an inverse measure of functionality or usefulness. When entropy maximizes, functionality and usefulness minimize.

The entropy content of a system is defined as the quotient of an extensive variable, one that depends on the size of the system (heat content) divided by an intensive variable, one that is independent of the size of the sample (temperature). Entropy, itself, however is an extensive variable and it establishes a balance over the system. We will spend a lot of time understanding the properties of entropy in later pages of this book. Equation 1 expresses the definition of entropy:

$$S = Q/T \qquad \text{(Equation 1)}$$

Where S is the entropy content of the system
Q is the heat content of the system
T is the temperature of the system

115

Chapter Five
The Laws of Thermodynamics

An entropy gradient is a driving force for the flow of order. Matter and energy spontaneously flow from an ordered state to a disordered state. Since a disordered state is defined as a higher entropy state, the natural flow of entropy is always from lower entropy content to higher entropy content. This is rather counterintuitive since this has the appearance of flowing "uphill". Still, the tendency for entropy is to flow from lower, more ordered conditions to higher, more disordered conditions.

Thermal Entropy: The concept of entropy is a difficult one. It is counterintuitive in the sense that it is measured on an inverse scale. Higher entropy implies less order, while lower entropy implies greater order. This definition leads to the peculiar characteristic that entropy flows "uphill". While all other differentials are resolved by flow from areas of higher concentration to areas of lower concentration (down-hill flow), entropy differentials induce flow from areas of low entropy to areas of high entropy (apparent uphill flow). It appears that entropy naturally flows "uphill".

While all other kinds of energy gradients tend to resolve themselves, entropy gradients naturally tend to increase. As entropy flows from ordered areas to disordered ones the disorder in the disordered areas increases, and the order in the ordered areas increases as well. The Second Law of thermodynamics says that the increase in disorder produced in the disordered areas must be greater than the increase in order produced in the ordered areas.

If the increased order is trapped by a system boundary such as a cell membrane, order will accumulate within a system. The entropy discharged will disperse into the greater universe while the order will be retained and increased within the system.

If the increased order is trapped by a system boundary such as a cell membrane, order will accumulate within a system. The entropy discharged will disperse into the greater universe while the order will be retained and increased within the system.

A Thought Experiment: Consider if you will, a deluge of entropy that rains down upon a planet and flows across the surface, up a gradient toward higher and higher entropic conditions. Ultimately, it radiates away from the planet toward even more entropic conditions in the universe beyond. In the environment of the planet there exists an infinitude of resistances to the flow of entropy that direct the flow toward certain areas and away from others, limiting the entropy level in any part of the system. Some kinds of resistances allow entropy to pass easily leaving behind an ordered pool of matter. Other types of resistances cannot pass much entropy, but retain it keeping it within a region as a source of disorder. The distribution and effectiveness of these resistances determine a pattern of ordered areas that become impounded behind the resistances or constraints in the system.

You and I are puddles of ordered matter retained by constraints that easily pass entropy, and readily retain order as the deluge of disorder passes by us. If our boundaries fail to discharge enough disorder, we will become disordered ourselves, we will not survive. If our boundaries change in such a way as to easily pass additional disorder, we will suddenly experience an increase in potential for greater order and complexity through the process of evolution.

The Density of Entropy: Dispersion of entropy into the universe produces ever more entropy, but it spreads out over a larger and larger volume resulting in a decreased entropy density.

In order to visualize how this seeming absurdity could be true, let us look at the mathematical definition of entropy presented above. Entropy is defined as the heat content of a system divided by its absolute temperature.

$$S = \frac{Q}{T}$$

Where: S is the entropy content of the system
T is the absolute temperature
Q is the heat content of the system

Chapter Five
The Laws of Thermodynamics

Since entropy is inversely related to the temperature, a BTU of heat at a higher temperature has less entropy than a BTU of heat at a lower temperature does, and conversely, a BTU of heat at a lower temperature has more entropy than a BTU of heat at a higher temperature does. In a thermal system heat flows from areas of high temperature to areas of low temperature (see Figure 14) and it carries entropy with it in the amount of $\Delta Q/T$ where ΔQ is the amount of heat flowing to the area of lower temperature. So entropy has the peculiar property that it spontaneously flows uphill. It flows from an area of higher temperature (lower entropy) to an area of lower temperature (higher entropy).

And since entropy, is associated with energy, it flows from a hot area to a cold area; it increases in quantity as it goes. Like a snowball rolling downhill heat picks up entropy as it progresses from hot to cold. Entropy is a vector quantity flowing in the direction of lower temperature.

Energy Flow and Order: When energy flows from a hot area to a cold area, the entropy change for the hot area is defined as the heat transferred divided by temperature. Since heat always flows out of a hot area the energy change for the hot area is negative, heat is removed. For the hot area the change in entropy is

$$\Delta S = \frac{\Delta Q}{T_h}$$

Where: ΔS is the change in entropy
ΔQ is the heat transferred
T_h is the temperature of the hot area

Note that the entropy change when heat flows out of a hot area is always negative. The hot area always winds up in a more ordered state. As it loses energy, it loses entropy.

For the cold area the change in entropy is:

$$\Delta S = \frac{\Delta Q}{T_c}$$

Where: T_c is the temperature of the cold area

Note that the entropy change when heat flows into a cold area is always positive. The cold area always winds up in a more disordered state as it picks up entropy.

Since T$_h$ is always greater than T$_c$, $\frac{\Delta Q}{T_h}$ is always less than $\frac{\Delta Q}{T_c}$ So the entropy change for the whole system ($\frac{\Delta Q}{T_c}$ - $\frac{\Delta Q}{T_h}$) is always positive. The entropy of the universe always increases in any spontaneous thermal process as shown conceptually in Figure 14.

Figure 14

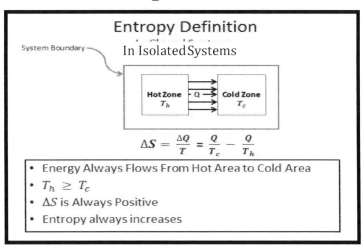

Entropy Definition

In Isolated Systems

Energy Always Flows From Hot Area to Cold Area
- $T_h \geq T_c$
- ΔS is Always Positive
- Entropy always increases

But the entropy change in the cooling portion of the system is always negative resulting in a more ordered state. Heat flowing out of a cooling system carries entropy away with it.

Whenever thermal energy flows into a system it carries entropy with it, warming the system and making it more disordered at the same time. Whenever thermal energy flows out of a system it carries away entropy, cooling the system and making it more ordered at the same time.

> Whenever thermal energy flows out of a system it carries away entropy, cooling the system and making it more ordered at the same time.

The order generated in the system by exiting energy is always greater than the disorder brought into the system with the entering energy because the energy discharges at a temperature lower than that at which it came in. Hence the flow of energy through a system is always an ordering process.

> The flow of energy through a system is always an ordering process.

As energy flows downhill its entropy content flows uphill, it increases. The entropy increase is associated with decreasing differentials. The smaller the differential becomes, the closer the system approaches to uniform temperature. Entropy is always associated with uniformity.

At this point it is worth noting that since heat carries entropy with it as it flows, the entropy increase always ends up on the cooler end of the flow. It's as if the heat flow pushes the entropy along ahead of it. When heat is transferred across a membrane, the entropy always ends up on the downstream side of the membrane. When heat is flowing out of a cell, disorder is projected out with it. Order is always left behind, within the boundaries of the cell.

An Example: Because of the definition of entropy (see equation 1) the entropy content of a system has units of energy divided by absolute temperature. In the English system this would be expressed as BTU/°R. In the international system it would be Joules/°K. Where °R and °K are temperatures on the Rankin and Kelvin scales respectively.

If it is the rate of entropy flow we are expressing, the units are energy/temperature·time, or BTU/°R Hr in the English system and Watts/°K in the international system.

To cite an example of entropy increase, let us consider heat flowing through a block which has been placed between a heat source (hot reservoir) and a heat sink (cold reservoir) like that shown in Figure 15. The heat flowing through the block is carrying entropy with it at a rate of $\Delta Q/T$.

Suppose the heat source is at a temperature of 110°C (383°K or 690°R) and the heat sink is at a temperature of 100°C (375°K or 672°R). Also suppose that heat is flowing through the block at a rate of 1 BTU/hour (0.293 Watts).

Entropy is entering the block along with the heat at a rate of

$$1 \text{BTU/Hr/690}^{\circ}\text{R} = 0.00145 \text{ BTU/Hr} \cdot ^{\circ}\text{R}$$

Or in international units:

$$0.293 \text{ Watts/383}^{\circ}\text{K} = 0.000765 \text{ Watts/}^{\circ}\text{K}$$

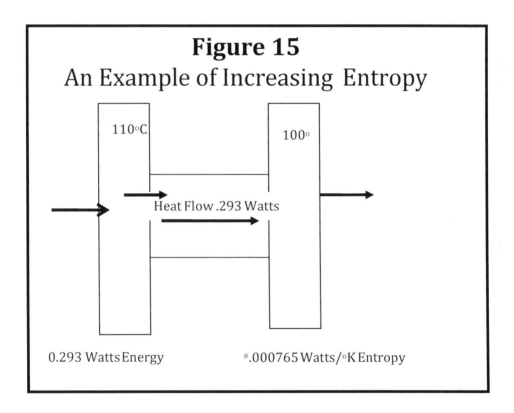

Figure 15

An Example of Increasing Entropy

110°C

100°

Heat Flow .293 Watts

0.293 Watts Energy   #.000765 Watts/°K Entropy

The heat flow is adding this amount of entropy to the warm end of the block. It will alter the condition of the block to some more disordered state. If the heat source is hot enough, for example, it will melt the end of the block. Otherwise, it will just add to the disorder of the block by warming it.

Entropy is leaving the block along with the heat at the cold end. But at the cold end of the block the energy contains more entropy, so the block loses entropy at a rate of:

$$1BTU/Hr/672°R = 0.00149 \ BTU/Hr·°R$$

Or in international units:

$$0.293 \ watts/375°K = 0.000781 \ watts/°K$$

This amount of entropy is leaving the block at the cold end, and it will alter the state of the block to some more ordered state. If the cool reservoir is cold enough it will freeze the end of the block. Otherwise, it will just add to the order of the block by cooling it.

Since more entropy is leaving the block than is entering it, the block, as a whole, is experiencing an overall loss of disorder equal to the difference between the entering disorder minus the leaving disorder.

$$0.00145 \ BTU/Hr·°R - 0.00149 \ BTU/Hr·°R = 0.00004 BTU/Hr·°R$$

Or in international units:

$$0.000765 \ Watts/°K - 0.000781 \ Watts/°K = 0.000016 \ Watts/°K$$

This is a measure of the energy that has been spent ordering the system. It may not seem like much energy, but if the order can be made permanent, for example by establishing it in a resilient solid or semisolid state it will persist and become cumulative. Like Sequoyah's Syllabary, it will fix information and allow it to spread for use by others and stabilize the life processes of the future.

The Inevitability of Order Generation: At this point it should be clear that any closed system that is in steady state with respect to energy flow is experiencing an entropy imbalance, discharging more entropy than it takes in, and therefore it is creating order within itself. The only way for such a system to be in entropy balance is for it not to be in energy balance but to take on more energy than it discharges in which case it warms up.

Order will always rise in a closed system unless the entropy discharge is less than the sum of the entropy generated in the system plus the entropy input. But we know that the entropy discharge is always more than the entropy input, so unless there is a lot of entropy generated within the system the order in a steady state, closed system always increases.

> Unless there is a lot of entropy generated within the system the order in a steady state, closed system always increases.

Order does not have to accumulate in a non-isolated system, but it always will unless the system can discharge ordered matter as well as ordered energy. In this case, the system becomes an open system.

Entropy Discharge: As energy leaves a closed system through the system boundary, it carries entropy with it. The release of this entropy is what creates order within the system. In a closed system, this order is manifested in the matter that is retained within the system.

If ordered matter is allowed to leave the system (as in an open system) the order that is in the matter leaves with it diminishing the rate at which order will be accumulated. If all the order generated in a system leaves with the matter and energy leaving the system, no order accumulates. This is the situation that thermodynamicists were contemplating in the 18th century calling it a heat engine.

States of Matter: The state that matter is in (solid, liquid or gas) has a major effect on its ability to leave a thermodynamic system. In general, solids (low entropy) have a harder time passing through a cell membrane than liquids (moderate entropy) or gases (high entropy) do. Therefore, any process that results in the precipitation of order in a solid form facilitates the retention of that order within the cell. This is also true of larger, more complex molecules. They cannot permeate the cell membranes as easily as smaller molecules. By this means biological systems generate order within their cells by building large, complex, functional molecules internally that cannot escape the boundaries of their closed systems.

Entropy and Information... Information is non-uniformity. If a system is totally uniform (the same everywhere), there are no differentials to identify in order to tell one part of the system from any other, hence there is no information. But if different parts of a system are different from each other (if differentials exist) it is possible to tell what part of the system you are in, and so there is, by definition, information in the system. By this reasoning, it should be clear that information is antithetical to entropy. Systems with lots of information, such as structures, symbols, differentials and gradients, have low entropy content or a high degree of order. Systems with low information content show a low degree of order or high entropy content.

> Information is antithetical to entropy. Systems with lots of information, such as structures, symbols, differentials and gradients, have low entropy content or a high degree of order. Systems with low information content show a low degree of order or high entropy content.

Structures: Even in an isolated system, differentials can be maintained against the flow toward entropy by structures, i.e. compartmentalization, or constraints within the system (see Figure 16).

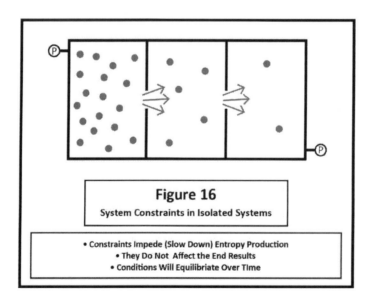

Figure 16

System Constraints in Isolated Systems

- Constraints Impede (Slow Down) Entropy Production
- They Do Not Affect the End Results
- Conditions Will Equilibriate Over Time

Any structure is a barrier as described in Chapter 4. Structure imposes constraints on the system limiting the flow of energy or matter within the system and allowing it to maintain the differentials necessary for information and activity over a longer period of time. Otherwise the system will equilibrate (resolve the differentials) and entropy will increase rapidly to maximum uniformity.

The second law determines that, unless constrained by structure or other internal constraints, material flow in any isolated system will always occur from areas of high potential to areas of low potential, that is, from areas of high pressure to areas of low pressure, from high concentration to low concentration; energy flow will always occur from areas of high temperature to areas of low temperature; information will always degrade; organization will always lapse into chaos. These changes lead to destruction of differences, resolution of differentials, increasing uniformity, maximizing entropy and minimizing information content.

Structures impose constraints on flows within a system, preserving differentials and increasing the statistical probability that more organized states may appear decreasing the uncertainty about the state of the system. This limiting of randomness or uncertainty opens the door to organization, variety and the existence of differentials, all states other than maximum entropy. So in this sense, the addition of constraints actually opens the system to a plethora of new and different states of being.

> the addition of constraints actually opens the system to a plethora of new and different states of being.

Students of complexity recognize systems of complex constraints that display steady state flows of energy or mass as "far from equilibrium systems". These systems actively solicit energy flow into themselves and they discharge it to achieve more order and greater dissipative capacity. Like a snowball rolling downhill picking up speed and mass as it goes, these systems proliferate order, complexity and energy dissipation capacity as they push entropy into the greater universe and build order and complexity within themselves.

Chapter Five
The Laws of Thermodynamics

Stewart A. Kauffman, a professor at the University of Calgary with appointments in biological sciences, physics and astronomy has written extensively on how complex living systems "self-organize". In his book, "Origins of Order – Self-Organization and Selection in Evolution"[1] he details physical, chemical and biological factors that contribute to the build-up of order and complexity in thermodynamic systems.

The Purpose of Life: The prevailing scientific view seems to be that transitions between phases and flow regimes work to improve the rate of transfer of energy. The growth of entropy or the resolution of differentials seems to be the major purpose of life. Those who are spiritually inclined see this as a reason for existence. Organization precipitates to enhance the flow of energy speeding up the production of entropy, resolving differentials in the universe.

But I have pointed out that complex structures impede progress and slow down the flow of energy and stabilize it giving it continuity. This seems to represent a major disagreement between my work and the prevailing scientific view. For some further discussion on this I recommend a book by Eric D. Schneider and Dorian Sagan called "Into the Cool – Energy Flow, Thermodynamics and Life"[2]

After pondering this dichotomy, I have reached a degree of satisfaction in an analogy with the Department of Transportation that I will elaborate here. As traffic increases on the back roads of our country, traffic jams become more and more frequent, and progress becomes slower and slower. Eventually the Department of Transportation comes along and does a study that shows that this road has become a bottleneck, and a new road should be built. The new road opens up the bottleneck and increases traffic flow in the whole region served by the road. This much of the analogy is consistent with the prevailing view. The complexity associated with the new highway has increased the rate of flow of all the traffic in town.

But as the population grows and conditions change, traffic inevitably increases still further, and it soon reaches a point where the new road is itself becoming a bottleneck. The new road, built to last decades, has now become obsolete; it no longer can handle the traffic flow. This part of the analogy is consistent with my point of view. The complex system at this point; built to increase flow, alleviate flow patterns and reduce differentials has now become a point of resistance once again. The Department of Transportation does another study and finds a new road, or a different kind of road should be provided. The new highway must now be upgraded or replaced.

State-of-the-art technologies when the highway was built are now no longer used, population patterns have changed, and highway standards now call for different types of construction. The highway structure has now outlived its usefulness.

If this analogy is correct, both points of view are right. Complexity can be an enhancement to energy flow and entropy creation, or it can be a constraint depending upon what stage of its life cycle you are looking at.

One key point here is the state of matter in which the complexity occurs. Complex fluid flows are persistent only as long as energy flows exist. They collapse when energy flows decline again. Changing regimes is as easy as walking by a new route. But when more resilient forms appear, flow regimes are locked in by the persistence of structure. This makes it possible for a flow regime to become obsolete, like the highway does. Its presence holds up progress. What started out as a solution has now become the problem. Changes occur when a new path is found that releases enough Gibbs free energy to dismantle the existing path. This sounds remarkably like a mechanism by which evolution might take place.

Maximization of Entropy in an Isolated System... In an unconstrained isolated system the contents will soon come to equilibrium. Equilibrium is the state where entropy is at its maximum under the system conditions and the operative constraints inherent in the system. This was the point of view of French engineer and physicist, Sadi Carnot in 1824 and German physicist Rudolph Clausius in 1850, pioneers of the science of thermodynamics.

Chapter Five
The Laws of Thermodynamics

If structure exists in an isolated system it will slow down the rate at which differentials will dissipate and equilibrium will be attained. This extends the time it takes to reach equilibrium and gives the process direction and continuity. Still, the inexorable march toward equilibrium will continue.

Entropy in Non-Isolated Systems: In 1943 at a meeting of the Dublin Institute for Advanced Studies at Trinity College in Dublin, Ireland, Nobel Laureate Dr. Erwin Schrodinger[3] presented an analysis that showed that the approach to equilibrium that happens in isolated systems did not occur in flow systems. In a closed system that passes energy but not matter across its boundaries, such as a planet, or in an open system that passes matter and energy across its boundaries, like an ecosystem or a living organism, energy is brought into the system from outside and used to maintain order in a metastable condition of steady-state disequilibrium (see Figure 17).

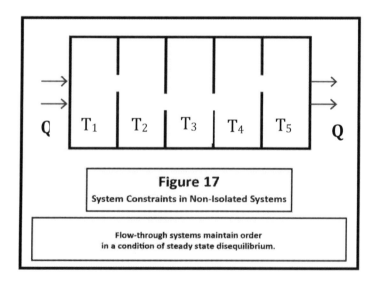

Figure 17

System Constraints in Non-Isolated Systems

Flow-through systems maintain order
in a condition of steady state disequilibrium.

Energy brought into the system from outside sources can continuously maintain differentials allowing energy flow to continue, resisted only by system structures and other constraints. It goes without saying that the energy must be discharged from the system to the outside environment at a lower potential.

By utilizing the flow of energy from the outside an organism can maintain its structures and create new ones without succumbing to the inevitable Second Law as isolated systems do. The structures of living systems serve to constrain entropy production making it smooth, continuous and stable. This allows life to sustain itself on intermittent energy inputs.

Dr. Schrodinger's views on this were published in 1944 in a book with the title, "What is Life?". These ideas inspired the great biochemists, James D. Watson and Francis Crick in their quest to unlock the genetic code and the structure of DNA.

Maximization of Entropy Production Rate: Being accustomed to the idea that physical systems always increased in entropy content, physical scientists were reluctant to accept the idea that entropy might spontaneously decrease, or order increase, in physical systems. As it became increasingly clear that energy inputs might be useful in increasing the order in a system the theorem of minimum entropy production was developed.

The Belgian physical chemist and Nobel Laureate, Ilya Prigogine, addressed this problem very succinctly in his book, "From Being to Becoming – Time and Complexity in the Physical Sciences"[4]. He identifies a group of linear, non-equilibrium processes that operate in systems near the equilibrium condition. In this realm they obey the principle of minimum entropy production rate. But he compares them to other processes that operate in entropy states that are farther from equilibrium with the following words:

> *It was clear when this theorem was formulated that it was strictly valid only in the neighborhood of equilibrium, and for many years great efforts were made to extend this theorem to systems further from equilibrium. It came as a great surprise when it was shown that in systems far from equilibrium the thermodynamic behavior could be quite different – in fact, even directly opposite that predicted by the theorem of minimum entropy production.*

Prigogine demonstrated that entropy production rates far greater than the minimum were to be expected in these types of systems.

Chapter Five
The Laws of Thermodynamics

In 1989 Dr. Rod Swenson, then at the University of Connecticut observed the emergence of "spontaneous order" in living matter and sociological systems. He coined the Law of Maximization of Entropy Production.[5] This law states:

Entropy will be maximized as rapidly as allowed by system constraints.

This new thermodynamic principle was soon recognized as a corollary to the Second Law. It asserts that in unconstrained open systems entropy production will occur very rapidly, while in a heavily constrained open system entropy production is a slow, steady process. In inadequately constrained systems, entropy production may even be violent and cause great damage as we have seen in Chapter 4 in the case of a supernova or in plant cells over-pressurized by osmosis. Alternatively, it may just cause violent, unstable heat and mass transfer as we have seen in recent recurrent violent weather events.

Biomass structures made from carbon dioxide, water and energy from the sun act as significant internal constraints to entropy production. Energy captured by biomass is forced to flow smoothly and continuously through biological constraints rather than erupting violently and turbulently toward uniformity. Energy expended without biomass quickly promotes entropy and equilibrium.

As Biomass structures proliferate, continuity of processes increases as does the complexity of the constraints that control the process. Complexity and stability proliferate in living systems. We will now look at some quantitative data that show how the process of biological proliferation works and how the characteristics of complexity grow

Chapter Five References

[1] Kauffman, Stewart, A.: "Origins of Order – Self Organization and Slection in Evolution", Oxford University Press, NY, NY, Copyright 1993

[2] Schneider, Eric, D. and Sagan, Dorion: "Into the Cool – Energy Flow, Thermodynamics and Life": University of Chicago Press, Chicago, Ill: Copyright 2005

[3] Schrodinger, Erwin: "What is Life", Cambridge University Press, Cambridge, UK, Copyright 1967

[4] Prigogine, Ilya: "From Being to Becoming – Time and Complexity in the Physical Sciences"W. H. Freeman Company, San Francisco, Copyright 1980

[5] Swenson, Rod: "Emergence and the Principal of maximum Entropy Production": Multi-level System Meeting, 32 Theory , Evolution and Non-Equilibrium Thermodynamics: Proceedings of the 32nd Annual Meeting of the International Society for General Systems Research.

Chapter Six
Mass and Energy Flows on Planet Earth

Chapter Summary

The temperature of the planetary surface is a function of the balance between the energy that impinges on the planet from sources in outer space and the energy that radiates away from the planet to return to the void. Energy entering and leaving the earth's surface must pass through the emptiness of space and the gaseous atmosphere, and it is dominated by radiative transfer mechanisms.

Energy circulates around the planet to make up for regional radiative imbalances. The mechanism for circulation of energy around the globe is convection, and it involves movement of huge masses of atmospheric gases and ocean waters.

The order and complexity at the surface of the earth are controlled by an entropy balance. Entropy is molecular disorder, and the more it can be removed from the earth and rejected into outer space, the more complex functions the earth can support. Complexity and evolution are controlled by the entropy balance.

Because of the mathematical relationships that define energy and entropy, these two factors cannot be in balance at the same time. If the earth is cooling its complexity is stable or increasing. If the earth is warming, its complexity is diminishing.

Energy and entropy balances for the earth are illustrated to demonstrate the relative magnitudes of these effects.

Carbon occupies reservoirs of hugely varying entropy content on the earth's surface. The system responds to entropy changes by exchanging carbon between these reservoirs. A carbon cycle diagram is presented to illustrate the overall cycle, and a Keeling Curve shows the carbon dioxide levels measured in the atmosphere at the observatory on Mount Mauna Loa in Hawaii.

Huge reserves of methane are stored in methane clathrate accumulations in sea ice. The potential disastrous release of this potent greenhouse gas through warming and melting clathrate deposits is discussed.

Sequestration of carbon in soils by manipulation of the soil carbon reservoir and enhancement of biomass productivity is another kind of carbon redistribution with significant potential. The whole biosphere can be used to enhance carbon storage. The use of charcoal or "biochar" to enhance this process is discussed.

Chapter Six
Mass and Energy Flows on Planet Earth

The Earth's Energy Budget: The laws of equilibrium thermodynamics accurately predict the behavior of isolated systems, that is, systems in which no matter or energy can enter or leave the system. The earth is not an isolated system; in fact, it behaves more like a closed system. Radiant energy from the sun bathes the earth in energy at a rate of 174 petawatts (one petawatt is 10^{15} watts). This total influx is called the solar constant. When this energy is distributed over the entire cross sectional area of the earth of 1.28×10^{14} square meters, the average intensity of the incoming energy is 1.36 KW/square meter. Since the actual area of the earth's surface is four times greater than its cross sectional area the average energy intercepted by the average square meter of ground is one quarter the average intercepted by the cross section or 340 Watts per square meter.

After adjusting for reflection back into outer space and absorption by the atmosphere and clouds, about 48% of this energy or 163 watts per square meter penetrates to the land and oceans and is absorbed at the surface.

This energy is not uniformly distributed. It is far more concentrated at the equator where its angle of impingement is more nearly perpendicular to the surface. It may increase the temperature or entropy of the earth, or it may be converted into biomass by photosynthesis. If it falls on areas devoid of life it is quickly converted into heat and then to entropy. This process leads to desertification of wide areas of the earth's surface. Eventually it must be radiated back into outer space or it will be stored as increased heat or entropy in the earth.

Other sources of energy also provide heat to the earth. These include geothermal energy generated internally by nuclear reactions in the earth's interior (about 47 terawatts), lunar or tidal energy (about 3 terawatts), and waste heat from human activities (about 13 terawatts) (one terawatt is 10^{12} watts). All of these sources combined are less than .035% of the solar influx. Solar energy influx dwarfs all the other energy sources combined. Figure 18 shows the energy flows that constitute the energy balance of the earth.

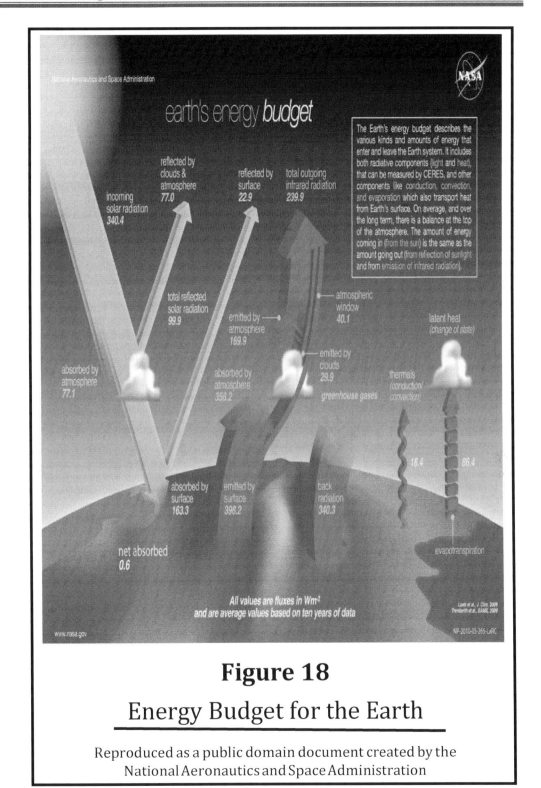

Figure 18

Energy Budget for the Earth

Reproduced as a public domain document created by the
National Aeronautics and Space Administration

Chapter Six
Mass and Energy Flows on Planet Earth

The Equilibrium Temperature of the Earth: The earth behaves like a thermodynamic closed system. It gains or loses virtually no material through its atmospheric boundaries, but energy from the sun floods over its surface and is radiated back into space.

Because it is a closed system and not an isolated system, the earth is not in equilibrium and so it has no equilibrium temperature. Literally, the equilibrium temperature occurs only when no bulk flow of energy exists. Because of the flooding of solar energy across the earth's surface, the earth maintains a condition of "steady state" which is entirely different from equilibrium. An isolated system in equilibrium tends to maximize disorder or uniformity, while a closed system in steady state tends to maximize order or complexity.

The flow of energy into and out of the earth's surface is depicted in Figure 18. The sum of the discharges and the sum of the influxes are approximately equal meaning that the energy budget of the earth is in balance.

The Law of Maximum Entropy Production says that a closed system produces entropy at a maximum rate, and this can only be achieved if the state of the system differs from its maximum entropy. In order to support entropy production a system must be to some degree ordered. In fact, the rate of entropy production is proportional to the degree of deviation from maximum entropy of the system. This is why a closed system tends to become maximally ordered. These ideas are discussed elsewhere in the book.

What is being described as the equilibrium temperature of the earth is really the steady state, thoroughly mixed temperature of the earth, and it represents the average temperature of the earth's surface under the steady state conditions imposed by the sun as an energy source and outer space as an energy sink. The earth would not organize into an ordered, complex system if it were at equilibrium.

For the temperature of the earth to stabilize in steady state, the energy of the shortwave (light) radiation absorbed by its surface must equal the long wave (heat) radiation discharged into outer space. If the shortwave, incoming radiation increases, the earth will warm up until the outgoing, long wave radiation again equals the incoming radiation. Once the incoming energy and the outgoing energy balance, the temperature of the earth remains stable.

> The earth behaves like a thermodynamic closed system. It gains or loses virtually no material through its atmospheric boundaries, but energy from the sun floods over its surface and is radiated back into space.

The energy coming in from the sun impinges on the earth at very short wavelengths, which are characteristic of the very high temperatures of its origin (5600K at the surface of the sun). The energy leaving the earth leaves at relatively long wavelengths characteristic of temperatures at the surface of the earth (60°F average earth surface temperature).

The radiative energy impinging on the earth from the sun, P_{in}, can be easily calculated from the equation:

$$P_{in} = (4\pi R_s \sigma T_s^4)\,(1-\alpha)\,(\pi R_e^2/4\pi D^2)$$

Where: R_s is the radius of the sun
T_s is the absolute temperature of the surface of the sun
σ is the Stephan Boltzmann constant
α is the albedo of the surface of the sun
R_e is the radius of the surface of the earth
D is the distance from the sun to the earth

The surface of the earth behaves much like a black body radiator in discharging its energy through its atmosphere into space. A black body radiates energy in proportion to the fourth power of its absolute temperature in accordance with the Stefan-Boltzmann Law. This relationship is expressed by the mathematical equation:

Chapter Six
Mass and Energy Flows on Planet Earth

$$J = \sigma T^4$$

Where: J is the power emitted per unit area

T is the absolute temperature of the body

σ is the Stefan-Boltzmann constant

The radiative energy emitted by the earth can be calculated by multiplying the energy emitted per unit area times the surface area.

$$P_{out} = 4\pi R_e{}^2 \sigma T_e{}^4$$

Where: R_e is the radius of the earth.

T_e is the temperature of the surface of the earth

Since the power entering the earth and the power leaving the earth are the same at steady state we can set the right halves of these equations equal to each other and solve the resulting expression for the temperature of the earth (T_e).

$$T_e = T_s (1-\alpha)^{1/4} (R_s/2D)^{1/2}$$

This expression gives the temperature that the earth must be in order to radiate enough energy to balance the energy impinging on it from the sun. The temperature turns out to be – 18°C (-1°F), which represents the average temperature the surface of the earth would be if it were free to radiate its energy into space.

The equilibrium temperature of the earth turns out to be – 18°C (-1°F), which represents the temperature the surface of the earth would be if it were free to radiate its energy into space.

But the atmosphere presents certain constraints on the system such that longwave energy cannot freely radiate through it. The actual average temperature of the earth's surface is 57.2°F, about 60°F above its equilibrium temperature. The warmer temperature is due to the trapping of heat by greenhouse gases in the atmosphere. The presence of these

The actual average temperature of the earth's surface is 57.2°F, about 60°F above its equilibrium temperature. The warmer temperature is due to the trapping of heat by greenhouse gases in the atmosphere.

gases is necessary to maintain an environment that is hospitable to existing ecosystems.

The radiative energy emitted by the earth can be calculated by multiplying the energy emitted per unit area times the cross sectional area. Some gases, like oxygen and nitrogen, are virtually transparent to longwave radiation and offer no resistance to its passage to outer space. Other gases, like carbon dioxide are more opaque to long wave radiation. They absorb it and become warm as a result. This effectively blocks the passage of energy impacting on those molecules out of the system. As these gases warm from absorbing the long wave energy they re-radiate energy in all directions, some of which goes to space and some of which returns to the earth, raising the surface temperature.

The amount of carbon dioxide in our atmosphere that produces our present climate is 278 parts per million (0.04%). Add more and the temperature warms, less and the temperature cools.

> The amount of carbon dioxide in our atmosphere that produces our present climate is 278 parts per million (0.04%). Add more and the temperature warms, less and the temperature cools.

There are other naturally occurring greenhouse gases, notably methane and nitrous oxide. Together these gases produce less than half of the greenhouse effect, but their energy blocking character is much more potent. Methane is nearly 30 times more potent than carbon dioxide is, and nitrous oxide is about 300 times more potent. These gases are relatively short lived and exist in the atmosphere in very low concentrations, and therefore their contribution to the greenhouse effect is relatively small.

The effect of carbon dioxide on surface temperatures can be extreme. The atmosphere of the planet Venus is 96% carbon dioxide. The calculated equilibrium

> The effect of carbon dioxide on surface temperatures can be extreme. The atmosphere of the planet Venus is 96% carbon dioxide. The equilibrium temperature is 8.3°F, but the actual surface temperature of Venus is 840°F, hot enough to melt lead.

temperature is 8.3°F, but the actual surface temperature of Venus is 840°F, hot enough to melt lead.

The carbon dioxide content of the earth's atmosphere is just enough to make us comfortable, but not so much as to make the earth uninhabitable...yet!

Energy Differentials on the Earth: The general flow of energy on the earth is shown in Figure 19.

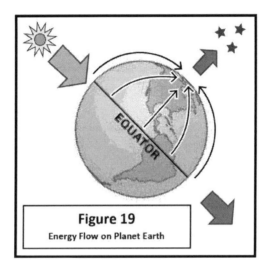

Figure 19

Energy Flow on Planet Earth

The equator receives the most intense solar energy because its angle of incidence is closest to 90°. This tends to make the equator warmer than the poles. Heat from the warm equator migrates toward the poles by convective air circulation and by ocean currents. Heat is radiated into outer space in greater quantities at the equator because the equator is warmer than other areas of the earth. Since the equator is also the longest latitudinal circumference there is also more area at the equator to radiate energy.

The general radiant energy discharge is shown in Figure 20.

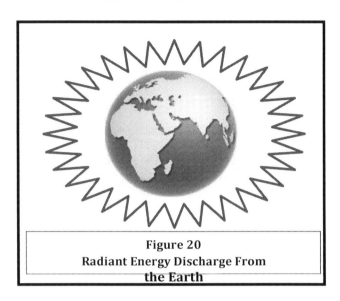

**Figure 20
Radiant Energy Discharge From
the Earth**

The equatorial regions dissipate energy by radiation to outer space as well as by convection to higher latitudes. The whole earth glows with a radiant energy discharge halo that is brighter in areas where the surface is warmer. More radiant energy is discharged at the equator than at higher latitudes.

Since more energy is extracted from the earth at the equator, and since entropy flow is defined by the equation $\Delta S = \Delta Q/T$ More entropy is also extracted at the equator giving equatorial land masses greater potential for generating ordered states.

Influxes of solar energy ultimately increase the temperature or entropy of the earth or they get rejected into space. The biosphere converts some of it into biomass, a more stable and complex (low entropy) form, and temporarily stores it in the earth's surface layers.[1]

Actual radiant energy discharge measurements are shown in Figure 21 an illustration of outgoing long wave radiation

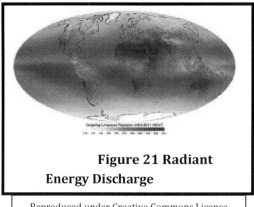

Figure 21 Radiant Energy Discharge

The greater energy discharge from warmer areas of the biosphere is quite apparent in the darker shading over the Sahara Desert, the Middle East, Australia and parts of Patagonia. The lighter band at the equator is due to the rain forest and its associated cloud belt. These differences in radiant energy discharge are very relevant to the appearance of complexity in warm areas of the biosphere as we shall see in later chapters. (Author: Giorgiogp2; File Airsorg.png). The text from this file states:

> *"Radiative cooling by outgoing longwave radiation is the primary way the earth system loses energy. The balance between this loss and the energy gained by radiative heating from incoming shortwave radiation determines global heating or cooling of the earth system. ... Local differences between radiative heating and cooling provide the energy (differentials) that drive (s) atmospheric dynamics.*

Note: Insertion of the word *"differentials"* is my addition

The Entropy Budget: As discussed in Chapter 5, entropy is an extensive property of a system, and so it establishes an entropy balance around the system. Entropy accumulation in a system is equal to the entropy entering the system plus the entropy generated from the processes within the system minus the entropy leaving the system.

If the entropy leaving the system is less than the entropy entering the system plus the entropy generated within the system, entropy increases in the system (disordering the system). If the entropy leaving the system is greater than the entropy entering the system plus the entropy generated within, the system is being depleted of entropy (becoming ordered). Figure 22 shows this entropy balance.

> If the entropy leaving the system is less than the entropy entering the system plus the entropy generated within the system, entropy increases in the system (disordering the system). If the entropy leaving the system is greater than the entropy entering the system plus the entropy generated within, the system is being depleted of entropy (becoming ordered).

The earth is a system that approximates a thermodynamically closed system, that is, it is bathed in energy from the sun, which it receives and

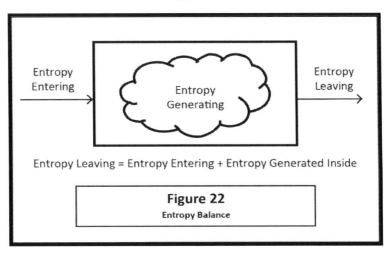

Entropy Entering → Entropy Generating → Entropy Leaving

Entropy Leaving = Entropy Entering + Entropy Generated Inside

Figure 22
Entropy Balance

re-radiates back into outer space, but it neither receives nor discharges any appreciable amount of mass.

Heat flowing into a system carries entropy into the system with it. Like the proverbial snowball, as it adjusts to the cooler environment the energy increases its entropy content. When the heat flows out of the system again it carries the extra entropy burden with it leaving the planet depleted in disorder.

Radiant energy has entropy content inversely proportional to its wavelength. Solar radiation carries with it entropy consistent with wavelengths emitted by the 5600K temperatures at the surface of the sun. Radiation emitted by the earth carries with it entropy consistent with wavelengths emitted by the 288K temperature of the earth.

The entropy balance of the earth has been measured and calculated and it is depicted in Figure 23. It can be seen that the entropy carried by solar energy impinging upon the earth is of the order of 40 MW/$^\circ$K·meter^2, and energy radiated away from the earth carries an entropy burden of 940 MW/$^\circ$K·meter^2. This leaves a net entropy decrease on the surface of the earth of 900 MW/$^\circ$K·meter^2, an immense imperative for developing order and complexity on the surface of the earth.

Entropy is an inverse measure of the usefulness of energy. Energy is very useful if it is at a high temperature (low entropy content). Energy is not useful if it is at a low temperature (high entropy content). Organizing the surface of the earth increases the functionality of the earth as it depletes the usefulness of the incoming energy.

The Biosphere: The biosphere, the collection of all living things on earth, acts like a heat engine. It receives energy from a hot source (the sun), converts some of it into useful, biochemical energy (biomass), and discharges the remaining heat to a cold heat sink (the earth itself).

The earth itself is a heat engine taking heat from several sources. It takes waste heat from the biosphere, it takes internally generated geothermal heat and it takes direct radiation from the sun. The work output from this heat engine is mostly in the form of material displacement such as volcanic activity, shifting continents, wind and weather, ocean currents and the hydrologic cycle. Waste heat is radiated into outer space.

These two heat engines operate in series. The biosphere feeds on the energy from the sun, discharges its waste heat to the earth and atmosphere, which radiate their waste heat to outer space.

As long as radiative pathways from the sun to the earth and biosphere, and from the earth to outer space are unimpeded and the basic structure of the system remains intact, a healthy biosphere performs its function as a heat engine producing biomass from solar energy with ease.

If the biological structure of the ecosystem or of the earth is damaged or destroyed the organization of the machine is gone and so the system fails. Energy is no longer recovered as useful biomass. Incoming energy accumulates as heat that degrades, sometimes very rapidly, into entropy. Entropy then reigns supreme consuming all available energy. That is why it is best to avoid excessive damage to the earth or the ecosystem from our daily activities.

If the biological structure of the ecosystem or of the earth itself is damaged or destroyed the organization of the machine is gone and so the system fails. Energy is no longer recovered as useful biomass. Incoming energy accumulates as heat which degrades, sometimes very rapidly, into entropy. Entropy then reigns supreme consuming all available energy.

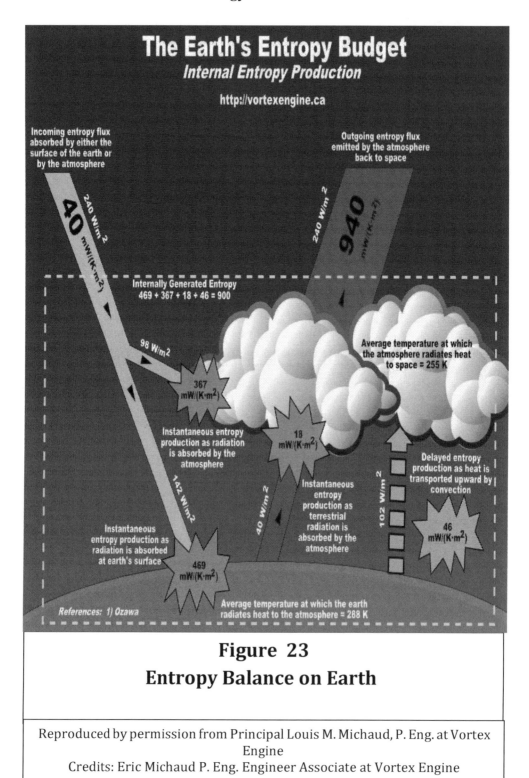

Figure 23
Entropy Balance on Earth

Reproduced by permission from Principal Louis M. Michaud, P. Eng. at Vortex
Engine
Credits: Eric Michaud P. Eng. Engineer Associate at Vortex Engine

Additional Credits for Figure 23

Credit for Figure 23 is given to Eric Michaud, engineer assistant at Vortex Engineering in Sarnia, Ontario, Canada.

Data were taken from research by:

- Hisashi Ozawa at the Institute for Global Change Research, Frontier Research System for Global Change, Yokohama, Japan
- Atsumi Ohmura at the Institute for Atmospheric and Climate Science, Swiss Federal Institute of Technology, Zurich Switzerland
- Ralph D Lorenz at the Lunar and Planetary Laboratory, University of Arizona, Tucson, AZ
- Toni Pujol at the Department de Fisica, Universitat de Girona, Catalonia, Spain.

The Second Law of Thermodynamics and the Global System: A Review of the Maximum Entropy Production Principle
Published in Volume 41, 3 Reviews of Geophysics © 2003 by the American Geophysical Union.

It is also clear that cutting off either the heat source or the heat sink would obviate the functioning of the machine. If the sun, for example, were unable to provide the energy necessary for photosynthesis, the biosphere would soon cool and be snuffed out. Likewise, if the waste energy with its entropy burden could not be discharged into space, it would accumulate as entropy in the biosphere such that it would overheat and could not continue to function.

Recent evidence shows that carbon dioxide and other gases discharged to the atmosphere clog the pathway for spent energy to radiate into outer space, with the result that the earth is warming and parts of our biosphere are beginning to malfunction.[2] This discovery adds urgency to the need to keep the energy/entropy discharge pathway clear of carbon dioxide and other greenhouse gases.

Chapter Six
Mass and Energy Flows on Planet Earth

The Carbon Cycle: Carbon circulates through the biosphere continuously flowing back and forth between several major reservoirs. The rates of flow and the content of the reservoirs have been fairly well established. A diagram of the cycle is shown in Figure 24 (next Page). Figure 24 is reproduced from the work of the National Oceanic and Atmospheric Association/Earth Systems Laboratory/Global Monitoring Division.

Photosynthesis removes carbon in the form of carbon dioxide from the atmosphere and, using energy from the sun, converts it to glucose, a sugar. Respiration extracts energy from the sugar and uses it to build and organize cellulose, a sugar polymer and other biological materials. The sugars are converted back into carbon dioxide through respiration, and discharged back to the atmosphere.

Major reservoirs of carbon include the atmosphere, the biomass, the soil the oceans and the geosphere. The carbon stored in each reservoir is relatively constant but subject to changes as the flows between them vary.

The atmosphere, for example, contains about 5.5 million gigatons of gas. (One gigaton is a billion tons.) It is 78% nitrogen, 21% oxygen and .04% carbon dioxide. Before the Industrial Revolution the atmosphere contained .027% carbon dioxide. The total Carbon Dioxide in our atmosphere has increased by 44% in the past 200 years. This is mostly due to the combustion of fossil fuels and discharging the resulting CO_2 into the atmosphere. The most commonly accepted figure for the total amount of carbon dioxide in the atmosphere today is 750 gigatons.

> The total Carbon Dioxide in our atmosphere has increased by 44% in the past 200 years. This is mostly due to the combustion of fossil fuels and discharging the resulting CO_2 into the atmosphere. The most commonly accepted figure for the total amount of carbon dioxide in the atmosphere today is 750 gigatons.

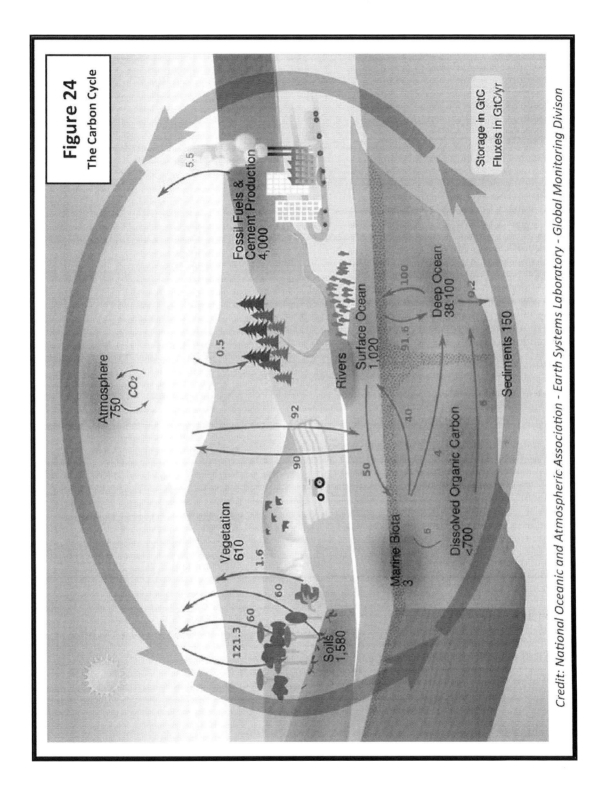

Figure 24
The Carbon Cycle

Atmosphere
750

CO_2

Fossil Fuels &
Cement Production
4,000

5.5

0.5

Vegetation
610

1.6

60

60

121.3

Soils
1,580

92

90

Rivers

Surface Ocean
1,020

50

40

Marine Biota
3

5

Dissolved Organic Carbon
<700

91.6

100

Deep Ocean
38,100

6

4

0.2

Sediments 150

Storage in GtC
Fluxes in GtC/yr

Credit: National Oceanic and Atmospheric Association - Earth Systems Laboratory - Global Monitoring Divison

149

Chapter Six
Mass and Energy Flows on Planet Earth

The biosphere constitutes another reservoir of carbon. The above ground biomass contains about 610 gigatons of carbon (similar to the amount found in the atmosphere). Subterranean biomass (roots, soil microbes, etc.) contains another 1,560 gigatons for a total terrestrial biomass carbon of 2170 gigatons.

The oceans contain carbon as living organisms, as dissolved organic matter, as biological detritus and as dissolved carbon dioxide and various forms of carbonates. The surface layers that remain in equilibrium with the atmosphere contain about 1020 gigatons of carbon, and the ocean depths that receive all the debris from above contain about 38,100 gigatons of carbon
Finally, the geologic structure of the earth itself contains about 100,000,000 gigatons of carbon, mostly as carbonate rocks, and about 10,000 gigatons of carbon as fossil fuels.

Each year terrestrial green plants soak up about 111,000,000,000 metric tons (111 gigatons) of carbon from the air in the form of carbon dioxide and convert it to biomass.[18] Respiration of the plant material produced by photosynthesis provides the energy necessary to sustain life and returns most of the carbon dioxide back to the atmosphere. Respiration returns 110 gigatons of carbon a year to the air in the form of carbon dioxide.

Cool ocean water absorbs carbon dioxide from the atmosphere at a rate of about 92 gigatons per year and converts it to biomass, mostly through photosynthetic phytoplankton. This carbon dioxide is recovered through decay and is emitted from warmer areas of the ocean.

So all in all, biomass (both terrestrial and oceanic) absorbs about 213 gigatons of carbon from the atmosphere and returns about 210 gigatons of it through decay. This balance shows a net decrease in carbon from the atmosphere of about 3 gigatons per year, a loss that is balanced by such things as volcanic outgassing of CO_2, wild fires, atmospheric oxidation of methane and other minor sources.

The difference between the carbon absorbed by photosynthesis and the carbon released by respiration, about 1 gigaton, is a natural net flux of carbon from the carbon dioxide reservoir in the atmosphere to the carbon reservoir in terrestrial biomass. This means that the biosphere must be expanding or densifying which is obviously not the case. Land use changes, desertification, deforestation and biomass fuel use are all depleting the world's biomass. Carbon dioxide from these sources accumulates in the atmosphere.

There is another, strictly non-biological, inorganic chemical pathway for carbon to leave the atmospheric reservoir and go directly to the geological reservoir. The pathway involves the weathering of bedrock by interaction with carbon dioxide dissolved in rainwater. The CO_2 in the atmosphere has a small solubility in rainwater. When it dissolves it makes carbonic acid, which reduces the pH of the rain. Acidified rain corrodes carbonate rock making bicarbonate, which is more soluble than carbonate and also contains more carbon. By this mechanism carbon is continuously removed from the atmosphere and washed into the soil and streams at a rate of about 0.4 to 0.5 gigatons per year..

The size of this carbon flow is somewhat variable. Dr David Schwartzman says that weathering of bare bedrock has been measured. But there is much evidence to demonstrate that biomass enhances the weathering rate of bedrock by a hundredfold or more.

Removal of biomass from the biosphere diminishes carbon dioxide removal from the atmosphere by virtue of reduction of biomass growth rate. It also diminishes carbon dioxide removal by reduction of the weathering process.

Biomass creation removes CO_2 from the atmosphere for the short term, a few seasons to the lifetime of the plant. Bedrock weathering is a long-term removal for geologic time frames. A plentiful inventory of living biomass is an important carbon reservoir and a necessary component of both CO_2 removal processes.

Anthropogenic (human caused) additions of carbon dioxide to the atmosphere include fossil fuel burning, land use changes (converting forest lands to agriculture or other uses) and industrial chemical emissions (primarily from concrete making); add about eight gigatons of carbon to our atmosphere each year. Measurements of atmospheric carbon dioxide concentrations atop Mount Mauna Loa in Hawaii and at other monitoring sites around the world confirm these numbers.[3] Figure 25 shows the results of measuring atmospheric carbon dioxide at Mauna Loa. Seasonal variations appear as spike-like teeth on the curve, but the constant increase in CO_2 levels over the years is readily apparent. Environmental and climate monitoring data collected at sites around the world confirm the predicted thermal and environmental effects resulting from the measured carbon dioxide increases

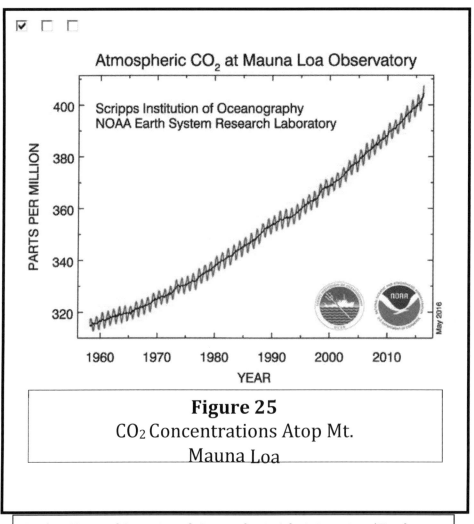

Figure 25
CO_2 Concentrations Atop Mt.
Mauna Loa

Credits: National Oceanic and .Atmospheric Administration / Earth System Research Laboratory / Global Monitoring Division

Dr. Jonathan Overpeck leads the World Data Center for Paleoclimatology of the National Oceanic and Atmospheric Administration[4]. Using data derived from tree rings, ice cores, corals, ocean and lake sediments they have generated an archive of weather and climate information covering a time span of hundreds to millions of years. Testing of air bubbles trapped in ice cores from glacial ice confirms the increase in atmospheric carbon dioxide concentrations in recent decades and centuries. They can now clearly identify the carbon dioxide levels in the atmosphere over more than 800,000 years.

Carbon dioxide excursions can also be related to natural phenomena and to human activities throughout the historical sequence. William Ruddiman, a paleo-climatologist and professor emeritus at the University of Virginia has researched climate history for many years. He has produced a book called "Plows, Plagues and Petroleum: How Humans took Control of the Climate". Dr. Ruddiman has demonstrated how forest removal by slash-and-burn agriculture by large populations initiated climate warming about 8,000 years ago. Subsequent decimation of populations in Europe and the Americas led to large scale regrowth of forests which absorbed large amounts of carbon dioxide that interrupted the warming trend and produced significant periods of cooling. [5]

The decimation of native populations in the Americas in the 16th and 17th centuries, for example, led to the cool period commonly known as the "Little Ice Age". The Bubonic Plague that repeatedly swept the populations of Asia and Europe produced cooling periods as well.

> The decimation of native populations in the Americas in the 16th and 17th centuries, for example, led to the cool period commonly known as the "Little Ice Age".

The Clathrate Gun: The evidence is clear and convincing that increased atmospheric carbon dioxide concentration causes warming of the surface of the earth, perhaps even catastrophic warming as suggested by many members of the scientific community. But an even greater calamity may await us if we don't heed the warnings of our scientists.

Chapter Six
Mass and Energy Flows on Planet Earth

Biomass decomposes anaerobically in many places of the biosphere where oxygen is lacking because of environmental constraints that prevent its access. This anaerobic decomposition produces methane gas as a its primary product. The sites where anaerobic decomposition occurs are often wet or under water preventing oxygen from accessing the site.

Methane emissions from anaerobic decomposition contribute to a significant baseline concentration of methane in the atmosphere. In the year 2010 this level was about 1900 parts per billion – up from about 1500 in 1990.

Methane is a greenhouse gas with approximately 30 times more heat trapping potential than carbon dioxide. It contributes significantly to global warming, but since the concentration of methane in the atmosphere is only about 0.05% that of Carbon dioxide, its effect on overall warming is less significant.

When methane is generated by biological decomposition in freezing water it interacts with the ice crystals as they form. This interaction traps the methane in a methane hydrate crystal formation called clathrate. Clathrates are denser than seawater and they form and decompose on the bottom of the ocean according to constraints determined by temperature and pressure relationships.

As the ocean absorbs heat from the changing climate it warms and melts the clathrate crystals accumulated at the bottom of the sea and releases the trapped methane, which rises to the surface and escapes

> As the ocean absorbs heat from the changing climate it warms and melts the clathrate crystals accumulated at the bottom of the sea and releases the trapped methane which rises to the surface and escapes into the atmosphere.

into the atmosphere. The release of methane, 30 times more potent as a greenhouse gas than carbon dioxide, exacerbates global warming creating a positive feedback loop that could lead to a runaway overheating of the planetary surface. Such an event could lead to ecosystem heating far above the currently accepted maximum allowable rise of 2°C or even the expected 6°C rise that might result from an excursion of carbon dioxide concentrations.

A methane clathrate release could overheat the earth by 15°C wiping out the majority of life on earth and eliminating ecosystems everywhere.

Dr. James P. Kennett, professor of earth sciences at the University of California, Santa Barbara, has spent his career studying the methane clathrate problem. He has written a book, published by the American Geophysical Union, and called, "Methane Hydrates in Quaternary Climate Change: The Clathrate Gun Hypothesis"[6] in which he describes this problem in depth.

Thomas Hartman,[7] an award winning radio talk show host produced a book called, "The Last Hours of Humanity: Warming the World to Extinction" in which he points out that the six great extinctions of life on earth were all preceded by global warming. He hypothesizes that warming from the release of carbon dioxide will always culminate in the catastrophic release of methane from the melting of clathrates if it exceeds 6°C.

Many paleo climatological and geological studies support the Clathrate Gun Hypothesis.

Carbon Sequestration: Concern about the implications of these data for the future of our planet has led scientists and engineers to search for alternative energy sources that do not produce carbon dioxide and for the means to remove carbon dioxide from

Carbon sequestration will not effectively reverse the existing climate problem.

fossil fuel burning sources. Both types of carbon dioxide remediation would be beneficial to the world because they would reduce the rate of carbon dioxide build-up. Neither would effectively reverse the existing climate problem.

That is because the real problem is entropy build up in the atmosphere and biosphere, the accumulation of disorder from destruction of biomass complexity that causes our far-from-equilibrium environment to drift toward equilibrium. As long as our biosphere is being removed or is allowed to become too uniform, it will lose structure, become dysfunctional and eventually it will be unable to support complex life.

Complexity is as critical to continuity as flow is to quasi-stability. It is order accumulated and compounded into higher states of function. Without the structure provided by biomass the functioning of the climate

> Complexity is as critical to continuity as flow is to quasi-stability. It is order accumulated and compounded into higher states of function. Without the structure provided by biomass the functioning of the climate system collapses. An equilibrated planet will not support ice, nor will it support complex life at any temperature.

system collapses. An equilibrated planet will not support ice, nor will it support complex life at any temperature.

Current Carbon: Nor can the problem of climate change be alleviated by switching from fossil carbon to current carbon. Fossilized carbon combustion consumes high entropy, non-functional carbon in the form of fuel and converts it into high entropy, non-functional carbon in the form of gaseous carbon dioxide. The combustion of fossil fuels depletes the functionality of the biosphere by resisting the escape of energy and entropy allowing the world to disorganize through heating.

The combustion of current carbon is far more destructive. It destroys functioning current complexity depleting the reserve of structure in the biosphere and forcing the world to disorganize by removal of its complex functional order.

> The combustion of current carbon destroys functioning current complexity depleting the reserve of structure in the biosphere and forcing the world to disorganize by removal of its complex functional order.

By either mechanism the functioning of the biosphere, upon which we all depend, is impaired. The difference is that if we destroy current carbon, we destroy living, reproducing biomass; obviating all its ecological services and damaging its ability to reproduce in proportion to the amount we destroy, while if we destroy fossil fuels we merely consume an already entropic non-living material.

Cyclic Carbon: The eight gigatons of carbon emitted into the atmosphere each year by anthropogenic sources pales into insignificance next to the 111 gigatons absorbed out of the atmosphere by terrestrial green plants each year.

When the biosphere was full of biomass, 10,000 years ago, in the middle of the interglacial period it contained roughly 1000 gigatons of carbon in functional biomass. Such a reservoir of functional biomass must have withdrawn more like 182 gigatons of carbon as carbon dioxide from the atmosphere each year, 71 gigatons more than it does now.

This, of course, is only circulating carbon dioxide. The amount withdrawn and made into biomass is returned when the biomass decays. But a reservoir of 1000 gigatons of stable biomass is a lot better able to buffer the climate from deviations in the physics and chemistry of its surroundings than the present 610-gigaton reservoir can.

Advances and retreats of the overall biosphere are much more important to the long-term climate composition than annual cycles are. The terrestrial

> A reservoir of 1000 gigatons of stable biomass is a lot better able to buffer the climate from deviations in the physics and chemistry of its surroundings than the present 610 gigaton reservoir can.

biosphere 10,000 years ago had 390 gigatons more carbon (64%) than today's biosphere has. This carbon was absorbed in the atmosphere, the

> The terrestrial biosphere 10,000 years ago had 390 gigatons more carbon (64%) than today's biosphere has. This carbon was absorbed in the atmosphere, the oceans and the geosphere, and it lost all its functional complexity in the transition.

oceans and the geosphere, and it lost all its functional complexity in the transition.

Biochar: Using biochar as a soil amendment creates a significant improvement on the productivity of biomass. Functional, physical complexity is retained in the charcoal following the carbonization process by which it

> Using biochar as a soil amendment creates a significant improvement on the productivity of biomass.

was made. This gives a boost to biomass productivity, which offsets some of the depletion of living, functional biomass reserves used to make the biochar.

The carbon cycle could be balanced if we were to harvest a fraction of the 111 gigatons of carbon in the biomass created each year by photosynthesis and stabilize it before it can be lost back into the atmosphere through respiration (decay). This capture (sequestration) and stabilization can be done by carbonizing (making charcoal out of) the biomass. It would require capture, recovery and stabilization of less than 8% of the annually created biomass to offset all anthropogenic (human caused) carbon dioxide production with stable, inert, elemental soil carbon (biochar).

Charcoal is long lasting and forms a long-term reservoir of carbon in the soil with a residence time of thousands of years. Biochar increases the fertility of soils and causes additional biomass to be created in the

> Charcoal is long lasting and forms a long term reservoir of carbon in the soil with a residence time of thousands of years.

biochar enhanced soils. The biomass is not elemental carbon, but it is organic matter containing about 40% carbon. This carbon is subject to decay and it cycles through the biosphere with a period of a few decades. Because of it's continuously cycling nature the biomass becomes a permanent, short cycle reservoir in the soil.

The structure of biochar decreases the entropy of the soil. The structure of biomass decreases the entropy of the biosphere. These two factors reduce entropy, increase order and promote complexity and structure in the environment. Both reservoirs improve the thermodynamic efficiency of photosynthesis. This kind of functioning sequestration causes more biomass to accumulate in soils and the terrestrial biosphere.

The incremental enhancement of carbon in such soils may produce many times more biomass carbon in the soil and the biosphere than the biochar that initiated it. The stable reservoir of biomass reduces the biomass carbonization requirement even further, perhaps to 2% of annual photosynthesis or even less.

Sources of biomass for carbonization may include all types of biological wastes as well as virgin biomass. Carbonization of biomass and using the resulting carbon as a soil amendment produces energy that can offset some of the carbon dioxide currently created through combustion of fossil fuels, and it stimulates plant growth, increasing the biomass reservoir. Efficient recovery and utilization of energy from the process will replace some fossil fuel generated power.

Charcoal has been found to promote biomass production and it may be

> Charcoal has been found to promote biomass production. The ability of biochar to kick-start an ecosystem is significant.

applied to agricultural soils to boost soil quality and enhance crop and biomass yields. It may also be used on damaged ecosystems to remediate soils and increase the growth of biomass and biological diversity. The ability of biochar to kick-start an ecosystem is significant.

Sequestration of elemental carbon from biomass in the form of biochar removes carbon dioxide from the atmosphere and stores it in the soil. It also has the potential to increase the agricultural production of the earth and to restore ecosystems as well, all the while providing a supplemental energy source to replace some of our fossil fuel demand.[8,9,10]

Chapter Six
Mass and Energy Flows on Planet Earth

Environmental Biomass Productivity: Dr. Park S. Nobel, in his textbook, "Physicochemical and Environmental Plant Physiology"[10] describes an "environmental productivity index" that determines how fast a plant will produce biomass relative to environmental conditions. The environmental productivity index is the product of indices for each environmental component. For example, the environmental productivity index based on water, temperature and light level is the product of the water index, the temperature index and the light index.

The value of each index is one when the concentration of each factor is optimal and is zero when the concentration of each factor is too low to support any growth. Indices are based on data generated for each factor in laboratory studies. Growth rates predicted by these indices are quite accurate.

This concept can be expanded to apply to any number of environmental growth factors. Increased concentrations of carbon dioxide, for example, tend to drive the photosynthetic reaction forward resulting in more rapid biomass production. Increasing the concentration of nutrients by adding fertilizers tends to increase biomass production as well.

Under natural conditions the index of one or more factors can be quite low. The factor that has the lowest index is the limiting factor. Adding more of the limiting factor will have the greatest effect on plant growth.

Irrigation, fertilization, lighting and temperature control all effect their own individual growth index. Under natural conditions it is nearly impossible to optimize all indices at once. Under controlled conditions such as such as in a greenhouse or through hydroponic techniques in is possible to produce environments that give very high rates of plant growth.

 Aquatic plants, for example, and algae, tend to produce biomass much faster than terrestrial plants do because they grow right in their water supply, which is often their source of nutrients as well.

Photosynthesis Amplification: Flooding of the atmosphere with carbon dioxide from fossil fuels loads the gas phase of the biological cycle (the atmosphere) with high entropy carbon dioxide. The increased carbon dioxide concentration in the atmosphere increases the photosynthesis rate and produces more biomass in a self-regulating cycle. Horticulturists under controlled conditions in greenhouse environments use the increase in plant growth at enhanced carbon dioxide levels.

Although soil conditions, atmospheric temperatures, light levels as well as carbon dioxide levels control plant growth rates, the soil/plant interface is the limiting factor in the rate of plant growth in most cases.

Charcoal (biochar) has been found to operate effectively in this growth-limiting niche to increase soil fertility and to stimulate plant growth in the bio-cycle. A small addition of biochar to the soil has been demonstrated to lead to increased plant yield, soil biomass, cation exchange capacity, fertilizer efficiency, soil moisture retention, fungal density, bacterial populations, nitrogen fixation rates, and more.[17,11]

All of the above are manifestations of improved soil/plant interface effectiveness leading to more efficient utilization of the energy from the sun to produce more biomass in the biospheric heat engine and less waste heat or entropy. This amounts to an amplification of the ordered output of the photosynthetic heat engine. Amplifying biomass production by adding small amounts of biochar is like doping the junction of a transistor with traces of metallic elements to greatly improve the conductivity response to voltages imposed on the junction. The structure is improved, the functionality is increased and the whole system performance is improved.

The stimulation of plant growth that biochar provides is much greater than the biomass consumed in biochar production. Many arguments are being made that the overall

> The stimulation of plant growth that biochar provides is much greater than the biomass consumed in biochar production

process is sustainable. It is urgent that field tests demonstrate quantitative increases in biomass production through biochar use. Leaders in this effort include: Dr. Johannes Lehmann at Cornell

Chapter Six
Mass and Energy Flows on Planet Earth

University, Dr. Rattan Lal at Ohio State University, Dr. Richard Perritt at North Carolina State University, Dr. James Amonette at Pacific Northwest National Laboratory, and many others.

The effect of biochar on photosynthesis is like the ability of a small voltage to modulate the flow of a large current in a vacuum tube or transistor. A small amount of structured soil carbon is regulating the use of solar power by the biosphere. A few million tons of biochar may be sufficient to control the output from a 111-gigaton biomass production machine.

It should be noted that all the carbon dioxide that has ever been emitted for energy production by the human race throughout history amounts to only a few hundred gigatons of carbon. Stimulating the sequestration of no more than a few gigatons a year would balance the entire biosphere in less than a century. Data indicate that removal of more than this amount could cause the earth to cool so much as to bring on another Ice Age. So if biochar is to be the solution to the climate crisis it needs to be done with a great deal of planning and research to determine which areas of the earth are to be bio-optimized and which are not.

As we have shown, enhancing global biomass production by 2% to 8% and carbonizing the result for use as biochar will offset all of the fossil fuel burning, deforestation, and industrial carbon dioxide production taking place on earth today. Biochar testing in agricultural soils regularly demonstrates biomass production increases of 20% to 100% and more. It could be

Biochar testing in agricultural soils regularly demonstrates biomass production increases of 20% to 100% and more. It could be concluded that biochar use may be an effective tool in controlling carbon dioxide build-up in our atmosphere.

concluded that biochar use may be an effective tool in controlling carbon dioxide build-up in our atmosphere.

Using concepts and mathematical models borrowed from electrical engineering such as those in Figure 1 and Figure 52 to define the effects of biochar on the biosphere, the environment and agricultural production might be a fruitful approach to understanding biochar dynamics.

Chapter Six References

[1] Smil, Vaclav: "The Earth's Biosphere – Evaluation, Dynamics and Change": MIT Press, Cambridge, MA, Copyright 2002

[2] Gore, Al: "An Inconvenient Truth – The Crisis of Global Warming": Viking Press, NY, NY Copyright 2007

[3] National Oceanic and Atmospheric Administration (NOAA), "Trends in Atmospheric Carbon Dioxide": Earth System Research Laboratory, Global Monitoring Division: www.esrl.noaa.gov/gmd/ccgg/trends

[4].Overpeck, Jonathan, National Center For Environmental Information: ftp://ftp.ncdc.noaa.gov/pub/cata/palec/about/wd

[5] Ruddiman, William: "Plows, Plagues and Petroleum – How Humans Took Control of the Climate": Princeton University Press, Princeton, NJ, Copyright 2005

[6] Kennett, James P.: "Methene Hydrates in Quaternary Climate Change: The Clathrate Gun Hypothesis":: American Geophysical Union, Washington, DC, Copyright 2003

[7] Hartman, Thom: "Last Hours of Humanity – Warming the World to Extinction" Published by Thom Hartman

[8] Lal, Rattan; Kimbal, JM; Fallet, RF and Cole, CV: "The Potential of US Croplands to Sequester and Mitigate the Greenhouse Effect": Sterling Bear Press, Chelsea, MI, Copyright 2008

[9] Taylor, Paul: "The Biochar Revolution – Transforming Agriculture and the Environment": Global Publishing Group, Mt. Evelyn, Victoria, Australia, Copyright 2010

[10] Bates, Albert: "The Biochar Solution, Carbon Farming and Climate Change": New Society Publishers, Gabriola Island, BC, Canada, Copyright 2010

[11] Leahmann, Johannes and Joseph, Stephen: "Biochar for Environmental Management, Science and Technology": Earth Scan Publications, London, UK, Copyright 2010

Part Three

Entropy and Order

Chapter Seven

Energy Flow, Order and Persistence

Chapter Summary

The production of entropy (disorder) is always associated with the flow of heat through any thermodynamic system. However, system boundaries are variable in their ability to pass ordered materials. A boundary that is highly resistant to the passage of entropy retains disorder within the system, increasing its level of disorder, while a boundary that freely passes disorder tends to retain ordered materials within the system, making it more ordered. By this mechanism a system in steady state may become highly ordered simply by the ability of its boundaries to pass entropy.

The flow of heat energy down a temperature gradient, from hot to cold assures us that disorder increases as energy flows downstream. At a system boundary this process continues, increasing the entropy outside the system by extracting entropy from within the system.

By this means the flow of energy through a closed system produces an ordering effect on material and energy retained within the system. Energy entering the system brings entropy with it, but energy leaving the system carries more entropy away with it since it leaves the system at a lower temperature. The most order is produced at the energy discharge point where entropy is finally rejected.

In this chapter we will try to explain this process in more detail.

Chapter Seven
Energy Flow, Order and Persistence

The flow of energy through a thermodynamic system is an inherently ordering process. This is not necessarily an intuitive idea, but I will try to develop some understanding of the rationale behind it by the arguments that follow.

In an isolated system, where neither matter nor energy can enter or leave the system, the temperature of the system tends to equilibrate eliminating differentials throughout the system. The entropy content of the system is given by the equation:

$$S=Q/T$$

Entropy is disorder. As discussed in Chapter 5, and when heat flows within an isolated system, the entropy change is defined as:

$$\Delta S= \frac{\Delta Q}{T}$$

Where: ΔS is entropy change

ΔQ is heat transferred

T is absolute temperature

Heat flowing out of a warm region within a system reduces the entropy content in that region, but increases the entropy content of the cooler region

> Heat flowing out of a warm region within a system reduces the entropy content in that region, but it increases the entropy content of the cooler region toward which it is flowing.

to which it flows. Since the cooler region has a lower temperature, the quantity ΔQ/T is greater in the cooler region than in the warmer region. This means that the flow of energy produces more entropy in the cooler region than it takes away from the warmer region. For this reason, the flow energy in any thermal process in an isolated system always increases the entropy content of the system.

For a non-isolated system, where heat flows into the system, it increases the entropy content of the system by the amount:

$$\Delta S = \Delta Q / T_h$$

Where T_h is the temperature on the hot side of the system

When this heat flows out of the other side of the system, it decreases the entropy content of the system by the amount:

$$\Delta S = \Delta Q / T_c$$

Where T_c is the temperature on the cool side of the system

Since the temperature on the hot side (T_h) is always greater than the temperature on the cool side (T_c), the quantity $\Delta Q / T_h$ is always less than the quantity $\Delta Q / T_c$, so more entropy is withdrawn with the heat exiting the system than is brought into the system with the heat that enters the system. The passage of heat, therefore always reduces the entropy content of any non-isolated system. The reduction of entropy is manifested as increasing order within the system.

> The passage of heat always reduces the entropy content of any non-isolated system. The reduction of entropy is manifested as increasing order within the system.

Entropy change equals heat flow divided by temperature. This relationship tells us that a given quantity of heat has more entropy when it leaves the system at a lower temperature than it did when it came into the system at a higher temperature. Because an entropy balance applies over any system; that is, the entropy entering plus the entropy generated in the system minus the entropy leaving must equal the entropy accumulation. The fact that more entropy leaves the system than enters it gives the system an entropy deficit created by the flow of energy that must be made up for by entropy generation within the system. Otherwise the entropy in the system will continuously decrease resulting in more and more order building up within the system. Such an entropy deficit is, by definition, a decrease in disorder, or conversely, an increase in order.

The system adjusts to the entropy deficits by becoming more ordered. Order can be created by several means including condensation reactions like changes of state from liquid to solid or from gaseous to liquid. Other condensation reactions include building larger molecules, filling adsorption sites and folding large molecules into complex structures.

> The entropy in the system will continuously decrease resulting in more and more order building up within the system. Such an entropy deficit is, by definition, a decrease in disorder, or conversely, an increase in order.

Some structures are more resistant to degradation than others. Like the Syllabary of Sequoya that fixes the sounds of the Cherokee language into permanent transferable symbols, entropy is constrained by the persistence of a resilient format. Such resilient internal ordering emerges from an entropy deficit and manifests itself as complex, resilient internal molecular structure.

> Some structures are more resistant to degeneration than others. Such resilient internal ordering emerges from an entropy deficit and manifests itself as complex, resilient internal structure.

When energy (heat) flows through a system it enters the system from a source that must have a higher temperature than the system does. The entropy produced by the heat entering the system at the higher temperature is $\Delta S = \Delta Q / T_h$ where T_h indicates the higher temperature of the source.

> When you discharge disorder, you leave order behind. If you discharge more disorder than you bring in you decrease the state of disorder in the system.

It is assumed that the system is in steady state so that the amount of energy leaving the system at other places is the same as the amount entering the system. The heat that leaves the system is rejected by the system to an area of lower temperature. The entropy produced by the heat leaving the system at the lower temperature is given by the equation $\Delta S = \Delta Q/T_l$ where T_l indicates the lower temperature of the energy sink to which the heat is discharged.

Since ΔQ ,the heat flowing through the system, is the same at both points, the entropy entering the system at the higher temperature, $\Delta Q/T_h$ is less than the entropy leaving the system at the lower temperature, $\Delta Q/T_l$. This means that less disorder is entering the system in the incoming stream than is leaving the system in the outgoing stream.

When you discharge disorder, you leave order behind. If you discharge more disorder than you bring in you decrease the state of disorder in the system. To put it another way, you accumulate order within the system. Figure 26 is a depiction of this concept.

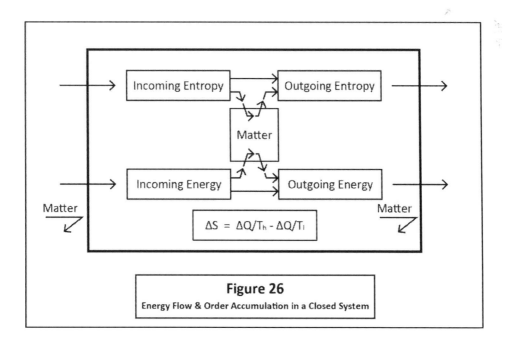

Figure 26

Energy Flow & Order Accumulation in a Closed System

Chapter Seven
Energy Flow, Order and Persistence

Entropy is a state function and displays a balance when heat flows through a non-isolated system (either open or closed). Such a balance can be expressed as "the entropy change in a system is equal to the entropy entering plus the entropy generated within the system minus the entropy leaving the system". This implies that as long as heat flows in steady state from hot areas to cooler areas, more entropy leaves the system in cooler areas than entered the system in warmer areas. Whenever the internal entropy production is constrained by persistent constraints and cannot make up the difference, the amount of disorder in the system always goes down.

The entropy deficit may stay in the system and accumulate as increased order or it may not, depending upon the nature of the system boundary. If the boundary allows order to escape, it will not accumulate within the system, but if the boundary does not allow the order to escape it will accumulate within the system.

If the boundary allows order to escape, it will not accumulate within the system, but if the boundary does not allow the order to escape it will accumulate within the system.

The accumulation of order will take place through chemical reactions, phase changes, complexity formation and molecular re-configuration. The products of these reactions are progressively more ordered and constrained and less random. At various levels of complexity, new forms of functionality and responsiveness begin to emerge.

The accumulation of order will take place through chemical reactions, phase changes, complexity formation and molecular re-configuration. The products of these reactions are progressively more ordered and constrained and less random. At various levels of complexity, new forms of functionality and responsiveness begin to emerge.

By this reasoning, any energy flow through a partially closed system will tend to increase the order within the system. It doesn't matter whether the system is a living system or a biologically inert system, order increases. This may cause a phase change or an ordered flow pattern in an inert mechanical system. In a living system it causes the growth of complex macromolecules and processes like adsorption and protein folding, which contribute to order while maintaining a mass balance.

All thermodynamic systems maintain an entropy balance. The difference between the entropy entering the system and the entropy leaving the system is always equal to the entropy change within the system. Since energy flows always carry more entropy at the discharge, than they do at the entrance point, the entropy content of the system always goes down unless the system boundary can be made to retain more disorder. The decrease in entropy is manifested in a more and more ordered system interior.[1]

All thermodynamic systems maintain an entropy balance. The difference between the entropy entering the system and the entropy leaving the system is always equal to the entropy change within the system. Since energy flows always carry more entropy at the discharge, than they do at the entrance point, the entropy content of the system always goes down unless the system boundary can be made to retain more disorder. The decrease in entropy is manifested in a more and more ordered system interior.

Flowing systems might be thought of as analogous to a set of sieves or semi-permeable membranes. Sand of mixed particle size is poured through the sieves. Large particles are scalped off on the first sieve. Coarse graded sand is retained on the second sieve. Fine graded sand is retained on the third sieve, and fines pass through all the sieves. What started out as mixed (disordered) sand emerges as segregated grades of sand, ordered to meet size requirements for several different purposes or functions.

In this analogy, the sieves themselves are analogous to internal constraints like the complexity of molecules, solid structures and material properties of the system, the trays that spatially orient the sieves are structural constraints analogous to the carbon structures in biochar, or the cellular porosity of wood, and the mechanism that elevates the sand to the entrance of the sieves is analogous to the energy source that drives the process.

A system and a process can be defined by its constraints. Open and closed systems are always permeable to matter and energy to some degree, and the escape of entropy from them will always impart order to materials flowing through, or contained within them. In an open system the ordered matter leaves the system along with the energy. The order may dissipate outside the system and go unnoticed. But in a closed system, where the matter becomes too ordered to be discharged from the system, it is retained and it accumulates. As order accumulates in a limited amount of matter, it compounds and becomes more and more complex.

In passive, non-living, mechanical systems, ordering may produce phase changes like condensation from a vapor or crystallization from a liquid. In

In passive, non-living, mechanical systems, ordering may produce phase changes like condensation from a vapor or crystallization from a liquid. In living systems condensation reactions are more sophisticated and subtle and include such things as increases in molecular size (proteins, DNA, carbohydrates) or complexity (protein folding, gene formation). In the absence of disruptive effects, order will grow in quantity and complexity.

living systems condensation reactions are more sophisticated and subtle and include such things as increases in molecular size (proteins, DNA, carbohydrates) or complexity (protein folding, gene formation). In the absence of disruptive effects, order will grow in quantity and complexity.

This order is produced purely as a result of thermodynamic concepts resulting from the Second Law as applied to non-isolated systems. It has nothing to do with "Life Force", supernatural input or teleological factors – intended or otherwise.

A special case is realized when the system boundaries are semi-permeable. As entropy is drawn out of the system with escaping energy, it is denied re-entrance into the cell by continuous energy flow and by the boundary. The order left behind in the matter contained in the system by the exiting entropy is denied exit by the boundary. Thus, you have cell contents continuously accumulating increasing order, which compounds itself creating complexity and ultimately, responsiveness. This type of thermodynamic process is entirely consistent with the Second Law and with the emergence and evolution of life[2]

Chapter Seven References

[1]Schneider, Eric D. and Kay, James J: Life as a Manifestation of the Second Law of Thermodynamics: Mathematical and Computer Modeling, Volume 19, No. 6-8, pp. 25-48

[2]Sagan, Dorion and Whiteside, Jessica Hope: "Gradient Reduction Theory: Thermodynamics and the Purpose of Life"
From: Schneider, S.H., Miller, J.R., Crist, E., and Boston, P.J.: "Scientists Debate Gaia: The next Cebtury": MIT Press, Cambridge, Mass., pp 173-186

Chapter Eight

Complexity and Emergence

Chapter Summary

Order precipitates from chaos when the permeability to entropy of a system boundary is great enough to allow entropy to escape the system. Virtually any system boundary will selectively retain larger, more ordered collections of molecules and pass smaller, lighter, simpler molecules of greater entropy content. By this mechanism, entropy tends to escape from selectively closed systems while order accumulates within them.

As order increases within a system, ordered molecular relationships multiply and patterns appear in the system contents. Gradually, new properties of order and structure emerge.

One such new property that emerges as ever more entropy is removed from the system is complexity. Systems that are constrained into complexity by their entropy balance, will accumulate order within themselves as fast as they can rid themselves of their entropy.

Other emergent properties that appear in complex systems include the capacity for self-replication and responsiveness. In this chapter we will discuss some of the details of the processes that allow this to happen.

Chapter Eight
Complexity and Emergence

Complexity is the result of a condensation reaction like a change of state. The reacting entities give up randomness in favor of a more ordered, reduced energy state. This condensation endows them with an enhanced degree of functionality.

Unlike oxidation-reduction reactions that deal with interactions between atoms to form molecules, condensation reactions deal with weaker forces between molecules to form or configure molecular groupings, or to alter their sizes or shapes. These reactions tend to force collections of molecules to act in unison, or in bulk, rather than independently.

For example, when water condenses from steam it gives up the ability to expand and contract in response to pressure and the ability to fill an entire container and it also gives up a great deal of energy in favor of a more compact and ordered liquid state. Upon

> Larger molecular assemblages constrain more matter imposing more order on a system. Protein molecules are very large assemblages of atoms containing sites that can interact with other sites on the same molecule resulting in shapes and structures of molecular entities that multiply functionality in all kinds of ways.

further cooling the water crystallizes to ice, a form in which the intermolecular relationships are even more ordered and constrained, again with the release of a great deal of energy.

Larger molecular assemblages constrain more matter imposing more order on a system. They also have more and subtler ways to interact with each other that constrain and functionalize matter at higher and higher levels. For instance, protein molecules are very large assemblages of molecular subgroups called amino acids. They contain active sites that can interact with other active sites on the same molecule resulting in twisting and shaping of the molecules causing shapes and structures of

> Carbon has an unusual ability to interact with itself and produce a huge array of constraints, which make it very functional. From this property of carbon comes a tremendous capacity for complexity including the potential for self-replicating responsive systems.

molecular entities that multiply functionality in all kinds of ways.

How does complexity emerge from simplicity? How does order emerge from disorder? These are questions that have puzzled scientists from the time of the Greek philosophers to the present day. Some of the answers are beginning to be found by people who study complexity as a science.

Part of the answer lies in the scale of the sample under observation. Relationships between entities increase faster than the number of entities increases. Larger samples contain larger numbers of entities. As relationships skyrocket, complex groupings of relationships emerge and reinforce one another, and new properties emerge. Robert Costanza, Director of the University of Maryland Institute for Ecological Economics, addresses the scale factor in his book, *"An Introduction to Ecological Economics"*,[1] this way.

> *The difficulties of negotiating an agreement among individuals are a function, in part, of the number of connections between individuals. Two people have one connection, three people have three, four people have six, and five people have ten, thus increasing geometrically.*

As the number of interacting entities increases, the number of relationships increases disproportionately. New relationships establish themselves, groups of similar and dissimilar relationships emerge, and the collection of entities takes on characteristics that only express themselves in the collection.

An example of this scale factor is found in our Indo-Arabic numeral system developed by mathematicians 2000 years before Christ and still the most popular and common symbolic representation of numbers in the world today.

In the Indo-Arabic numeral system, a different symbol or mark is used to identify each different quantitative concept up to the number ten. As long as the sample of items is below ten, there is no reason to think that there is any limit to the number of symbols and that a different symbol will be devised to identify each and every quantity as far as can be counted. But as soon as the quantity exceeds nine a change in procedure occurs. Suddenly there are two digits in the symbol that represents each number.

Chapter Eight
Complexity and Emergence

This is clearly different, but at this sample size, it is not clear that there are not an infinite number of symbols. The two-digit symbol for ten may be just an outlier, with no significance in the scheme of things.

As the sample size climbs toward twenty a pattern emerges that shows the digits in the first decimal place repeating the digits in the original set from one to nine. At a sample size of twenty it becomes clear that the symbols in the first decimal place have become exhausted and a change has occurred in the second decimal place. In this sample size range a pattern is emerging, and a thoughtful person might be able to predict symbols for subsequent quantities.

At a sample size of one hundred, a third column opens up, and the cycles repeat themselves. At sample sizes this large the emerging pattern is becoming clear, and a reasonable person might be able to predict what will happen at sample sizes of one thousand and greater. This system and its patterns have emerged simply because a large sampling of numbers has been considered.

This is how properties emerge in a complex system. A view that includes just a few molecules shows no hint of the macroscopic state of a sample. But as the sample becomes large enough it becomes clear that the molecules are interacting in such a way that the sample is a solid, a liquid or a gas. These properties may not be discernable from a few molecules, but from a large collection of molecules properties such as physical state become clear. More ordered physical states precipitate from states of lesser order as entropy is removed from a system.

Another example of how pattern and properties emerge from a

> More ordered physical states precipitate from states of lesser order as entropy is removed from a system.

system only in large numbers and sample sizes comes from digital photography. A few pixels of light, hue and texture seem not to be related at all. But as the number of pixels increases, patterns and detailed relationships emerge. At a sufficient size and pixel quantity it is possible to reproduce a whole photograph complete with details of shape size, color, light and spatial relationships.

A final example comes from Charles Darwin's theory of evolution. Scientists have suspected that something was wrong with Darwin's theory for a long time. The issue had nothing to do with pre-conceived notions from early literature, but with the direction and variability of evolving systems. Darwin's ideas did not quite line up with the observed facts.

In Darwin's view, species change or mutate randomly due to minor variability of conditions during reproduction. Mother Nature is a tough taskmaster, and unfit changes are pruned away by natural selection.

In Darwin's time, the number of observations was quite small, and the theory, as expressed by Darwin fit the observations quite well. But modern scientists recognize that biological replication follows the laws of chemistry and physics including thermodynamics.

> The next step in evolution is determined by the present state of evolution, the entropy balance, and the constraints imposed by the rules governing molecular interactions.

Molecules do not interact randomly; they are constrained to interact by rules that can be predicted by the laws of physics and chemistry including the Periodic Table of the Elements, among other things. By this means, evolution does not follow a random pathway, but a pathway that is somewhat predetermined by the rules of molecular interactions. The future is determined by the past. The next step in evolution is determined by the present state of evolution, the entropy balance, and the constraints imposed by the rules governing molecular interactions.

When scientists take an accounting of

> When scientists take an accounting of these constraints on a system their predictions about evolution agree more closely with observed facts. biological patterns emerge when the number of observations is increased enough so that the patterns can be recognized. In the same manner, molecular groupings evolve complexity and functionality as they increase in size.

these constraints on a system their predictions about evolution agree more closely with observed facts. [2] As with our numerical accounting system and pixelated pictures, biological patterns emerge when the number of observations is increased enough so that the patterns can be recognized. In the same manner, molecular groupings evolve complexity and functionality as they increase in size.

It only takes a minor selective resistance to disassembly and dispersion to turn the direction of entropy formation around to favor accumulation of

It only takes a minor selective resistance to disassembly and dispersion to turn the direction of entropy formation around to favor accumulation of order and complexity. A selective membrane will do the trick. Any degree of system closure may be adequate. Even something so nebulous as a gravitational field that selectively attracts more massive bodies or an electrical gradient that selectively orders charged particles. The permeability of the boundary to more complex structures determines the equilibrium level of complexity retained within the system.

order and complexity. A selective membrane will do the trick. Any degree of system closure may be adequate. Even something as nebulous as a gravitational field selectively attracts more massive bodies. An electrical gradient selectively orders charged particles.

The permeability of the boundary to more complex structures determines the equilibrium level of complexity retained within the system. The gravitational field of the sun, for instance releases a huge amount of short wavelength, low entropy radiation, while retaining almost all forms of mass, no matter how high the entropy. As a result, the sun's level of complexity is quite low.

The gravitational field of a planet is selectively retentive of matter, allowing the lighter, more entropic, fractions of matter to escape while retaining the heavier elements and allowing some order to be generated by phase changes and other types of energy flows. The amount of order that can be captured and retained by this type of system is significant, but limited.

The gravitational field of the earth is such as to allow the escape of gases such as hydrogen, hydrogen sulfide, ammonia, while retaining heavier gases such as bimolecular oxygen and nitrogen, trimolecular carbon dioxide and solid and liquid phases such as elemental carbon and water. The atmosphere of the earth is transparent to high entropy, low temperature, radiation, allowing it to escape freely into space leaving a large potential for order accumulation behind on the surface. The chemistry of carbon allows a huge array of order-creating reactions to take place as the entropy escapes with the energy required to balance the energy input from the sun. Some of these reactions create order that is resistant to decay and dispersal, and hence it will accumulate if it is enclosed in a system from which it cannot escape.

The earth is truly a "Goldilocks Planet". If we continue to disrupt the Goldilocks reactions that keep it all functioning properly, we will find that it can be easily destabilized. Like the wave off the shore of "West Running Brook", the rock, the basis of order in the stream of life can be eroded, and we will do ourselves out of a home.

Chapter Eight References

[1] Costanza, Robert, et al: "<u>An Introduction to Ecological Economics</u>": St Lucie Press, an imprint of CRC Press, Boca Raton, FL, Copyright 199

[2] Kauffman, Stewart, A.: "<u>Origins of Order – Self Organization and Selection in Evolution</u>", Oxford University Press, New York, NY; Copyright 1993

Chapter Nine

Heat Engines

Chapter Summary

A heat engine is an open system, one in which the boundary allows the passage of both matter and energy into and out of the system. Entropy also discharges freely from a heat engine leaving the potential for accumulating order which can be recovered from the discharge as organized energy or work.

The amount of useful, organized energy that can be recovered from a heat engine is expressed by the efficiency, and it is limited by physical constraints.

Like all other thermodynamic systems, a heat engine is vulnerable to the ability of its boundary to discharge entropy. If the ability of its boundary to discharge entropy is diminished, the energy associated with waste heat is retained with the inevitable consequence that a temperature excursion will result. Such an excursion can be destructive to the organization and structure of the engine itself leading to a meltdown or malfunction.

It is essential to maintain the entropy extraction pathway of the system so that all entropy generated in the process is freely discharged in order to maintain the continuity of system function. All thermodynamic flow systems operate under this same constraint. In this chapter, we will examine some of the details of how this works in heat engines.

Chapter Nine
Heat Engines

Heat engines are open systems that take energy in at a high temperature (large differential from the environment) and provide the structure to convert some of it to the ordered state we call work (see Figure 27). The cost of the ordering process is to deplete the Temperature differential of the remaining energy to a higher entropy state (lower discharge temperature). The diminished temperature at the discharge of the heat engine is equivalent to an increase in entropy.

More entropy is discharged from a heat engine than enters it. This fact maintains

More entropy is discharged from a heat engine than enters it. This fact maintains and preserves the ordered functioning of the

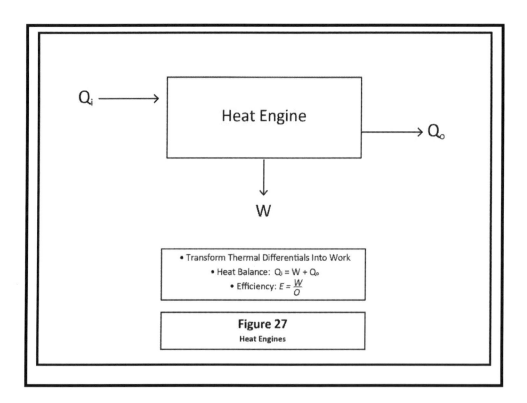

Q_i → Heat Engine → Q_o

W

• Transform Thermal Differentials Into Work
• Heat Balance: $Q_i = W + Q_o$
• Efficiency: $E = \frac{W}{Q}$

Figure 27
Heat Engines

Note: Remember that $S = \frac{Q}{T}$ so that the heat leaving the engine at low temperature contains more entropy (is more disordered) than the heat entering the engine at high temperature. More entropy leaves the engine than entered the engine. This circumstance leaves order behind. The order left behind is able to do useful work.

and preserves the ordered functioning of the engine.[1]

Efficiency: The energy efficiency of a heat engine is the ratio of the ordered shaft energy output (useful work) to the total energy input of the system. The difference between the total energy input and the shaft energy output is energy wasted, and it adds to the total entropy of the universe. Elaborate structures can be designed to increase the efficiency of the engine. More turbine blades, more heat transfer surface, more pistons will all extract more useful energy from a given system. In general, greater efficiency in a heat engine requires more elaborate and relevant structures.[2]

> In general, greater efficiency in a heat engine requires more elaborate and relevant structures.

Structures and Energy Recovery: The same properties of solid structures that allow them to isolate differentials in an isolated static system also allow them to direct the resolution of differentials in an open dynamic system. They constrain the flow of energy and matter through them or around them as they race toward uniformity (maximum entropy levels). In fact, structures can be designed to guide or force the flow of fluids into ordered paths in their search for uniformity. This fact allows us to extract ordered energy, or work, from a system as it rushes up its entropy trajectory toward its maximum state of disorder.

Heat engines are designed to extract work from thermal differentials. They cause the flow of matter toward increasing entropy (randomness) to redirect a portion of the flow into a lower entropy, more ordered, state. In this form the extracted energy can do useful work.

The tendency for mass flows to redirect a small portion of themselves in the direction of decreasing entropy is commonplace in nature. It is analogous to an eddy thrown off by a stream, like the

> The tendency for mass flows to redirect a small portion of themselves in the direction of decreasing entropy is commonplace in nature. It is analogous to an eddy thrown off by a stream, an ordered swirl of current, a portion of which flows counter to the main portion of the stream.

wave in West Running Brook, an ordered swirl of current, a portion of which flows counter to the main portion of the stream.

Robert Frost sees such an eddy as a *"Tribute of the current to the source"*. The water encounters *"some strange resistance in itself"*, its flow constrained by *"catching on a sunken rock, flung backward on itself in one white wave"*. The wave is persistent and sustains itself in spite of persistently increasing entropy. As Frost says, *"The sun runs down in sending up the brook"*. As long as the rock remains and the flow of the brook dissipates its energy over it, the system is quasi-stable.

It is not even necessary to have a "sunken rock". When the inertial gradient of a flowing fluid exceeds the viscous limits of the fluid, a constraint is surpassed that causes eddies to form and the flow becomes turbulent. Entropy production rate increases in satisfaction of the Law of Maximum Entropy Production.[3] Entropy production is enhanced by increased inertial gradients, and at the same time, constrained by the increasing order of the flow pattern. The Law of Maximum Entropy Production allows the entropy production rate to escalate even though wonderfully elaborate, low entropy, ordered flow patterns are created.

> The Law of Maximum Entropy Production allows the entropy production rate to escalate even though wonderfully elaborate ordered flow patterns are created. Under some physical and chemical conditions, resilient solid structures may precipitate along the flow lines or shear planes. These structures give permanence to the patterns of flow, an essential step in the development of complex solids.

Under some physical and chemical conditions, resilient solid structures may precipitate along the flow lines or shear planes. These structures give permanence to the patterns of flow, an essential step in the development of complex solids.

Like Sequoya's Syllabary, the precipitated complex structures stabilize information content in a resilient form that persists in spite of the dispersive properties of entropy generation. As long as these complex structures persist, they hold entropy generation at bay and combat the degeneration of living complexity into chaos and uniformity.

> As long as these complex structures persist, they hold entropy generation at bay and combat the degeneration of living complexity into chaos and uniformity.

Eddies are caused by structures that oppose or redirect the flow causing fluid shear in excess of the viscous limits of the fluid to maintain laminar flow. Such structures may exist naturally such as a boulder at the bottom of a stream, or they may be carefully designed such as a piston in an internal combustion engine or a blade in a turbine.

Alternatively, they may be self-generated, caused by properties of the fluid itself, constraints that allow entropy to be produced faster only if some increase in order is produced as well. Robert Frost calls it, "some strange resistance in itself". Scientists may call it

> Structures may be self-generated, caused by properties of the fluid itself, constraints that allow entropy to be produced faster only if some increase in order is produced as well. This is an expression of Dr. Rod Swenson's "Law of Maximum Entropy Production rate".

Benard's Cells, convection cells, or biomass depending upon its source and upon how intricate and resilient and permanent it is.

Carnot Efficiency: The efficiency of a heat engine is limited by thermodynamic considerations. Even under ideal conditions with no energy losses, an engine can never convert all of its input energy into work. Heat engines are notably inefficient as expressed in the following discussion.

Sadi Carnot demonstrated in 1824 that the efficiency of a heat engine can be no greater than a certain function of its inlet and outlet temperatures (see

Figure 28). His famous efficiency relationship is now a well-established law of thermodynamics.

$$\eta = (1 - \frac{To}{Ti})$$

Where: η is the engine efficiency (percent)
T_o is the outlet temperature (degrees K)
T_i is the inlet temperature (degrees K)

This equation defines the maximum theoretical efficiency possible in an ideal frictionless heat engine. Any real engine has an efficiency less than this, but efficiencies close to this can be achieved by careful design. Let's see how this works in a few representative situations.

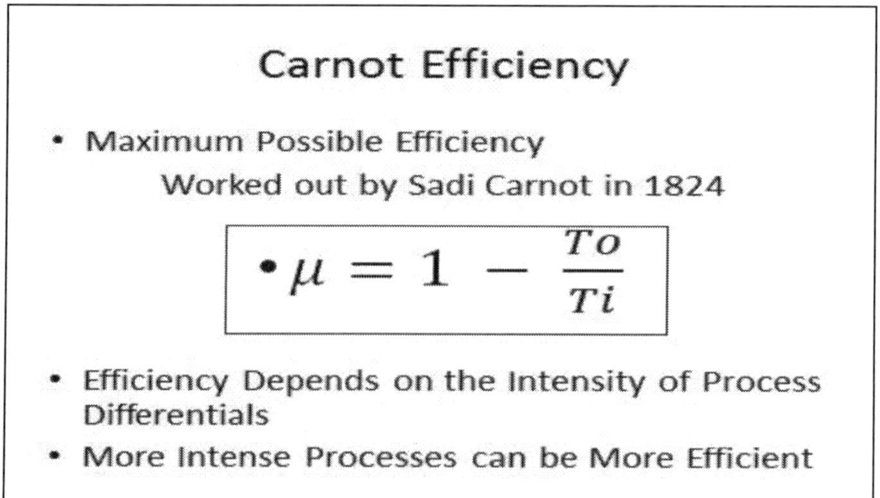

Carnot Efficiency

- Maximum Possible Efficiency
    Worked out by Sadi Carnot in 1824

$$\bullet \mu = 1 - \frac{To}{Ti}$$

- Efficiency Depends on the Intensity of Process Differentials
- More Intense Processes can be More Efficient

Figure 28

Efficiency of Industrial Heat Engines It is informative to consider an industrial boiler that is used to generate steam and to drive a turbine producing rotating shaft work. These devices taken together constitute a thermodynamic heat engine.

If the boiler produces saturated steam at 500 psi (470°F or 516K), and the turbine discharges saturated steam at 15 psi (250°F or 394K), the Carnot equation for the system shows that the maximum possible system efficiency is:

$$\eta = 1 - \frac{394K}{516K} = 23.6\%$$

For every 1000 BTU of energy put into the system only 236 BTU of useable energy can be recovered. 764 BTU is thrown away as waste heat adding its entropy to the universe. This may not seem very efficient, but it is the best one can do under the conditions. For years engineers tried to increase the efficiency of their engines by increasing the inlet temperature. For instance if the boiler pressure were increased to 1000 psi (558K), the Carnot efficiency increases to:

$$\eta = 1 - \frac{394K}{558K} = 29.13\%$$

Efficiency of Electric Power Plants: Power plants consume massive amounts of energy solely for electric power generation and so they are interested in maximizing their production efficiency[3]. In these cases it is effective to heat water to its critical point where there is no longer any difference between the liquid and the vapor phases. The pressure of water at its critical point is 3200 psi and the temperature is 705°F or 647K. Under these conditions, the Carnot equation gives an efficiency of:

$$\eta = 1 - \frac{394K}{647K} = 39.1\%$$

Efficiency Enhancement from Vacuum Condensers: To improve the efficiency still further a large cooler can be used to condense the discharge steam. This leaves a vacuum at the turbine discharge, which reduces the resistance at the exit point. If the pressure at the turbine discharge can be reduced to $\frac{1}{3}$ atmosphere (5psia) the temperature of saturated steam will be reduced to 160°F or 344K. The Carnot efficiency will then be:

$$\eta = 1 - \frac{344K}{647k} = 46.8\%$$

This type of efficiency enhancement system draws down the temperature at the turbine discharge, which means that the heat flow is leaving the system in a higher state of entropy. This leaves still more order behind to produce a higher proportion of work, or greater efficiency. It is interesting to note that the condenser also produces order in the condensate discharge by condensing it into the liquid phase. This condensation reaction produces order manifested by the phase change. The entropy decrease in both the turbine discharge and in the condenser discharge must be made up for by the entropy increase from warming the cooling water consumed by the condenser. This results in huge requirements for cooling water and related equipment in the electric power industry.

Power plants that utilize vacuum condensers produce huge plumes of evaporated cooling water that re-condense in the atmosphere and can be seen for miles as droplets of condensate.

Conclusions About Efficiency: These examples show that even under the most carefully engineered conditions the efficiency of heat engines that use steam as a working fluid is very low. Half or more of the energy input to thermal energy systems is lost as increased entropy. Process parameters can be manipulated to increase efficiencies to near the 50% mark.

More than half the energy consumed by a heat engine is discharged as increased entropy

> Even under the most carefully engineered conditions the efficiency of a heat engine is low. Half or more of the energy input to thermal energy systems is lost as increased entropy. To maintain order or complexity in the system, all of this entropy must be discharged from the system

or disorder (waste heat). To allow order or complexity to prevail in the product, or work, stream; all of this entropy must be discharged from the system. It can be discharged as waste steam if the turbine discharges directly to the atmosphere, or it may be discharged as warmed cooling water if a discharge condenser is used.

Discharging Entropy: In a mechanical system the entropy is discharged as hot exhaust gas, steam, hot air, warm water and radiated energy. If the system cannot discharge enough disordered waste energy to balance the entropy produced the engine will overheat and its own structure will degrade into disorder.

In a biological system the entropy is discharged through warm fluids excreted by cells, tissues and organs; by evaporation of water or radiation from body surfaces. If excretion, evaporation and radiation are not able to discharge enough entropy, a living system will heat up with a fever until the functions of its proteins are no longer able to keep it alive.

In a biological system the entropy is discharged through warm fluids excreted by cells, tissues and organs; by evaporation of water or radiation from body surfaces. If excretion, evaporation and radiation are not able to discharge enough entropy, a living system will heat up with a fever until the functions of its proteins are no longer able to

A planet discharges its entropy through radiation to outer space. When this process is not sufficient to discharge all the entropy generated by activities on its surface, the surface heats up, pushing out more radiation until the entropy balances once again. If the planet still cannot discharge enough entropy, its complex structures and macromolecules begin to break down and its order starts to dissipate.

In any of the above cases if the entropy discharge system is unable to discharge all the entropy generated by the system, the system will heat up until the entropy balances once again even if it means that the system degenerates into disorder. But on the other hand, as we have seen, if the system is able to discharge more entropy than the system generates it will do so, and the system will demonstrate an increase in order, complexity and stability.

Chapter Nine
Heat Engines

In a mechanical system this reduction of entropy may manifest itself through cooling of the system or a condensation or phase change such as precipitation of water from steam or ice from water. The cooled or precipitated phase has reduced entropy to balance the entropy discharge. A refrigerator or freezer works on precisely this principle. Entropy extracted by the work performed by the motor, causes water to organize, or freeze, in the ice cube trays.

In a biological system entropy discharge may manifest itself through adsorption, protean folding, increasing size and complexity of biological molecules or precipitation of complex biostructures, all of which are different types of condensation phase changes, ordering is caused by the discharge of entropy from the biological system.

In a planetary ecosystem discharging of entropy may manifest itself as reduced surface temperatures, stabilized climate zones, precipitative phase changes, increasing molecular sizes, evolution of ecosystems through building complex biostructures, or all of the above. Decreasing the ability of a planet to discharge its accumulated entropy promotes the destruction of its climate zone stability, molecular complexity, biostructural diversity, molecular stability and precipitated phases. That is exactly what we are seeing now. Global warming is only one manifestation of the inability of our atmosphere to discharge the entropy load that we generate by our activities on earth

Chapter Nine References

[1] Ewing, J. Alfred: "The Steam Engine and Other Heat Engines": Cambridge University Press, Cambridge, UK: Fourth Edition, 2013

[2] Senft, James, R.:"Mechanical Efficiency of Heat Engines": Cambridge University Press, Cambridge, UK, Copyright 2007

[3] Breeze, Paul:"Power Generation Technologies: Second Edition": Newnes, an Imprint of Elsevier, Waltham, Mass., Copyright 2014

Chapter Ten

Biological Energy Conversions

Chapter Summary

Biological systems behave somewhat more like closed systems than open systems. The passage of matter is regulated across biological membranes while the flow of energy is less affected.

In a biological system the accumulation of entropy is expressed by condensation reactions in the system interior that lead to order, complexity, and eventually self-replication and responsiveness.

These condensation reactions lead to increased concentrations of large molecules that eventually exceed the solubility limits and precipitate as solid or semi-solid structures within the system.

In this chapter we will discuss a few of the specifics of these processes.

Biological Heat Engines: The biosphere is a different kind of heat engine[1, 2]. It is self-emergent from the accumulation of order and complexity in natural environmental ecosystems. It operates on minute, low

> The highly ordered product of the biological engine persists in the environment rather than dissipating spontaneously into entropy as kinetic energy does. The biosphere replicates itself by producing more biomass with more of the same order and complexity and the same self-emergent properties. So the process is autocatalytic and proliferates exponentially.

intensity differentials instead of the high-energy erosive differentials of industrial engines. These are conditions that make for reduced efficiency in industrial engines, but they produce an output of static, chemically or structurally bound order instead of the dynamic order of kinetic energy. The highly ordered product of the biological engine persists in the environment rather than dissipating spontaneously into entropy as kinetic energy does. Figure 29 summarizes these differences.

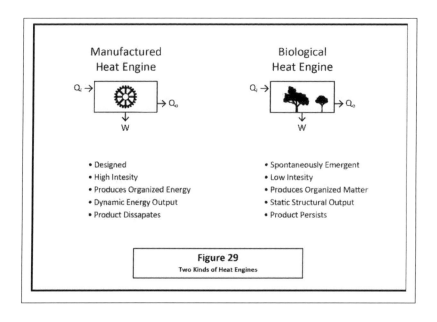

Manufactured Heat Engine

$Q_i \rightarrow$ [ ] $\rightarrow Q_o$
W

Biological Heat Engine

$Q_i \rightarrow$ [ ] $\rightarrow Q_o$
W

- Designed
- High Intesity
- Produces Organized Energy
- Dynamic Energy Output
- Product Dissapates

- Spontaneously Emergent
- Low Intesity
- Produces Organized Matter
- Static Structural Output
- Product Persists

Figure 29
Two Kinds of Heat Engines

Industrial VS. Biological Heat Engines

The industrial heat engine acts like an open system. Material and energy stream through the borders leaving no order to build up in the system. They operate on high intensity turbulence that is distructive to material order generation.

The biological engine works like a closed system. Matter is retained within the system. Any order it acquires is retained inside the system and accumulates. The accumulated order is resiliant and compounds itself producing complexity and,, ultimately, functionality within the system.

The biosphere replicates itself by producing more biomass with more of the same order and complexity and the same self-emergent properties. So the process is autocatalytic and proliferates exponentially.

The resiliency and persistence of the high chemical energy product of the biospheric heat engine causes it to have a lasting effect on the environment.[3] The structural nature of biomass causes it to act as a deterrent to the dissipating forces of entropy generation. It also carries information in its structures that informs subsequent generations of life.

In order to produce high energy, persistent, solid products, biological processes must be gentle enough to prevent the destruction of the products as they are made. Living processes are carried out in tiny resilient vessels, living cells, which spread out differentials over a large number of individual cell boundaries thereby preventing any destructive accumulation of stresses that might destroy the developing tissues.

This huge multiplicity of semi-permeable boundaries also provides resistances that smooth out flow conditions and make life a continuous process.

These processes can only take place in a thermodynamically closed system. The complex living solids that are formed by biological processes cannot be allowed to dissipate into the surrounding environment. If they escape their complexity is lost and can never accumulate to the levels necessary to achieve self-emergent functionality. In a biological system the increased entropy in the energy discharge is taken from the developing matter in the cell depleting the entropy within and creating order in the form of larger, more complex molecules. The larger molecules are even more resistant to passage through the boundaries of the cells. They accumulate, become ever more complex, and display more and more complex functionality within the system.

As soon as the cellular system becomes open enough for the molecular structure to escape the system, the internal complexity and functionality of the living system is lost.

For living systems to survive, internal complexity must be maintained, and it can only be maintained if the environment remains cool enough for the system to reject excess heat, which carries away entropy, leaving order within the system boundaries. External high temperatures or insulating boundary layers prevent the discharge of heat from the system, and as soon as heat flow subsides, entropy discharge diminishes and internal order cannot be maintained. This process is fundamental to all systems, living or not.

> External high temperatures or insulating boundary layers prevent the discharge of heat from the system, and as soon as heat flow subsides, entropy discharge diminishes and internal order cannot be maintained. This process is fundamental to all systems, living or not.

All systems show symptoms of entropy accumulation when they experience trouble discharging entropy into the environment. Internal entropy starts to build up, measurable as an increase in temperature of the system. In mechanical systems it shows as overheating of engines, increasing pressures and other symptoms. In biological systems, it shows up as a fever or inflammation and the breakdown of biological order. In planetary systems it shows as melting ice and snow and the breakdown of climatic order.

When the internal entropy build-up becomes too great, the system breaks down, leading to loss of function, the machine breaks down. In the case of living systems, life ceases and decay starts. In the case of planets, climatic cycles cease to function. In some cases, completely new regimes of order, like glaciers, emerge made up of different, less complex, forms of molecular organization.

 We will discuss some of the advantages and limitations of persistence and information content in the following section.

When the internal entropy build-up becomes too great, the system breaks down, leading to loss of function, the machine breaks down. In the case of living systems, life ceases. In the case of planets, climatic cycles cease to function. In some cases, completely new regimes of order emerge made up of different forms of organization.

Chapter Ten References

[1] Caplan, Roy S., Essig, Alvin: "Bioenergetics and Linear Nonequilibrium Thermodynamics: The Steady State (Harvard Books in Biophysics)": Harvard University Press, Cambridge, Mass.: Copyright 1999

[2] Haynie, Donald T.: "Biological Thermodynamics": Cambridge University Press, Cambridge, Mass. Copyright 2008

[3] Walker, Brian; Salt, David and Reid, Walter: "Resilience Thinking: Sustaining Ecosystems and People in a Changing World": Island Press, Washington DC: Copyright 2006

Chapter Eleven

Flow Systems

Chapter Summary

Two properties are required for complexity to flourish, order and persistence. Order is produced by flow systems. Persistence resists flow. The conditions of temperature, pressure and concentration required by compounding order occur at the interface between flow conditions and solid state structure.

This chapter recapitulates the idea of flowing systems producing and retaining order and adds the concept of ordered flow regimes emerging to maximize the production of entropy.

When resilient structures precipitate within complex flow regimes, persistent complex structures result. This chapter presents some of the details of the mechanics of such phenomena.

Chapter Eleven
Flow Systems

Thermodynamically non-isolated systems are flow systems. Just like the prehistoric peoples gazing into their campfires, scientists are beginning to understand that it is necessary for matter and energy to flow in order for them to be creative. Matter and energy stream into and out of non-isolated systems and interact within the system as they pass through. Entropy enters the system with the matter and energy coming in, and entropy leaves the system with the matter and energy flowing out. Matter and energy flow down an energy gradient while entropy flows up an entropy gradient. As a result it is normal for a non-isolated system to lose more disorder than it gains with the potential to become a more ordered system as it does.

If the entropy flowing out is greater than the entropy flowing in plus the entropy generated by processes in the system, there is a decrease in entropy within the system.[1] In engineered systems this entropy reduction appears as a phase change in the system such as water condensing from vapor or ice crystallizing from liquid or as work performed by the system.

> If the entropy flowing out of the system is greater than the entropy flowing into the system plus the entropy generated by processes within the system, there is a deficit of entropy, or an increase in order, produced

But phase changes can be subtle in biological systems as expressed earlier. Adsorption, protein folding and macromolecular growth are all examples of entropy reduction reactions. In biological systems intermediate complex structures can be created. In living systems the precipitation of these structures is adaptive and autocatalytic as well[2].

Radiation from the sun is the primary source of energy required to run the processes of life on earth. This is effective because the sun is so hot. Radiative insolation wavelengths are very short reflecting this high temperature source and low entropy content.

At the more modest temperature differentials incurred at the surface of the earth, radiation makes a comparatively small contribution to heat transfer. Convection and conduction, which govern the passage of energy through matter, are more common modes of energy transfer here. As we discussed in Chapter 6, radiant transfer is the only mode available to reject energy through empty space. Wavelengths leaving the surface of the earth for outer space are long wavelengths, reflecting these more modest temperatures and higher entropy content.

The primary mode of energy transfer on earth is convection, which is intimately related to the flow of fluids. Fluid flow is induced by pressure differentials, which, in turn may be induced by dynamic energy input, elevation, density or temperature differentials. Fluid will flow from areas of high pressure to areas of low pressure in order to resolve or eliminate the differential.

These facts are clearly demonstrated by the energy and entropy diagrams in Chapter 6. The rejection of high entropy energy into outer space leaves the earth with a 900 milliwatt/Kelven square meter entropy deficit. The entropy deficit drives processes that generate order.

> The rejection of high entropy energy into outer space leaves the earth with a 900 milliwatt/Kelven square meter entropy deficit. This power must be absorbed by ordering processes on the earth's surface.

Ordering processes on the earth's surface must absorb this power.

Flow Regimes: In the analysis of fluid flow systems it is recognized that at low-pressure differentials and mild gradients a flow regime called "laminar flow" (see Figure 30) predominates. In this condition the velocity of the flow is at a maximum along the central axis of the conduit, and it tapers smoothly in a parabolic fashion to a velocity of zero at the wall of the conduit.

At high-pressure differentials and large gradients the flow pattern changes to a condition called "turbulent flow" (see Figure 31). In this condition the viscous resistance of the fluid causes a break in the parabolic continuity of the flow velocity curve. The edges bulge outward allowing a larger portion of the pipe area to experience maximum flow velocity. Eddies form and cause swirling masses of fluid that create a thoroughly mixed cross section with a flow velocity decreasing rapidly near the wall and forming a nearly flat profile over a large portion of the conduit. The turbulent flow profile allows higher flow velocities across a larger portion of the cross section of the pipe.

The transition from laminar to tu rbulent flow is a change in entropic regime like those discussed at the end of Chapter 10. It is also a manifestation of Dr. Adrian Bejan's Constructal Law,[3] which states that systems construct themselves so as to maximize the ease of transport of

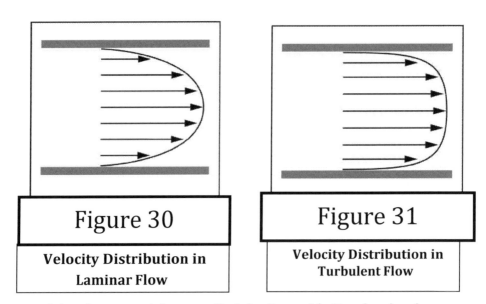

Figure 30	Figure 31
Velocity Distribution in Laminar Flow	**Velocity Distribution in Turbulent Flow**

material and energy. A factor called the Reynolds Number has been devised to predict the conditions under which the transition will occur. Each different system; a smooth pipe, an elbow, a sudden expansion; may experience this transition at a different Reynolds Number, but when all the parameters are known and accounted for, the transition to turbulent flow can be predicted with a fair degree of accuracy.

Many analogs to this phenomenon may occur in nature. For instance, a river exhibits meandering behavior when it flows through level flatlands where elevation gradients are gentle and flows are smooth, but it will cut deeper, straighter paths when grades are steeper and flow is more turbulent as in Robert frost's "West Running Brook". Steep gradients encourage scouring of river channels while flatter gradients encourage deposition of solids. Flows run perpendicular to contours in steep gradients, while meanders run more parallel to gross contours.

Meanders force a river to follow a much longer path to its mouth. They are a structural ordering formed by flow under low energy gradients just as large biological molecules, cell walls and membranes are structures formed by energy flow under low entropy gradients. Additional research may discover that a factor such as a Reynolds Number might be devised to define the conditions necessary for forming biological structures in living systems.

Chapter Eleven References

[1] Schneider, Eric D. and Dorion Sagan: "Into the Cool: Energy Folw, Thermodynamics and Life": University of Chicago Press, Chicago, Ill. : Copyright 2005

[2] Holland, John H.: "Signals and Boundaries: Building Blocks for Complex Adaptive Systems": MIT Press, Cambridge, Mass.: Copyright 2012

[3] Bejan, Adrian: "Design in Nature – How the Constructal Law Governs Evolution in Biology, Physics Technology and Social Organizations": Anchor Books Division of Random House Inc., NY, NY, Copyright 2012

Chapter Twelve

The Expanding Universe

Chapter Summary

Since the discovery of the expanding universe by Edwin Hubble, the science of thermodynamics has been turned on its head. The expansion of space implies that the Universe is not an isolated "fixed" system at all but an expanding system in which the amount of entropy might increase forever but still not become more concentrated. If space is created faster than entropy increases, the entropy per unit volume continuously diminishes.

This chapter is a very brief discussion of the effects of these discoveries on current thought.

Chapter Twelve
The Expanding Universe

The First Law of thermodynamics states that matter and energy can neither be created nor destroyed. This broad statement has always been interpreted as being equivalent to saying that the gross concentration of matter and energy in an isolated system always remains the same.

The second law of thermodynamics says that the amount of entropy in an isolated system always increases to a maximum. This would imply logically that entropy in an isolated system becomes more and more concentrated until it reaches a maximum concentration.

Any thermodynamic system that contains a fixed amount of matter and energy and is bounded by a fixed boundary preventing interchange of matter and energy with the outside environment is considered an isolated system. The Universe itself was considered an isolated system since it followed the first two laws and was conceptually "fixed".

Most scientists have felt confident that the universe could be considered an isolated system, since it follows these two laws. But in 1929 Edwin Hubble, working at the Mount Wilson Observatory analyzed the spectra of light emitted by distant astronomical objects and found them to be shifted toward the red end of the spectrum. This he interpreted as an indication that they were moving away from the earth and were subjected to a reduction in frequency due to some kind of electromagnetic Doppler Effect.[1]

Hubble observed that the rate of recession of astronomical objects was a function of their distance from the Earth. They receded faster when they were further away. He formulated a relationship for the velocity of recession of any two objects in intergalactic space that indicated that all heavenly bodies were receding from each other. This relationship is now known as Hubble's Law. Hubble's discovery of this law is described in a book by Gale E. Christianson called "Edwin Hubble: Mariner of the Nebulae"[2]

Hubble's Law demonstrates that the Universe is not a system of fixed boundaries. In fact, the Universe is a system whose boundaries are always expanding.

The expanding Universe is a system whose volume gets larger and larger as time goes on. This implies that new space is continuously created within the Universe. New space arises where none existed before.

> Hubble's Law demonstrates that the Universe is not a system of "fixed" boundaries, but a system whose boundaries are always expanding. The expanding Universe provides existing matter and energy with a plethora of new, vacant space at zero potential into which to flow.

If matter and energy are to be neither created nor destroyed as indicated by the First Law, this new space must be devoid of matter and energy. This means that the new space created by the expanding Universe has zero mass density, and zero energy potential. The expanding Universe therefore provides existing matter and energy with a plethora of new, vacant space to which to flow.

The implications of Hubble's Law are great for the science of thermodynamics. An isolated system, by definition, has a limited capacity for entropy due to its defined size, its internal constraints and the entropy content of a completely random system. As that maximum entropy is approached in an isolated system, activity slows down, and entropy cannot be increased. But in a system that is expanding, new space becomes available for the entropy generated to expand into.

> A system that is forever expanding provides new space at zero potential forever available for the entropy generated to flow into.

Depending upon the rate of entropy generation and the rate of space

Depending upon the rate of entropy generation and the rate of space generation, entropy may be seen to increase in quantity forever and never increase in density or concentration. The flow of entropy into newly created space tends to leave order behind in the older areas of space, precipitating various forms of matter

generation, entropy may be seen to increase in quantity forever and never increase in density or concentration. The flow of entropy into newly created space tends to leave order behind in the older areas of space, precipitating various forms of matter and organization through the process of adiabatic expansion.

This process does not prevent a "heat death" or running down of the Universe, but it does provide an intermediate stage, a stage of organized matter, for matter and energy to pass through before it can reach complete dispersion, equilibrium or maximum entropy content.

Chapter Twelve References

[1] Hubble, Edwin: "A Relation Between Distance and Radial Velocity Among Extra-Galactic Nebulae": Proceedings of the National Academy of Sciences, 15 (3), pp.168-173

[2] Christianson, Gale E.: "Edwin Hubble: Mariner of the Nebulae": The University of Chicago Press, Chicago, Ill., Copyright 1995

Part Four

Physical Manifestations of Entropy

Chapter Thirteen

Entropy, Physical State and Structure

Chapter Summary

The physical condition of material tells us a lot about its entropy content. The transition from solid to liquid to gas involves step-changes in entropy content. Energy flow is required to counteract and prevent the normal increase in entropy content.

This chapter introduces the reader to the relationship between entropy and the rigidity of organization in the three states of matter, the progression of increasing entropy as materials change from solid to liquid to gas, and the energy through-put required to maintain the physical state and prevent the order in the system from diffusing away into the equilibrium state.

Chapter Thirteen
Entropy, Physical State and Structure

In basic physics, we learn about the three states of matter, solid, liquid and gas. As we study materials science and become more and more familiar with the characteristics of these states a pattern emerges linking physical states with entropy content.

The entropy content of materials determines their physical properties[1]. Gas molecules are the most entropic and the least predictable on the molecular scale. Liquid substances are less entropic and are more predictable. Solids are rigid and predictable because they contain the least entropy.

Gas molecules are in constant independent motion throughout the entire

Gas molecules are the most entropic and the least predictable on the molecular scale. Liquid substances are less entropic and are more predictable. Solids are rigid and predictable because they contain the least entropy.

available space within the confines of a given container. In a mixture of gases, different molecules intermix with each other. There is no way to tell what part of the container a molecule will be in. In this form the order and information in the system is at a minimum. Entropy is at a maximum.

Even in this high entropy state, the system is constrained. Gas molecules of different kinds have different weights. Under the constraints of gravitational force at the surface of the earth, there is a tendency for heavier molecules to diffuse to the bottom of the container, so you can see that even this simple, high entropy system is not random or uniform. It is constrained by the molecular weights of the gases to have the heavier gas concentrate on the bottom of the container.

In the liquid state, a material occupies only the part of the container required by its volume. You can tell a great deal about the location of its molecules just by observing that they are in the lower portions of the container. By understanding the constraints on a liquid you can tell where the liquid is. The system in a liquid state is much more ordered than it would be in a gaseous state. Even though it flows, it is more compact, more ordered and contains less entropy. In the liquid state the probability that molecules will occupy a layer at the bottom of the container is much higher than it was in the gaseous state.

Molecules of a solid are rigidly connected to each other. They are in fixed positions. The location of each molecule can be specified relative to any other. Such a system is highly ordered and contains minimal entropy. The predictability that a molecule of a solid occupies a specified position relative to other molecules is almost a certainty.

The three states of matter described above have properties that emerge in the macro-scale and that determine their usefulness in different applications. Gases, for instance, are free to flow in all directions. They fill all the space available to them. They expand when heated if they are unconfined, and they produce increased pressure when they are confined. These are properties that are useful in converting heat energy into work energy. When the gas expands it absorbs heat, and when it pushes against a piston it performs work. This process may convert heat into work. This capacity is a characteristic of high entropy level materials.

Liquids are a condensed phase, constrained only to flow in the bottom of their container. They are relatively incompressible. They do not perform work in the same way that gases do. To get a hydraulic system to perform work you must input an equal amount work at another point. A hydraulic system conveys work from place to place, but it does not convert heat energy into work. This is characteristic of intermediate entropy level conditions.

Solids do not expand or flow. They transport dynamic energy only by virtue of their rigidity. They are rigid and structural materials. Because of these properties they make good structures, and specifically, good containers. They can contain, obstruct, manipulate, direct and generally constrain flows in the other two states of matter. This is characteristic of low entropy conditions.

There are conditions other than physical state that have analogous effects on order and entropy. Mixing of two fluids is one example. When two fluids are mixed they are in a higher entropy state than they are when they are separated. The molecules are more randomly distributed when the two fluids are mixed. Their individual positions cannot be identified. Only when they are separated is it possible to tell the two fluids apart and to identify different positions for each. The pure, separated state is a lower entropy state than the mixed state.

Separating mixed fluids into their individual constituents is a difficult process requiring the flow of energy through the system and the differentiation of characteristics of the individual components. Some examples follow:

- A solution of salt and water can be separated by evaporation of water from the mixture and drying the precipitated salt. Energy is required to evaporate the water. It is a characteristic of the salt to have limited solubility and to precipitate as a solid.
- Hydrocarbons can be separated from a mixture by evaporation of the mixture and taking advantage of the tendency for lighter hydrocarbons to concentrate in the vapor phase.
- Ionic contaminants can be removed from dilute solutions by selective adsorption onto ion exchange resins. These resins have a very high affinity for ionic forms of matter. They will attract the ions to their surface and anchor them by electrostatic bonds. The anchoring of the ions to the solid surface is much like the positioning of molecules in the solid state. It reduces the entropy of the adsorbed ions.
- Activated carbon has a strong affinity for ionic and organic molecules in solution at low concentrations. By a process of adsorption it will anchor the organics to its surface like the ion exchanger adsorbs ions. This reduces the entropy of the organic materials by fixing their location on the surface of the carbon
- A semi-permeable membrane allows smaller, simpler molecules to pass through, but retains larger, more complex molecules.

All of the above processes require energy flow to make them work. Energy is required to evaporate the liquid mixtures, and energy is also required to regenerate the adsorbent materials. Energy is also required to force fluids through semi-permeable membranes. As soon as the energy stops flowing the order producing process stops working and the progression toward disorder resumes.

Cessation of energy flow allows entropy to start to increase again, and order immediately starts to deteriorate. A minimum energy flow is required simply to maintain the reduced entropy state. The greater the flow of energy, the more order can be maintained in a system. A

A minimum energy flow is required simply to maintain the reduced entropy state. The greater the flow of energy, the more order can be maintained in a system. A reduction in energy flow leads to a corresponding reduction in the amount of order that can be maintained by the process.

reduction in energy flow leads to a corresponding reduction in the amount of order that can be maintained by the process. Carbon dioxide in our atmosphere reduces the rejection rate of radiant energy from the earth. The earth retains more entropy under these conditions, and so the elaborately complex and functional state of order on its surface, the biomass, deteriorates.

A constraint to entropy discharge such as carbon dioxide build-up in the atmosphere serves as a ratchet mechanism promoting the deterioration of order and increasing the energy required to maintain order in a system.

A constraint to entropy discharge such as carbon dioxide buils-up in the atmosphere serves as a ratchet mechanism promoting the deterioration of order and increasing the energy required to maintain order in a system.

Dr. Eric Chaisson[2] observes that energy flow density is a direct measure of the complexity of any thermodynamic system, a relationship that may be used to relate the intensity of energy flow to the complexity of any thermodynamic system. This insight is useful in demonstrating energy flows required for processes in any system from the astrophysical through the geological to biological, sociological and economic. Dr. Chaisson and his work are discussed in more detail in Chapter 30.

Chapter Thirteen References

[1] Dugdale, J. S. :"Entropy, and its Physical Meaning": Taylor and Francis Publishers, Philadelphia, PA: Copyright 1996

[2] Chaisson, Eric: "Cosmic Evolution – The Rise of Complexity in Nature": Harvard University Press, Cambridge, Mass. : Copyright 2001

Chapter Fourteen

Structure and Information

Chapter Summary

Information itself is a low entropy condition. Patterns of kinetics and structure reduce the entropy content of a system and maintain it in a reduced entropy state. Constraints on the regularity and meaning of patterns allow a system to convey information. Precipitation of patterns into a resilient, lasting format secures their information into a persistent form.

The conditions that promote precipitation of information are found at solid-liquid interfaces such as within the interstices of a granular substance. Repeatable patterns and extensive surface area tend to maximize the potential for information content. Persistence tends to protect the information from fading from order into the increased entropy state.

Matrices of solid structures are ideal places for information to accumulate. Granular soils such as those that emerge from the weathering of rocks have some of these characteristics. Fragments of biomass have even more.

Biomass is made up of repeated cellular structures that form a cellular matrix ideal for containing and preserving information.

Extra cellular matrices form an information carrying matrix that has valuable properties for use in the medical profession in such practices as regenerative medicine and tissue engineering. Extra-cellular matrices from plants have similar properties that can be stabilized by thermal carbonization into functional, complex matrix of biochar. This chapter describes some of these ideas further.

One aspect of entropy is that it represents an absence of information. A highly entropic system is a very uniform one. In a uniform system with no structure all atoms and molecules are similar or the same. Since they are all the same and there is no spatial definition, it is impossible to tell the position of one molecule from any other. You have no information about which molecule is which and where they are located. By definition the system is lacking information.

Information and Structure: When structure is added to the system it becomes possible to identify and differentiate spaces (see Figure 32). Just as if it were in a solid structure, a molecule is retained in a definite space relative to all the other spaces and molecules. It therefore becomes possible to identify the location of molecules by the spaces they are in, and it becomes possible to put molecules of different types into different spaces. Such systems have inherently more information content and less uncertainty than systems that are uniform. They are more ordered and less entropic.

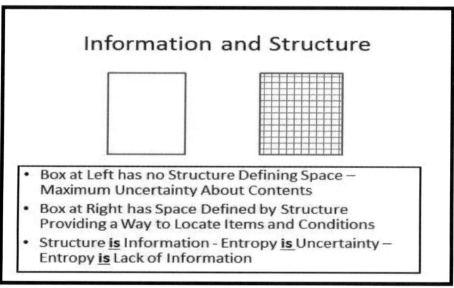

Figure 32

Systems that have microstructure have more definable spaces in a given volume than systems that have macrostructure so they have greater information density. That is why microchips can contain more information in less space than power grids.

In the physics of statistical mechanics, entropy is related to the number of "microstates" that could exist within the macro-condition of the whole system. Part of the definition of "constraints" is that it is "something that decreases the number of possible microstates" a system can be in. Structures that increase the number of definable spaces in a system diminish the number of possible microstates, and so reduce the entropy of the system (see Figure 33)

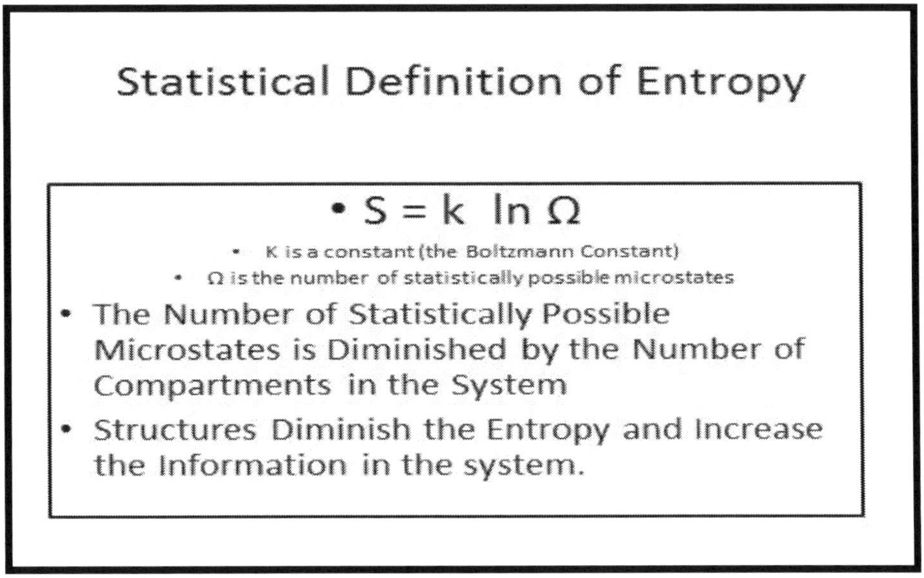

Statistical Definition of Entropy

$$\bullet \ S = k \ \ln \Omega$$

- K is a constant (the Boltzmann Constant)
- Ω is the number of statistically possible microstates

- The Number of Statistically Possible Microstates is Diminished by the Number of Compartments in the System
- Structures Diminish the Entropy and Increase the Information in the system.

Figure 33

Cellular level bio-systems are highly constrained by microstructures that carry densely packed information. This information with its associated structures stabilizes the system against entropy intrusion.

Cellular level bio-systems are highly constrained by microstructures that carry densely packed information. This information with its associated structures stabilizes the system against entropy intrusion.

Since one space can contain material with a different composition or energy condition than its neighboring spaces, the structures allow energy gradients to exist in close proximity maintaining a "far-from-equilibrium" condition without equilibrating to a high level of entropy or uniformity. This is equivalent to a high information density or low entropy content.

Biomass is therefore a great hedge against entropy proliferation. When

Biomass is a great hedge against entropy proliferation. When biomass is removed from an ecosystem, the system becomes more amenable to diffusion and turbulent dispersion of gradients, and so it is more likely to lapse into entropy or uniformity over order or life.

biomass is removed from an ecosystem, the system becomes more amenable to diffusion and turbulent dispersion of gradients, and so it is more likely to lapse into entropy or uniformity over order or life. (see Figure 34).

Figure 34

Characteristics of Biological Systems

- Combine the Flow Properties and Entropy Balancing of Non-Equilibrium Thermodynamics With the "Self-Organizing" Tendency of Complex Adaptive Systems to Generate and Proliferate Biological Micro-Structure.
- Biological Microstructure Opposes Entropy Build-up in the Environment.
- Creates Continuous, Constrained Differential Resolution Replaces Turbulent, Violent Differential Resolution

Structure in Biological Systems: Biological scientists have been fascinated by the ability of species to pass on the information defining their physical characteristics to their offspring. Gregor Mandel began to uncover the mechanisms by which this happens when he discovered the laws of genetics. When Watson and Crick elaborated the structure and function of the double helix, it was easy to assume that we had at last found the repository for all the information necessary to build and operate immensely complex biological systems. However, it was also understood that biological systems respond to their environment by changing their shape and function. The famous "nature vs. nurture" debates ensued. Now we are finding that large amounts of information are carried in tiny structures that were never dreamed of before.

An example of this kind of structural information can be observed in the medical profession in a discipline called "Tissue Engineering" or "Regenerative Medicine". This practice relies on information stored in structures taken from one patient to produce growth of similar structures in another patient. To describe

> Tissue Engineering or Regenerative Medicine relies on information stored in structures taken from one patient to produce growth of similar structures in another patient.

this process we will start with an understanding of the basic structure of organs in animals.

A muscle is a relatively simple organ with a relatively obvious function, so muscles will be the organs used to exemplify the tissue engineering process in this text. However, the principles can be applied to most any other organ in the mammalian body.

An organ is a collection of cells that have specialized shape and function such that they work together in synchronized fashion to produce the desired functional result in harmony with the other organs. It is essential that the cells of an organ be able to act in harmony with each other to produce the desired result. This requires that information be transferred throughout the organ as a whole as well as between individual cells.

As the cells of a muscle multiply, they are positioned next to each other and aligned to effectively function as contractile tissue. In the developing fetus, the information from DNA sequences is compared with environmental conditions to organize the structure of the developing muscle. This organizing function is extensive and time consuming, and it is advantageous for the process to be abbreviated and streamlined so that repairs to the adult organism can be made more efficiently when necessary in the adult body.

The process of "repair" in existing tissues in an adult is quicker and simpler than the process of "creation" in a fetus from the raw information encoded on DNA molecules. The

> Repair in existing tissues is quicker and simpler than the process of "creation" in a fetus from the raw information encoded on DNA molecules. The reason repair is quicker and easier than creation is because a pre-existing structure or pattern already exists to guide the repair process.

reason repair is quicker and easier than creation is because a pre-existing structure or pattern already exists to guide the repair process. Creation requires that raw encoded information must be interpreted to establish the pattern and organize the cells.

Extra-Cellular Matrix: As an organ grows by cell division, adjacent cells secrete a fibrous protein material called collagen and an amorphous mixture of polysaccharides between themselves and their neighbors. As the cells mature the collagen-polysaccharide mixture dehydrates and becomes firmer. Eventually, it becomes a flexible structural scaffold that surrounds each cell and keeps it oriented and functioning in harmony with its neighbors.

The collagen scaffold is not a living tissue but it is flexible and permeable enough to allow the living cells to interact with each other by communicating through the collagen layer to carry out their

> The Extra-Cellular Matrix is a structure that contains a great deal of information about the form and functioning of the living cells that occupy it.

coordinated life functions. The non-living scaffolding has been given the name "Extra-Cellular-Matrix". It is a structure that contains a great deal of information about the form and functioning of the living cells that occupy it.

The power of the extra-cellular-matrix to direct and coordinate the biological repair process is gaining recognition and acceptance in the medical profession. In the case of muscle tissue, the matrix consists of a series of pockets, each of which hold a living cell. Muscle matrix pockets may be 100 microns wide by a few millimeters long, just the right size to contain and nurture a living muscle cell. The matrix is more resistant to damage or other change than the living cells that occupy it so it acts as a protective

> The matrix is more resistant to damage or other change than the living cells that occupy it so it acts as a protective sheath for individual cells. Cells live and die, but the matrix is relatively permanent and retains its structure and function beyond the life cycle of the cell.

sheath for individual cells. Cells live and die, but the matrix is relatively permanent and retains its structure and function beyond the life cycle of the cell.

When cells of an organ die, decompose and are absorbed into the system, new cells that mature into the vacant space left in the matrix by the old cell replace them. This process is easy to comprehend. Nevertheless, the potential of the matrix to direct the development of a replacement cell is much greater than that. The matrix contains all the information necessary to tell the new cell what kind of a cell it is to become.

Suppose a stem cell rather than the progeny of an adjacent muscle cell occupies the vacant space in a muscle matrix. The power of the matrix is such that the undifferentiated stem cell develops into a muscle cell compatible with the muscle cells in its surroundings.

How does the stem cell know that it is to develop into a muscle cell rather than all the other types of cells it is genetically capable of becoming? What signals from its surroundings inform it that such a transition is necessary? Some factors of shape, or surface texture, or chemistry, or location of active sites triggers the transformation of the stem cell into a muscle cell.

The stem cell contains all the genetic information that any other stem cell has, but the information telling it to differentiate and what to differentiate into is provided by the extra-cellular-matrix!

Medical Applications of the Matrix: Dr. Steven Badylak, Director of the McGowan Institute for Regenerative Medicine in Pittsburgh, PA,[1] uses extra-cellular-matrix from muscle tissues to repair damaged muscles of injured soldiers and accident victims (see Figure 35). Muscle tissue is removed from a donor organism and prepared by physically removing the living muscle cells leaving only the matrix scaffolding. The matrix is then installed in the damaged muscle areas of the patient.

Signals from the installed muscle matrix attract the patient's stem cells to the site, and they fill the vacancies in the matrix and develop into new muscle tissue in a matter of days instead of weeks or months that may be required for healing of the damaged tissues. Physical therapy can begin to strengthen the regenerated tissue in just a few days.

Figure 35

Dr Steven Badylak

- McGowan Institute for Regenerative Medicine
- Treats Soldiers and Accident Victims
- Repairs Severe Muscle Damage
- ECM is Layered Into Damaged Area
- Stem Cells Occupy the Matrix and Mature Into Muscle Cells
- Patient Can Use Repaired Muscle Within

One interesting aspect of this type of reparative procedure is that the matrix is specific to organ type and function, but not necessarily to species. Matrix from a pig, for example, has been used to repair tissues in human beings.

Dr. Doris Taylor, a cardiac surgeon and Director of Regenerative Medicine Research at the Texas Heart Institute[2] can custom build a heart using the patient's own stem cells and extra-cellular-matrix form a cadaver (see Figure 36). The cells are stripped from a cadaver heart and replaced with the patient's stem cells, which, quickly take up positions within the extra-cellular-matrix. The stem cells mature into heart muscle, and if all goes well, the heart begins to beat. The beating heart can them be installed into the patient.

Figure 36

Dr. Doris Taylor

- Director, Regenerative Medicine Research at Texas Heart Institute.
- Removes living cells from cadaver hearts
- Entire heart becomes Scaffold for New Cells
- Infuses Scaffold with Stem Cells From Patient
- Stem Cells Mature into Heart Muscle Cells
- Heart Starts to Beat
- Heart can be Transferred to Patient Without Fear of Rejection Since All Living Cells Have Patient's Own Genetics

---

Since the living cells in the heart are the product of the patient's own stem cells, they are genetically identical to the patient's cells. This means that they are fully compatible with the patient's genetics and there is little or no risk of rejection of the new heart.

These examples demonstrate how information about development and function can be carried in the cellular microstructure of biomass. The information can be successfully transmitted across species boundaries and inserted into a new environment. Details of structure and function can be carried to new locations and used to establish functioning new systems where others have failed.

This transfer of information in the constrained spaces offered by complex structures is reminiscent of the information transfer offered by the constrained sounds of a language or by the

> Information about development and function can be carried in the cellular microstructure of biomass. The information can be successfully transmitted across species boundaries and inserted into a new environment.

constrained images or symbols of Sequoya's Syllabary

Plant Extra-cellular-matrix: Plants too have an extra-cellular-matrix. Dr. J.W. Kimball, in a web site called "Kimball's Biology Pages"[3] describes the extra cellular matrix in plants. As the plant grows the living cells surround themselves with a layer of structural cellulose embedded in an amorphous mixture of compounds like lignin and pectin (see Figure 37). This scaffold-like structure is rigid and durable, and it becomes the heartwood of a tree as new layers of sapwood are layered upon the exterior of the trunk. The cellulose matrix is embedded with spatial, structural and functional information about the plants from which it came.

Figure 37
Plant Extra-Cellular-Matrix

- Chemically Composed of Cellulose Embedded in an Amorphous Mixture of Lignin, Pectin and Others
- More Rigid and Durable Than Animal Matrix
- Resistant to Degradation and Decay
- Source of Regenerative Information for New Cell Construction and Function.

The once-living fraction of biomass can be removed from the extra-cellular-matrix by thermal decomposition (pyrolysis) just as the living cells are removed from animal tissues by physical and chemical means. The resulting structure, made of elementary carbon, retains many of the information bearing patterns and some of the functional properties of the original matrix.

The Biochar Matrix: The structure of biochar is an extra-cellular-matrix of plant tissue that has been cleansed of its volatile components by thermal decomposition rather than by physical or chemical means. Information required for nucleation of plant populations, ecologies and functioning - in short, entire ecosystems – may be contained within its complex pore structure. Each available macropore is an environmental niche that can be filled with microorganisms contributing to the health and stability of the biosphere.

In Dr. Johannes Lehman's book on Biochar, *Biochar for Environmental Management, Science and Technology*, a paper authored by Downie, Croski and Monrowe[4] describes the porosity of biochar in three different size ranges. Pores with diameters less than 2 nanometers are called micropores, pores with diameters between 2 and 50 nanometers are called mesopores, and pores greater than 50 nanometers in diameter are called macropores (see Figure 38).

Figure 38
Biochar Matrix
Three Sizes of Pores:

- Micropores: < 2 Nanometers
- Mesopores: > 2 < 50 nanometers
- Macropores: > 50 nanometers

These dimensions are extremely small, they are useful in describing dimensions on an atomic scale. A carbon atom, for example is about 0.15 nanometers in diameter. A ribosome (the region of the human cell where proteins are made) is about 20 nanometers across.

The diameter of a large micropore is about thirteen times as large as the diameter of a carbon atom (see Figure 39). A mesopore can be up to 300 times as wide as a carbon atom, and a macropore is larger still, similar in size to living bacterial cells, and even greater.

> # Figure 39
> # Micropores and Mesopores
> - Micropores Can Admit Small Molecules Such as Mineral Nutrients, Water and Low MW Solvents
> - Mesopores Can Admit Biologically Active Molecules Such as Proteins and Carbohydrates.
> - These pores have 90% of the Surface Area of the Carbon
> - Mass Transfer is Governed Largely by the Adsorptive Properties of the Carbon

Mineral ions and low molecular weight solvent molecules, such as water, can penetrate into the micropores. Mesopores are large enough to accept complex biological molecules such as amino acids and small proteins, enzymes, complex sugars and polynucleotides. Mass transfer in

> The presence of living organisms occupying the macropores tends to drive mass and energy transfer mechanisms by biological metabolism rather than by diffusion' which tends to keep their surfaces farther from equilibrium, decreasing their degree of saturation and increasing their effectiveness as adsorptive surfaces. The metabolism of the occupying organisms and not the adsorptive properties of the carbon may be the driving force for mass transfer in the macropores, making the macropore surface more effective even though its surface area is much smaller.

these small pores is governed by the adsorptive properties of the carbon, an equilibrium driven process.

Viruses and small bacteria may be able to enter the smaller macropores. Larger bacteria and fungal hyphae may be able to enter the larger macropores. Fungal hyphae may be between 2 and 10 micrometers in diameter (2000 to 10,000 nanometers). These living systems may fit into the largest of macropores.

The combined surface area of the micropores may be ten times as large as that of the macropores. But the presence of living organisms occupying the

---

Figure 40
Macropores

- Macropores Can Admit Viruses, Bacteria, Fungal Hyphae, Even Protozoa and Small Multicellular Organisms.
- Mass Transfer is Influenced by the Metabolism of the Occupying Organisms
- This May Increase the Relative Importance of the Macropores in Spite of Their Small Surface Area.

---

macropores tends to drive mass and energy transfer mechanisms by biological metabolism rather than by diffusion' which tends to keep their surfaces farther from equilibrium, decreasing their degree of saturation and increasing their effectiveness as adsorptive surfaces. The metabolism of the occupying organisms and not the adsorptive properties of the carbon may be the driving force for mass transfer in the macropores (see Figure 40). This may make the macropore surface more effective even though its surface area is much smaller.

Patterns of Cellular Life: In order to convey the patterns of cellular life to successive generations and proliferate ecosystems the pores must be big enough to allow penetration by soil microbes. To take advantage of the matrix mechanism the larger macropores are extremely relevant.

 In his book, "Incomplete Nature – How Mind Emerged From Matter",[5] Dr. Terrence Deacon, Professor of Biological Anthropology at the University of California at Berkeley, after an exhaustive survey of the physical and informational characteristics of emergent systems, puts it this way:

> *Whether it is embodied in separate information-bearing molecules (as in DNA) or merely in the molecular interaction constraints of a*

> *simple autogenic process, information is ultimately constituted by preserved constraints*

Dr. Deacon's observation that "preserved constraints" constitute information that may be used to direct autogenic processes is consistent with the analysis of constraints interacting with energy flows expressed in Chapter 4 of this book. The cellular structures of biomass are constraints that direct the autogenic processes of regeneration. These structures may be preserved by transforming them into decay resistant elemental carbon as in the pyrolysis of biomass to make biochar.

Dr. Deacon goes on to say:

> *There is no reason to assume ... that the only information transmitted from generation to generation is genetic. ...Biological information is not an intrinsic attribute of that substrate...it is precisely this non-intrusive character of information that must be accounted for.*

> *Genetic information arises from the shifting of dynamically sustained constraints on to structurally embodied constraints that have no direct dynamical role to play... The dissociation of this molecular pattern from the dynamics that it influences additionally protects these constraints from the thermodynamic unpredictability of the dynamical context.*

> *So the capacity of a... system to generate and transfer constraints from substance is the key to open-ended evolution involving ever more complicated dynamics and ever more diverse substrates.*

The macropores of biochar act as the necessary "preserved constraints" on entropy production in the environment to maintain the consistency of life processes in the biosphere. They also contain an informational content to define the biological potential for the coming generation appropriately sized to regenerate plant cells and preserved by the carbonization process.

Genetic information is preserved on a molecular scale and is interpreted and implemented by the production of proteins that implement the construction of biological chemistry. Structural and functional information is preserved on a cellular scale by the extra-cellular-matrix, and it is interpreted and implemented by intervening biological processes on both the molecular and the cellular scales.

Photomicrographs of biochar structure identify a rich profusion of macropores in the 20 to 30 micron (20,000 to 30,000 nanometer) range (see Figures 57-60). These pores will admit some soil bacteria and fungal hyphae. Also evident are numbers of macropores in the 50 to 200 micron (50,000 to 200,000 nanometer) range. These macropores will host a wide range of soil microbes from bacteria to protozoa and small multicellular organisms. Biochar properties and their processing techniques should be chosen to preserve and enhance the structure of these macropores.

Biochar properties and their processing techniques should be chosen to preserve and enhance the structure of these macropores.

Chapter Fourteen References

[1] Stephen Badylak: Mcgowan Institute for Regenerative Medicine: mirm.pitt.edu/badylak

[2] Dr. Doris Taylor: Texas Heart Institute – Regenerative Medicine Research: texasheart.org/research/regenerative medicine/director.cfm

[3] Kimball, JW: "Kimball's Biology Pages – The Extra Cellular Matrix(ECM)": 5/19/2013

[4] Downie, Adrian; Croski, Alan and Monrowe, Paul: "Physical Properties of Biochar", Earth Scan Publications, London, UK, Copyright 2010 (see reference *18)

[5] Deacon, Terrance W.: "Incomplete Nature – How Mind Emerged From Matter": W.W. Norton & Company, London, UK, Copyright 2013

Part Five

Energy Induced Ordering

Chapter Fifteen

Patterns Without Structure

Chapter Summary

Energy flows through a system by different flow mechanisms depending upon the intensities of the differentials involved. For low temperature differentials conductive heat transfer mechanisms are dominant. For intermediate temperature differences convective mechanisms predominate, and for higher temperature differentials radiative processes take over.

The change from conductive heat transfer mechanisms to convective mechanisms allows greater heat flow or entropy generation to occur. It also shifts the dynamics to a more ordered flow regime. The more order a system contains, the faster it will generate entropy. This is a statement of Dr. Rod Swenson's Fourth Law of thermodynamics, The Law of Maximum Entropy Production.

In this chapter, we will discuss how ordered patterns are produced from the flow of energy through fluid media.

Chapter Fifteen
Patterns Without Structure

Up to this point, we have implied that structures were required for the maintenance of differentials. However, structures are by no means the only way energy differentials can be generated and preserved in open systems. Just as chemical properties in the Periodic Table determine which molecules will react with each other and gravity keeps heavier molecules at the bottom of a container, fluid properties dictate the modes with which momentum and or heat can be transferred in physical systems.

Fluids, though not rigid like a solid, are not completely without constraints. Fluids have properties like density, viscosity, surface tension, heat capacity, coefficient of thermal expansion and diffusion coefficient, which determine limits on modes of resolution of differentials. If a liquid is stressed beyond the limits of shear allowed by its viscosity, eddies will form. Eddies are a form of active momentum transfer that disperses energy gradients faster than can be done by laminar flow. As long as the momentum gradient persists eddies continue to form and turbulent conditions arise and continue.

Eddies are a flow pattern that arises only from the properties of the fluid and the applied shear stresses. No solid surfaces are required, only momentum differentials and fluid properties. They are quasi-stable and will persist only as long as energy is input to the system.

Convection Cells: Thermal currents form in heated fluids whenever the temperature gradient is too great to be satisfied by conduction alone.[1] A pan of water on a stove exhibits a rising column of heated water in the middle, which spreads across the surface and descends at the sides to be heated again and recirculated. A large flat-bottomed pan will generate multiple circulating cells like those shown in Figure 41 (next page).

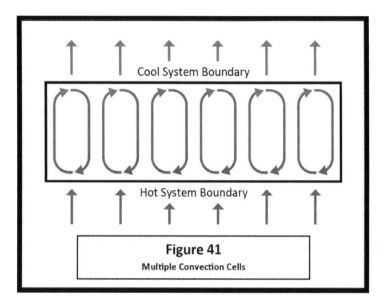

Figure 41

Multiple Convection Cells

The phenomenon of convection cells is very common in nature. The atmosphere performs this way whenever the surface air becomes heated

The phenomenon of convection cells is very common in nature. The atmosphere performs this way whenever the surface air becomes heated to the extent that it becomes unstable and begins to rise. On a hot, humid summer afternoon a thunder storm is the likely result. Thunder storms are an example of convection cells in the atmospheric fluid

to the extent that it becomes unstable and begins to rise. On a hot, humid summer afternoon a thunderstorm is the likely result. Thunderstorms are an example of convection cells in the atmospheric fluid.

Heat from the core of the earth causes the magma layers to circulate which pushes the continents around causing shifting of tectonic plates. Continental drift is another example of convection cells that occur in the fluid magma that supports the continents.

Benard's Cells: The same pattern arises from thermal convection when a viscous fluid is placed between two flat plates and heat is applied to the bottom plate. At low temperature differentials heat is transferred from bottom to top by simple conduction. But as the bottom plate is made hotter a point may be reached where the temperature gradient is too great to be dispersed by pure conduction alone. At his point convective currents begin to form, rising up from hot zones and spreading out on the upper surface. Spreading currents cool again on the upper surface.

Benard's Cells

Figure 42
Photo Credit: E. L. Koschmiedr

They meet and begin to flow downward in response to cooling in contact with the upper plate. They reach the bottom and spread out until they are heated enough to rise again. This action takes place all across the surfaces of the plates and the conductive heat transfer is converted into convective transfer in multiple cells of circulating currents called Benard's Cells or Benard's Hexagons. This pattern of hexagons is caused by the physical properties of the fluids and the temperature gradient between the plates. No walls separate them. Only the energy input and the properties of the fluids determine their shape, size and function. A photograph of Benard's Cells is shown in Figure 42.

Cyclones: Rotating atmospheric circulation systems form when warm, moist, low-pressure air erupts into cooler unstable stratospheric layers.[2] Condensation of the moisture in the rising air mass releases energy that heats, spreads and expands the cold air layer creating a positive feedback loop that draws more moist air into the system. The resulting circulation is like the circulation in a Benard's cell, but because of the Coriolis effect the whole circulating system rotates.

Cyclones are stable weather events as long as they are in warm ocean areas where the temperature and depth of the ocean are sufficient to provide the energy flow necessary to keep it going. As soon as the cyclone wanders onto land or into cooler waters the system no longer has access to its energy source so it becomes unstable and dissipates.

A diagram of cyclonic circulation is shown in Figure 43. Conditions in the upper atmosphere are such that moisture precipitates as liquid water and descends as rainfall. If the conditions were such as to allow water to precipitate as a solid and to remain in a solid sheet, the process would generate a cell of stable solid structure.

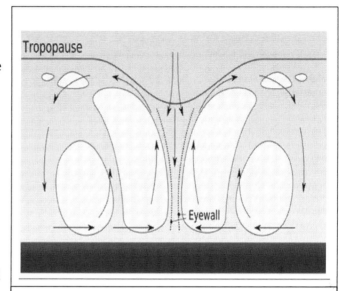

Figure 43
Cyclonic Circulation
Illustration from: Kerry Emanuel: "Anthropogenic Effects on Tropical Cyclone Activity"

A series of these cells would look something like the pattern of Benard's cells on a large scale, a pattern of storm-sized cells agglomerating across the countryside. Because the properties of ice crystals don't allow them to grow into solid sheets as they tumble through the air, but constrain them to grow into hexagonal crystals, they come down as snow rather than agglomerating into solid sheets and creating cellular structures across the countryside.

Monsoons: Because the shortwave radiant energy from the sun penetrates through the earth's atmosphere with little resistance and imparts most of its energy to the terrestrial surface, it creates conditions like those in the Benard's Cell apparatus. Some areas of the earth experience this surface warming only in the summer when the angle of inclination of the sum is direct and not in the winter when the sunlight approaches the earth obliquely[3].

The updraft resulting from long periods of heating from direct sunlight draws air across nearby water bodies and feeds moist air into a convection cell resulting in intense periods of rainy weather. These rainy seasons are called monsoons. They are seasonal, regular, and often severe. As soon as the energy from the sun becomes less intense, when the summer season ends, the rainy season subsides.

This is another example of an organized circulation pattern created solely by the application of energy to a thermodynamic system.

Gyres: Gyres are large scale circulating currents in the ocean surface driven by winds. They are a two-phase phenomenon driven by momentum transfer from the gas phase into the liquid phase. In general they don't involve solid structures. They occur in large ocean basins with minimal effects from adjacent landmasses.

Gyres involve no phase changes. We might not even be aware of them except for their tendency to concentrate floating debris at their centers. The accumulation of large masses of non-biodegradable floating matter at the centers of rotation of gyres is becoming a pollution problem in the open ocean.

These are some examples among many found in nature of patterns of fluid behavior that emerge from physical properties and energy input without structural constraints. Other examples include wave motion, hurricanes and tornados, and stream meanders.

Precipitation of a solid containment matrix will help preserve the patterns, but it is not necessary to have such a matrix to initiate them or

Precipitation of a solid containment matrix will help preserve the patterns, but it is not necessary to have such a matrix to initiate them or for them to continue their existence. Energy throughput is sufficient to enable them to persevere.

for them to continue their existence. Energy throughput is sufficient to enable them to persevere.

In biological systems the chemical versatility of carbon to interact with itself and many other chemical entities through covalent bonding causes structural matrices to precipitate in areas that have just the right conditions. This characteristic enables the system to continue to function

In biological systems the chemical versatility of carbon to interact with itself and many other chemical entities through covalent bonding causes structural matrices to precipitate in areas that have just the right conditions. This characteristic enables the system to continue to function through a wide range of energy flow fluctuations.

through a wide range of energy flow fluctuations.

[4]Chapter Fifteen References

[1] Koschmieder, E. L.: "Benard Cells and Taylor Vortices (Cambridge Monographs on Mechanics)": Cambridge University Press, New York, NY: Copyright 1993

[2] Longshore, David: "Encyclopedia of Hurricanes, Cyclones and Tornadoes" Facts-on-File Science Library, September 2007

[3] Clift, P. D.; Tada, R.; and Zheng, H.: "Monsoon Evolution and Tectonics - Climate Linkage in East Asia: Special Publication 342 (Geological Society of London Special Publications)" Geological Society of London Special Publications, September 2010

Chapter Sixteen

Climate Zones

Chapter Summary

Circulating flow patterns on a rotating sphere such as the earth receiving energy from a point source like the sun become latitudinal circulation patterns like the climate zones that cause atmospheric circulation on earth.

In this chapter we will discuss some of the details of these processes.

When solar energy impinges on the earth it sets up a situation that resembles the horizontal plate configuration that generates the Benard's Hexagons. Solar radiation warms the surface of the Earth, which transfers the warmth to the lower atmosphere. Warm air rises to the upper atmospheric layers where it spreads out releasing its heat through adiabatic expansion and conduction to the outer atmosphere, and through radiation to the blackness of outer space. Loss of heat causes it to become cooler, denser and dryer so that it descends again to the surface of the Earth where it once again begins to pick up heat.[1]

On a flat, uniformly heated surface a similar process generates hexagonal Benard cells, but on the surface of a rotating globe heated by a point source like the sun the cells formed are shaped like latitudinal bands around the surface of the Earth. These bands of climate circulation are well understood by navigators and weathermen on the earth, and they are responsible for consistent winds like the trade winds and the easterlies that used to reliably propel sailing ships back and forth between continents.[2]

On a flat, uniformly heated surface a similar process generates hexagonal Benard cells, but on the surface of a rotating globe heated by a point source like the sun the cells formed are shaped like latitudinal bands around the surface of the Earth. These cyclic air currents are the Benard's Cells of our planetary heat transfer system.

Figure 44m (next page) represents the circulating atmospheric climate cells on the surface of the earth. The first such cell, the equatorial cell, called the Hadley Cell, starts with warm, moist air rising from the equator. Air rising from this zone cools and loses its moisture in the upper atmosphere, a process responsible for the tropical rain forests that surround the world at the equator.

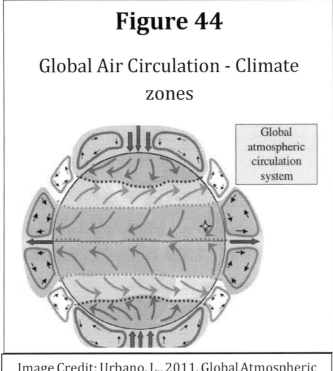

Figure 44

Global Air Circulation - Climate zones

Global atmospheric circulation system

Image Credit: Urbano, L., 2011. Global Atmospheric Circulation and Biomes, Retrieved June 4th, 2016, from Montessori Muddle http://MontessoriMuddle.org/.

The cooler, dryer air aloft at the equator spreads out and loses its heat as it dissipates and expands. Ultimately it becomes so cool, dry and dense that it begins to fall back to earth. This happens in a band about thirty degrees from the equator. In regions affected by these descending air currents there is an abundance of dry, clear weather. Desert biomes are common in these zones.

Dry air circulating earthward from the Hadley Cell divides in the lower atmosphere sending some air south to complete the Hadley Circulation and directing some air northward to start another circulation cell, this one called the Ferrel Cell.

Picking up heat and moisture from the surface of the earth, this north flowing air rises again in regions around 60 degrees from the equator.

Rising air currents drop their moisture and create temperate and boreal forests. The updraft divides again in the upper atmosphere sending some air south to complete the Ferrel Circulation and some north to create a Polar Cell. Finally, cold, dry air converging at the top of the globe falls to the arctic surface and contributes to the dry deep freeze of the arctic weather.

These cyclic air currents are the Benard's Cells of our planetary heat transfer system. The pattern that emerges is a function of the earth's rotation, the properties of the air, the shape of the Earth, the application rate of solar heat to the earth's surface and the resistance to flow along the surface of the earth as well as other factors[3]. They are patterns without structures caused and preserved by energy input from the sun.

Solid barriers like mountain ranges get in the way of the circulating cells and cause variations of their shape and intensity in many areas of the surface. Surface roughness like vegetation causes drag on the lower air currents slowing the circulation pattern. When these air currents flow across a smooth surface they flow rapidly and disperse gradients quickly creating entropic conditions easily. Surface roughness resists flow patterns in the lowest and densest layers of the atmosphere, interfering with entropy expansion and preserving ordered conditions. The grand sweep of the circulation cells is a pattern dependent on the physical properties of fluids, resistances, conditions, and energy input to insure its continuing activity.

> Surface roughness like vegetation causes drag on the lower air currents slowing the circulation pattern.

As stated in the United Nations Intergovernmental Panel on Climate Change Report[4], it is commonly known that the boundaries of these cells shift poleward as the climate warms. This fact leads me to surmise that during warmer climate periods (inter-glacials) the polar front might migrate northward all the way to the pole. This

> It is commonly known that the boundaries of these circulation cells shift poleward as the climate warms.

would reduce the number of climate cells from three to two. If this were to occur the descending air at the pole would shift to ascending flow. This would reverse the climate at the pole from dry to wet. Instead of desert regions with next to no precipitation the poles would become regions of high precipitation. The moisture falling in Polar Regions would be frozen, and as such it would accumulate as ice and snow, forming glaciers that would push southward, only melting when they reached warmer climates.

A climate cycle such as this is an example of an entropy cycle that could cause glaciation cycles and Ice Ages. This idea may be speculative, but as noted in Chapter 1, Edward O. Wilson says:

> *"Scientific theories are a product of the imagination – informed imagination. They reach beyond their grasp to predict the existence of previously unexpected phenomena."*

During glacial periods the fresh water content of the earth is in a low entropy state (ice) while the atmosphere is in a high entropy state (mixed) and the complexity of the biosphere is pushed back toward the equator. During interglacial periods the fresh water is in a higher entropy state (liquid and gas), the biosphere (low entropy) is extensive and the atmosphere is partitioned into climate zones (also low entropy). This interaction, exchange of entropy between climate media, easily explains glacial cycles. When the atmosphere is mixed (a high entropy state) equatorial heat is dispersed to the poles and no part of the earth can support ice. But when biomass expands a low entropy state (isolated, unmixed) descends over the globe, the poles become cold because both ordered biomass and ordered climate resist convective heat transfer across the surface

When the atmosphere is mixed (a high entropy state) equatorial heat is dispersed to the poles and no part of the earth can support ice. But when biomass expands a low entropy state (isolated, unmixed) descends over the globe, the poles become cold because both ordered biomass and ordered climate resist convective heat transfer across the surface.

Chapter Sixteen References

[1] Marshall, John and Plumb, Allen R.: "Atmosphere, Ocean and Climate Dynamics: an Introductory Text (International Geophysics)": Elsevier Academic Press, Burlington, Mass. Copyright 2008

[2] Randall, David: "An Introduction to the Global Circulation of the Atmosphere": Princeton University Press, Princeton, NJ, Copyright 2015.

[3] Dutton, John A.: "Dynamics of Atmospheric Motion" Dover Publications, 1995

[4] Mann, Michael E. and Krump, Lee R.: "Dire Predictions – Understanding Climate Change – The Visual Guide to the Findings of the IPCC", Second Edition, DK Publishing House, NY, NY, a Penguin Random House Company, Copyright 2015

Chapter Seventeen

Energy Induced Patterns That Cause Structure to Accumulate – Biostructure and Biomes

Chapter Summary

Just as ice freezes on the cold surfaces of a refrigerator, solid structures tend to precipitate and grow whenever entropy is withdrawn from a system.

The reactions that cause this to happen depend on the concentration of reactants in the solution, so the rate of solids growth is inherently self-limiting. Solids that have precipitated act as seed material, nucleation sites and templates for more solids precipitation, so the process can also be self-replicating and auto-catalytic.

This chapter discusses the conditions under which these processes occur.

Chapter Seventeen
Energy Induced Patterns

In Part 2 we learned how disorder or entropy increases in every interaction or process universally, and how in isolated systems where material and energy flows are prevented, entropy increases to a maximum and ultimately prevails. In Part 3 we learned how order and complexity emerge and accumulate when matter and energy are allowed to discharge from enclosed systems. In Part 4 we learned how order could be manifested in physical states of matter – more immobile states having increased order and diminished entropy content than more fluid forms.

In the last two chapters we learned how changes of state are not the only consequences of ordering. Ordered patterns of activity can emerge in energy flow systems without any emerging structure to support or preserve the flow pattern. These activity patterns are quasi-stable and persist like the wave in Robert Frost's "West Running Brook" as long as the energy flow and configuration constraints continue to exist. But as soon as the energy flow ceases and/or the configuration changes, the flow patterns dissipate and become random once more.

The precipitation of solids and the emergence of flow patterns are both manifestations of order resulting from entropy extraction from systems[1]. If the system is of a type that retains matter but allows energy to escape, order will accumulate in the

> The precipitation of solids and the emergence of flow patterns are both manifestations of order resulting from entropy extraction from systems. If the system is of a type that retains matter but allows energy to escape, order will accumulate in the system.

system. Ordered circulation patterns in high entropy states of matter (gasses and liquids) provide the bulk fluid flow necessary to bring reactants together, and molecular interactions establish the bonds necessary to hold together large complex associations of molecules into solid structures.

Minor amounts of bulk flow are necessary to bring together the components to build solid structures. Intense flows generate shear stresses and turbulence that tear solids apart. It follows that for any physical and chemical paradigm an optimal condition of flow exists that will most successfully encourage the growth of complex structures. Where these conditions exist in a cooling medium, one in which heat and its associated entropy are being removed, organized flow, solids and structure will emerge in a system.[2]

The emergence of solid structures is a significant occurrence in a system. Solid structures are resilient and have the ability to resist dissipation.

> For any physical and chemical paradigm an optimal condition of flow exists that will most successfully encourage the growth of complex structures. Where these conditions exist in a cooling medium, organized flow, solids and structure will emerge in a system.

They carry in their shape the same information that existed in the flow patterns they replaced, but they do not dissolve into randomness when the flow stops. So it could be said that the emergence of solids offers the same function in natural systems that Sequoyah's Syllabary did for language. Information in solid form is resilient and more permanent than the information in circulating patterns of flow. The information in

> Information in solid form is resilient and more permanent than the information in circulating patterns of flow. The information in patterns of fluid flow is dynamic, changing and short lived like the patterns in spoken language. The information in solid structures is static, structured and permanent like a message in written language.

patterns of fluid flow is dynamic, changing and short lived like the patterns in spoken language. The information in solid structures is static, structured and permanent like a message in written language.

The energy released during the transition between the two states (heat of fusion) is significant. The transition from a fluid to a solid releases energy, that has to be removed from the system in order for the condensation/precipitation cycle to continue. Such a condensing system tends to preserve the temperature of the reacting medium even as it gives up heat and the associated entropy to some other sink. The discharge of entropy imparts order and complexity to the precipitated solids. The low entropy and the resilience of the solids buffer the system establishing order over time as well as in space.

Circulating flow patterns have very specific shear patterns within them. Shear is greatest where the patterns encounter static surfaces or opposing currents. Shear is the factor that brings solids forming reactants together. So shear increases the probability of solids formation.

But shear also provides fluid stresses. Beyond a certain level, shear stresses tear solids apart again. Within the spectrum of shear stresses there exist conditions that are optimal for solids production and growth. Solid structures will begin to form at these surfaces of optimum shear, and they will grow by depleting concentrations of reactants in adjacent layers of fluid. Solid surfaces once formed will present nucleation sites for deposition of additional solids so that solid masses will grow. Depletion of concentrations at the surface of the solids will draw reactants from adjacent areas by diffusion reconstituting adjacent solutions and enabling deposition of more solids, thickening and strengthening solid structures.

As long as stresses don't reach levels that tear apart the structure, and as long as the concentration of reactants is not depleted below the level required to precipitate solids, structures will continue to grow and to fix order and organization into solid form when entropy is withdrawn from the system.

As long as stresses don't reach levels that tear apart the structure, and as long as the concentration of reactants is not depleted below the level required to precipitate solids, structures will continue to grow and to fix order and organization into solid form when entropy is withdrawn from the system.

Industries that grow crystals from solutions depend on these processes. Water treatment systems that remove solids by growing an insoluble floc to absorb contaminants and settle the mixture also operate in this way.

The balance of entropy over a non-isolated system determines the amount of entropy generated within the system, and therefore the amount of ordering that happens in the system's interior. If the entropy leaving the system is greater than the sum of the entropy entering the system and the entropy generated by the processes going on within the system, the system is diminishing its entropy content and becoming more ordered. See the entropy balance chart in Chapter 6 to understand how this process encourages biomass complexity and accumulation on Planet Earth.

As we learned in Chapter 6, energy flow through a closed system always discharges more entropy than it takes in. So unless these systems generate a lot of entropy internally, they are always producing ordered interiors. This implies the production of larger and larger, more complex and structured molecules and the precipitation of solids with more complex shapes and structures in regions where circulation, shear force and concentrations allow.

Chapter Seventeen References

[1] Lagzi, Istvan, "Precipitation Patterns in Reaction-Diffusion Systems":
Research Signpost, 2010

[2] Ball, Phillip: "Patterns in Nature: Why the Natural World Looks the Way
it Does": University of Chicago Press, Chicago, Ill., Copyright 2016

Chapter Eighteen

Pattern and Complexity

Chapter Summary

Complexity is an emergent property of a system that is emitting more entropy than the sum of what it takes in and what it creates. Order tends to emerge in such systems at rates determined by their entropy balance. When all possible order has been generated at one molecular entropy level, new forms of order emerge in response to continued entropy removal. Order thus compounded is the basis for the emergent property of complexity.

This chapter will present some relevant facts that will help us understand this process.

Chapter Eighteen
Pattern and Complexity

Complexity is also a result of entropy reduction. It is comprised of molecular variability on a macroscale. In the solid state it is characterized by high surface areas and void volumes resulting from tortuous porosity. In molecular structures it is caused by ordered molecular groupings and macromolecular structures. In both cases complexity is an indication of low entropy content or high levels of order. [1]

We have already considered how complex solids might precipitate from swirling flow patterns and energy extraction from fluid media. Now let's consider how complexity might grow from mixtures of smaller molecules. To do this we need to call on some concepts from chemical kinetics.

Chemicals interact with each other at rates that are highly dependent upon the concentration of reactants and products. If we take the combustion of natural gas (methane) as an example, we find that a molecule of methane reacts with two molecules of oxygen to give a molecule of carbon dioxide and two molecules of water. This is expressed by the following chemical equation:

$$CH_4 + 2O_2 \longrightarrow CO_2 + 2H_2O$$

Obviously the reaction mixture must contain some methane and some oxygen for this reaction to take place at all. If either gas is lacking in the reaction mixture the reaction will not occur.

If we start out with a sample of air and add to it a trace of methane, we can ignite individual methane molecules one at a time, but the distance to another methane molecule is too great for the heat released to have any effect on the neighboring methane molecules. In this case the methane concentration is too low for the reaction to propagate itself through the mixture. It is said to be below the lower combustible limit.

If we increase the methane concentration gradually we will reach a point where the heat released by combustion of the first molecule is sufficient to ignite the one next to it. At this point ignition of the first molecule will initiate the ignition of surrounding molecules and combustion will proceed until all the methane in the mixture is converted into carbon dioxide and water vapor. A significant surplus of oxygen will be left over.

This methane concentration is called the lower combustible limit. For a combustible gas like methane it may be called the lower explosive limit, for obvious reasons.

Once the lower combustible limit is surpassed, all mixtures of methane and air will react to completion. Such mixtures are extremely hazardous, especially when exposed to an ignition source, because they will react with explosive violence and the potential to do extreme damage.

As the concentration of methane is increased a point will be reached where there is no oxygen left over in the reaction products. At this concentration ratio (called the stoichiometric ratio) the maximum amount of combustion energy is dispersed into the minimum amount of reaction products producing the greatest destructive force.

Further increasing the methane concentration leads to a situation where the reaction consumes all the oxygen before all the methane is consumed leaving some unreacted methane behind in the reaction products.

Finally, on increasing the methane concentration still further, a point will be reached where the methane is so concentrated that the energy effects of ignition will no longer propagate to the site of another oxygen molecule. At this point the mixture is said to be above the upper combustible limit, and so it will not support the combustion process.

Methane mixtures that are above the upper combustible limit can be very hazardous even though they do not support combustion because as soon as mixing with air dilutes them they will become combustible and/or explosive again.

From this simple example it can be seen that reaction rates are intimately related to the concentration of the reactants, a very rational conclusion if you can accept the idea that

> Reaction rates are intimately related to the concentration of the reactants.

molecules have to encounter one another if they are to react, and the frequency of these encounters is proportional to concentration.

Chapter Eighteen
Pattern and Complexity

As molecules increase in size and molecular weight interactions tend to involve specific reaction sites on molecules. Larger molecules may have numerous reaction sites, and they may interact in many different ways with other sites on other molecules or even with other sites on the same molecule. Bonding

> Bonding between sites on the same molecule effects the way the molecule has to bend, twist or fold to bring the reaction sites together.

between sites on the same molecule effects the way the molecule has to bend, twist or fold to bring the reaction sites together.

In Chapter 8 we discussed the relationship between numbers of interacting entities and the emergence of properties that characterize the collection. Large molecules that have numerous reaction sites demonstrate a similar property of emerging characteristics. Interactions become predictable and functional as numbers of interacting molecular sites increase.

In his book "Origins of Order"[2], Stu Kauffman considers many of these functions and concludes that the number of ways macromolecules can interact increases faster than size of the molecule does. This implies that complex macromolecules tend to interact with increasing frequency and rate as they grow bigger in size and molecular weight. Like a snowball rolling down a hill they increase in mass and complexity as they grow and opportunities for novel interactions

> Complex macromolecules tend to interact with increasing frequency and rate as they grow bigger in size and molecular weight.

proliferate. This gives rise to the emergence of properties and characteristics that never would have existed on smaller molecular scales.

This tendency to grow and complexify as molecules shed entropy leads to functionality in mixtures, and life emerges from a mix of complex, functioning molecules.

Functionality occurs in direct proportion to the entropy balance in a flowing system.[3] The entropy balance is entirely controlled by the ability of the system boundary to pass entropy out of the system and the ability of the system to assume and retain ordered configurations.

Functionality occurs in direct proportion to the entropy balance in a flowing system. The entropy balance is entirely controlled by the ability of the system boundary to pass entropy out of the system and the ability of the system to assume and retain ordered configurations.

Chapter Eighteen References

[1] Bourgine, Paul and Lesne, Annick: "Morphogenesis: Origins of Patterns and Shapes (Springer Complexity)": Springer, Copyright 2011

[2] Kauffman, Stewart A.: "Origins of Order   Self-Organization and Selection in Evolution": Oxford University Press, NY, NY; Copyright 1993

[3] Polis, Gary A. and Winemiller, Kirk O.: "Food Webs: Integrations of Patterns and Dynamics": Springer, Copyright 1996

Part Six

The Biosphere

Chapter Nineteen

Cycling of Biosphere Stores

Chapter Summary

The growth and distribution of the biosphere is directly related to rejection of entropy into outer space which leaves order and complexity behind on the surface of the earth. Warm regions of the globe reject more energy and entropy than cold regions do, and so they accumulate more order in the form of biomass wherever other constraints permit. This is the reason tropical rain forests cover the terrestrial portions of the equator while plant productivity becomes minimal at extreme latitudes.

One of the additional constraints that prevents productivity in some areas of the globe is the exponential population growth dynamics of most species and ecosystems. When populations are diminished below a critical level, the recovery rate is reduced too much for an ecosystem to effectively recover.

This chapter will analyze how destruction of the planetary biomass reserve allows the earth to equilibrate toward a "heat death" scenario and recovery of the biomass restores stable temperature differentials to the climate system.

Chapter Nineteen
Cycling Biosphere Stores

How does one determine the mass of the biosphere? Most commonly it is sufficient to focus on the mass of plant material (phytomass). Since plants are autotrophs (create their own food by acting on mineral compounds [carbon dioxide and water]) and sunlight, and since they also serve as food for all of the heterotrophic organisms on earth (those that obtain their food by eating other organisms) plants make up more than 90% of the total biomass of the earth.

A common practice is to sample small areas of the earth's surface and measure all the phytomass in the sample[1]. The resulting number can be reasonably applied to all the areas having similar vegetative components and densities. The larger the number of samples and the more discerning the description of plant communities, the more accurate is the estimate of phytomass. Similar plant communities and climate types are classified as biomes or ecosystem types and assumed to have similar phytomass densities which may range from less than 5 tons per hectare for deserts and arctic tundra to more than 1000 tons per hectare for mature forests.

Mapping the extent of various biomes and ecosystems produces detailed information on the area covered by each type[2]. Multiplying the areas by the mass densities and adding the results gives the total global plant biomass (phytomass). As more and more data are developed, the estimates of global phytomass become more and more accurate.

Estimates of global phytomass are often given in terms of the amount of carbon they contain. This facilitates comparisons with the carbon content of the atmosphere, the oceans, the geosphere, etc. Current estimates indicate that the total phytomass of the biosphere is about 1350 billion tons (gigatons) containing about 650 billion tons of carbon in the year 2000.

It is informative to review estimates of biomass during earlier periods of history. Figure 2 on page 35 gives a rough idea of how the biomass content of the earth varies throughout extended periods of history. Estimates of total global phytomass during the last glacial maximum, about 20,000 years ago, indicate that the biosphere contained about 500

Giga-tons of carbon. This was a period of glacial maximum when the entire boreal forest was obliterated by glacial ice.

10,000 years later, in the middle of the Holocene period, when glaciers retreated and phytomass retook the surface of the planet; the earth's phytomass had doubled to more than 1000 gigatons of carbon. Early agricultural and other biomass removal activities gradually reduced this maximum amount to about to about 900 gigatons of carbon by the beginning of the industrial era.

The Industrial Revolution is generally considered to have started with the use of the improved steam engine invented by James Watt in 1776. Since

> Estimates of total global phytomass during the last glacial maximum, about 20,000 years ago, indicate that the biosphere contained about 500 Giga-tons of carbon. This was a period of glacial maximum when the entire boreal forest was obliterated by glacial ice. 10,000 years later, in the middle of the Holocene period, when glaciers retreated and phytomass retook the surface of the planet, Earth's phytomass had doubled to more than 1000 gigatons of carbon.

then the use of biomass carbon for food, fuel, construction and industrial purposes, as well as its removal for living space, farming, transportation, mining and other land clearing operations has increased at an exponential pace, only to be relieved by the advent of coal and other fossil fuels as competitive sources of energy. This continued consumption of wood for fuel along with its destructive removal for agricultural and community developmental purposes reduced the carbon content of the biosphere to about 650 Giga-tons by the year 2000. Present estimates indicate global biomass carbon content to be around 610 gigatons.

Glacial Retreat: What caused the glaciers to recede 20,000 years ago? Were there changes in energy input to the planet from increasing solar radiation caused by sunspot cycles or planetary axis shifts or orbital variability? All of these things may have had something to do with the demise of the glaciers. But it's hard to relate observed glacial cycles to variations in solar radiation from these sources.

In this book I am suggesting that the glaciers were the cause of their own destruction. They destroyed the biomass in front of them as they moved south, and they constrained the subsequent production of new biomass on the surface of the earth. But as glaciers moved further and further south they had to absorb the full impact of convective transfer of tropical heat without the buffering effect of the forest biomass they had destroyed. The forests in the temperate and arctic zones that had isolated and protected the glaciers during their growth phases were no longer present to resist the convective transfer of heat from the tropics. Without the biological structures and complexity of the phytomass, the earth went through an entropy maximum that equilibrated the conditions in the tropics with the polar conditions in the arctic. Since the solar influx of energy is most intense in the tropics and since the tropical zones make up most of the surface of the globe, huge amounts of energy could be released by the tropics without having much effect on tropical temperatures. This allows melting of huge amounts of ice in the higher latitudes from the spreading of tropical energy to glaciated surfaces.

When glaciers remove biomass it causes the demise of the structural complexity that resists convective circulation and heat transfer in the atmosphere. Advancing thermal circulation from the tropics forces the glaciers to retreat, exposing fresh fertile soils as they go. Opportunistic biomass advances to take over newly exposed territory reclaiming more and more area and rebuilding the biological buffer that isolates the climates in the higher latitudes and keeps them cool protecting the glaciers. Properly protected from tropical heat, high latitude climates begin to cool again and the glaciers begin to regrow.

With the biomass communities and the climate zones stabilizing and the temperature differentials increasing, the planet goes through an entropy minimum or structural complexity maximum, which the scouring action of the glaciers degrades once more.

In this scenario the earth is seen as an entropy oscillator powered by the energy input from the sun. The whole cycle takes many generations of plants, many cycles of ecological succession amid changing climax communities, and many thousands of years.

Earth is an entropy oscillator powered by the energy input from the sun. The whole cycle takes many generations of plants, many cycles of ecological succession amid changing climax communities, and many thousands of years.

Twenty thousand years ago the glaciers had advanced throughout the entire boreal forest and they were bulldozing their way through the forests of the temperate zone. The changes in climate and the relentless scraping had reduced planetary phytomass carbon content to 500 gigatons. Warm air from the tropics was released to wash over the glaciers, which retreated, and phytomass retook control, advancing behind the retreating frost line so that the forests could reclaim their territory. The phytomass recovered its carbon content rebuilding the global biosphere to more than 1000 Giga-tons of carbon.

At this point the glaciers were no longer confronting tropical heat. Thousands of miles of complex structures stood between the glaciers and the tropics, blocking the convective advance of energy so the poles again cooled. The Arctic Ocean froze, glaciers formed on mountain ranges and other areas of high elevation. But the isolation of the Polar Regions and the formation of continental glaciers have never had a chance to be completed in our current cycle.

Another destroyer of biomass has arisen. Before the glaciers could build to the point of an onrushing ice age mankind has become an even bigger destroyer of biomass. By mid-Holocene, 10,000 years ago, the biosphere had grown to 1000 Giga-tons of carbon – not enough to effectively isolate the poles, but enough to stabilize the climate system. With the advent of the Industrial Revolution the biosphere was already experiencing a 100 Giga-ton deficit of carbon. Isolation of the poles was not yet complete, and already complexity and structure were being destroyed faster than they were growing. Convective dispersion of energy was already interfering with the cycle.

At this point, biosphere destruction began in earnest. Biomass removal proceeded at exponentially increasing rates. In the 250 years since the Industrial Revolution biomass has been reduced by about 30% to 610 Giga-tons of carbon. A similar level of biomass (500 gigatons) on the planet 20,000 years ago initiated enough atmospheric convective heat transfer to reverse the advance of continental glaciation. It is little surprise that diminishing biomass is causing the same condition today, even if melting continental glaciers cannot absorb the heat transfered, and even if it is the result of anthropomorphic activities.

> Mankind has become an even bigger destroyer of biomass. With the advent of the Industrial Revolution the biosphere was already experiencing a 100 Giga-ton deficit of carbon. In the 250 years since the Industrial Revolution biomass has been reduced by about 30% to 610 Giga-tons of carbon. A similar level of biomass on the planet 20,000 years ago initiated enough atmospheric convective heat transfer to reverse the advance of continental glaciation. It is little surprise that diminishing biomass is causing the same condition today

Dr. Vaclav Smil, Distinguished Professor at the University of Manitoba sensed these relationships when he wrote his recent book, "Harvesting the Biosphere – What We Have Taken from Nature"[3]. He makes the following comment on the work of J. Rockstrom, "*A Safe Operating Space for Humanity*"[4] published in the scientific journal "Nature".

> Before the advent of human modification of the earth's surface, entropy cycles were purely natural phenomena. But when mankind emerged, the natural cycle was superseded and an alternative cycle was imposed on the biomass and the climate by mankind.

Curiously, a recent assessment of a safe place for humanity, one that identifies (and) quantifies the planetary boundaries that must not be transgressed if unacceptable climate change is to be prevented, does not list either a minimum phytomass stock or primary productivities among its top ten concerns. Rather these concerns are climate change, disturbances of the nitrogen and phosphorous cycles, stratospheric ozone depletion, ocean acidification, global fresh water use, atmospheric aerosol loading and chemical pollution, and they address phytomass stocks and productivity only indirectly, via the categories of biodiversity loss and changes in land use (explicitly defined as the percentage of global land cover converted to cropland, with a proposed limit of no more than 15% compared to the present 12%).

Smil's assertion that 12 % of global land cover is converted to cropland obscures the fact that the land selected for conversion is the most densely occupied by, and productive of, biomass. The proportion of global biomass production that is currently allocated to human use is therefore much greater. Most current estimates put this figure at 40% to 50%.[5]

In this book, I am contending that the terms "minimum biomass stock" and "climate change" used by Rockstrom are closely, and probably causally, related; if not the same problem.

Before the advent of human modification of the earth's surface, entropy cycles were purely natural phenomena, a battle between biomass-destroying glaciers and biomass stimulating tropical warmth. But when mankind emerged with his tool making skills and his ability to modify the earth's surface, presumably to his own advantage, the natural cycle was superseded and mankind imposed an alternative cycle on the biomass and the climate.

To analyze the effects of this change of cycles, I want to refer to a book by several experts in the field of ecological economics. The book, published in 1999, is called, "An Introduction to Ecological Economics"[6]. The authors are:

Chapter Nineteen
Cycling Biosphere Stores

- Robert Costanza, Director of the University of Maryland Institute for Ecological Economics

- John Cumberland, Professor Emeritus in Economics at the University of Maryland

- Herman Daily, Associate Director of the University of Maryland Institute for Ecological Economics

- Robert Goodland, Environmental Advisor to the World Bank, Chair of the Ecological Society of America, and President of the International Association of Impact Assessment.

- Richard Norgaard, Professor of Energy and Resources at the University of California, Berkeley.

The book opens with a discussion of two conflicting paradigms of the finite global ecosystem, which serves as both a source for economic/industrial raw materials and a sink for the waste products of human industry. The first paradigm the authors call the "Empty World" scenario. It visualizes a time when biomass resources were virtually omnipresent on the surface of the earth, and human intervention was virtually non-existent. At this time industrial resources were virtually non-existent as well. In this situation human activity is limited by a lack of industrial resources, and so industrial resources are considered vastly more valuable than natural resources. Under these conditions there is a great incentive to convert natural resources to industrial resources.

The second paradigm, called the "Full World" scenario occurs when industrial resources proliferate and become cheap at the expense of natural resources, which have been depleted and become dear. In this scenario the relative value of the two types of resources is reversed.

If the inflection point or the transition in values happens too quickly to be assimilated by perception and integrated into our social system, we have no way to measure the comparative values of the two types of resources; natural and industrial. We find ourselves coping with shortages of natural resources with no way to adjust our perception of their relative value.

We view the shortage of natural resources as just an annoyance, a limitation on the supply of raw materials that can be converted into more valued manufactured products. The value of a manufactured product is, at least in part, dependent on the fact that you have some natural resource to use it on. So the shortage of natural products tends to increase the value of industrial products. But what good is a saw, for example, if you have already cut down all the forest? The authors draw their conclusion with the following statement.

> *The role of Economic Development Banks in the new era would be increasingly to make investments that replenish the stocks and increase the productivity of natural capital. In the past, development investments have largely aimed at increasing the stock and productivity of human made capital. Instead of investing mainly in saw mills, fishing boats and refineries; development should now focus on reforestation, restoration of fish populations and renewable substitutes for dwindling reserves of petroleum.*

This approach to economic sustainability through restoring natural capital stocks is entirely consistent with restoring climate stability through restoration of the earth's biomass. A reversal of the relative economic values owing to an excessive increase in the level of industrial capital over natural capital completely changes the dynamics of capital accumulation without human consciousness ever taking note of the changed paradigm.

 The two world paradigms stem from entirely different growth dynamics that occur at different population densities[7]. The "Empty World" dynamics represent a world where natural resources are plentiful – more than sufficient to support species growth. These growth dynamics lead to exponential population growth as shown in Figure 45. Under these conditions, the ability of a species to multiply is exponentially related to the number of reproducing individuals in the population.

If the population is reduced by half, the rate of growth is reduced exponentially to a fourth of the initial value. Under these conditions removal of biomass can push plant populations rapidly toward extinction while severely diminishing their potential for recovery.

The "Full World" scenario represents a world where a species density is beginning to overrun the carrying capacity of its environment. In this world the reproductive potential of the species is no longer limited by its capacity to reproduce. Species reproduce at rates much faster than the environment can carry, and the population is controlled by the individual's ability to survive in an environment that is unable to support the sheer numbers of the species. These dynamics lead to a logistic or sigmoid growth curve as shown in Figure 46.

In the lower range of the sigmoid population dynamics curve, population growth rate is almost solely dependent on the number of reproducing individuals in the present population. The carrying capacity of the environment is far greater than existing populations, and the ability of the organism to reproduce and "fill the void" is the only thing controlling the rate of population growth.

In the upper range of the sigmoid population dynamics curve, future population size is a function almost solely of the capacity of the environment to support population densities. The ability of an organism to produce new individuals is no longer relevant because the environment provides limits on the population size.

Most of the world's plant populations operate in the "Full World" scenario, a paradigm in which the plant's natural reproduction capacity is more than sufficient to replace individuals lost through natural attrition.

However, once the population is depleted below the inflection point in Figure 46, we enter a realm of population dynamics where the ability of a species to replace lost individuals is entirely dependent on the density of the existing population. As "Harvesting the Biosphere" is increased beyond this point, the ability of biomass species to regenerate the biosphere is depleted in geometric proportion to the amount of biomass left behind after the harvest.

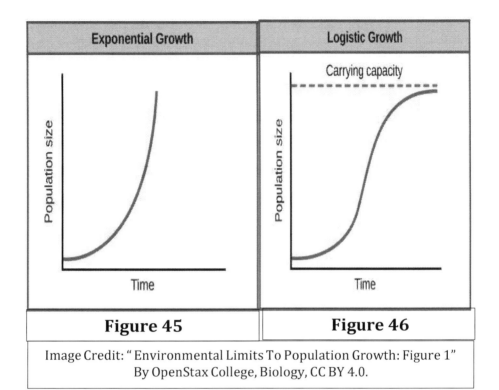

Figure 45

Figure 46

Image Credit: " Environmental Limits To Population Growth: Figure 1"
By OpenStax College, Biology, CC BY 4.0.

In this regime the vitality of a species is entirely dependent on its numbers. The ability to overcome natural constraints to reproduction

> In the exponential growth regime the vitality of a species is entirely dependent on its numbers.

depends on interactions between individuals. Just as methane and oxygen can't react if the concentrations are too small, biological populations can't maintain themselves if the numbers of individuals are insufficient to provide the necessary physical and social interactions to facilitate reproduction.

An example of a species controlled by this dynamic can be found in the Passenger Pigeon, a species that once existed in huge flocks containing millions of birds. The species went extinct when populations fell below a level that enabled the reproductive process to function.

Chapter Nineteen
Cycling Biosphere Stores

It has been customary (without very much quantitative justification) to display the graph in Figure 46 with the inflection point toward the higher end of the population scale. However, the data in Figure 2 indicate that the biomass of the earth is already depleted toward the midpoint of the scale. This should be a potential cause for concern that without human intervention on behalf of the biomass, the biosphere may have already been depleted beyond its ability to quickly recover.[8]

This brings into question the assumption that biomass carbon is a renewable resource. In fact, it is becoming more and more clear that just

> This brings into question the assumption that biomass carbon is a renewable resource. In fact, it is becoming more and more clear that just the opposite is the case. Biomass, because of its dependence on the mechanics of reproduction, is a resource that can be critically reduced to a level from which it cannot recover. Therefore it is a particularly vulnerable resource that is prone to depletion beyond its ability to recover.

the opposite is the case. Biomass, because of its dependence on the mechanics of reproduction, is a resource that can be reduced to a critical level from which it cannot recover. As proximity to willing mates is reduced by diminishing numbers, the ability of a species to reproduce is exponentially degraded. Species extinction is the inevitable result of this process. Biomass is a particularly vulnerable resource that is prone to depletion beyond its recovery potential.

Paul Hawkin, entrepreneur, founder of the gardening supply store Smith and Hawkin, has teamed up with Amory and L. Hunter Lovins, founders of the Rocky Mountain Institute, to write a book called "Natural Capitalism – Creating the Next Industrial Revolution".[9] They express the biomass dilemma in this way:

> The industrial revolution that gave rise to modern capitalism greatly expanded the possibilities for the material development of

humankind. It continues to do so today, but at a severe price. Since the mid eighteenth century, more of nature has been destroyed than in all prior history. While industrial systems have reached pinnacles of success, able to muster and accumulate human-made capital on vast levels, *natural capital*, on which civilization depends to create economic prosperity, is rapidly declining, and the rate of loss is increasing proportionate to gains in material well-being. *Natural capital* includes all the familiar resources used by humankind: water, minerals, oil, trees, fish, soil, air, et cetera. But it also encompasses living systems which include grasslands, savannas, wetlands, estuaries, oceans, coral reefs, riparian corridors, tundras, and rainforests. These are deteriorating worldwide at an unprecedented rate. Within these ecological communities are the fungi, ponds, mammals, humus, amphibians, bacteria, trees, flagellates, insects, songbirds, ferns starfish and flowers that make life possible and worth living on this planet.

This paragraph captures the biomass dilemma very well, and it provides the background for an entire revolution in the way humanity must evaluate the resources we consume to make our lives worthwhile. An emphasis on the value of sustainable, renewable natural resources is essential if we are to sustain ourselves and the habitability of our planet.

The Aral Sea:...An extreme example of ecosystem collapse is the abrupt change of climate in the region of the Aral Sea[10]. Once the fourth largest freshwater lake on the planet, the Aral Sea covered 26,000 square miles between Kazakhstan and Uzbekistan. It was fed by two free flowing rivers, the Syr Darya flowing in from the North, and the Amu Darya, flowing in from the South. These free-flowing rivers were tapped to provide irrigation for agriculture in the surrounding country side. The conversion to agriculture caused irreparable damage to regional ecosystems. The diversion of water caused the entire Aral Sea to dry up. Ships that once carried freight and a fishing industry now lie as relics in the desert. A biomass ecosystem that once was adapted to this semi-arid biome has completely succumbed to the human manipulation of water and soils leaving nothing but a stagnant salty lake.

Figure 47-Shows NASA images of how the Aral Sera looked from space in 1989 compared to the outline of the sea in 2014. Figure 48 shows an example of one of the Ships remaining in the desert, a relic of the vibrant shipping industry that used to ply the sea.

Satellite Views of the Aral Sea

Figure 47

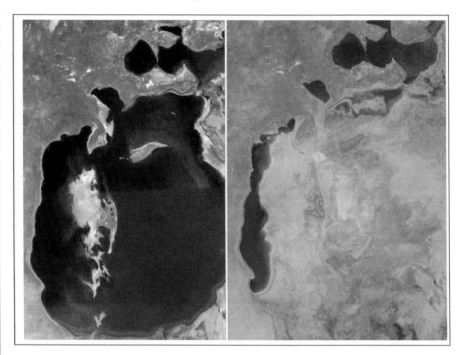

Credits: NASA Collage by Producercunningham Public Domain by Wikipedia

Altering the water balance of the Aral Sea lead to drying out of this large area of Central Asia and the demise of the ecosystems there. Removal of the river flow that entered the sea completely changed the water balance and thermal flow regime that controlled the ecosystem of the Aral Sea. Figure 48 shows just one of hundreds of Commercial ships left high and dry by the evaporating sea.

In a similar manner, pre-glacial, "Biomass-Full World" energy distribution operates on completely different dynamics from post-glacial, "Biomass-Empty World" energy distributions. Pre-glacial energy distribution is achieved through heavily constrained, low entropy, ecosystems, resulting from full development of the biomass, enabling wide and persistent temperature differentials and the accumulation of low entropy forms of water (ice). Post-Glacial energy distribution is much more uniform, without biomass, and with thoroughly mixed climate systems and energy differentials.

Remnants of Commercial Shipping on the Aral Sea

Figure:48

Credits: Wikipedia Commons File: Aralship2.jpg Author: Staecker

Chapter Nineteen
Cycling Biosphere Stores

A glacier functions as a transition mechanism from a "Biomass-Full World" (low entropy) state to a "Biomass-Empty World" (high entropy) state. Biological constraints to convective heat transfer act as impediments to equilibration. They are at a minimum when the earth is fully glaciated. Without these constraints, according to the Law of Maximum Entropy Production, entropy increases at the maximum possible rate allowing the earth to surge toward equilibrium. Once equilibrium has destroyed the biological complexity and enabled Tropical warmth to penetrate into more northern climates, biomass is restored to its original ability to restrain convective energy transfer. This re-imposes the constraint between the equator and the poles and allows the equator to warm and the poles to cool, restoring the ovoid shape of the radiative discharge shown in Figure 49.

When the planet approaches thermal equilibrium, uniformity takes over and the surface of the earth tends to approach its equilibrium temperature of 57°F. Radiative energy discharge assumes the equal distribution shown in Figure 50. Accumulations of ice can no longer exist leading to glacial retreat. With glacial retreat, biomass takes over again and thermal differentials are reestablished allowing the poles to cool once again and ice sheets to grow again.

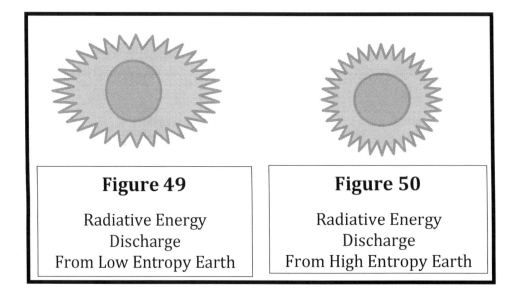

Figure 49	Figure 50
Radiative Energy Discharge From Low Entropy Earth	Radiative Energy Discharge From High Entropy Earth

Biomass is the reservoir of order that imposes a non-equilibrium condition on the atmosphere. It doesn't matter what the biomass removal

> Biomass is the reservoir of order that opposes equilibration of the atmosphere. It doesn't matter what the removal mechanism is, the result is the same, disorder, warming, and equilibration of the atmosphere.

mechanism is, the result is the same, disorder, warming, and equilibration of the atmosphere.

With half of the biomass in the world destroyed, as it is today, the higher latitudes of the planet will warm. If it is cool and glacier covered to begin with, the warming will melt the glaciers and re-establish the biosphere. As the biosphere re-establishes itself, the inflection point on the sigmoid growth curve rises and the earth accommodates greater and greater biomass populations. If it is already too warm and disorganized to begin with, the warming will raise the planetary temperatures, melt ice, vaporize water and drive the planet closer to equilibrium as Tropical warmth beats back the glaciers.

A planet already deprived of half of its biomass is below the inflection point on the sigmoid biomass growth curve. At this point biomass recovery is entirely dependent on population density. Because its density is already depleted, its ability to recover is already severely depressed.

A fundamental change in economic philosophy is necessary to reestablish the value of biomass resources and replace the 40-50% of the biomass

> A planet already deprived of half of its biomass is below the inflection point on the sigmoid biomass growth curve. At this point biomass recovery is entirely dependent on population density. Because its density is already depleted, its ability to recover is already severely depressed.

that has been removed by human activity if we are to prevent equilibration of the earth and the resulting "Heat Death" Greater biomass populations are required to stabilize the climate and to restore improved living conditions for all species on earth.

.

Chapter Nineteen References

[1] West, P. W.: "Tree and Forest Measurement": Springer, 2015

[2] Myneni, Ranga B. and Ross, Juhan: "Photon-Vegetation Interactions: Applications in Optical Remote Sensing and Plant Ecology": Springer – Verlag, Berlin Heidelberg, 1991

[3] Smil, Vaclav: "Harvesting the Biosphere – What We Have Taken From Nature": MIT Press, Cambridge, Mass. Copyright 2013

[4] Rockstrom, J. et al. 2009, "A Safe Operating Space for Humanity", Nature 461: 472-475

[5] Krausmann, Fridolin; Bondeau, Alberte, et. al.: "Global Human Appropriation of net Primary Production Doubled in the 20th Century" Biomass

[6] Costanza, Robert, et al: "An Introduction to Ecological Economics": St Lucie Press, an imprint of CRC Press, Boca Raton, FL, Copyright 199

[7] Rockwood, Larry L.: "Introduction to Population Ecology": Wiley – Blackwell, Cichester, West Sussex, UK; Copyright 2015

[8] Bolton, Melvin: "Populations: Growth and Control": Ribbonwood Publications, Queensland, Australia; Copyright 2011

[9] Hawkin, Paul; Lovins, Amorey and Lovins, L. Hunter: "Natural Capitalism – Creating the next Industrial Revolution": Little, Brown and Company, New Your, NY; Copyright 1999

[10] Zaviolav, Peter O.: "Physical Oceanography of the Dying Aral Sea": Springer – Praxis, Chichester, UK; Copyright 2005

Chapter Twenty

Biosphere Productivity

Chapter Summary

The carbon content of CO_2 in the atmosphere is a function of the size of the biosphere and other carbon reservoirs. Since the biosphere expands and contracts more rapidly than other carbon reserves, it has the most immediate effect on the carbon content of the atmosphere.

Decreasing the carbon content of the biosphere drives up the carbon content of the atmosphere. Increasing the carbon content of the biosphere depletes the carbon content of the atmosphere.

In this chapter we will consider how these ideas determine the extent of climate change

Chapter Twenty
Biosphere Productivity

How much phytomass does a biosphere with 650 gigatons of carbon storage produce in a year?[1] Plants produce sugars through photosynthesis. Some of these sugars are transformed into new plant tissues, and some are consumed to provide the energy necessary to support the metabolism of the plant. The total fixation of carbon into sugars is termed gross primary productivity (GPP). The amount of carbon that is converted into plant structures and tissues is called net primary productivity. The carbon in sugars consumed in support of metabolic function is called respiration (R_a). Net primary productivity is equal to gross primary productivity less the carbon required for respiration:[2]

$$NPP = GPP - R \qquad \text{(Equation 1)}$$

Vaclav Smil tells us that

> *"the NPP of major biomes ranges from negligible amounts in extreme environments (hot and cold deserts) to nearly 1 Kilogram of carbon per square meter (20 tons per hectare) in the richest tropical rain forests".*

Net primary productivity is the phytomass productivity of an ecosystem after the losses of respiration are removed, but before other environmental losses are considered. These other loses include things like litter-fall, root death, exudation, predation and natural physical losses. These losses may be designated as "L". A new term called "net ecosystem productivity" (NEP) is then defined as

$$NEP = GPP - R - L \qquad \text{(Equation 2)}$$

Losses, both respiratory (R) and non-respiratory (L) return carbon compounds to the atmosphere as carbon dioxide, to complete the natural carbon cycle. In a completely mature ecosystem the return stream approaches equality with the productivity so that net ecosystem productivity is zero, and gross primary productivity is equal to the sum of the losses. Thus in a mature ecosystem:

$$NEP = 0 \qquad \text{(Equation 3)} \quad \text{or:}$$

$$GPP = R + L \qquad \text{(Equation 4)}$$

Carefully mapping ecosystems and evaluating the above parameters for each ecosystem can obtain an estimate of global carbon circulation.

Present technology indicates that global gross primary productivity is about 120 gigatons of carbon per year. This represents the total amount of carbon drawn out of the atmosphere to replace losses, to provide for respiration and to accumulate biomass on the earth's surface.

If this figure is compared with the total atmospheric carbon content (about 750 gigatons) it is found that the entire atmospheric reservoir would be used up in about 7 years if it were not replaced by an equal amount from respiration and losses. The respiration and losses create enough carbon dioxide to balance the entire gross primary production. This is the lesson of equations 3 and 4. The net change to the carbon dioxide content of the atmosphere due to biological activity is zero

> In a balanced biosphere net ecosystem productivity is zero no matter how large the biosphere is. NEP was zero during the Wisconsin Glaciation, and it was zero during the last interglacial maximum.

(Equation 3). These large flows of carbon through the atmosphere have near zero effect on the amount of carbon in the atmosphere.

In a balanced biosphere net ecosystem productivity is zero no matter how large the biosphere is. NEP was zero during the Wisconsin Glaciation, and it was zero during the interglacial maximum. The only thing that changes this balance is actual changes in the size of the biosphere.

During the last interglacial biospheric maximum there were 500 gigatons more carbon in the biosphere than during the glacial maximum. Carbon lost from the biosphere passes through the atmosphere to be absorbed by the oceans and passed on to the geosphere. But it may take a thousand years for the atmosphere to equilibrate with the oceans, so a loss of biomass strongly affects the composition of the atmosphere.

Chapter Twenty
Biosphere Productivity

The biosphere today contains about 610 gigatons of carbon, 390 gigatons less than it contained at the glacial minimum 10,000 years ago. If thebiomass could be recovered to glacial minimum levels, 390 gigatons of carbon could be recovered from the atmosphere. Since the atmosphere has only 750 gigatons of carbon in the first place, the removal of 390 gigatons would leave only 360 gigatons of carbon in the atmosphere, less than existed before the Industrial Revolution.

The biosphere today contains about 610 gigatons of carbon, 390 gigatons less than it contained at the glacial minimum 10,000 years ago. If the biomass could be recovered to glacial minimum levels, 390 gigatons of carbon could be recovered from the atmosphere. Since the atmosphere has only 750 gigatons of carbon in the first place, the removal of 390 gigatons would leave only 360 gigatons of carbon in the atmosphere, less than existed before the Industrial Revolution.

Carbon dioxide from burning fossil fuels enters the atmosphere on a non-circulating basis. This forces the atmosphere to accumulate carbon dioxide, increasing the concentration in the atmosphere by approximately 6 gigatons, as carbon, per year (almost 1%). Carbon dioxide from other sources such as concrete making add another 2 gigatons, pushing the annual carbon dioxide accumulation well above 1%.

Although these contributions from anthropogenic sources seem small, they are non-cyclical, they are cumulative. Their effects on the atmospheric composition are compounded, leading to the exponentially increasing carbon dioxide levels shown in Figure 25 in Chapter 6.

Restoring the long-term atmospheric carbon dioxide content by increasing the carbon content of the biosphere is a practical means for restoring the thermal transfer processes on the planet. The carbon in our biosphere comes immediately out of the atmosphere. Increasing the carbon content of the biosphere reduces the carbon dioxide content of the atmosphere, and it restores order and complexity and therefore the heat transfer processes of the earth

In the book, "Natural Capitalism – Creating the Next Industrial Revolution"[3] by Paul Hawkin, Amory Lovins and L. Hunter Lovins they express the idea of order and usefulness in natural systems very well as follows:

> Science provides a necessary basis for business to comprehend the emerging economics of living systems and ecosystem services. In scientific terms there is no phenomenon called production, only transformation. No matter how energy or resources are used, scattered or dispersed, their sum remains essentially the same, as dictated by the Law of Conservation of Matter and Energy. This law is of more than passing interest because it means that the term "consumption" is the abstract figment of economists' imagination – that it is physically impossible in all processes or transformations. What is consumed in the environment is not matter or energy but order or quality – the structure, concentration or purity of matter. This is a critically important concept, because it is "quality" that business draws upon to create economic value. Instead of focusing on whether physical resources will run out, it is more useful to be concerned about the specific aspects of the quality that natural capital produces: clean water and air, healthy soil, food, animals, forests, pollination, oceans, rivers; available and affordable sources of energy; and more. If industry removes concentrates and structured matter from the system faster than it can be replaced, and at the same time destroys the means of its creation, namely ecosystems and habitats, it introduces a fundamental problem in production.

This insight is essential to understanding the sustainability of human existence on earth. The premise of this book is that the fundamentals of thermodynamic and ecological sciences taken together explain the climate change phenomenon and suggest a means for its correction.

Chapter Twenty References

[1] ~~Smil, Vaclav: "The Earth's~~ Biosphere – Evaluation, Dynamics and Change": MIT Press, Cambridge, Mass; Copyright 2002

[2] Leith, H and Whittaker, R. H.: "Primary Productivity of the Biosphere": Springer, 2011

[3] Hawkin, Paul; Lovins, Amorey and Lovins, L. Hunter: "Natural Capitalism – Creating the next Industrial Revolution": Little, Brown and Company, New Your, NY; Copyright 1999

Chapter Twenty-One

Natural Biomass Depletion Cycles

Chapter Summary

There are three major causes of biomass destruction resulting in devastating reduction in the amount of carbon contained in biomass. The first two changes involve water in entropic forms that make it unavailable in its necessary liquid state. Glaciation converts all available water to its solid, low entropy, form in which it decimates the landscape. Desertification converts all available water into the vapor phase, a high entropy form, in which state it is also unavailable to plants. Both of these form constraints that will not allow the biomass population to expand.

The third cause of wholesale biomass destruction is anthropogenic biomass removal in which the human species destroys the biomass reservoir for his own benefit.

This chapter approaches these three mechanisms of biomass removal in more detail.

Chapter Twenty One
Natural Biomass Depletion Cycles

Many deserts across the globe are expanding. Increasing aridity and destruction of biomass at their perimeters lead to receding ecosystems and the advance of lifeless conditions. Once destroyed these ecosystems may not have the ability to re-establish themselves.

The demise of the constraint system associated with biomass takes away the ecological continuity needed for stable environments. Direct impingement of solar energy on the surface of the earth in the absence of biomass produces large temperature differentials and unstable atmospheric density gradients that turn over violently. These processes damage ecosystems and prevent their recovery in several ways:

- Surface temperature excursions cycle through temperature ranges that are beyond those that life can tolerate.
- Differentials resolve themselves through violent, turbulent means creating shear stresses that are damaging to soils and living structures.
- Resolution taking place without constraints approaches equilibrium so closely that life can't utilize the energy differences in the remaining differentials.

> An ecosystem that has been damaged in this way requires the moderation of differentials and a constraint system that maintains those differentials long enough for them to be useable by emergent life.

An ecosystem that has been damaged in this way requires the moderation of differentials and a constraint system that maintains those differentials long enough for them to be useable by emergent life. Nature's approach to this problem is to provide plants with the ability to produce seeds. A seed is a package of customized constraints and differentials that allow new plants to germinate and survive with relative independence in a barren environment inadequate to support mature plants. But some environments that have been more than so depleted of life supports are too hostile even for seeds and other propagation methods. In this case mankind must supply intervention. Otherwise the ecosystem has little chance of recovery.

Deserts usually occur in water short areas, and so they are frequently found around 30° latitude where cool, dry air at high elevations settles toward the surface of the earth. Low humidity leads to cloudless skies, and direct sunlight heats the surface of the ground. As the dry air descends it contracts, becoming warmer because of increasing pressure. When it contacts the warm ground it heats up further and absorbs moisture from the soil. Since the molecular weight of water is less than that of air, the act of absorbing water makes the air lighter and so it rises to be replaced with more dry air from above. This constant circulating of dry air across the surface of the earth desiccates the soil to the point of inhospitality to plant development. Moisture, then, is a critical constraint in the ecology of most desert environments.

The Sahara Desert and the Arabian Peninsula are massive deserts perpetuated by the meteorological cycles described above. Yet the ability of these deserts to support life varies drastically in response to climate cycles. Paleontological investigations show that pastoral hunter-gatherers who lived off the productivity of the land once occupied these places. [1]

During interglacial periods, according to climate models, the Southwest Asian Monsoon may shift, directing moisture-laden air from the Arabian Sea across Yemen and Oman. The redirected winds produce rainfall-feeding dozens of rivers and tens of thousands of wetlands and lakes throughout Arabia and northeast Africa. Dr. Andrew Lawler attributed these shifts in monsoons to Milankovitch Cycles, and he produced a technical paper in the August 29, 2014 issue of Science Magazine[1] in which he states:

> *The most pronounced period of wet and warm weather in the past few hundred thousand years took place about 125,000 years ago during the height of the interglacial. Less dramatic monsoon shifts came about 80,000 and 55,000 years ago.*

Compelling evidence has also emerged linking the direction of the Southeast Asian Monsoons and the climate in the Sahara Desert and the Arabian Peninsula to the precession of the tilting of the axis of rotation of the earth. A paper by Peter B. deMenocal and Jessica E. Tierney in the journal Nature Education[2] describes the wet periods and the lake levels that resulted. The precession guides the Monsoon winds to bring moisture-laden air from the Indian Ocean and the Arabian Sea across the coastal mountains to water the continental deserts. It takes approximately 20,000 years to complete a precessionary cycle, which would place the last greening of the Sahara about 5000 years ago. Sediment samples of dust blown into the Atlantic Ocean from North Africa confirm these dates. If this theory is valid, we are about half way to the peak of the dry end of the cycle, and we should experience another peak of greening in about 15,000 years.

Gilbert Walker discovered linkages between regular oscillations in the Indian Ocean Monsoons and the Southern Oscillation phenomenon that creates the El Nino-La Nina cycles in 1904[3]. These fluctuations in ocean surface temperature affect the climate and the ecology of countries bordering the Pacific Ocean in the Americas including Mexico and the desert Southwestern United States. Expanding deserts and diminishing agricultural productivity combined with inefficient use of irrigation water and diminishing groundwater supplies is causing crises in food production in these regions.

The evidence suggests that these deserts are capable of producing a rich diversity of biomass if the right conditions exist to sustainably generate and retain persistent complexity from the discharge of its solar energy input.

Water is a major constraint of any developing ecological system. Under the present conditions the thermodynamic entropy of ecosystems in most deserts is so high that water exists primarily as a vapor, a highly entropic form unsuitable for sustaining living systems.

Cold climates may be even more destructive of biomass than deserts. Water in its solid form is equally unable to support plant life. In addition, accumulations of snow in cold climates result in glaciers that carve their way through northern climate zones carrying away boreal forests, soils, rocks and even the very mountains that support them. Deprived of its bio-structure and the climatic continuity it provided, the ecology of northern climates cannot readily recover.

This book identifies three different factors that affect climate systems by destroying biomass and allowing the climate structure to collapse regionally or globally. The first is glacial ice, which physically tears the surface of the earth apart removing biomass by brute force.[4], [5] The second is vaporization, which removes water from extensive regions leaving the climate unsuitable to proliferation of plant species. The third is mankind who physically removes the plant cover. The result of each process appears to be warming, or at least redistribution of thermal energy on the planet.

Each of these processes creates an entropy surge, an excursion of entropy content on the earth's surface through the removal of the complexity associated with biomass.

A watershed event is usually required to tip the scales in the direction of biomass production and provide the necessarily ordered conditions or

> Each of these processes creates an entropy surge, an excursion of entropy content on the earth's surface through the removal of the complexity associated with biomass.

constraint patterns that encourage life to return. In the case of glaciation, such a watershed event may come from the deterioration of ecosystems that constrain convective heat transfer and allow solar energy to escape the tropics and melt the glaciers leading to repopulation of the temperate and boreal zones with biomass on a global scale. In the case of desertification it may come from the restoration of low entropy liquid water on a regional or continental scale through the return of monsoon weather patterns. In the case of human removal of biomass, it must come from a change in the destructive behavior of mankind, the primary destroyer of biomass since the glaciers.

Chapter Twenty One References

[1] Lawler, Andrew: "In Search of Green Arabia": Science, August 29, 2014

[2] deMenocal, P.B. &Tierney, J.E.: "African Humid Periods Paced by Earth's Orbital Changes": Nature Education Knowledge 3(10):12: (2012)

[3] Mock, Donald R.: "The Southern Oscillation: Historical Origins": Unpublished Tern Paper, University of Washington, Seattle, Washington May 1981: National Oceanic and Atmospheric Administration, Earth System Research Laboratory, Physical Sciences Division

[4] Imbrie, John and Imbrie, Katherine Palmer: "Ice Ages – Solving the Mystery": Enslow Publishers, Short Hills, NJ; Copyright 1979

[5] Benn, Douglas and Evans, David J. A.: "Glaciers and Glaciation, Second Edition": Routledge, New York, NY; Copyright 2010

Chapter Twenty-Two

Anthropogenic Biomass Depletion

Chapter Summary

Anthropogenic biomass depletion has turned out to be the largest cause of biomass removal from the surface of the earth including the glaciation of the Ice Ages. A biomass removal system that started out small has grown to the point where it threatens the sustainability of all life on earth. This chapter will describe some of the effects of this problem.

Chapter Twenty Two
Anthropogenic Biomass Depletion

Into this mix of Phytomass generation, storage and depletion we must overlay the activities of mankind, which modify natural cycles to access phytomass for his own use. Such uses include consumptive uses such as food for himself, fuel for his comfort, and feed for his animals as well as the use of phytomass as a raw material for tools and construction purposes[1].

Harvesting phytomass for these purposes is as old as mankind himself. Hunting-gathering societies pursued phytomass for weapons, for nutrition and for its heat content more than 20,000 years ago. However, low population levels and low individual consumption rates resulted in a low impact on natural phytomass stores and productivity.

The transition from hunter-gatherer life styles to more permanent, sedentary living such as pastoralism and farming increased the consumption of phytomass for shelter construction, animal feed and tool making as well as for fuel for space heating within structures. The agricultural transition also emphasized clearing land of natural phytomass to make room for growing crops and pasturing animals. This wholesale destruction of phytomass cover was usually carried out by slashing and burning phytomass or by simply burning standing phytomass. The result was destruction of habitat for animals (zoomass) as well as above ground phytomass.

Improved farming methods and development of superior crop varieties increased crop productivity from limited land areas. But increasing economic prosperity led to higher meat consumption rates, which reduced the caloric productivity of the land.

Use of wood as a fuel for heating increased during the agricultural transition and began to grow exponentially during the industrial revolution. The rise of

> Use of wood as a fuel for heating grew exponentially during the industrial revolution.

fossil fuels reduced the pressure on the global forest phytomass crop as a source of energy. However, recent developments in biofuels from phytomass have increased the demand for all types of phytomass.

A group of research scientists at the Potsdam Institute of Climate Impact in Potsdam, Germany led by Fredolin Krausmann and Alberte Bondeau,[2] in an article in the Proceedings of the National Academy of Sciences asserts that global biomass has been reduced by 24% from agricultural expansion in the 20th century alone. Dr. Vaclav Smil, in his book "The Earth's Biosphere: Evaluation, Dynamics and Change"[3] states phytomass removal during the industrial revolution reduced global phytomass carbon by about 200 gigatons or 22%. Together, these two estimates indicate biomass losses of 46%

Large areas of the earth are permanently relieved of their phytomass cover for urban development including buildings, impervious surfaces and water and energy infrastructure. Smil states that urban infrastructure in the United States occupies a land area the size of the State of Vermont, and that globally the urban infrastructure covers a land area equivalent to that of Italy. He makes a point of noting that half of this figure is due to water reservoirs for hydroelectricity generation.

An assessment of the total human appropriation of the products of photosynthesis published in the peer reviewed scientific journal Bioscience, in 2012 by P.M. Vitousek[4] states:

> "humans now appropriate nearly 40% of potential terrestrial productivity.'

He also estimates that human activity affects much of the remaining 60%.

By this estimation, humans are using 48 gigatons of phytomass out of a total photosynthetic capability of 120 gigatons for the entire earth, and their activities are having deleterious effects on the remaining 72 gigatons.

There is a deep-seated denial of the importance of man-made destruction of ecosystems. Each year we are impressed with the rising extent of flooding of rivers in the American Midwest. Communities along the

305

Chapter Twenty Two
Anthropogenic Biomass Depletion

Mississippi-Missouri river system endure high costs in destruction of property and loss of life.

The cause of this havoc is well known. The ecosystems across the entire Midwest have been completely denuded and converted into agricultural enterprises of impressive productivity. The loss of structure in the atmosphere, ecosystems and soils in this vast area causes it to produce increased runoff and decreased absorption of water. The entire region has become untethered from the buffering effects of healthy ecosystems as it has been given over to the extremes of agricultural productivity and increased concentration of runoff from natural precipitation.

The cost of this behavior in terms of loss of life and property and eroded soil and nutrients is clear. It has been assessed and calculated many times, and it is demonstrated in annual reports of disasters along the river system. But there is no cognizance devoted to linking the cost of these disasters and the price of the food produced. Floods are considered weather events and therefore an "act of God". Insurance companies won't even include these risks in their insurance policies. Causal relationships are ignored, or worse, denied, and the liability is externalized from the agricultural industry and absorbed by the general society as a whole. This obviates the need to take corrective action in our agricultural practices or even to understand and control the mechanisms that produce them.

This denial mechanism is an effective way to diffuse the responsibility for climate change away from causal factors and toward simplistic mechanisms that will only be partly effective in correcting the problem. One such diversion is to consider climate change a material and energy balance issue related to the buildup of carbon dioxide in the atmosphere neglecting the reservoir of biological complexity that establishes differentials and continuity on the surface of the earth. By this means, global warming is viewed as simply a material and energy balance problem with atmospheric carbon dioxide providing resistance to energy dispersion from the surface of the earth causing it to warm.

With this simplistic point of view, suggestions are made to eliminate carbon dioxide from the atmosphere as a solution to climate instability. These

> If the earth is cooled by removal of carbon dioxide from the atmosphere without replacement of biomass complexity, productivity of the biosphere will not be enhanced, climate instability will not be alleviated and global habitability will not be ensured.

carbon dioxide removal projects will only remove from the atmosphere an essential reactant in the production of future biomass. It will not increase the stability of the climate, nor make the planet more habitable. Only replacement of biological complexity can do that.

If the earth is cooled by removal of carbon dioxide from the atmosphere without replacement of biomass complexity, productivity of the biosphere will not be enhanced, climate instability will not be alleviated and global habitability will not be ensured.

Recent advances in agricultural practices have reduced the land area devoted to agriculture and increased the forested area in certain parts of the globe. Huge areas of the continents of Asia and Africa have been planted in trees. These developments have made a significant difference in correcting the effects of the carbon imbalance described above.

Improvements in the productivity of American farms have allowed many areas with marginal utility to return to near-natural ecosystem conditions. Ecosystem recovery and climate restoration are progressing in these areas.

If global disorder can be the watershed event that pushes back the glaciers, a resurgence of natural order may be the watershed event that can reverse the desertification process. This may also reverse an anthropogenically caused disorder crisis. Man has become the master biomass destroyer; he can also become that necessary watershed event. Policies and behaviors that preserve and proliferate biomass can "restore order to natural carbon" and enhance the constraints that preserve the differentials on Planet Earth. It's time that people accepted that responsibility and took up their role as stewards of our planet.

Chapter Twenty Two References

[1] Daly, Ryan: "Biomass Resource Allocation (Energy Science, Engineering and Technology: Energy Policies Politics and Prices": Nova Science Publishers, UK ed. Edition, 2013

[2] Krausmann, Fridolin; Bondeau, Alberte, et. al.: "Global Human Appropriation of Net Primary Production Doubled in the Twentieth Century": Proceedings of the National Academy of Sciences, Vol 110 No 25, June 18, 2013

[3] Smil, Vaclav: "The Earth's Biosphere – Evaluation, Dynamics and Change": MIT Press, Cambridge, Mass.; Copyright 2002

[4] Vitousek, Peter; Ehrlich, Paul R.; Ehrlich , Ann H. and Matson, Pamela A.: "Human Appropriation of the Products of Photosynthesis", Bioscience 36: 368-373

Part Seven

The Soil

Chapter Twenty-Three

Agriculture and Soils

Chapter Summary

Three quarters of the carbon content of the biosphere is contained in soil biota. The complexity and structure associated with living systems in the soil constitutes a huge reservoir of order that combats entropy generation below our feet. Unfortunately, this reservoir has been degraded by agricultural activity for nearly 10,000 years.

This chapter describes the soil food web and the mechanisms by which it has been depleted. It also describes some hopeful signs that the complexity of the soil may be reinstated to the benefit of climate stability and global order.

Chapter Twenty Three
Agriculture and Soils

Soil Science: Agricultural and Environmental scientists like Dr. Rattan Lal[1,2] of Ohio State University and Dr. Johannes Lehmann[328] of Cornell University are breaking new ground in understanding how to apply thermodynamic principles to the soil matrix in which green plants grow and to effect substantial improvements in plant health, growth and yield. In his book "*Soil Quality and Agricultural Sustainability*"[1], Dr. Lal states:

> "*The goal of sustaining agriculture and ecosystems is to strive for minimal production of entropy i.e. minimization of dissipative processes caused by soil and land perturbations such as excessive erosion, nutrient losses, soil compaction, soil structure deterioration, and salinization. This model can be used also to understand the concept of ecosystem resilience when man-induced ecological perturbations push an ecosystem away from its steady state condition.*"

Loss of complexity and structure is responsible for degradation of large areas of farmland in the United States every year.[4] The discoveries by these men demonstrate the importance of maintaining a low entropic, highly ordered, condition in agricultural soils as well as in our atmosphere. Demonstrations have shown that plants grown in soils with low entropic conditions may produce 3 times as much biomass and food harvest as compared with plants grown in soils with high entropic conditions. This shows the importance of minimizing the entropy function (maximizing biological activity and structure) in soils devoted to agricultural production and ecological preservation.

Studies have also shown that the accumulation of greenhouse gases in our atmosphere is not just a function of industrialization but began nearly 9000 years ago with the advent of agriculture.[5] The impoverishment of soil carbon content has been a major contributor to atmospheric carbon dioxide. Agricultural sources contributed at least a third and perhaps as much as two thirds of the excess carbon dioxide in the atmosphere. This realization has led to a great deal of research work to evaluate how much atmospheric

> Agricultural sources contributed at least a third and perhaps as much as two thirds of the excess carbon dioxide in the atmosphere.

carbon could be reduced by increasing the carbon content of the soil through biochar addition and enhancement of soil biological activity. Albert Bates describes how this is done in his book, "The Biochar Solution: Carbon Farming and Climate Change".[6] Dr. Rattan Lal discusses this in some detail in his book, "Soil Carbon Sequestration and the Greenhouse Effect".[7]

Natural Soils: Natural soils are low-entropic environments containing large amounts of biological structure that utilizes, maintains and controls many types of gradients, reactions and activities.[8, 9, 10, 11] Specific surface areas, moisture content, void volume and aeration levels vary considerably from place to place. Organic matter in various states of decay pervades the soil matrix. Living systems grow and recede in the open spaces. Their membranes contain a rich variety of substances with varying physical, chemical and electrical properties creating gradients in concentration, electrical charge, and temperature. Membrane permeability and enzyme concentration provide controls over chemical migration and reaction rates and maintain gradients within the requirements for life. These structured, ordered, low-entropic conditions support

> Membrane permeability and enzyme concentration provide controls over chemical migration and reaction rates and maintain gradients within the requirements for life. These structured, ordered, low-entropic conditions support continuous activity, function and change.

continuous activity, function and change.

Chapter Twenty Three
Agriculture and Soils

Soil Food Web: A rich soil food web occupies the interstices in the soil matrix, beginning with Bacteria, Archaea and Fungi at the bottom of the size and simplicity range and proceeding through Algae, Slime Molds, Protozoa, Nematodes, Annelids (earthworms), Gastropods (slugs and snails) and Arthropods (insects, spiders, mites, ticks, etc.) and ending with the largest and most complex creatures such as reptiles, mammals, and birds.[10,12]

The web of life in the soil creates additional structure in the soil itself such as channels through which water, air, and nutrients can travel to areas where they are needed. Structure also includes the granular consistency that results from clumping or agglomeration of fine soil particles into an organic matrix of exudates called glomalins that are secreted by plant root tips and fungal hyphae. This clumping of soil particles promotes water and air drainage and/or retention. Membranes that contain and differentiate chemical concentrations are also an inherent part of the biology of the food web.

Soil Fungi, Bacteria and Archaea: The soil food web is supported by the creatures at the very bottom, the Bacteria, the Archaea and the Fungi.[9, 11, 12] Bacteria and archaea are single celled prokaryotic microorganisms. They are simple and primitive and in general have no structures such as nuclei or other organelles within their cells.

Soil fungi are collections of long, root-like filaments called hyphae that run beneath the soil surface. These filaments are extensive, covering wide areas in search of soil nutrients. When a nutrient source is located the nutrient is ingested into the hypha and carried to all parts of the fungus.

Fungi have no chlorophyll of their own with which to make food. They rely on relationships with other organisms to feed. Some fungi are parasitic, taking their nutrition from living plants and animals and causing disease and distress as they do so. Some are saprophytic, absorbing their nutrition from decaying tissues of dead organisms. Others are symbionts, which form mutually beneficial relationships with their host organism.

Symbiotic fungal hyphae interact with plant roots wherein an exchange occurs. Plants take up excess nutrients from the fungi and give up some of their excess food, which supports further growth of the network of hyphae.

Collections of hyphae associate into bundles called mycorrhizae. These bundles are large enough to be evident to the naked eye. The network of mycorrhizae beneath the soil surface is called the mycorrhizal mat. In some cases it contains more organic carbon than all other soil life combined.

Fungal hyphae or mycorrhizae provide a source of carbonaceous materials and nutrients for a lush community of bacteria

> In some cases the mycorrhizal mat contains more organic carbon than all other soil life combined.

and archaea. These lower echelons of the soil food web are the underpinnings of all of the biology in the rest of the soil.

Green Plants: The array of living creatures in the soil, the food web, supports the community of green plants, the photosynthetic canopy that captures radiant thermal energy from the sun and converts it into biomass (biochemical energy). Release of this energy through the process of respiration provides the work that is necessary to create new biomass and structure to offset what is lost to the production of entropy in the environment. This process offsets the deterioration of order and structure on its march toward the entropic state and replaces the dissipated chemical energy in the soil beneath.

The Effect of Tillage (Soil Depletion): When native soil is converted to farmland, accepted practice is to remove all of the existing above ground vegetation, stems, branches, leaves, etc. This is done on the premise that the existing vegetation competes with the intended crop for space, sunlight, water, air and nutrients. It may also be done to make the soil accessible and workable, but it is done at the expense of removing structure, order, and stored energy, a cost that must be recognized, understood and evaluated.

Removal of above ground vegetation begins a process of conversion of the carbon content of the vegetation from a low entropy

The removal of vegetation is done on the premise that the existing vegetation competes with the intended crop for space, sunlight, water, air and nutrients. It may also be done to make the soil accessible and workable, but it is done at the expense of removing structure, order, and stored energy, a cost that must be recognized, understood and evaluated.

state, biomass, to a very high entropy state, carbon dioxide. As we have seen from the previous discussion, carbon dioxide is a disorganized, high entropy gas, and a dissipated and unstructured form of carbon, very highly entropic. By removing vegetation we have favored the disordered, unstructured, low-energy, high entropy form of carbon over the ordered, structured, high energy, low-entropy form necessary for life. We have also destroyed the ecological environment that used to host the higher forms of the soil food web, reptiles, mammals and birds.

In removing the above ground vegetation we have created an environment from which the entropy resistant structure has been removed. We have also removed the photosynthetic canopy in which the entropy resistant structure is created, and with it the potential for the site to act as a heat engine and convert energy to new ordered forms. Sunlight impinging on the modified surface will no longer be converted into biomass and life supporting structures, but only into high entropy heat.

Removal of above ground vegetation initiates the removal of below ground vegetation. Roots, stumps, etc. begin to decay as the entropic progression continues in the subterranean arena. In the subsurface we have not only increased the entropy content of the carbon and the air, we have also removed structures from the soil. Roots that used to separate mineral matter from organic structures and serve as reservoirs of water, carbon and nutrients begin to dissipate and decay. The soil becomes more entropic, losing its structure and order as these components decay, and so does the atmosphere. The mid-range portions of the soil food web (earthworms, insects, nematodes, protozoa, etc.) that depend on soil structure, moisture, air and nutrient distribution are destroyed as well.

Now, enter the plow, the final insult to the natural low entropy condition of soil organization. Tilling rips up the very structure of the soil itself. The channels that worms and nematodes create are destroyed. The glomalins that hold mineral soil particles together into a granular structure are exposed to oxidation and destroyed. Fungal mycelia that transport water and nutrients over long distances are torn up and destroyed. All the lower food web creatures are themselves exposed to oxygen in the air and oxidized.

In healthy soils the structures in the food web contain more carbon than the above ground biomass. Destruction of this living subsurface system releases large amounts of carbon dioxide and creates a highly entropic, mineral soil environment with no biomass, no structure, no physical, chemical or electrical gradients and no stimulus for biologically supportive reactions.

Rehabilitation of Depleted Soil: To reclaim a soil that has high entropy content requires that the soil structure be replaced.[10, 11, 13,] The membranes that support variability in soil composition and create the driving forces for life processes have to regrow to become viable again. Restoration of these structures and differentials requires energy and an energy conversion apparatus like the one that has been destroyed. Fortunately new seeds contain in their DNA all the information necessary to create a nucleus of a membrane structure and of an energy capture mechanism of their own. A seed is the ultimate low entropy nucleation system. Once it starts to grow it will utilize energy from the sun to create low entropy biomass, which contains both the structure and the energy source necessary for life.

> To reclaim a soil that has high entropy content requires that the vegetation and soil structure be replaced.

If all the necessary nutrients are present, the seed will recreate a structure sufficient for its own survival as a monoculture, but without a stable ecosystem structure in the soil; water, air and nutrient gradients are not consistently present. Water that enters the soil, dissolves soluble nutrients, and percolates down out of reach of the growing plants. Air that enters the soil evaporates water drying the soil. Unless water and nutrients are monitored and replaced through irrigation and fertilization, seedlings may encounter environmental variability beyond their ability to sustain themselves. Under these conditions, natural restoration of the soil food web and structure is slow and inconsistent.

Rehabilitation of depleted ecosystems through human intervention is possible and, in fact, has been practiced in arid climates for many years. A severely damaged ecosystem is hard to recover, and failure of plant starts has been a major problem making progress painfully slow and success rates spotty. But advances in irrigation and growing technologies, and selection of hardy native species have resulted in a surge of successful reforestation projects in recent decades. Among the areas where successful rehabilitation projects have been completed are China, Africa, Australia, the United States, Israel, Egypt and several European, Middle Eastern and Southeast Asian countries.

Chapter Twenty Three References

[1] Lal, Rattan: "Soil Quality and Agricultural Sustainability": Sleeping Bear Press, Chelsea, MI, Copyright 1998

[2] Lal, Rattan; Sobecki, Terry; Livari, Thomas and Kimbal, John: "Soil Degredation in the United States, Extent Severity and Trends": Lewis Publishers, Boca Raton, FL, Copyright 2004

[3] Lehmann, Johannes and Joseph, Stephen: "Biochar For Environmental Mhagement, Science and Technology": EarthScan Publications, London, UK; Copyright 2010

[4] Lal, Rattan; Kimbal, JM; Fallet, RF and Cole, CV "The Potential of US Croplands to Sequester and Mitigate the Greenhouse Effect": Sleeping Bear Press, Chelsea, MI; Copyright 2008

[5] Ruddiman, William: "Plows, Plagues and Petroleum – How Humans Took Control of the Climate": Princeton University Press, Princeton, NJ, Copyright 2005

[6] Bates, Albert: "The Biochar Solution, Carbon Farming and Climate Change": New Society Publishers, Gabriola Island, BC, Canada, Copyright 2010

[7] Lal, Rattan and Follett, Roland: "Soil Carbon Sequestration and the Greenhouse Effect":

[8] Heminway, Toby: " Gaia's Garden – A Guide to Home Scale Permaculture":Chelsae Green Publishing Company, White River Junction, VT, Copyright 2009

[9] Stamets, Paul: "Mycellium Running – How Mushrooms Can Help Save the World": Ten Speed Press, Division of Random House, NY, NY, Copyright 2005

[10] Edwards, Clive A.; Lal, Rattan; Adden, Patric; Miller, Robert and House, Gar:"Sustainable Agricultural Systems": Soil and Water Conservation Society, Ankey, Iowa, Copyright 1990

[11] Ladygina, Natalia and Rineau, Francois: "Biochar and Soil Biota": CRC Press, Boca Raton, FL; Copyright 2013

[12] Lowenfels, Jeff; and Lewis, Wayne: "Teeming With Microbes – The Organic Gardener's Guide to the Soil Food Web": Timber Press, Inc, Portland, Oregon, Copyright 2010[12]

[13] Solaiman, Zakaria M. and Abbott, Lynette K.: "Mycorrhizal Fungi: Use in Sustainable Agriculture and Land Restoration": Springer, New York, NY: Copyright, 2014

Chapter Twenty-Four

Structural Expressions of Thermodynamic Order in Soils

Chapter Summary

Structures are essential to maintain order and functionality in thermodynamic systems. Microstructures are more effective than macrostructures in maintaining the continuity of steady state processes.

This chapter elaborates on these ideas.

Chapter Twenty Four
Structural Expressions of Thermodynamic Order in Soils

The most important expression of thermodynamic entropy is uniformity. Any thermodynamically isolated system that has uniform characteristics at all points is incapable of macroscopic change. Such a system can do no work, nor can it participate in any activity whatsoever. Maximum entropy, or equilibrium, is a terminal state in an isolated system.

Utility implies a deviation from maximum entropy. To be utilized in any way, a system must have less than maximum entropy. Utility comes from variability of conditions from place to place across the system. Consider a steam engine, for example. In order for a steam engine to do any work, it must have a source of high-pressure steam and a discharge area of low-pressure steam. The ability to do work and the efficiency with which it can be done are entirely dependent upon the pressure and temperature differential between the inlet and discharge points in the system.

Doing work increases the entropy of the Universe, depleting its order and utility. But the entropy of the system can also increase without any actual work having been done. This implies energy transfer at zero efficiency such as might happen through diffusion. High quality differentials can be degraded by random molecular motion causing them to equilibrate, dispersing temperature and concentration gradients, and facilitating uniformity without any useful work being done.

The loss of function and the increase of uniformity in any system is a measure of its degradation or loss of utility. A system without any structure, regardless of how rich in differentials it may be, soon diffuses into uniformity and loses its utility.

One way to maintain differentials within a system is to impose structures on it, structures that will contain material differences and impede diffusion and other kinds of flows. Structures are important in their ability to preserve differentials in a thermodynamically isolated system. In more open systems they allow differentials to become constant and flow to become continuous, resulting in the condition known as steady state.

Life is a steady state condition, and as such it requires a non-isolated system with throughputs of energy and/or matter flowing through the system. It also requires structures capable of maintaining differentials and establishing steady state conditions.[1]

Life is a steady state condition, and as such it requires a non-isolated system with throughputs of energy and/or matter flowing through the system. It also requires structures capable of maintaining differentials and establishing steady state conditions.

Small structures with a high degree of complexity establish a more continuous state of flow than do larger, simpler structures. It is typical of human cultures to construct large, simple structures that replace smaller, more complex systems. These large, simple structures are not as functional as smaller, more complex ones. They don't produce the same continuity and stability characteristics that define a steady state condition.

Small structures with a high degree of complexity establish a more continuous state of flow than do larger, simpler structures.

When a small, complex structural paradigm is removed and replaced by a larger scale structural paradigm, the continuity characteristic of biological systems breaks down, and it is replaced by dysfunctional, non-steady state interactions.

Steady state processes are continuous because they have evolved with inherent servomechanisms that

Steady state processes are continuous because they have evolved with inherent servo mechanisms that keep process stresses within the critical structural requirements of the process containment structures.

keep process stresses within the critical structural requirements of the process containment structures. Larger scale processes create larger scale stresses that are destructive of complex structures. Without its complex structures, a system has no means of resisting the collapse of the differentials that have maintained the steady state conditions. The differentials may then collapse turbulently and destructively, accelerating the collapse of the steady state process, and increasing the destruction of structure and the spread of uniformity.

Ecological systems have evolved into a steady state condition with their environment. Their complex structures and steady state energy flows balance each other creating a non-destructive, continuous flow system. Removal of biological structures from the ecological community damages the stability of the system and destabilizes the steady state condition. In its unstable condition the increase in entropy, the spread of randomness and uniformity, is rapid. The destruction of structure and the rise of uniformity spread throughout the ecosystem.[2]

Chapter Twenty Four References

[1] Sposito, Garrison: "Chemical Equilibria and Kinetics in Soils": Oxford University Press, 1994

[2] Anderson, G. M.: "Thermodynamics of natural Systems":Cambridge University Press Cambridge, Mass.; Copyright 1996

Chapter Twenty-Five

Matrices

Chapter Summary

A matrix is a close association of solid surface, air, water, nutrients and energy where conditions are created that promote the precipitation of complex solid microstructures. Using the glycoside condensation reaction as an example, this chapter demonstrates how complexity precipitates and builds. Cell membranes are an example of a semi-permeable system boundary that permits high entropy products like water to pass out of the system providing a ratcheting mechanism that prevents the complex, low entropy products from escaping or degrading back into a disordered state.

Through processes like capillary action, diffusion and adsorption, a matrix can charge itself with nutrients and biologically active molecules. By hosting microbes a matrix can use the energy in ATP to drive biological reactions.

This chapter explains some aspects of these processes.

Chapter Twenty Five
Matrices

We have discovered the importance of constraints in flow-through systems. The outflow of energy from a system is necessary, but not sufficient, to bring about the accumulation of order and complexity within a system. Bringing about order requires resistances to the flow of energy that cause differences in potential to arise within the system. To accumulate order requires that the system be bounded in some way such that the order formed is retained within the system.

A system is a region of space with its boundaries and its contents. A system boundary is presumed to have more resistance to flow than other parts of the system. But it is understood also that other resistances to flow pervade the system. Sometimes diffused, sometimes abrupt, these resistance patterns will direct and define the flow of energy and materials through the system.

In Chapter 14 (See Figure 32) we related patterns of resistances to structure and to information. A system with no constraints and no resistances has no information. The flow of energy through such a system won't result in any generation of order or complexity. In order for a thermodynamic system to work, it must have contents that interact with the matter and energy that pass through. The contents of the system and the resistances of the borders determine the accumulation of order and complexity that occurs.

Systems containing fluid contents without any solid structures to resist flows still interact with the matter and energy that pass through. They behave in accordance with the properties of their contents. Flow through these systems encounters constraints associated with gas laws, flow laws, expansion properties, thermal properties and so on.

Systems that contain solid structures encounter impedance to material and energy flows by virtue of the strength, rigidity, shape, size and placement of the solid structures. Flows through matrices of

Matrices of solid materials have a drastic effect on the material and energy flow characteristics of thermodynamic systems.

solids are impeded by the tortuosity of the path they must follow. To the extent that concentrations and compressibility respond to differentials in driving forces, tortuosity tends to make flow continuous[1].

And so we find that matrices of solid materials have a drastic effect on the material and energy flow characteristics of thermodynamic systems. Solids may precipitate from solutions in accordance with solubility relationships. They may be positioned or arranged into structures by circulating flow patterns, and they may grow in extent, density, and strength by intermolecular attractions.

Condensation reactions, like the glycoside bonding of soluble sugars into insoluble polysaccharides, can also form solids in biological systems. Polysaccharides, like cellulose; polyamides, like proteins; and polynucleotides, like the strands of a DNA double helix are all insoluble macromolecules that precipitate from solution and grow in size and complexity as they are assembled piece by piece by removing molecules of water and forming a glycoside bonds.

Removal of water from the reaction medium, such as might occur if the water defuses through a semi-permeable cell membrane, tends to lock in the order of such macromolecules preventing the hydrolysis that would break them down again if entropy were to be generated in the system or enter the system with incoming energy through the membrane.

Figure 51 (next page) shows a glycoside bonding reaction between sugar groups and the removal of water, locking in the order of the polysaccharide chain. As the polysaccharide chains become longer and longer their solubility decreases and they precipitate as solid materials.

The polymers precipitated by these reactions tend to interact to form activated structures on a molecular scale. At larger scales, such as the circulation patterns of the Benards Cells discussed in Chapter 15, solids can precipitate in areas where concentration and shear forces allow, and they survive and form matrices by following the shear planes of the circulating fluids.

Other matrices are more haphazard, being the result of dumping together solid particles of varying shapes and sizes. An example of such a matrix is the soil. The Mississippi State University Agricultural website calls soil "*a biological setting where differentials in air, water, nutrients and heat can interact.*"

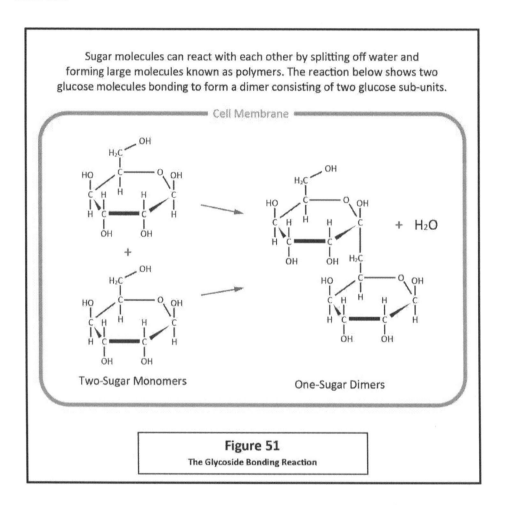

Sugar molecules can react with each other by splitting off water and forming large molecules known as polymers. The reaction below shows two glucose molecules bonding to form a dimer consisting of two glucose sub-units.

Two-Sugar Monomers

One-Sugar Dimers

Figure 51

The Glycoside Bonding Reaction

The chemical environment in the matrix is controlled by water flowing over solids that have significant capacity to modify conditions through processes like filtration, adsorption, ion exchange, etc. Flow that is controlled by soil texture, as determined by particle size and shape (sand, silt, or clay), and soil structure as determined by soil aggregation and channeling.

Surface effects largely determine the distribution of liquids in matrices. Water, for instance, distributes itself in accordance with an energy factor called water potential. Total water potential is the sum of 6 energy factors such as osmotic potential, pressure potential, gravimetric potential, and humidity potential. Another factor, the matrix potential is a function of the matrix size and complexity, and it may become dominant over all the other factors in matrices with small particle sizes and channel diameters.

Liquids tend to coat surfaces and penetrate into channels, by capillary action, dispersing themselves into matrices where they soak up, dissolve and distribute soluble materials from both the soil particles and the air. Liquids are the ideal reaction medium for dissolved materials both mineral and organic.

Depending on the saturation level of liquids in the matrix, gas phase materials may enter the matrix as well. The combination of high surface area and multiple phases makes matrices very active places. The large surface area densities in matrices make them the ideal location for surface chemistry. Surface chemistry is important because it condenses three dimensions down into two. Molecules on a surface have only two dimensions to move through rather than three, and so they are much more likely to encounter each other and to react.

Scientists and engineers have long recognized the value of matrices in mass and energy transfer operations. Chemical process engineers have access to a large variety of packings and media to increase surface area and distribute flows in process equipment from septic systems to petroleum fractionators.

The soil matrix is a meeting place for the three natural states of matter, solid, liquid and gas, and it is a natural place for the resolution of differentials between the three. Dr. David Schwartzman's book, "Life, Temperature and the Earth – The Self-Organizing Biosphere"[2], makes this point as follows:

> The evolution of the biosphere is geophysiological in the sense that self-regulation arises from the coupling of biota and its inorganic surface environment... The soil geomembrane is a critical site of this coupling. Markos (1995) pointed out that an extracellular matrix composed of mineral particulates, cell exudates, organic debris, and biofilms is a second structure of biological communities. As such it constitutes a mediating environment between the inorganic and organic bodies of the biosphere; the extracellular matrix of the soil is just such a mediator.

Schwartzman also says "A mineral soil 1 meter thick with individual grains (cubes) 1mm³ in volume has 6000 times the potential reactive surface area of a bare rock surface". This is indicative of the surface area enhancement of soil.

The activity and the functional specificity of matrices are inversely proportional to the size of their particles. Just as a microchip can contain more complexity than a printed circuit board, a DNA molecule can hold more complete, specific and exact information than a soil matrix. But this does not detract from the marvelous functionality and information holding capacity of a soil matrix.

In Chapter 14 we discussed the wonderful regenerative properties of the extracellular matrices from human and animal tissues. By manipulating these matrices and their regenerative information, doctors can work miracles of healing at unheard-of rates.

Perhaps we shouldn't be surprised to learn that the porous matrix of charcoal (biochar) contains a similar trove of information that can be enlisted to accelerate growth in green plants. The infinitude of pores, channels and crannies separated by rigid membranes of varying permeability creates a

We shouldn't be surprised that the porous matrix of charcoal (biochar) contains a similar trove of information that can be enlisted to accelerate the growth in green plants. The infinitude of pores, channels and crannies separated by rigid membranes of varying permeability creates a multitude of environmental niches that are inviting to mineral nutrients, macromolecules and microbial life.

multitude of environmental niches that are inviting to mineral nutrients, macromolecules and microbial life.

Through capillary action, diffusion and adsorption, this matrix charges itself with the essentials for living systems. In fact the matrix becomes a responsive, functional reservoir of growth factors including water, air, and nutrients. In times when these elements are plentiful, the matrix charges up; "breaths them in", if you will. When these elements of life become scarce, the biochar matrix "exhales", stimulating the soil matrix with measured amounts of nutrients. Life becomes abundant and healthy when its needs are met in this way.

The larger biochar structures, mesopores and macropores, become reservoirs of biologically active macromolecules and incipient life forms respectively. Microbes that enter the macropores find shelter and protection from predators. A mature biochar becomes an ecosystem, a civilization of living creatures, and a nucleus of healthy ecology that spreads to the soil matrix and supports life systems in regions beyond itself

.

Chapter Twenty Five References

[1] Lal, Rattan: "Principles of Soil Physics": Marcel Dekker, Inc., New York, NY; Copyright 2004

[2] Schwartzman, David: "Life, Temperature and the Earth – The Self-Organizing Biosphere": Columbia University Press, NY, NY, Copyright 2002

Part Eight

Climate Change

Chapter Twenty-Six

Global Warming

Chapter Summary

The entropy content of the matter on the surface of the earth is an inverse measure of the order and/or complexity it contains. Order and complexity are enhanced by the rejection of entropy across the atmospheric boundary into outer space. The more freely entropy is discharged across the atmospheric boundary, the more ordered the surface of the earth becomes.

This process maintains the complexity, stability, variability and activity of ecosystems on earth. In so doing it controls the complexity of the biological ecosystems that evolve. If the rejection of entropy is constrained in any way, disorder is retained on the surface of the earth and complex evolved organic systems can no longer sustain themselves.

This chapter describes some of the processes that make up the entropy balance.

Chapter Twenty Six
Global Warming

The geosphere, the atmosphere, the biosphere and all associated processes are run by the infusion of energy from the Sun at a low entropy level and the discharge of that energy from the surface of the Earth at a higher entropy level as discussed in Chapter 4.[1,2] It is the discharge of energy from a system at a high entropy level that carries disorder out of the system and imparts order to the system contents that are left behind.[3]

And as discussed in Chapter 9, if the entropy generated within a system cannot be discharged it will stay behind as heat or disorder in some other form within the system. The system will heat up until the entropy balances again and so the system will degenerate into disorder.[4,5]

Solar energy impinges on the Earth in a very low entropy form (short wavelength). It radiates away in a very high entropy state (long wavelength). The balancing of these two energy flows leaves the Earth with an entropy deficit (order surplus). Continuous passage of energy across the surface of the earth leaves the Earth in a highly ordered condition.

If the flow of entropy from the Earth is obstructed in any way it will cause the entropy content of the Earth to increase with a resulting increase of disorder in the environment.

> If the flow of entropy from the Earth is obstructed in any way it will cause the entropy of the Earth to increase with a resulting increase of disorder in the environment.

Short wave (low entropy) energy from the Sun easily penetrates the carbon dioxide in the atmosphere, heating the surface of the earth. But long wave (high entropy) energy radiated outward from the Earth is absorbed by carbon dioxide in the atmosphere causing it to warm. Because it is warmed, the carbon dioxide radiates some of its heat back to the Earth. This process traps high entropy energy on the surface of the Earth. As the energy dissipates, spreading its entropy across the biosphere, it dismantles the ordered materials there and reduces the level of order achievable in the system.

Life has evolved into an exquisitely ordered system, and it cannot sustain itself as the order around it recedes. The atmospheric boundary layer that passes radiant energy away from the Earth determines the complexity level that can be maintained by the materials it leaves behind. If the boundary cannot pass sufficient entropy to maintain the order within the system, entropy will be left behind, diminishing the order level in the system.[6]

Changes in the carbon dioxide level of the atmosphere are like an entropy control valve maintaining the level of order that will be left on the surface

Life has evolved into an exquisitely ordered system, and it cannot sustain itself as the order around it recedes. The atmospheric boundary layer that passes radiant energy away from the Earth determines the complexity level that can be maintained by the materials it leaves behind. If the boundary cannot pass sufficient entropy to maintain the order within the system, entropy will be left behind, diminishing the order level in the system.

of the Earth. Increasing CO_2 constrains the passage of entropy out of the system keeping order from forming and increasing the temperature in the system. Decreasing CO_2 clears the discharge pathway allowing the energy and entropy to discharge into outer space and leaving a cooler, more ordered planet behind.

Should the permeability of the atmosphere at long wavelengths diminish to zero the Earth would become a closed system for energy at these wavelengths. All activity would be converted into thermal disorder, and entropy would reign supreme. Short wavelengths would continue to penetrate the atmosphere and the temperature of the surface would rise until the outgoing wavelengths could penetrate the atmosphere and a balance could be restored once again.

To clarify these concepts the reader might want to review the energy and entropy balance depicted in Figures 18 and 23.

Chapter Twenty Six References

[1] Mann, Michael E. and Krump, Lee R.: "Dire Predictions, Second Edition: Understanding Climate Change": DK Publishing, Inc. ,New York, NY; Copyright 2008.

[2] Archer, David: "Global Warming: Understanding the Forecast": John Wiley & Sons, Inc., Hobokin, NJ; Copyright 2012

[3] Rod Swenson: "Thermodynamics, Evolution and Behavior": G. Greenberg and M.M. Haraway (Editors): "The Handbook of Comparative Psychology": Garland Publishing, New York, NY; 1998

[4] Chaisson, Eric: "Cosmic Evolution – The rise of Complexity in Nature" Harvard University Press, Cambridge, MA; Copyright 2001

[5] Schwatrzman, David: "Life, Temperature and the Earth – The Self-organizing Biosphere": Columbia University Press, New York, NY; Copyright 2002

[6] Matsuno, Koichiro and Rod Swenson: "Thermodynamics in the Present Progressive mode and its Role in the Context of the Origin of Life": Biosystems 51 (1999) pp. 53-61

Chapter Twenty-Seven

Global Equilibration

Chapter Summary

When the structure of ecosystems is lost, the entire heat transfer regime on the earth's surface is changed resulting in a lurch toward equilibrium in the environment. Suddenly the resistance to energy transfer on earth is reduced and radiant energy discharge through the atmosphere becomes the primary controlling factor determining global complexity.

There is a huge change in order production mechanisms when this happens. Order is no longer made by energy flowing across an infinitude of micro-constraints as it is in a biomass "full Earth". Order is only filtered out of escaping entropy by atmospheric constraints.

This is a totally different mechanism of order generation. This chapter will describe some of the different processes between the two systems.

Chapter Twenty Seven
Global Equilibration

The earth currently supports about 6 10 gigatons of phytomass carbon, much of which is in the tropic zone where as much as 80% of all incoming radiation impinges on the surface of the globe. The warmth of the tropics spreads largely by convection of fluids (air & water) toward the poles where only a small fraction of the total solar energy impinges on the surface where most of that energy is reflected back into space because of its low angle of inclination. Circulating currents in the atmosphere and the oceans distribute the excess heat from th e tropics to the poles, mixing masses, dispersing differences and generally encouraging the climate toward uniformity or equilibrium.

When conditions permit, phytomass grows on the land surface and in the oceans, generally, anchoring itself to solid attachment sites and presenting resistance to the circulating flows. Flows thus constrained are inadequate to spread entropy-causing thermal currents across the global surface, and so the areas where insolation is least, the poles, become cool. To compensate for this, warmer climates reject more heat from the globe through high entropy, long wave radiation.

Cooler climates over the higher latitudes that cannot radiate as much high entropy radiation and therefore cannot generate so much complexity grow less phytomass land cover and encourage ice and snow cover and accumulation, and, eventually, the formation of glaciers. Glaciers flow down mountainsides and across continents, scouring the last vestiges of phytomass from geological surfaces. Removal of surface phytomass allows the lowest reaches of the atmosphere to become active again, increasing the convective heat transfer from the tropics where 80% of solar radiation impacts the earth. By this means, glaciers promote their own destruction and promote a resurgence of biomass across the surface of the globe.

A globe without biomass tends to be turbulent and convective, promoting uniformity, a condition of high entropy content. A globe with phytomass cover tends to be organized,

A globe without biomass tends to be turbulent and convective, promoting uniformity, a condition of high entropy content. A globe with phytomass cover tends to be organized, structured, variable, and stable; a condition of low entropy content.

structured, variable, and stable; a condition of low entropy content. The input of energy from the sun, and the discharge of energy to the infinite energy sink of outer space cause energy to flow through the earth system. Cycles of energy input and discharge from daily fluctuations through annual cycles to Milankovitch cycles affect the conditions that cause the progression to shift direction, and so they affect the periodicity or frequency of glaciation cycles.

The earth is, in effect, an entropy oscillator driven by the thermal

The earth is, in effect, an entropy oscillator driven by the thermal differential between the sun and the infinite heat sink of outer space and controlled by the products of its own processes.

differential between the sun and the infinite and expanding heat sink of outer space and controlled by the products of its own processes.

Biology is an emergent property of physical matter subjected to the constraints of closed system thermodynamics, chemistry and physics and the energy flow enabled by the ambient conditions created by the relative location of the earth and the sun.

The flow of energy across physical constraints is an inherently ordering process. Order is generated by energy flow from systems, both simple and complex.

The flow of energy across physical constraints is an inherently ordering process.

Agitation from thermal molecular vibrations or from turbulent conditions is destructive to this order. When the flow of energy is stopped, as in thermodynamically isolated systems, the destruction of order takes over and entropy prevails. But whenever energy flow is allowed and gradients are not too extreme, as in thermodynamically closed systems, order and complexity emerge and accumulate in a system.

When energy flows out of a thermodynamically closed system, one that retains matter but allows energy to leave, the discharging energy has entropy associated with it. Discharging entropy leaves order behind which manifests itself as organization of the matter contained in the system. As more entropy is discharged, order accumulates and compounds itself resulting in complexity. [1]Under these conditions functionality emerges, and precipitation of life-like processes becomes highly probable if not absolutely certain.[2]

> When a system is open to flow of both matter and energy the ordered matter escapes with the energy and dissipates externally to the system. This order is no longer complex or functional.

When a system is open to flow of both matter and energy, as in open systems, the discharge of thermal entropy still produces order in the matter, but in this case the ordered matter escapes with the energy and dissipates externally to the system. This order is no longer complex or functional.

When a system is neither isolated nor fully open, but constrained, and this includes every known system on the earth including the earth itself; events that trend toward isolation of the system tend to increase the build-up of entropy within; while events that trend toward openness tend to increase the build-up of order.

So why aren't open systems ordered? A system must be closed enough to retain the order once it is created. Ordered materials that escape into space fly apart by thermal agitation. Order is not retained without system boundaries to retain it. A degree of closure must be maintained that allows energy and high entropy materials to escape the system but retains low entropy materials with their order and complexity within the system.

The release of carbon dioxide and other greenhouse gasses into the atmosphere restricts the radiation of energy

> Order is not retained without system boundaries to retain it. A degree of openness must be maintained that allows energy and entropy to escape the system but retains order and complexity within.

(waste heat) into space. This tends to isolate the earth system, which diminishes the discharge of entropy. This reduces the build-up of order and complexity (in the form of biological ecosystems) as it increases the build-up of entropy (low molecular weight materials, disorder, or waste heat) on the surface of the planet. Removal of greenhouse gases reverses the process, opens the system allowing energy to flow from the surface of the planet taking the built up entropy with it and allowing the natural build-up of order to prevail once again.

So, current science sees the greenhouse effect as the driver of global warming, climate change or

> Biological structures in parallel represent the bulk of the constraint on convective energy transfer on earth. Their proliferated resistances to energy flow establish differentials that enable an approximation of steady state conditions to exist.

global equilibration. But the resistance of the atmosphere to energy dissipation into outer space is just the last ditch resistance in a series of constraints to energy flow on the earth's surface. Order on earth is, in fact, the result of an interaction of a network of parallel resistances to energy and material flows.

Removal of biomass depletes the number of parallel resistances in the network, increasing the overall biomass resistance. But as biomass pathways are removed convective pathways replace them with equal numbers of more conductive pathways. The removal of biomass increases the thermal conductivity of the surface of the earth.

The complexity of the resistance pathway is simply reduced to the next highest complexity level. Atmospheric convection controls the heat transfer regime after biomass is removed. Depending on the composition of the atmosphere, the properties of the component gases, and the temperature differentials imposed on the surface of the earth by impacting sunlight, atmospheric turbulence will establish itself in a manner that controls the rate of energy transfer and entropy accumulation.

Figure 52 is a schematic rendering of a resistance network of the biospheric and convective resistances on planet earth.

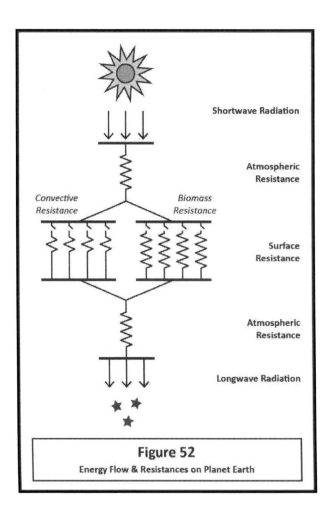

Figure 52
Energy Flow & Resistances on Planet Earth

Each resistance initiates its own entropy discharge and order build-up. If some of the biological constraints are removed the energy flow is shunted to another set of resistances with a lower overall impedance value, reducing the thermal difference between the equator and the poles and increasing the differential between the poles and outer space.

Biological structures in parallel represent the bulk of the constraint on convective energy transfer on earth. Their proliferated resistances to energy flow establish differentials that enable an approximation of steady state conditions to exist. When biomass is destroyed, the number of these parallel resistances is reduced, and so their collective resistance is increased.

At the same time the biomass resistances that are removed are replaced by atmospheric convective resistances of much smaller magnitude. This replacement process reduces the cumulative resistance of the network and allows more energy dispersion and entropy creation on the planet.

Removal of biomass resistance substitutes the lower atmospheric convective resistance which elevates the discharge temperature at the poles.

The removal of biomass resistance to energy flow, like opening the switches to the various biomass resistors, closes the switches on the convective resistors, enabling turbulent convective energy flow, to take over. The temperature of the exit point is thereby increased, raising the temperature of the poles.

The reduction of total resistance by removal of biomass diminishes the temperature differential across the earth's surface increasing the temperature of Polar regions at the bottom of the atmospheric interface. This is an insight that Vaclav Smil alluded to when he said in his book "Harvesting the Biosphere – What We Have Taken From Nature."[3]

> *Curiously, a recent assessment of a safe operating space for" humanity...does not list either a minimum phytomass stock or primary productivities among its ten causes.*

In their book, "*Natural Capitalism – Creating the Next Industrial Revolution*"[4], Paul Hawkin, Amory Lovins and L Hunter Lovins say it this way:

Chapter Twenty Seven
Global Equilibration

As the planet traps more heat, it drives more convection that transports surplus heat from equatorial to the polar areas (heat flows from hotter to colder), so temperature changes tend to be larger at the poles than at midlatitudes.

There is a recognition here that the heat transfer mechanism has changed, but it is not clear that removal of the low entropy condition at the heart of the planetary surface is the causal factor creating the transition.

The rape of the phytosphere by the human species is the primary cause of diminishing differentials and constraints to energy flows on Planet Earth. To blame it on carbon dioxide build-up and the resulting resistance to energy discharge is not totally wrong, but it is simplistic and misleading.

To rebuild conditions suitable for life on our planet we need to rebuild the creative constraint system that nature provided on the surface of the earth in the first place, a distributed system of

> To rebuild conditions suitable for life on our planet we need to rebuild the creative constraint system that nature provided on the surface of the earth in the first place.

resistances that causes energy to cascade over, under, around and through a network of constraints that defines the life process. The scale of the constraint system must be such that energy flow is convective but laminar, not too turbulent and destructive, and therefore conducive to proliferation of more modulating structural constraint systems. These ends are met by regeneration and expansion of the biosphere, and by no other means.

Chapter Twenty Seven References

[1] Eric D. Schneider and Dorion Sagan: Into the Cool – "Energy Flow Thermodynamics and Life": The University of Chicago Press, Chicago, Ill. ; Copyright 2005.

[2] Kleidon, Axel and Lorenz, Ralph D.: "Non-Equilibrium Thermodynamics and the Production of Entropy: Life, Earth and Beyond (Understanding Complex Systems)": Springer, New York, NY; Copyright 2005

[3] Smil, Vaclav: "Harvesting the Biosphere: What We Have Taken From Nature": MIT Press, Cambridge, MA; Copyright 2013

[4] Hawkin, Paul; Lovins, Amorey and Lovins, L. Hunter: "Natural Capitalism – Creating the next Industrial Revolution": Little, Brown and Company, New Your, NY; Copyright 1999

Chapter Twenty-Eight

Biomass and Climate

Chapter Summary

Life emerged in the disequilibrium of a cooling earth and evolved by accumulating complexity and by modifying the environment to suit its own needs. Inadvertently or intended, life modified the earth's climate to its own advantage.

By providing a system of biological constraints life ensures climate stability and variability so that a wide range of stable micro-environments came into being, assuring the greatest opportunity for different life forms. Through the advent of photosynthesis, life converted the atmosphere from a reducing condition to an oxidizing condition assuring itself of an endless supply of hydrogen from water to reduce carbon to organic forms and an endless energy supply from the sun.

This chapter discusses some of the details of this evolutionary process.

Chapter Twenty Eight
Biomass and Climate

Historically, scientists have held the view that biome types and ecological communities were controlled by the climate. There were assumed to be areas that were just too hot or too dry or too cold to host certain species.

But the more modern view recognizes that ecological succession modifies the climate as it proceeds, and that the final climate co-evolves with the ecology occupying an area and the geological factors that affect biomes and climatic conditions.

Dr. Lynn Margulis, Professor of Biology in the Department of Geosciences at the University of Massachusetts until her death in 2011, is considered a trail-blazing evolutionary theorist because of her development of the endosymbiotic theory of the origin of organelles in eukaryotic cells. She attributes the development of climatic conditions and atmospheric composition to the early biosphere. In her book, written with science writer Dorian Sagan, "Microcosmos – Four Billion Years of Microbiological Evolution"[1] she writes:

> *Microbes by themselves are thought to have maintained the mean temperature of the early earth so that it was hospitable for life, despite the much cooler "start-up" sun that astronomers believe existed then...only life itself seems powerful enough to have promoted the conditions favoring its own survival in the face of environmental adversity.*

Dr. Margulis describes how the original living systems required hydrogen to combine with carbon to make the myriad organic compounds that life

the original living systems required hydrogen to combine with carbon to make the myriad organic compounds that life requires, and that elemental hydrogen is too light to be retained on the earth by gravity so it floated away into outer space.

requires, and that elemental hydrogen is too light to be retained on the earth by gravity so it floated away into outer space. The only hydrogen sources that were left were those that had combined with other elements into compounds like methane (CH_4), water (H_2O), ammonia (NH_3) and hydrogen sulfide (H2S), gases that were abundant in the atmosphere in the Hadean Age from 4.5 billion to 3.9 billion years ago. Early life required hydrogen it could get from these materials at low energy cost.

The earliest life forms rearranged and recombined these sources of hydrogen into the complex molecules that compose living systems today. Even during these early times life was powerful enough to establish the composition of the atmosphere by removing the hydrogen bearing gases from it and using them in its own construction.

These early life forms emerged during the Archean Age, some 3.9 to 2.5 billion years ago, and they prospered covering the earth with soft mats of single celled organisms, the archaea and the bacteria. Large amounts of hydrogen rich gases spewed from vents between the tectonic plates of the earth and provided a rich source of hydrogen, nitrogen and sulfur containing raw materials for the Archean mat to use.

Methane, hydrogen sulfide and ammonia were the low hanging fruit for Archean life. The energy required to break the bonds holding these materials together was low enough to be within the capabilities of the cooler early sun and primitive microorganisms to manipulate. But as the earth cooled and settled it could no longer fill the demand of the Archean mat to absorb these materials. The concentration of these reducing gases in the atmosphere diminished, and the expansion of the mat became limited by this means.

The hydrogen starved biotic mat covering the earth was in need of other sources of hydrogen to reduce the available carbon into useable forms. That hydrogen source was found in water, an abundant material that covered most of the surface of the earth. Through the process of photosynthesis the energy in sunlight was used to provide the additional energy required to split water and use the hydrogen to

Through the process of photosynthesis the energy in sunlight was used to provide the additional energy required to split water and use the hydrogen to reduce carbon compounds to useful forms for continued growth of the microbial mat.

reduce carbon compounds to useful forms for continued growth of the microbial mat.

This process solved the shortage of reducing gases in the atmosphere for the microbes that could utilize it. But it caused a problem for all of the other microbial biomass of the planet. For the first time elemental oxygen was released in volume and it was heavy enough to remain in the atmosphere. Oxygen is a strongly oxidizing substance, and this makes it toxic to organisms that require a reducing environment including all the microorganisms that had evolved until that time. The balance of nature was shifting. By separating the oxidizing gas (oxygen) from the reducing material (hydrogen) the new microbes were able to utilize the hydrogen in water to their own advantage and the oxygen in water to the disadvantage of every competing organism.

This shift in chemical mechanisms enabled photosynthetic organisms to surge forth and dominate the globe while Archaic life forms were relegated to isolated areas where oxygen is not present to toxify their environment. It also changed the composition of the atmosphere once again. The oxygen content of air rose in proportion to the living mass of the biosphere driving susceptible organisms into isolation.

Archaic life forms were relegated to isolated areas where oxygen is not present to toxify their environment. It also changed the composition of the atmosphere.

The sequence of events illustrates the power of microorganisms to determine the composition and physical state of the atmosphere. Archaic life forms depleted the atmosphere of reducing gases necessary for their own growth and development. Photosynthetic forms utilized the hydrogen available in water, and by so doing introduced oxygen into the atmosphere in quantities that subdued their competition and ensured their own emergence as the primary producers in the biosphere.

The sequence of events illustrates the power of microorganisms to determine the composition of the atmosphere.

From the very beginning climax communities and their climate have co-evolved. Biomass comprises a system of constraints on the environment

From the very beginning climax communities and their climate have co-evolved. Biomass comprises a system of constraints on the environment that dictates the composition and variability of conditions enabling ecosystem development.

that dictates the composition and variability of conditions enabling ecosystem development.

Dr. E. O. Wilson, in his book, "The Future of Life"[2] makes the statement

> *Alone among the solar planets, Earth's physical environment is held by its organisms in a delicate equilibrium utterly different from what would be the case in their absence.*

I would prefer that Dr. Wilson had called the relationship a "delicate disequilibrium" because it is a flow system dependent upon energy flow to maintain its steady state. But Dr. Wilson's point is that the biosystem controls and stabilizes the conditions in the climate.

As we saw in the sections of this book covering thermodynamics, when constraints are numerous enough and energy input cycles are of adequate intensity and periodicity, a system of non-equilibrium patterns emerges and quasi-stable steady state results. This circumstance results in a quasi-stable system including a climate and an ecosystem, or climax community. Such a community can be destabilized by energy inputs or constraint frequencies that are beyond the survival limits of the ecosystem.

The collapse of an ecosystem may result in the development of a different climax community, or it may result in the demise of life forms and the creation of a desert. In the one case a system of constraints and energy inputs is re-established in a more stable configuration. In the other case the system of biological constraints is permanently removed, and a climate unconstrained by living systems results.

Removal of biological constraints creates a system in which energy inputs are no longer absorbed and released in accordance with a stable sequence of constrained patterns. Rather, energy inputs accumulate creating

Removal of biological constraints creates a system in which energy inputs are no longer absorbed and released in accordance with a stable sequence of constrained patterns.

excessive differentials that build up beyond the ability of the system to resolve them in the laminar mode. The resolution of differentials then takes place through destructive turbulence precluding the establishment of conditions suitable for life to re-emerge.

Microbes established themselves in hostile climates. They have evolved, spread, grown and complexified modifying the climate to their own

Microbes established themselves in hostile climates. They have evolved, spread, grown and complexified modifying the climate to their own advantage as they went. As a result, a stable climate that is compatible with the existence and persistence of the life forms that now occupy the planet exists today. When life forms are eliminated, the climate deteriorates, sometimes to the extent that it is beyond the recovery capabilities of the biomass

advantage as they went. As a result, a stable climate that is compatible with the existence and persistence of the life forms that now occupy the planet exists today. When life forms are eliminated, the climate deteriorates, sometimes to the extent that it is beyond the recovery capabilities of the biomass.

When life forms proliferate, the climate transitions are resisted as they carry energy from equator to pole and so it stabilizes. It becomes organized and enters a pattern of stabilized flow in which it resists the passage of energy. The poles cool, the number of microclimates increases, the variety of life forms broadens. Unfortunately, as life forms become more complex they also become more narrowly adapted to their environment and more vulnerable to elimination by changes in the climate.

We need to understand the limits of the constraints that accommodate life forms without creating ecologies that are so narrow and life forms that are so delicate that they succumb to the slightest changes in the ecology. Fortunately life forms control the environment within their own required limits. The deck is loaded in favor of stable ecosystems evolving from established ecological communities once they survive and become stable.

Like the standing wave in the flowing water off the point of shore in "West Running Brook", *The white water rode the black forever*, until such time as energy flows change or constraints collapse, the submerged rock at the bottom of the stream shifts, ending the energy balance and allowing entropy to take over once again

We must re-establish resilient, sustainable ecosystems over large areas of the biosphere that presently do not have the ability to support life, or exist in a depleted state. These objectives are solidly within the capabilities of the human occupants of the planet if we can muster the will to make it happen.

We must re-establish resilient, sustainable ecosystems over large areas of the biosphere that presently do not have the ability to support life, or exist in a depleted state. These objectives are solidly within the capabilities of the human occupants of the planet if we can muster the will to make it happen.

Chapter Twenty Eight References

[1] Margulis, Lyn and Sagan Dorian: "<u>Microcosmos – Four Billion Years of Microbiological Evolution</u>": Summit Books, NY, NY, Copyright 1986

[2] Edward O. Wilson: "<u>The Future of Life</u>": Vintage Books, A Division of Random House, Inc., NY

Chapter Twenty-Nine

Remediation Strategies

Chapter Summary

The climate is unstable not only because of the presence of CO_2 in the atmosphere, but also because of a shortage of solid biomass buffering climate instability. Replacement of the world's biomass reserve would benefit climate stability by mediating both conditions.

This chapter gives order-of-magnitude estimates of how much biomass must be replaced in a global scale biomass remediation scheme.

Chapter Twenty Nine
Remediation Strategies

The outstanding conclusion of the last chapter is that the major causal factor deteriorating the climate is destruction of the phytomass – not the build-up of carbon dioxide. Correction of carbon dioxide levels by means other than replacement of the phytomass will not restore climate stability.[1] Only restoration of the constraints offered by the thermodynamic structure of biomass can do that.

The solution to the climate crisis has to include replacement of the structure and function of phytomass thereby restoring the complexity of the biosphere that buffers energy transfer mechanisms on the surface of the earth.

The biomass graph (Figure 2, page 35) gives us an idea of how much biomass existed during the glacial minimum 10,000 years ago that shifted the climate trajectory in the direction of another ice age. This may give us an idea of how much biomass must be restored to the biosphere to re-establish a stable, livable climate. 400 gigatons would restore us to conditions that initiated an Ice Age (all other things being equal, of course). But this result is significantly beyond our goal.

Suppose we could regenerate 250-300 gigatons of biomass carbon taking it out of the atmosphere. This would draw down atmospheric carbon dioxide to 450-500 gigatons. The resulting atmospheric concentration would be 240-266 ppm, slightly below the level before the Industrial Revolution.

This would clear the pathway for long wave radiation to emanate from the surface of the Earth. It would allow the discharge of entropy and the restoration of order and complexity in the biosphere. By careful monitoring of climate variables we could tell if we wanted to create more biomass or not.

An educated guess would suggest that the drop in atmospheric carbon dioxide would initiate an extraction of dissolved carbon dioxide from the oceans. This would reduce the acidity of seawater and hasten the recovery of mollusks, arthropods, copepods and coral reefs. Once this process got started it would begin to elevate CO_2 concentrations in the atmosphere again, so we would have to generate more biomass to offset the CO_2 we were drawing out of the ocean.

Eventually we would find a biomass level that maintained atmospheric concentrations, oceanic concentrations and terrestrial biomass stores in reasonable balance, while still allowing enough entropy discharge to maintain order and complexity in living systems.

The fossil fuel energy generation systems of the earth release about 6 gigatons of carbon into the atmosphere annually. Concrete making releases another 2 gigatons or so. All other anthropogenic sources release about 2 more gigatons. To offset this anthropogenic carbon dioxide production we must remove all of this or about 10 gigatons of carbon from the atmosphere each year.

Under present conditions, photosynthesis from approximately 610 gigatons of carbon in green plants consumes carbon from carbon dioxide at a rate of about 110 gigatons a year to produce phytomass. Through respiration (R) and decay of biomass (L) an equivalent amount of carbon is returned to the atmosphere.

> Under present conditions, photosynthesis from approximately 610 gigatons of carbon in green plants consumes carbon from carbon dioxide at a rate of about 110 gigatons a year to produce phytomass.

If the biomass in the terrestrial biosphere were increased by 300 gigatons to a total of 910 gigatons, the amount of carbon circulating between the biosphere and the atmosphere would increase from 110 gigatons per year to 165 gigatons per year. The amount of carbon stored

> If the biomass in the terrestrial biosphere were increased by 300 gigatons to a total of 910 gigatons, the amount of carbon circulating between the biosphere and the atmosphere would increase from 110 gigatons per year to 165 gigatons per year. The amount of carbon stored in the biomass reserve would remain constant at 910 gigatons. This would allow 50% more growing biomass to provide ecosystem services such as cooling, water supply and purification to the Earth

in the biomass reserve would remain constant at 910 gigatons. This would allow 50% more growing biomass to provide ecosystem services such as cooling, water supply and purification to the Earth.

The amount of carbon released by fossil fuel burning is just 6% of the carbon absorbed by photosynthesis in growing green plants. If the net growth rate (NPP) of green plants could be increased by just 6% per year, it would absorb all of the carbon dioxide released by fossil fuel burning.

When carbonized phytomass (biochar) is used to increase the production of phytomass, it remains in the soil as elemental carbon for hundreds or thousands of years. The decay process is interrupted, and carbon storage in the soil is increased.

When carbonized phytomass (biochar) is used to increase the production of phytomass, it remains in the soil as elemental carbon for hundreds or thousands of years. The decay process is interrupted, and carbon storage in the soil is increased.

So the use of biochar for increasing yields of biomass not only increases net ecosystem productivity, (NEP) it also decreases non-respirational losses (L). By this means, carbon removal from the atmosphere through photosynthesis is enhanced and the proportion of soil carbon losses back to the atmosphere through decay of phytomass is reduced. As a result carbon stores build up in the soil without returning to the atmosphere through respiration.

In addition, carbon is withdrawn from the atmosphere by the process of weathering of silicate rocks. Recent research by Dr. David Schwartzman, at Howard University in Washington, DC has shown that biomass stimulates the weathering process by at least two to three orders of magnitude.[2] The increased biomass would therefore increase the CO_2 removal from the atmosphere by silicate rock weathering more than 100-fold. This carbon is returned to the geosphere by sedimentation to the sea floor and subduction.

The net result is an increase of phytomass carbon in the biosphere and an increase of elemental carbon in the soil and an increase of carbonates in the geosphere all of which came from the atmosphere. The increased phytomass carbon re-establishes the buffering system that ensures healthy thermodynamic

> The net result is an increase of phytomass carbon in the biosphere and an increase of elemental carbon in the soil and an increase of carbonates in the geosphere all of which came from the atmosphere.

differentials, which stabilize the climate. The increase of soil carbon stimulates more phytomass generation and helps to re-establish the carbon balance in the atmosphere. The sequestration of carbon as carbonates in the geosphere diminishes the carbon available for all surface phenomena including accumulation in the atmosphere and for biological growth.[3]

Chapter Twenty Nine References

[1] Sundquist, E. T. and Broecker, Wallace S.: "Carbon Cycle and Atmospheric CO_2: Natural Variations, Archean to Present (Geophysical Monograph No.32)": American Geophysical Union, January 8, 1991

[2] Schwartzman, David: "Life, Temperature and the Earth – The Self – Organizing Biosphere" : Columbia University Press, New York, NY;, Copyright 2002

[3] Sundquist, Eric T. and McPherson, Brian J.: "Carbon Sequestration and its Role in the Global Carbon Cycle (Geophysical Monograph Series)": American Geophysical Union, Geophysical Monograph Series, Book 183; January 12th 2009

Chapter Thirty

Biomass Replacement Projects

Chapter Summary

Many benefits accrue from revegetation of large areas of our planet, particularly in semi-arid regions that have been damaged beyond their ability to recover.

Some such projects have failed because they lack the elements of structure and function required to create self-sustaining ecosystems. But as experience on how to create self-sustaining ecosystems accumulates, successful projects are proliferating and lessons for establishing sustainable ecosystems are being learned.

This chapter is about large scale reforestation projects that are restoring ecosystems and changing climates in large regions of the world.

Chapter Thirty
Biomass Replacement Projects

The problem of biomass depletion has been evident ever since the use of biomass fuels created the shortages of biomass in 18th century England that led to the adoption of fossil fuels. Without regard for thermodynamic analysis, ecologists the world over have been recognizing the deleterious effects of phytomass removal in many areas of the globe. Reforestation has become a priority in virtually every nation in Europe, Asia, Africa, and Australia and in North and South America, including the United States.

Often the most vulnerable areas are in semi-arid regions that have supported healthy biomes in the past but have been stripped of their biological resources for economic gain. Once the biomass resource is gone and replacement mechanisms have been disabled, it may become clear that the ecosystem is unable to renew itself without human intervention in the recovery process.

The importance of phytomass restoration through afforestation has been recognized by dozens of countries around the world and on

The importance of phytomass restoration through afforestation has been recognized by dozens of countries around the world and on every continent.

every continent. Two areas in particular where large scale afforestation projects have been undertaken are beginning to reach a degree of maturity that they are beginning to provide data demonstrating how to maximize the success of such activities.

These projects are the Loess Plateau project in Northwest China and the Green Wall of the Sahel project in central Africa. Both of these projects are in arid to semi-arid regions where advancing desertification is an ever-present concern. A brief discussion of each of these projects follows.

The Loess Plateau: ...The rise of the Chinese civilization was enabled and enhanced by its ability to draw on many natural resources. Not the least of these was the large forest biomass resource and the fertility of their agricultural soils. China was among the earliest of the great agricultural civilizations along with the Fertile Crescent in Mesopotamia and the Lower Nile Valley in Egypt. All three of these areas are in arid to semi-arid climates threatened by nearby deserts, but all three areas contained fully developed ecosystems capable of supporting incipient civilizations.

But the two resources, phytomass and soils are interdependent and incompatible in development. Appropriation of the soils for agriculture obviates their use for phytomass ecosystems. Appropriation of soils for forest ecosystems obviates their use for agriculture. Exploitation of both resources at once destroys the ecosystem and produces a sterile, lifeless environment.

The abundant environmental resources of the Loess Plateau enabled the Chinese civilization to rise to heights equaled in few other places on earth. It was partly to take advantage of these resources that China moved its capital to Beijing in 1421. Timber from the Loess Plateau provided a seemingly endless supply of building materials for construction of the magnificent city. The same timber was used in construction of the mighty Chinese fleets that explored the world early in the fifteenth century. The growing biomass based Chinese civilization required food, fuel construction materials and growing space. As the land yielded its treasure of biomass it was used for grazing great herds of goats and sheep for meat and milk and leather and wool.

Wanton destruction of ecosystems for agriculture, living space, construction and fuel destroyed the ecosystem on the Loess Plateau. Removal of forests, destruction of grasslands for field crops, and widespread open grazing of animals denuded the area of all vegetative cover and left the vulnerable soils (loess) to erosion by wind and rain. By the twentieth century the area was known as the most eroded area in the world and was called "China's Sorrow".

The Loess plateau extends over 640,000 square kilometers, an area the size of the country of France. Re-establishment of mixed forest and grass cover on such a huge area is considered to be the largest afforestation project ever undertaken.

Chapter Thirty
Biomass Replacement Projects

A recent article in The Plaid Zebra Magazine,[1] calls the project by the name of the "Three North Shelter Belt Project" and claims that it is "the world's largest tree planting project" and that, "since 1978, 66 billion trees have been planted by Chinese citizens. By projects end, in 2050 it is intended to stretch 4,500 km (2800 miles) and cover 405 million hectares (42% 0f

> Since 1978, 66 billion trees have been planted by Chinese citizens. Each year China creates 3.3 million hectares of forests, afforests another 3.7 million hectares of mountains where hunting and grazing are prohibited, and plants 2.4 billion trees.

China's forested territory), and increase the world's forest cover by more than a tenth.

In the web page "Environmental Education Media Project"[2] (eempc.org/loessplateau.watershedrehabilitationproject) Dr. John D. Liu recounts the details of the project and the effect it has had on the production of biomass, the soils and the population and culture of the region. He says that, "Forest covered 9% of China's territory in 1949. That coverage has increased to 16% now and is projected to reach 20% in 2020". They also state, "Each year China creates 3.3 million hectares of forests, afforests another 3.7 million hectares of mountains where hunting and grazing are prohibited, and plants 2.4 billion trees".

Policy support from the Chinese Government, Financing from the World Bank, and cooperation from local farmers and landholders combined to drive this major effort to restore hydrologic cycles and phytomass productivity on the Loess Plateau. The project has helped to contain wind-blown dust from the Gobi Desert and reduced the air pollution problems in Beijing.

Numerous papers have been written criticizing Chinese afforestation projects citing the many failures experienced by demonstration projects. Some of these problems are being overcome by improved planting and watering methods and through improved varieties of plants and the use of native species.

Restoring Climate Stability by Managing Ecological Disorder

An article by Breanna Draxler in the March/April issue of Popular Science has the title "The Future of Trees is Looking Up"[3]. In this article it shows China and Europe as the two world leaders in reforestation projects with a total of 5.1 and 2.1 million acres reforested per year respectively. This kind of biomass recovery can have a significant effect on the world biomass shortage and climate change.

Brazil and Indonesia still lead the world in forest destruction with 5.7 and 2.7 million acres per year respectively. These figures represent a deficit that more than offsets the gains made in the most successful biomass recovering countries.

Afforestation projects in China are proceeding to increase China's forest cover and to benefit China's environment and economy with side benefits

> Afforestation projects in China are proceeding to increase China's forest cover and to benefit China's environment and economy with side benefits to China's standard of living, health and income levels. They are also significantly contributing to the restoration of the world's phytomass.

to China's standard of living, health and income levels. They are also significantly contributing to the restoration of the world's phytomass.

Figures 53 - 56 show the remarkable results of this huge restoration project. Such large-scale permaculture projects are demonstrating the potential for restoring the carbon balance of the earth by increasing the complexity and functionality of ecosystems worldwide.

Figure 53
Loess Plateau (September 1995)

Figure 54
Loess Plateau (September 2009)

Figure 55

Loess Plateau (September 1995)

Figure 56

Loess Plateau (September 2009)

Chapter Thirty
Biomass Replacement Projects

The Great Green Wall of the Sahel: In Africa, just south of the Sahara Desert lies a land of arid to semi-arid regions similarly imperiled by desertification from the nearby desert regions to the north. This is a tropical desert and more hostile to afforestation than the deserts in China. But still, the region has a history of forest and savanna ecologies many thousands of years ago. Sand, blowing southward from the wind-swept Sahara, claims a staggering 4 million hectares of dry-land ecology to desert annually.

In this land of choking dust and heat and drought, eleven nations have signed an agreement to plant a wall of trees across the entire continent of Africa in the southern reaches of the Sahara Desert in order to reverse the expansion of the desert, restore forest ecologies, enhance the hydrological cycle, improve agricultural yields and reduce poverty. The countries of Mauritania, Senegal, Mali, Burkina Faso, Niger, Nigeria, Chad, Sudan, Ethiopia, Eritrea and Djibouti have signed an agreement with the Global Environment Facility, (GEF) an organization originated by the World Bank in 1991. Since 1994 the GEF has operated as an independent funding organization with the World Bank as its major trustee. Since 1991 the GEF has funded environmental projects with grants worth more than $13.5 billion and leveraged more than $65 billion in co-financing for 3900 projects in 165 countries. The Ndjamena convention agreement created the Great Green Wall Agency with $108 million for the participating countries to further develop the Great Green Wall Initiative.

The Great Green Wall is planned to be a ribbon of forested land stretching from Djibouti on the west coast of the African Continent to Senegal on the east coast.[4] It is envisioned as a wall of trees 9 miles wide and 4,300 miles long blocking the advance of sand carrying winds from the Sahara Desert, restoring biodiversity and ecological stability to the area, and establishing improved hydrologic cycles needed for agriculture.[5] The finished project will cover 24 million acres with more than 2 billion trees.

The African Green Wall project is newer than the Chinese Loess Plateau project, and it is in an earlier stage of completion. About 50,000 acres of trees has been planted in the countries of Senegal and Eritrea on the east end of the wall, and large acreages of experimental plantings have been done in Nigeria to test tree species for hardiness under the prevailing conditions.

The difficulties of establishing a forest in the African Sahel are greater than those encountered on the Loess Plateau. It is a tropical desert with more extreme conditions of heat stress and water shortage. Careful selection of tree species, planting technologies and stewardship are required to ensure the success of the project.

The complexity of planning a project that includes parts of 11 countries, each with its own laws and cultures is more difficult than administering a project under one strong central government. Political instabilities in many places along the path of the project make implementation difficult. The European Public Affairs Magazine says Africa's Great Green Wall is expected to reverse land degradation trends by 2025, and lead to development of wide areas of the Sahara by 2050.[6]

John D. Liu, Director of the Environmental Education Media Project and International Fellow for the Communication of Science at Rothamstead Research is also the founder of the Commonland Foundation, an organization that works on large scale landscape restoration projects. He is developing an understanding of environmental economics from his vast experience that is similar to the "Empty World/Full World" ideas of Robert Costanza expressed in Chapter 19. He states:[7]

> *A very important problem we must overcome is that the economy creates a perverse incentive for the earth to be degraded by rewarding the behavior that increases energy consumption, extraction, production, consumption, pollution and degradation. The neoclassical economists believe that this is the way wealth is created. The truth is that this is not wealth at all. The only thing that is happening in the existing economy is that we are rapidly exhausting the resources of the earth. If we continue to plunder the earth, the ecosystems we depend on will eventually collapse, and human civilization as we know it will fail. This has happened before to other civilizations, but now we face this together on a planetary scale.*

Chapter Thirty
Biomass Replacement Projects

Recognizing that the ecological outcomes are not inevitable but are the result of mistakes in economic thinking suggests the solution. Essentially the economy is inverted. Things produced by human beings are derivatives of the earth's ecosystems. They have been inflated and the Source of Life has been said to be worth nothing. This is simply fundamentally untrue. In order to get a different result we must invert the economy again, putting the source of life at a higher value than the derivatives. If we invert the existing economy to recognize the value of natural ecosystem function, the economy will be much larger than it is now. The growth in the economy will be increased biodiversity, biomass and accumulated organic matter, which is also what nature wants. It will be impossible to pollute or degrade as to do this would reduce wealth.

This inversion of the economy puts human productivity on the same side as that of nature, eliminating the incompatibilities that confront the existing economic system.

Dr. Liu also demonstrates an understanding of the non-equilibrium thermodynamic approach to climate change, making the following statement about the Paris Climate Agreement;[8]

In Paris, we've started to turn the corner. Instead of just talking about greenhouse gas (GHG) emissions, we're now seeing [climate change] spoken about as a holistic problem. When you see it holistically, you find out that CO_2 and GHG emissions are a symptom of systematic dysfunction on a planetary scale... Human impact on the climate is not simply emissions, it is degradation.

The degradation of our ecosystems through biomass destruction has removed order, complexity and function from our environment to such an extent that the global biosphere can no longer function. The only way to reverse the trend is to repair the damage and replace the biomass.

The trees planted in the Shelterbelt project number 66 billion – more than ten trees for every man, woman and child on Earth. If each tree matures to sequester a quarter ton of carbon, the project will have already removed over 15 gigatons of carbon from the atmosphere and converted it to biomass, a quasi-stable, living form that prevents its return to the atmosphere as long as the ecosystem continues to exist.

In this book I am asserting that the "systematic dysfunction on a planetary scale" that Dr. Liu has identified is actually a failure of the function of the biosphere caused by continued excessive biomass removal. The thermodynamic chaos and disruption of ordered systems caused by this assault on planetary order is causing ecosystems to approach an inflection point tipping biosystems into disordered states.

Chapter Thirty References

[1] Lao, David: The Plaid Zebra, February 19, 2016: "China is Building a Great Green Wall of Trees to Stop Desertification"

[2] Liu, John D: Environmental Education Media Project: eempc.org/loessplateau.watersheadrehabilitationproject

[3] Draxler, Breanna: "The Future of Trees is Looking Up": Popular Science, March-April 2016

[4] Betancort, Silvia Curbelo: European Public Affairs, October 23, 2014: "A Great Green Wall at the Edge of the Desert"

[5] Koigi, Bob: Euractive.de, August 30, 2016: "Africa Builds 'Great Green Wall' Against Extreamism and Misery"

[6] Liang, Aislinn: The Telegraph, May 3, 2016: "Great Green Wall Thousands of Miles Long Could be Built Across Africa to Stop the Spread of the Sahara."

[7] Tucci, Ricardo: Jume 29, 2016: John D. Liu Interview: "It is Possible to Rehabilitate Large-Scale Damaged Eccosystems"

[8] Groome, Alexander, Regeneration International: Interview With John D. Liu, February 4, 2016, "Meet John D. Liu, the Indiana Jones of Landscape Restoration"

Chapter Thirty-One

Astrophysics and Order

Chapter Summary

The complexity of a system is directly related to the rate of energy dissipation per unit mass of the system. This simple relationship holds for celestial bodies, planetary systems, biological systems, economies and social organizations.

Planets undergo historical temperature cycles which include prolonged cool phases in which surface physical and chemical processes respond to energy input in ways that absorb heat and produce complex systems in a self-regulating, temperature-controlling feedback loop that keeps the planetary atmosphere cool and stable for prolonged periods.

In most systems complexity is a surface phenomenon, but in some biological systems the most intense complexity is internal. The human brain, for instance, is the most complex organ we possess, and it is located in the interior of the head, surrounded by other, less complex organs that serve to protect it from the entropy storm.

The most advanced creatures have evolved to protect their complexity by making it internal and surrounding it with body parts with less critical functions.

This chapter is about scientists on the cutting edge of complexity science and the discoveries they are making that change the way we think about complexity.

Chapter Thirty One
Astrophysics and Order

Recent work in astrophysics has established an understanding of the importance of "cosmic evolution", complexity generation and "big history" in non-isolated system thermodynamics. The expanding universe, discovered by Edwin Hubble gives insight into how entropy flows out of closed systems creating order and complexity as it goes. The complexity content of a system is related to how much energy flows out of a system, and such systems tend to be self-sustaining and stable. Some aspects of this theoretical work are exemplified by the work of three men working on different aspects of the problem.

Energy Flow Density and Complexity: Dr. Eric Chaisson, a research astrophysicist at Harvard University and the Harvard-Smithsonian Center for Astrophysics, studies complexity generated by energy flows. He has described the results of his work in a book he calls, "Cosmic Evolution – The Rise of Complexity in Nature"[1].

In his book, Dr Caisson recognizes that energy flow is a necessary condition for the emergence of order in nature. He observes that the universe is expanding according to Hubble's Law, and that the new volume created by expansion establishes a sink for matter, energy and entropy. This idea of newly created space makes possible the continuous entropy increase observed by

> New space created by expansion establishes a sink for matter, energy and entropy. This idea of newly created space makes possible the continuous entropy increase observed by Clausius and Carnot without increasing the entropy density in the Universe.

Clausius and Carnot without increasing the entropy density in the Universe. The trick is for the entropy produced by everyday processes to flow to the newly created space. This is the imperative that drives non-equilibrium thermodynamics. To quote Dr. Chaisson:

> *...a more modern analysis is not so dire* (as a heat death), *suggesting that the maximum possible entropy will likely never be attained. In an expanding Universe the actual and maximum entropies both increase, yet not at the same rate; a gap opens between them and grows larger over the course of time, causing the Universe to*

increasingly depart from Clausius' idealized heat-death scenario. We need not be so pessimistic; indeed it is this inability of the cosmos to ever reach true maximum disorder that allows order, or lack of disorder, to emerge in localized, open systems.

Then Dr. Chaisson discusses the existence of constraints in natural systems. Such a concept was discussed in Chapter 4 in some detail, and I think Dr. Chaisson and I mean exactly the same thing by it even though our expressions differ slightly. Dr. Chaisson says,

We need not look into space to find examples of unlikely events that actually did occur. Ample evidence here on Earth exists to show that natural phenomena can constrain chance, producing oddities in structure for which the a priori chances are slim....Clearly to assemble larger proteins and nucleic acid, let alone a human being, would be vastly less probable if it had to be done randomly, starting only with atoms or simple molecules... it is once again the natural agents of order that tend to tame chance....natural selection is a decidedly deterministic action that directs evolutionary change. The deterministic part can be considered a constraint – a physical, chemical or environmental boundary – that limits the role of chance...

Dr. Chaisson hints at the autocatalytic nature of biological systems with the statement: *"order itself can be considered a restraint on the way a system can arrange itself"*. This expression describes the constraining effect that biomass has on entropy creation. A biological system is freed from the need to explore the huge numbers of possible random ways to develop by the presence of a pre-arranged template or pattern that allows an ecosystem to reproduce itself.

> A biological system is freed from the need to explore the huge numbers of possible random ways to develop by the presence of a pre-arranged template or pattern that allows an ecosystem to reproduce itself.

Individual species can do this as well. This is the basis of regenerative medicine and tissue engineering using the extra-cellular matrix discussed in Chapter 14.

The passive functioning of biochar, through processes such as adsorption and chelation,

can interact with the active functioning of living microbes. For example, microbial

The passive functioning of biochar, through processes such as adsorption and chelation, can interact with the active functioning of living microbes. For example, microbial constituents can provide the ATP necessary to promote active functioning in the biochar structure while the passive biochar can provide the complex structure to direct the functioning of the ATP.

constituents can provide the ATP necessary to promote active functioning in the biochar structure while the passive biochar can provide the complex structure to direct the functioning of the ATP. This kind of synergy may be responsible for increased biomass production with biochar addition. Dr. Chaisson makes some tantalizingly similar statements as he considers an inanimate rock in orbit such as:

> Suppose, however, that the rock is in elliptical orbit, so that its temperature varies cyclically; the result is again a stable, methodical process of energy flowing in and out of the system, although the rock's temperature is now more complex while varying regularly with each orbit. Such cyclic behavior is typical of a dissipative structure that organizes (or reorganizes) itself in a way as to minimize the production of entropy – a disequilibrium process that, not coincidentally, mimics the metabolism of many living organisms whose cycles transport energy.

If we consider the cyclic behavior of conditions on such an orbital rock and apply this behavior to a glycoside bonding reaction such as we discussed in Chapter 25, Figure 49, we can see that the order produced on the rock as it recedes from its energy source can be "locked in" by the removal of water from the reaction medium. This prevents disorder from returning to the rock during its next heating cycle as it approaches its heat source again. The result is a ratcheting mechanism that "jacks up" the order on the rock as it orbits its energy source.

Dr. Chaisson describes in some detail how matter precipitated from energy in the early Universe before it was some 100,000 years old. Rapid expansion leads to adiabatic cooling and precipitation of ordered specs of matter. Prior to this point the Universe consisted solely of uniformly distributed radiant energy. Expansion led to a proliferation of space for the entropy to distribute itself into followed by the precipitation of more ordered forms of existence. Proliferation of space led to diminishing entropy density even while the total entropy content increased. Diminishing entropy density is the result of the flow of entropy into newly created space creating low entropy pockets in some areas even though the over-all entropy content of the Universe is increasing.

Adiabatic cooling is a process of entropy increasing since the decrease in temperature saps the utility of the heat content of the system. But pockets of order tend to precipitate out of the general entropy increase just as they do during the release of humid compressed air or the formation of raindrops in the cooling levels of the stratosphere. Once matter decoupled from energy, it cooled faster than the radiative fraction of the Universe because of the increase in volume available to it. This thermal differential between matter and radiation is responsible for the growth of complexity.

> Once matter decoupled from energy, it cooled faster than the radiative fraction of the Universe because of the increase in volume available to it. This thermal differential between matter and radiation is responsible for the growth of complexity.

The flow of energy through the various constraints and restrictions in the Universe is established as the source of complexity present in natural systems. It is rational to conclude that the quantity of energy flow through various types of structures is a good indicator of

> The flow of energy through the various constraints and restrictions in the Universe is established as the source of complexity present in natural systems. It is rational to conclude that the quantity of energy flow through various types of structures is a good indicator of their complexity.

their complexity. Dr. Chaisson proceeds to do this by identifying an energy rate factor he calls the Free Energy Rate Density, the rate of energy dissipation through a structure per unit mass measured in ergs per second per gram represented by the symbol Φ. This he establishes as a measure of complexity.

He then compares Φ for many different types of structures throughout the Universe. A star, for instance our sun, has a Φ of about 2 ergs per second per gram. A planet, such as our Earth: 75 ergs per second per gram. The biosphere: 900 ergs per second per gram. A human: 2×10^4 ergs per second per gram. Our brain: 1.5×10^5 ergs per second per gram. When he applies this analysis to human societies in general, he finds a Φ of 5×10^5. Through comparisons of the Free Energy Rate Density, Dr. Chaisson establishes a complexity scale that measures the degree of organization in each type of organized system.

He concludes that the type of organization that precipitates is dependent upon the conditions that exist at the time of its organization, and therefore the complexity of previous orders dictate the kind of complexity found in the present one. This is far from the assertion that evolution must occur by chance alone. The resulting data when plotted against time give a characteristic "hockey stick" graph of the rise of complexity in nature.

Dr. Chaisson then examines how Φ tends to be optimized in nature. Greater energy flow densities tend toward greater complexity. But he warns that excessive flows can be destructive as well. To quote Dr. Chaisson again:

> *This is not to say that indefinitely high values of Φ would in every case lead to ever more complexity. Examples abound in Nature where too much energy flow triggers just the opposite- namely an open system that suffers a breakdown, robbing the system of complexity and often returning it to equilibrium.*

Dr. Chaisson extends his argument to interactions between the biosphere and the climate. He discusses biological control of the carbon cycle:

> *The microorganism, for sure, excrete metabolic products that modify their environmental conditions, a property that has clearly enhanced their own species' survival, which, not coincidentally extends, and most impressively so, over billions of years. Accordingly living things have seemingly prevented drastic climate changes throughout much of Earth's history, as evolution has endowed organisms with improved ability to keep surface conditions favorable for themselves. For example, as our Sun ages, thus becoming more luminous and sending more heat toward Earth, Life responds by modifying Earth's atmosphere and surface geology to keep the climate fairly constant – a kind of "geophysiological thermostat" that basically adjusts CO_2 levels down by preferentially getting wrapped up in calcium carbonate under high temperatures, thereby cooling the atmosphere; if those temperatures go too low, the reaction to form carbonate decreases and the amount of CO_2 and the atmospheric temperature both rise, the whole CO_2 cycle acting as a positive feedback that keeps water liquid and Earth habitable.*

This paragraph clearly expresses how the biosphere controls carbon dioxide levels in the atmosphere by the rock-weathering process and stores excess carbon as carbonates in the geosphere. It is a good expression of how global warming may be a function of biomass levels in the biosphere. More will be said about this subject in the following discussion of Dr. Schwartzman's work.

Heat and Self-Organization: Dr. David Schwartzman, Professor of Biology at Howard University in Washington, DC, wrote another book along the same lines. Dr. Schwartzman calls his book, "Life, Temperature and the Earth – The Self-Organizing Biosphere"[2]

Dr. Schwartzman starts by describing a standard life cycle followed by all terrestrial planets, creation, cooling, homeostasis, and dissolution. A terrestrial planet is formed by the common gravitational attraction of regional solid masses that converge, collide, and accrete into a single mass. The resulting mass is very large, and the potential energy of each massive segment is converted into heat as collisions build and temperatures increase to very high levels. This gravitational contraction is the same energy source that provides heat to stars and gives them the extreme temperatures that make them shine. Gravitational contraction of solid masses is somewhat different from contraction of gas clouds, but the results are the same, a very hot mass with a surface that radiates thermal energy into the deep space that surrounds it.

Following the accretion phase in which the planet grows in mass and temperature, a cooling phase ensues in which the planet radiates its energy into space as it cools from its super-hot state. As it radiates its energy into its surroundings, its surface becomes cooler, and cooler until the amount of energy dissipated through radiative cooling approaches the amount of energy acquired from its mother star (the Sun). When the solar energy being absorbed by the planet becomes equal to the thermal energy being radiated out into space, the planet enters a stable phase of homeostasis through which the temperature will remain relatively stable for an extended period of time.

Depending upon the mass of the parent star, the star will precede toward a more mature phase, likely that of a Red Giant. As the star expands it becomes more and more luminous, imparting more and more energy to the planet. The planet's surface temperature rises in response to increased energy input from the star, and eventually it is stirred out of its homeostatic state and into a rising temperature mode again. Ultimately, the surface of the maturing star engulfs the planet, driving the surface temperature to extreme levels once again.

So the temperature, history curve of a terrestrial planet looks like a big U, very hot at first, dropping to a more-or-less steady state condition with mild temperatures, and finally rising again to extreme high temperatures at the end of its lifetime. The chemical and physical environment at the surface of the planet controls the details of the conditions on the planet during the cool, homeostatic phase.

We happen to be living in the cool, homeostatic phase of the temperature history of the Earth. One major mechanism controlling the homeostasis we experience is the carbon dioxide level in our atmosphere. Carbon dioxide controls the amount of energy leaving the planet since it is somewhat

We happen to be living in the cool, homeostatic phase of the temperature history of the Earth opaque to radiant heat transfer in the infrared wavelengths associated with temperatures on earth. Temperatures at the surface of the Earth increase in proportion to the opacity of the atmosphere to the discharge of long wave radiant energy.

> Temperatures at the surface of the Earth increase in proportion to the opacity of the atmosphere to the discharge of longwave radiant energy.

Schwartzman describes the long-term control of atmospheric carbon dioxide levels through the silicate-carbonate geochemical cycle in which carbon dioxide interacts with calcium and magnesium silicates (rocks) to produce calcium (or magnesium) carbonates and silicates.

$$CO_2 + CaSiO_3 = CaCO_3 + SiO_2$$

This process goes on in atmospheric weathering reactions on exposed rock surfaces. The reaction reverses itself at high temperatures releasing carbon dioxide in thermal vents and volcanoes. But the weathering process on the surface produces a net removal of carbon dioxide from the atmosphere increasing the transparency of the atmosphere to infrared wavelengths, allowing greater discharge of radiant energy and associated cooling of the surface of the Earth.

This reaction is represented as being entirely mineral and inorganic. But Schwartzman is quick to point out that:

> weathering involves biotic mediation." He continues, "chemical weathering requires a flow of water and carbon dioxide through a layer of soil, with a high reactive surface area of Ca and Mg silicates if consumption of atmospheric carbon dioxide is to occur at a rate similar to that on today's Earth. Thus, most chemical weathering occurs on vegetated continental surface in temperate and tropical climates because of moderate to high rainfall and temperatures.

This process is inherently self-limiting or homeostatic because the removal of carbon dioxide allows radiative cooling of the Earth's surface, reducing rainfall and chemical reaction rates both of which reduce

385

weathering rates. Reduced weathering rates preserve carbon dioxide in the atmosphere. But Schwartzman points out also that the rate of abiotic weathering is far too low to keep the Earth in steady state at present temperatures, and so he reviews the many ways that biological processes enhance weathering rates. He cites a 1970 study by Jackson and Keller[3] in which *"Lichens appeared to have increased weathering rates by one or two orders of magnitude compared with adjacent bare rock."*

He defines a biotic enhancement of weathering factor, B, as the ratio of weathering rates under biologically mediated conditions to weathering rates in abiotic conditions, and he finds that a value of B of 100 to 1000 is appropriate. Enhancement of atmospheric weathering of geophysical features by a factor of 1000 is no small matter. It means that carbon dioxide removal by biotically mediated weathering competes with photosynthesis as a cooling system for Planet Earth.

Enhancement of atmospheric weathering of geophysical features by a factor of 1000 is no small matter. It means that carbon dioxide removal by biotically mediated weathering competes with photosynthesis as a cooling system for Planet Earth.

Dr. Schwartzman then addresses the nature of soil structures bridging the gap between biological systems and physical surroundings. He presents the following paragraph:

> *The evolution of the biosphere is geophysiological in the sense that self-regulation arises from the coupling of biota and its inorganic surface environment. As emphasized in the discussion of the weathering process, the soil geomembrane is a critical site of this coupling. Markos (1995) pointed out that an extracellular matrix composed of mineral particles, cellular exudates, organic debris and biofilms is a second structure of biological communities. As such it constitutes a mediating environment between the inorganic and the organic bodies of the biosphere; the extracellular matrix of the soil is just such a mediator"*

Energy flow regimes in the soil are dependent for their functioning on structures in soil that act like extracellular matrices or physiological mediators between the biological and physical realms. Understanding this fact is essential to developing an understanding of biochar and how and why it works. The medical profession has done wonderful things by using extracellular matrices to guide the process of healing and repair of tissues. Understanding the workings of matrices in soils as a guidance system for developing ecosystems may provide equally exciting progress in the design and development of ecosystems. It is a wide-open field regarding enhancement of biomass generation on the surface of the Earth.

Schwartzman then ties biological evolution to planetary evolution by linking the resilience of biological membrane construction to the temperature of the planet surface at the time when they evolved. I find this approach to be quite logical and very worth pursuing because the resiliency of the membrane that may be required at an early time in planetary evolution may require too much thermodynamic closure to allow for the passage of entropic wastes needed to allow complexity to bloom. More sophisticated, but less resilient membranes that would be more amenable to the excretion of entropic waste materials and retention of complex materials could have emerged when the temperature of the earth's surface was lower, allowing complexity to compound itself in living systems. He expresses it this way:

> *The upper limit for growth of organismal groups is apparently determined by the thermolability of biomolecules, organellar membranes, and enzyme systems...*

> *The progressive increase in the biotic enhancement of weathering as a product of biotic and biospheric evolution intensified the carbon sink with respect to the atmosphere/ocean system, leading to the transition of climate from a hothouse in the early Precambrian to an*

icehouse in the Phanerozoic. By the late Proterozoic, the rise of atmospheric oxygen may have resulted in a substantial increase in terrestrial biotic productivity, which along with the onset of frost wedging substantially increased the biotic enhancement of weathering. Climate and life co-evolved as a tightly coupled system, constrained by abiotic factors (varying solar luminosity and the crust's tectonic and impact history). Self-regulation of this coupled system is a property of geophysiology.

The fact that long-term carbon dioxide removal from the atmosphere is mediated by the biosphere is well presented here. This revelation is very supportive of the assertion that the shortage of biomass in today's world is more fundamental to the essence of global warming and climate change than atmospheric carbon dioxide levels are. The totality of the world's biomass is responsible for not only short-term carbon dioxide uptake through photosynthesis, but also the long-term uptake through atmospheric weathering of rock. Depletion of the world's biomass damages every mechanism by which nature cools the surface temperature of the earth.

Schwartzman then goes on to talk about some other matters concerning complexity that we have discussed before, such as the creation of order and complexity through the extraction of entropy from a thermodynamic system. He says:

Finally, a potential indicator of the biosphere's self-regulation is proposed, namely, the trend in the net entropic flow from its effective physical boundary (i.e., the boundary of the biota itself), the surface of the ocean and land, compared with the trend for an abiotic surface.

He continues:

Ebeling (1985) and Lesins (1991), among others, have pointed out that the net entropic flow from the Earth's surface and atmosphere is a necessary condition for biospheric self-organization. The flow is possible because of the existence of a heat sink in outer space; low entropy solar radiation comes into the biosphere, and high entropy heat radiation leaves it to the heat sink.

Here Schwartzman is introducing the idea that self-regulation of the biosphere is a function of the extraction of entropy through the atmospheric thermodynamic boundary of the system. This is a conclusion that I have settled on many times, and it is clearly shown in Figure 23 in Chapter 6. I am satisfied that it is true and accurate. If this fundamental fact could be recognized at the start of every research effort, I think much time could be saved and much better understanding could be gained. Schwartzman has a winner here!

He combines some of these ideas as follows:

> *Thus, the Earth's surface system can be self-organized, whether it be geochemical or geophysical, because it possesses feedback and disequilibrium (Ortoleva et al 1987). If the early, pressure-cooker atmosphere at 3.8 Ga was in steady state, geochemically balanced between a volcanic source and a weathering sink, assuming plausible limits on continental area and volcanic out-gassing rates, then the present biotic enhancement of weathering (B)is likely two orders of magnitude (see discussion in Chapter 8). This requirement for a high present B follows directly from the need, under steady state conditions, to balance the higher volcanic flux of carbon by weathering on somewhat smaller continents, some 4 billion years ago, necessitating high atmospheric carbon dioxide levels (and correspondingly high surface temperatures) to speed up weathering, work now done by biotic enhancement at a much lower carbon dioxide level.*

Combining the ideas of complexity resulting from entropy extraction and weathering enhanced by complex biological systems leads to a stronger understanding of how effective the ecological system can be as a homeostatic control mechanism keeping an otherwise warm planet cool and how likely it is that tampering with the system by massive biomass removal will result in planet-wide warming of the climate.

In his final chapters Schwartzman concludes:

> *In conclusion, the biotically mediated cooling arising from biotically enhanced chemical weathering is postulated to have been crucial to the emergence of complex life on Earth.*

Chapter Thirty One
Astrophysics and Order

Big History: A third person that is working on the generation of order by energy systems is Dr. Fred Spier, Senior Lecturer at the University of Amsterdam in the Netherlands. Dr. Spier, the author of several books on the emergence of order in nature, has authored a paper in the journal, "Social Evolution and History" entitled, "How Big History Works: Energy Flows and the Rise and Demise of Complexity"[4]. In this paper Dr. Spier makes several key observations that contribute to the understanding of order. For example he identifies complexity as a surface phenomenon. In his words:

> From the perspective of Big History, the highest complexity appears to exist on the surfaces of celestial bodies situated on the outer edges of galaxies. In other words, higher complexity is typically a marginal phenomenon, both in the sense that it can be found on the margins of larger regimes and in the sense that it is exceedingly rare. Most of the universe consists of lesser forms of complexity. To be sure, as Eric Caisson observed, this is not true for life itself. The highest biological complexity, most notably DNA and brains, are to be found in or near the center of their regimes and not on their edges. Apparently this type of complexity needs to be protected against matter and energy flows from outside that are too big, in which case it would be destroyed, or too small, in which case it would freeze. In other words, life has created a space suit for its own highest complexity. In fact, terrestrial life may have well succeeded in turning the entire biosphere into a space suit. This is, in my view, the essence of James Lovelock's Gaia Hypothesis, which states that terrestrial life has evolved feedback mechanisms that condition the biosphere in ways that are advantageous for life's continued existence on our planet.

From Dr. Spier's point of view, damaging the biosphere is tantamount to compromising our own space suit that protects us from energy flows greater than our physiology can sustain. He embellishes his argument with the following paragraph:

> Damaging the biosphere is tantamount to compromising our own space suit that protects us from energy flows greater than our physiology can sustain.

> Surprisingly little attention has been devoted to the demise of complexity. Seen from the highest level of generality, complexity is destroyed when the energy flows, and/or energy levels, (temperature and pressure) become either too high or too low. For instance without energy flow no biological regime will survive. Yet if

such an organism experiences energy flows that are too big it will succumb to them too. This is also true for lifeless forms such as rocks, planets or stars. All matter regimes are, therefore, characterized by certain bandwidths of energy levels and flows within which they cannot exist.

From my point of view, the "bandwidth of energy levels and flows" is controlled by living biomass on the surface of the earth. Excessive biomass resists energy flows and creates excessive differentials that lead to glaciers that destroy the excess biomass. The deficiency of biomass releases energy flows diminishing differentials and restoring energy flow dynamics to levels within the "bandwidth" once again.

There is an overshoot from this process in which the deficiency of

Deficiency of biomass leads to reduced differentials approaching equilibration which leads to energy levels and flows that are too low to support plant growth. When this happens evolution is driven back to an earlier level of ecological succession. It may be necessary, in the most extreme cases, to intervene in the process by injecting some artificial form of complexity into an excessively equilibrated system to jump start a system of energy differentials and rebuild an ecosystem.

biomass leads to reduced differentials approaching equilibration, which leads to energy levels and flows that are too low to support plant growth. When this happens evolution is driven back to an earlier level of ecological succession. It may be necessary, in the most extreme cases, to intervene in the process by injecting some artificial form of complexity into an excessively equilibrated system to jump-start a system of energy differentials and rebuild an ecosystem.

When this process is fully understood and refined it may be possible to identify an optimal level of entropy content, or complexity for any system that will result in rapid and complete restoration of any damaged ecosystem.

Dr. Spier then differentiates between material entropy and energy entropy. His argument is based on the earth as a thermodynamically closed system, one from which energy escapes but material does not. He makes the following argument:

> The matter and energy flows that our species has sought to master, had to be neither too large, because humans would have succumbed to their effects, nor too small, because they would not have supported human life sufficiently. As I have argued, this is not only true for human history, but also for "Big History" as a whole.
>
> All human efforts to capture matter and energy flows have inevitably generated entropy. While the low level radiation produced by human activities could comparatively easily be radiated out into the cosmic trashcan, for matter flows this was not the case. As a result of human activities, therefore, material entropy on the surface of the earth has relentlessly increased.

To Dr. Spier, the destruction of material order on the earth's surface is more intractable than the energetic disorder retained by our atmosphere. From my point of view, the restoration of the biosphere restores order to both energy and matter. It restores order and continuity to energy flows by replacing the constraint system that controls turbulence and equilibrium in the ecosystem, and it restores order to matter by enhancing the process of photosynthesis that creates ordered molecular structures out of smaller, more chaotic molecular groups.

The history of human societies on Earth has been simultaneous with the destruction the Earth's biomass. The very thing that enabled our emergence to begin with, and our continued existence now, is being systematically destroyed, by the new Bio-Economy, and with it the chemical-physical feedback mechanism that enables biotically enhanced chemical weathering and the resulting biotically mediated cooling. I think Caisson, Schwartzman and Spier have it right, and it supports my conclusion that the removal of biomass is more significant even than industrial carbon dioxide emissions in the effort to combat global warming. In the light of this understanding it boggles my mind that we continue to justify the consumption of our bio-systems by calling them "renewable carbon" as opposed to "fossil carbon". It won't matter which it is after we burn it all up

Chapter Thirty One References

[1] Caisson, Eric : "Cosmic Evolution – The Rise of Complexity in Nature": Harvard University Press, Cambridge, Mass.; Copyright 2001

[2] Schwartzman, David: "Life, Temperature and the Earth – The Self-Organizing Biosphere": Columbia University Press, New York, NY; Copyright 2002

[3] Jackson, T.A. & Keller, W. D.: American Journal of Science 269, 446-466 1970: "A Comparative Study on the Role of Lichens and "Inorganic Processes" in the Chemical Weathering of Recent Hawiian Lava Flows

[4] Spier, Fred: "Big History and the Future of Humanity": John Wiley and Sons, Oxford, UK; Copyright 2015

Chapter Thirty Two

The Rise and Fall of Complexity

Chapter Summary

Complexity is achieved in a natural thermodynamic system by discharging more entropy than the sum of what comes into the system and what is created within the system. As long as this balance is maintained, the order in the system will grow and the complexity of a system will increase. Evolution is the process by which the complexity of species increases over time.

Death is the result of failure of an individual to discharge enough entropy to support its complexity. Extinction is the result of failure of a species to discharge enough entropy to support its accumulated complexity.

This chapter will discuss how this works and some significant examples.

Chapter Thirty Two
The Rise and Fall of Complexity

A thorough understanding of thermodynamic entropy balance is paramount to describing the effects of evolution and the state of complexity on the surface of the earth. The beauty of this approach is that events that are inexplicable by other means seem to be obvious when viewed in the context of an entropy balance. The process of proliferating constraints by biomass expansion providing growing resistance to convective energy transfer across the surface of the earth while increasing the production of order at the same time is inherently obvious when viewed in this way. The accumulation of order in systems whose boundaries can readily pass entropy but retain ordered material is an obvious extension of this idea. The development of complexity as a higher level of order when all lower levels of order are filled and

> Complexity as a higher level of order that emerges when all lower levels of order are filled and the entropy balance demands a still more ordered system.

the entropy balance demands a still more ordered system is another logical extension of this thought process.

We have seen how matter becomes functional when it reaches a certain level of complexity and how self-replicating systems emerge motivated by the imperative of rejected entropy. Matter seeks through available constraint systems to find new levels of complexity advantageous to its own survival. Evolution is a search for the most effective combination of

> Matter seeks through available constraint systems to find new levels of complexity advantageous to its own survival. Evolution is a search for the most effective combination of complexity and persistence to accomplish the survival of the species.

complexity and persistence to accomplish these ends.

Complexity tends to be vulnerable and persistence tends to be inflexible and resistant to change. Evolution is a delicate balance between these two properties.

> Evolution is a delicate balance between vulnerable complexity and flexible resilience.

Complexity grows as the rate of entropy rejection

from a system increases. When the entropy rejection rate balances the entropy intake rate plus the entropy production rate the complexity level in a system becomes constant as well.[1]

If the entropy rejection rate is reduced from this balance point, the complexity level in the system cannot be sustained. Such a system must relinquish some of its order.[2]

> If the entropy rejection rate is reduced from this balance point the complexity level in the system cannot be sustained. The system must relinquish some of its order.

The process of backing down from a highly complex state of order involves giving up the most highly ordered features first. For example, the water in an ice cube doesn't evaporate appreciably until all the ice melts. Only when the temperature is increased well beyond the melting temperature does evaporation take place. In a biological ecosystem this means loss of the most elaborate, complex species at the top of the evolutionary tree first. These species of maximum complexity will be the first victims of increasing disorder.

An evolving ecosystem adjusts to changes in its ability to discharge entropy by changing the rate at which it evolves. As the entropy discharge rate declines the evolution rate declines as well.

A significant entropy rejection rate is required just to maintain the existing complexity level of the planet, even if further evolution weren't occurring at all. If the entropy rejection rate falls below that critical level, the evolutionary process will start to work in reverse. Complex, highly evolved species will start to disappear from the very top of the evolutionary tree as planetary entropy increases and complexity begins to simplify.

The Megafauna: One of the inadequately explained mysteries of the biological record is the relatively abrupt disappearance of the megafauna. These large animals are often defined as species with an adult weight of greater than 100 pounds. This would include humans, so it behooves us to take notice when this class of organisms is threatened or stressed.

Chapter Thirty Two
The Rise and Fall of Complexity

These large creatures included species such as the Giant Sloths, Short Faced Bears, American Lion, Giant Tortoises Saber Toothed Cats, Mammoths and Mastodons. They all became extinct about 12,000 years ago, many during the American Megafauna Extinction Event that claimed more than 90 genera of mammals.

There is much contention over what caused the extinction of all these mega-species. Their demise seems to be somehow related to the appearance of mankind in the Americas. Were the megafauna hunted to extinction by the interlopers who crossed the Bering Strait on the exposed land bridge? Or did they succumb to climate change in the abrupt cooling at the onset of the Younger Dryas, a period of pronounced climate cooling about 12,000 years ago?

Questions of this sort can be addressed by understanding that they relate to the entropy balance of the earth. Anything that interferes with the projection of entropy into outer space is going to have consequences in the level of complexity the earth can support. Reductions in entropy discharge result in diminishing numbers and complexity of species, starting with the largest and most complex and working its way downward as the entropy discharge diminishes, entropy content increases and order declines.

The Thermodynamics of the Megafauna: The megafauna were a peak in mass-complexity, or Free Energy Rate Density as described by Dr. Eric Chaisson in Chapter 31. When energy discharge flow rate diminishes, entropy will no longer be carried away from the system, and the mass-density peak will no longer be supportable. Left unsupported, the mass-complexity peak of the megafauna collapses. The complexity of several species may collapse in this way before the entropy balance is sufficient to support the ecosystem again.

> Left unsupported by entropy discharge, the mass-complexity peak of the megafauna collapses. The complexity of several species may collapse in this way before the entropy balance is sufficient to support the ecosystem again.

Dr. David Schwartzman says that weathering of carbonate and silicate rocks absorbs carbon dioxide, so the ability of the earth to reject entropy recovers with time. Removal of carbon dioxide allows the earth to cool and reorganize by re-establishing the "net entropic flow from the earth's surface". Weathering of rock is one method by which entropy extraction is restored and vulnerable complexity is saved from entropy build-up.

Dr. Fred Spier points out that internalized centers of complexity are, to a degree, protected from the entropy storm outside, and that successful complex species have devised ways to "pump" entropy away from their centers of complexity and dispose of it in the outside environment.

But if entropy build-up is caused by a species that willfully increases the entropy of the earth by wanton destruction of the ordered condition while preventing the escape of the resulting entropy as well, neither the weathering of rock nor the protection of our order by internalization will be sufficient to protect ourselves from dissolution.

Changing Entropy Discharge Requirements: Every degree Fahrenheit increase in the temperature of the surface of the earth increases the thermal driving force with which entropy is discharged into outer space. The difference between the temperature at the surface of the earth and the background temperature of outer space is 511°F. Every degree that the earth warms increases this driving force by 0.2%. All other things being equal, this represents a relatively small increase in the potential for complexity generation on earth.

However, the driving force for sustaining the complexity level of individual species is based on the difference between the species metabolic temperature and the temperature of their environment. For a species with an internal temperature of 98.6°F the driving force for complexity generation and maintenance is 41.4°F. Every degree F increase in global temperature decreases this driving force by 2.4%.

The situation is even worse during warm seasons of the year when the differential for entropy rejection is at its minimum. This means that global warming actually increases the potential for entropy discharge and order generation on earth, but it diminishes the ability to satisfy that demand for order generation through the present mass-complexity hierarchy. The most massive and complex species are unsuited to survival under the new conditions. Some other means to convert energy flow into complexity must be found or heating will continue. Instead of being homeostatic, the system has become thermally accumulating unless some new arrangement for thermally resistant complexity can evolve or some chemical feedback mechanism such as weathering of rocks can be found as demonstrated by Dr. Schwartzman.

This is one reason why megafaunal species have gone extinct. Environmental changes have modified their entropy balance

This is one reason why megafaunal species have gone extinct. Environmental changes have modified their entropy balance requirements and prevented them from passing enough entropy to satisfy the complexity level they achieved.

requirements and prevented them from passing enough entropy to satisfy the complexity level they achieved.

Mankind doesn't have to hunt the megafauna into extinction. All he has to do is modify the environment to change their entropy discharge rate and prevent them from passing enough entropy to satisfy their complexity requirements, and then wait for them to disappear. Historically this has been done by anthropogenic removal of biomass reserves, and as long as the general problems it caused were less that the apparent benefits of the practice, it appeared to be OK.

Now the situation is different. Half of the earth's biomass reserve is already destroyed. The potential for recovery is diminished greatly, and the remaining complexity reserves are under assault by anthropogenic restrictions on planetary entropy discharge and by anthropogenic destruction of existing earthly complexity.

The most successful complex species have found that the best way to assure continuous entropy discharge is to operate at an internal temperature that is greater than the temperature of the surrounding environment. Internalizing chemical energy (eating food), and releasing its heat internally, maintains an elevated internal temperature. By this means, continuous heat flow to the outside environment is maintained and entropy is rejected maintaining the internal order of the system.

All this entropy removal comes at a cost. The entropy that must be removed to maintain order in living species must be dumped into the external environment where it interferes with ordered ecosystems, and the entropy that must be removed to maintain ordered ecosystems must be dumped into outer space.

Some species in some climates cannot discharge enough entropy to maintain their internal order as climate conditions change. These species go extinct.

> Some species in some climates cannot discharge enough entropy to maintain their internal order as climate conditions change. These species go extinct

The human species has chosen another survival strategy altogether. We have sought shelter from the entropy storm, minimizing our exposure to natural processes that may be erosive to our order by living in structures both naturally occurring or of our own construction. When that isn't enough for our comfort, we fabricate our own low entropy environments where we can safely discharge our entropy. We expend energy to keep the entropy low in our living spaces dumping our excess entropy overboard into the immediate environment. We even make some of these living spaces portable so that we can carry them around with us. The entropy that we extract from these spaces we dump on the environment burdening the order of the ecosystem with it.

Every bit of the order we create in these systems involves the flow of energy, now artificially created energy, which produces CO_2 that obstructs the passage of entropy into the universe and causes it to further deteriorate the order of our ecosystems.

It is becoming clear that destruction of the order of our ecosystems leads to the demise of complex species and equilibrium of our climate system, a process that starts with the most complex, massive and vulnerable species and works down to simpler, more resilient forms as it pushes heat from equatorial climates toward the poles causing the greatest warming in the arctic regions.[3]

Chapter Thirty Two References

[1] Zurek, Wojciech H.: "Complexity, Entropy and the Physics of Information (Santa Fe Institute Studies in the Sciences of Complexity Proceedings":Santa Fe Institute Studies in the Sciences of Complexity Proceedings (Book 8) , January 26, 1990

[2] Prigogine, Ilya and Stengers, Isabelle: "Order Out of Chaos (Radical Thinkers): Verso (October 10, 2013)

[3] ACIA (Arctic Climate Impact Assessment) (Author): "Arctic Climate Impact Assessment – Scientific Report": Cambridge University Press, November 7, 2005

Part Nine

Biochar – a Tool

Chapter Thirty-Three

Understanding Biochar

Chapter Summary

Biochar is a storehouse of resilient, functional complexity that hosts micro-organisms increasing its functionality, complexity and energy relationships. Its microstructures constrain the generation of entropy on earth.

This chapter explains how it interacts with mineral and biological systems as an intermediary between the mineral world and the soil food web.

Chapter Thirty Three
Understanding Biochar

Biochar: An emerging agricultural tool is charcoal, also known as biochar. Heating wood or other biomass vaporizing the volatile fractions and leaving elemental carbon structures behind creates the residue called biochar.[1] During heating the carbon residues retain the structural nature of the biomass which is so critical to minimizing entropy in ecosystems. The result is a solid material with an intricate structure and a massive surface area, two characteristics of complex, low entropy solids. Biochar has a third characteristic of complexity – a proliferation of chemically reactive sites that bond with mineral nutrients in soils. It provides a plethora of nuclei of the necessary structures that promote and encourage any biological reactions that may be initiated by natural phenomena. Biological reactions, once started, are supported by the biochar structure and chemistry until they become self-supporting. The growth process becomes autocatalytic when structures and chemical differentials necessary for life are further created by the growing organism itself. In this way biochar acts initially as a catalyst, providing an environmental structure capable of hosting a living environment until it becomes capable of reproducing and sustaining itself.

The huge surface area of biochar is activated; it adsorbs and holds nutrients and other biologically active materials through loose chemical bonding mechanisms to bonding sites on the carbon surface. The affinity of biochar for mineral nutrients and other bioactive materials acts as a food store and growth stimulant utilizing the adsorptive properties of carbon to act as a resource for ecosystem life. Living organisms in the environment can reduce surrounding concentrations of nutrients and biologically active materials to low enough levels to reverse the adsorption of nutrients on the carbon. The desorbed nutrients can then be taken up by plants and used for metabolism and assimilation into the soil food web. Upon the death and decay of the living organisms, nutrients are released again into the soil and may be re-adsorbed by the biochar. This creates a localized nutrient cycle that stimulates the health of the plants and reduces nutrient loss to the greater environment, and so it reduces the need to add artificial nutrients (fertilizers) to the soil. It also reduces the tendency of the nutrients to disperse into a higher entropy state (groundwater pollution, soil gas emissions).

> Biochar adsorption creates a localized nutrient cycle that stimulates the health of the plants and reduces nutrient loss to the greater environment, and so it reduces the need to add artificial nutrients (fertilizers) to the soil. It also reduces the tendency of the nutrients to disperse into a higher entropy state (groundwater pollution, soil gas emissions).

The structure of biochar also accommodates living structures that are symbiotic with green plants. The hyphae of mycorrhizal fungi permeate the intersticies and the macropores of the biochar and pick up adsorbed nutrients and carry them to points of symbiotic interaction with green plants, enhancing the mutually beneficial relationships for both organisms by acting as a carrier for nutrients. The expansion and densification of the mycorrhizal mat drastically increases the surface area available for nutrient uptake, and it also increases the organic carbon content of the soil.

The beginning of a healthy mycorrhizal mat stimulates bacterial profusion by providing a source of energy and nutrients, living and dead, upon which bacteria may feed. With the base of the food web thus established, an entire food chain is initiated. Healthy soil is thereby stimulated, reducing the time required to return a depleted soil to functional health and enhancing the productive potential of the soil.

Biochar, being resistant to decay, may remain in the soil for thousands of years.[2] [3, 4] the biochar thus establishes a stable, long term, low

> Biochar is resistant to decay and may remain effective in the soil for thousands of years.

entropy, structural carbon reservoir in the soil removing a high entropy carbon reservoir from the air. The biological growth that biochar promotes establishes a stable, short term carbon cycle in the soil as well, promoting and maintaining an even larger carbon reservoir. The build-up of these two soil carbon reservoirs removes carbon dioxide from the air, clearing the energy discharge pathway from the biosphere allowing the escape of entropy from the earth, and enabling the accumulation of order and complexity in the biosphere.

Investigations of ancient agricultural sites, most notably in the Amazon River basin, have uncovered areas of particularly high fertility, even when the surrounding soils are heavily leached and devoid of essential plant nutrients. These fertile areas have one thing in common, a high concentration of elemental carbon, charcoal from charred biomass.

Biochar increases the nutrient availability of almost any soil. This it does by adsorbing nutrients out of the surrounding soil and releasing them when the plants need them. The way it does this is through a chain of complex symbiotic relationships with soil microbes. It makes the nutrients more available to plants than they would be if they were simply present in the soil or dissolved in the groundwater. Drs. Johannes Lehmann and Stephen Joseph express this in their book "Biochar for Environmental Management"[18] this way:

> Biochar is not only more stable than any other amendment to soil....it increases nutrient availability beyond a fertilizer effect....These basic properties of stability and capacity to hold nutrients are fundamentally more effective than those of any other organic matter in the soil.

The Process of Adsorption: Adsorption of plant nutrients is a surface phenomenon. The surface of charcoal has many molecular irregularities that attract and hold mineral nutrients of all kinds. Such irregularities may be centers of electrical charge that attract dissolved ionic materials like metal ions, or they may be non-ionic chelation sites that physically "fit" complementary sites on larger, less soluble molecules like amino acids and protein fragments, polynucleotide chain fragments or carbohydrate sugar groups. In either case adsorptive bonding removes nutrients from groundwater solution and stores them on solid surfaces for recovery by soil microbes and transportation to green plants.

Biochar macropore structure is very complex and filled with pores, hollows, voids and discontinuities. Many of these are vestiges of the original structure of the plants the biochar came from. A section of the surface area in a piece of biochar is shown in Figures 57-60. These images were generously supplied

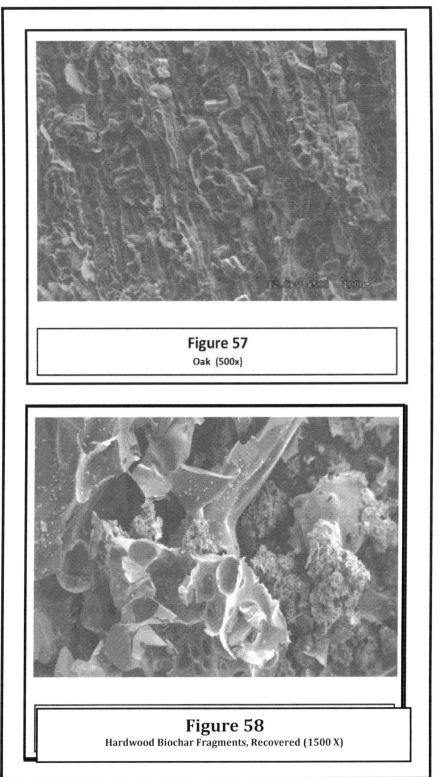

Figure 57
Oak (500x)

Figure 58
Hardwood Biochar Fragments, Recovered (1500 X)

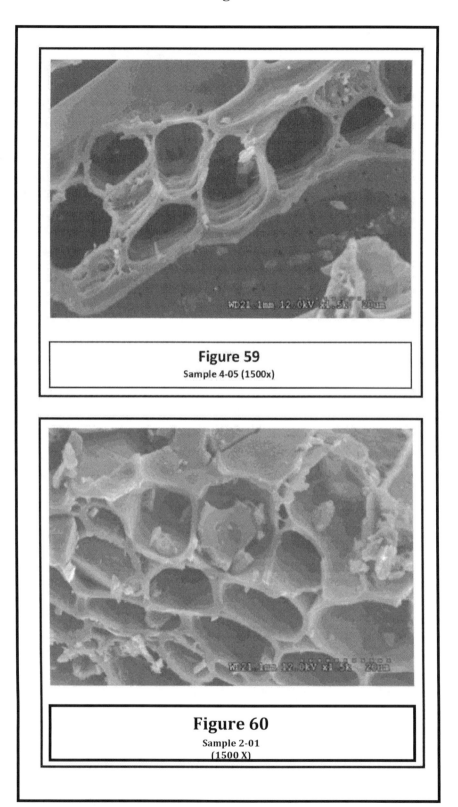

Figure 59
Sample 4-05 (1500x)

Figure 60
Sample 2-01
(1500 X)

by Kurt Spokas, Research Soil Scientist at the USDA-ARS Soil and Water Management Unit in Saint Paul Minnesota. Parts of this work were carried out at the Characterization Facility, University of Minnesota which receives partial support from NSF through the MRSEC program. Biochar pores are classed according to their size range. Micropores are those that are less than 2 nanometers in diameter. They are atomic in scale. A carbon atom is about 0.15 nanometers in diameter. Although they are individually small, they collectively possess most of the surface area of the biochar (about 60-80% of the total). The large surface area of the micropores gives them most of the adsorptive capacity of the biochar, but their small size makes them inaccessible to anything but relatively small molecular entities. The micropores adsorb mineral nutrients and small organic molecules such as amino acids and nucleic acids.

Midsized pores, or mesopores, are those between 2 and 50 nanometers in diameter, and they are much more accessible to larger molecular entities. Their size can accommodate biological macromolecules such as proteins and collections of peptide chains. This size molecule includes extremely active types of biological macromolecules such as enzymes that control the rate and direction of biological reactions.

Macropores are all those with diameters larger than 50 nanometers. These pores are accessible to soil microbes, some single cell types like bacteria and protozoa, and some multicellular types such as fungi, algae and nematodes. These living organisms in the macropores have access to the mineral nutrients in the micropores through the biomolecules in the mesopores. This chain of supply puts the stores of nutrients into a format that is very compatible with the needs of plants and microbes in the soil.

Fungal Mycorrhizae: This underground symphony of symbiosis supplies nutrients from biochar stores to photosynthetic plants in a more effective form than nutrients attain by themselves in the soil. A special example of the symbiotic relationships that develop is the life of soil fungi. Soil fungi consist of very large networks of root-like filaments underground. The mushroom represents only a tiny percentage of the overall mass of a fungus, and it is only the fruiting body or reproductive organ. The major portion of the fungal organism is in the root-like hyphae whose function is to scour the countryside for mineral nutrients. Hyphae often travel long distances, often bundled together in readily visible white bundles called mycorrhizae that can be seen traversing through the soil.

But because fungi are heterotrophs and have no chlorophyll or any other means of producing their own food for the energy needed to sustain their metabolism, they must go to some source of organic materials that have already been made for the purpose. Green plants, being autotrophs, make high energy sugars in their leaves through photosynthesis, which they use for their own metabolic consumption and as raw materials for construction of more plant material. Normally, green plants make excessive amounts of sugars beyond their own needs. The excess sugars circulate in the plant tissues including the roots where their presence contributes to the concentration differential between cellular contents and groundwater that enables osmotic pressure to deliver water back to the top of the plant

Fungi, searching for sugars to support their own metabolism, have evolved a way to cooperate with green plants to satisfy their needs. Because of their vast hyphal network absorbing mineral nutrients from wide areas in the soil, fungi have an excess of mineral nutrients to share. Because of their abundant photosynthetic capabilities, plants have an excess of sugars to share. Fungi have devised a way to penetrate plant roots and affect an exchange of nutrients for sugars that benefits both parties.

> Fungi, searching for sugars to support their own metabolism, have evolved a way to cooperate with green plants to satisfy their

Endomycorrhizal fungi have developed specialized organs called arbuscules that penetrate plant root cell walls and absorb sugars directly from inside the cell. Ectomycorrhizal fungi can absorb sugars from root tip exudates outside the plant cells. Both types acquire their energy from sugars obtained in this process, which they use to build new hyphae and to support their metabolism.

On the other end the micorrhyzae branch out into individual hyphae, which are strands of tissue only one cell wide and having lots of surface area through which to absorb nutrients. These hyphae are so small they can invade the macropores of a biochar particle and absorb the concentrated nutrient content from within the pores. In this way the fungi act as a direct route, a highway, for nutrient transfer between the biochar and green plants.

Soil bacteria also are stimulated by the presence of biochar. Most bacteria are heterotrophic and dependent on ready-made biomolecules for their energy supply. These bacteria are attracted to the richness of biomolecules adsorbed in the mesopores. They find not only a diet to their liking, but also cover that protects them from the grazing of predator species.

> Bacteria are attracted to the richness of biomolecules adsorbed in the mesopores. They find not only a diet to their liking, but also cover that protects them from the grazing of predator species.

Biochar Base of the Soil Food Web: The constant shedding of bacteria from biochar macropores creates a nutrient-rich zone surrounding the biochar to which plant roots and soil predatory microbes are attracted. This process establishes another link from the biochar to green plants. By these means and others biochar acts to adsorb nutrients from the soil and distribute them to green plants both nearby and far away. Bacteria and fungi are the bottom of the food chain and the building blocks of healthy ecosystems.

Biochar virtually takes the function of a bottom layer of the food chain being a substrate where bacteria and fungi can feed.

> Biochar takes the function of a bottom layer of the food chain being a substrate where bacteria and fungi can feed.

Once biochar adsorbs nutrients they are held securely against the tendency for dispersion into the groundwater or the atmosphere. This prevents the loss of nutrients from the soil through leaching or evaporation. It also reduces the conversion of nitrogen to nitrous oxide gas through the nitrification-denitrification bacterial process, reducing the release of this greenhouse gas, 300 times more potent than carbon dioxide, into the atmosphere.

While the adsorption of nutrients to biochar prevents their dispersion into the environment, it keeps them available for consumption by soil microbes and green plants that support the entire ecosystem.

Pre-charging Biochar with Nutrients: Adsorption of nutrients is a condensation reaction imposing order on the nutrients much as if they were being condensed from a gas or anchored into a crystal structure. A small Heat of adsorption will release the nutrients to satisfy the nutrient demand of plants. When the soil warms in the spring it floods the subterranean environment with nutrients that had remained adsorbed on biochar surfaces all winter.

To be most effective biochar should be saturated with plant nutrients before being applied to the soil. The affinity of biochar for plant nutrients can be so strong that it can tie up all the nutrients in the soil before the plants get to use them. This can have a negative effect on biomass production, so it is important to satiate the biochar to equilibrium with the environment before applying it to field or forest. Fortunately the adsorptive properties of biochar make it useful in many ways that can satisfy its nutrient demand.

> To be most effective biochar should be saturated with plant nutrients before being applied to the soil.

Other Uses For Biochar: Elemental carbon is a nutritional supplement. Pharmaceutical companies make charcoal dosages to relieve digestive disorders. If biochar is fed to cows it improves their digestive health, sometimes resulting in better milk and beef production. When biochar fed cows are let out to pasture they spread the biochar (which is now filled with nutrients) across the pasture improving forage production. When biochar fed cows are kept in the barn, as they are during cold months in northern climates, the presence of biochar in the gut reduces flatulence and produces manure with less moisture content, lower odor levels and easier handling characteristics.

When biochar is mixed with bedding in stables and stalls it reduces odors, insects and diseases and improves handling characteristics of the used bedding. The bedding is then a more potent amendment when spread on the soil.

Biochar can also be used for treatment of wastes. It adsorbs ammonia and sulfur compounds. Liquid manure can be made virtually odor free by treatment with biochar. Brownfields soils can be reclaimed by applications of biochar. Wastewaters can be treated with biochar.

When biochar has been used in these ways it becomes charged with nutrients and equilibrated with the environment. It can then be used on fields and gardens with maximal results. Biochar that is applied directly in its raw state may take years to charge with nutrients, but treating it with fertilizer solutions may easily charge it.

Water Retention: Biochar is also retentive of water. Plants that have been treated with biochar will sustain good health in dry conditions during draughts. And because biochar drains well, the plants will also do better during periods of wetness including saturation.

> Plants that have been treated with biochar will sustain good health in dry conditions during draughts. And because biochar drains well, the plants will also do better during periods of wetness including saturation.

Biochar soaks up water (by a<u>b</u>sorption, not a<u>d</u>sorption). Water is drawn into pores by capillary action, which is stronger in smaller capillaries than in larger ones. So as the water is drawn into mesopores and micropores it is held more strongly than it is in the macropores. Water in the macropores drains away more easily leaving the smaller pores filled with water that is more tightly bound. The water is still available to plants, but physical forces less easily remove it. The larger pores are filled with oxygen (air), which helps the plants survive periods of inundation.

Reducing Dispersion: Mineral nutrients, oils and solvents, heavy metals and all kinds of contamination disperse and spread out in the soil matrix.

It's an expression of the Second Law. Dispersion reduces differentials as it increases entropy or uniformity.

But adsorption is a condensation reaction, removing the adsorbed materials from solution by attaching them to a solid surface. This increases differentials and decreases uniformity and entropy.

> Adsorption is a condensation reaction, removing the adsorbed materials from solution by attaching them to a solid surface. This increases differentials and decreases uniformity and entropy.

Heat Effects: Biochar making also releases large amounts of heat. Approximately two thirds of the heat produced by complete combustion is retained in the heat of combustion of the gas that is driven off in the production of biochar, heat that can be recovered by burning the gas and used to heat homes and businesses, do work or generate electricity. So the production of biochar can provide useful heat without consuming fossil fuels.

Growth Stimulation: The use of biochar stimulates increased production of biomass in an ecosystem. With the increase in biomass, atmospheric carbon dioxide is reduced, habitats are restored, and the entropy state of the earth is set on track again. If biochar can tip the entropy cycle toward production of biomass instead of reduction of it the world can be shifted toward order generation and climate stabilization once more.

In the agricultural context, biochar has been shown to be capable of increasing annual biomass generation from a few percentage points to hundreds of percent, far more than is necessary to swing the entropy cycle in favor of biomass production.

The beauty of controlling the climate through biomass production using biochar is that it is an entirely reversible process. If we should happen to find that we are shifting the production of biomass too far, and moving towards a new glaciation cycle, we can correct the problem by burning biomass, or biochar, to convert the fixed carbon back to CO_2 and increase the entropy again. We would then only have to find a use for the excess energy we would generate in the process. We have no shortage of uses for energy!

On the other hand, if we find we can cause deserts to bloom, the climate to stabilize, habitats to re-emerge, agricultural abundance to proliferate and global warming to recede; we can work on optimizing living conditions for all living inhabitants of Planet Earth.

Chapter Thirty Three References

[1] Bates, Albert: "The Biochar Solution, Carbon Farming and Climate Change": New Society Publishers, Gabriola Island, BC, Canada, Copyright 2010

[2] Stamets, Paul: "Mycellium Running – How Mushrooms Can Help Save the World": Ten Speed Press, Division of Random House, NY, NY, Copyright 2005

[3] Edwards, Clive A.; Lal, Rattan; Adden, Patric; Miller, Robert and House, Gar:"Sustainable Agricultural Systems": Soil and Water Conservation Society, Ankey, Iowa, Copyright 1990

[4] Gore, Al: "Our Choice - A Plan to Solve the Climate Crisis": Rhodale Press, Emmaus, PA, Copyright 2009

Chapter Thirty-Four

Making Biochar

Chapter Summary

This chapter discusses my own experience with making biochar through simple tin can methods and with more sophisticated thermal feedback control systems.

Chapter Thirty Four
Making Biochar

Making biochar is a relatively simple process. Wood that is heated to 100°C begins to dry as the water it contains evaporates. When all the water is gone the temperature rises further until the wood reaches about 200°C at which point it begins to decompose.

The decomposition is a result of increasing thermal agitation of the wood molecules to the point where fragments of molecules fly off and become independent moieties or smaller molecules. The decomposition products are primarily low molecular weight gases, but some are liquids at room temperature and some are even solid particles, or smoke.

The decomposition gases are small gas molecules like carbon monoxide (CO), hydrogen (H), Methane (CH_4) and other flammable components as well as some carbon dioxide (CO_2), a non-flammable gas and larger molecules such as condensable gases and smoke. The mixture, called synthesis gas, or syngas, is an energy intensive combustible gas.

At first the syngas is produced at a concentration below the combustible limit as discussed in Chapter Eighteen on Page 264 & 265, too small to support combustion. But at a temperature of about 225°C the mixture becomes combustible and will burn if an ignition source is present. When the temperature reaches 250 to 300°C the syngas combustion becomes self-sustaining, once ignition occurs the gas will continue to burn until the gasification is complete.

At low temperatures, below self-sustaining levels, the process is Smokey, but as soon as sustainability is reached all smoke is consumed in a clean-burning flame. A pilot light can provide continuous ignition, which reduces smoke production during the pre-self-sustaining phases.

Thermal decomposition at low temperatures is an endothermic process requiring the input of heat to break molecular bonds and release gaseous products. Beyond about 300°C the wood releases some of its oxygen content, which reacts with the syngas producing heat and making the reaction exothermic. The heat release will drive the carbonization reaction to completion without further oxygen or energy input.

Making biochar from wood is an easy process because the syngas can be ignited to provide the heat that is needed to gasify more wood. If the oxygen input is controlled, the gases that are released will consume the excess oxygen before it can attack the carbon. A simple reactor configuration that accomplishes all of these ends is the top-lit-up-draft (TLUD) reactor.

TLUD can be made out of a steel can by punching holes in the bottom to

Figure 61
A One Can TLUD

allow a draft of incoming air for combustion of the wood. Holes are also provided about 2/3 of the way up the sides to provide additional air to combust the gases released. A typical one can TLUD is shown in Figure 61

This simple can, will carbonize biomass batches of about a half can full. A second can, with the ends removed, may be placed atop the first to provide increased residence time in a separate, secondary, combustion chamber. This allows the first can (reaction chamber) to process a full batch. It also provides a taller stack that increases the draft pulling air through the container and speeding up the process while stabilizing the

423

combustion and reducing the smoke output. A typical TLUD with a separate secondary combustion chamber is shown in Figures 62 & 63.

Air drawn into the TLUD reactor through the perforated bottom plate is used in combustion of a portion of the biomass fuel. This provides the

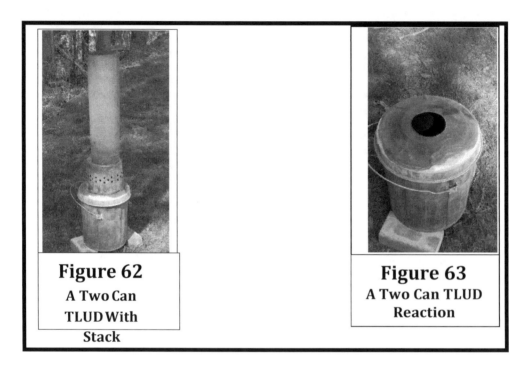

Figure 62
A Two Can
TLUD With
Stack

Figure 63
A Two Can TLUD
Reaction

heat necessary to gasify more biomass, and soon the gaseous product of the process is continuously burning while the carbon biochar product is left unconsumed. As more air becomes available the increased heat release carbonizes biomass further down into the reactor. The reaction with the syngas quickly consumes the oxygen protecting the biochar from being oxidized to ash. By the time the reacting layer reaches the bottom of the reactor, the entire biomass charge has been converted to biochar.

Quenching the Reaction: Once the reacting layer has reached the bottom of the reactor it is important to quench the entire mass of hot charcoal. This can be achieved by dousing the reaction chamber with cold water. This method is superior to simply shutting off the air because the reacting mass of charcoal retains heat for a long time, and it may reignite unless and until after it has thoroughly cooled. Once the reacting mass has been thoroughly quenched with water you can be sure that the reaction has ceased, and the wetted biochar is safe to handle and store and to use with little or no risk to health or property.

The heat of the reacting charcoal will flash-vaporize the quench water at first, creating a violent escape of steam and a hazard of scalding. Care should be taken to use plenty of cold quench water and to keep clear of the escaping steam.

Reactor Design Variables

Aspect Ratio: The most common choice of a reactor container is a tin coated steel can. A #10 can is about 4.25 inches in diameter by 7 inches high on the straight side. This gives an aspect ratio of 7/4.25 or 1.65. A smaller aspect ratio promotes more mixing of combustion gasses while a larger aspect ratio promotes more laminar, unmixed flow. Laminar flow is most effective and should be encouraged in the reactor design. Larger aspect ratios are better than smaller ones.

Bottom Open Area: Bottom holes should be small enough to retain the biomass fuel within the reactor, but large enough to admit the necessary air flow, and not so large that the biochar product burns. If the holes are too big, the biomass charge will fall out the bottom of the reactor. For fuel of small particle size, such as wood pellets, the holes must be small but numerous. For larger chips or chunks, the holes may be quite large, up to perhaps an inch or so in diameter.

I have used holes as small as 5/32 inch in diameter placed on 1 inch centers. Such an arrangement gives an open-area-to-total-area ratio of about .02. This appears to be about the minimum open area for good char production. This hole size was chosen for wood pellet fuel.

At open area ratios much smaller than .02 the amount of air admitted may be too small to sustain carbonization. Such a system may produce a lot of smoke but not enough syngas to sustain secondary combustion. Larger open areas will allow more combustion air to enter the reactor consuming the syngas and releasing enough heat to promote more gasification. The excess released syngas will discharge to the secondary combustion chamber to react with the secondary air.

Very large open area ratios will produce such a conflagration within the reactor that it will consume the carbon fraction of the fuel as well as the syngas leaving nothing but ash remaining.

The range of open areas that will produce good, continuous , sustainable process conditions appears to be quite large. The amount of gas released by carbonization will react with the incoming air, releasing more heat and carbonizing more biomass. Excess oxygen appears to be discharged to the secondary chamber before it can oxidize much biochar. Only after the gasification reaction is complete do you start losing biochar to oxidation.

The whole system is somewhat self-regulating across a wide spectrum of operating conditions. But if gas velocity gradients in the reactor get more than so high, it is possible for the carbon fraction to begin to oxidize resulting in decreased biochar yield and, in the extreme case, no biochar at all.

Secondary Combustion Chamber

The heat required to char biomass is really quite small compared to the heat content of the syngas released in the carbonization reaction. As a result there is a lot of unburned gas left over which escapes the carbonization chamber and goes to the secondary combustion chamber. Air that is drawn into the secondary chamber sustains combustion of the syngas.

Syngas combustion is a gas-gas reaction that is faster, more complete and efficient than the gas-solid reaction going on in the gasification reactor. Therefore, on a BTU basis the secondary combustion chamber can be smaller than the primary reactor. But the heat release from the combustion of the syngas is so much greater than the heat release from the gasification reaction that it is best to have at least as much reaction volume in the secondary chamber as in the carbonization reactor.

The amount of air required to support secondary combustion is also larger than the air required in the carbonization reactor. The total open area provided for secondary air intake should be twice the area provided in the carbonization reactor. The exact ratio is not critical because any unburned syngas that exits the secondary chamber will continue to burn in the ambient air at the system discharge.

Also gas flows are to a considerable degree controlled by the exit temperature and the height of the stack as will be discussed below.

Stack

The biochar reactor system can be fitted with a stack that will produce a draft that will draw additional air into the system. The taller the stack, the greater the draft produced and the more air will be drawn into the system. Sometimes, if the system has been built with intake holes that are too small and cannot take in enough air giving lackluster performance, additional stack will increase the air flow and improve performance.

Other Process Configurations

The TLUD biochar maker is just one of several configurations that can be designed for different applications depending on fuel type, heat recovery, and syngas use.[1] A TLUD is simple and it makes biochar as it produces heat. It has no controls on it to make adjustments for variations in operating conditions.[23] I call methods like these "Light it, and let it rip" methods. They are quite reliable, cheap and simple.

These methods utilize the heat from combustion of part of the biomass to gasify the rest of the biomass. There is plenty of excess heat for recovery if the application has a need for heat and if the operator has enough technical expertise to utilize it.

These methods discharge a mixture of combustion gasses and syngas from the same opening. These mixed gases exit at a lower temperature having lower thermal potential and lower purity than a discharge of syngas alone would have. Greater heat recovery is possible if the syngas is collected separately from the mixed waste gases.

Indirect Heating

Another process configuration is to remove a slipstream of the syngas which is burned to provide heat to carbonize the biomass while the majority of the syngas is used to provide heat for some other purpose. This arrangement recovers the heat of combustion of some of the syngas to carbonize the biochar, but it keeps the bulk of the syngas separate from the combustion gas. The bulk of the syngas is made available in its purest form to provide heat for some other purpose. This process configuration utilizes a larger proportion of the heating value of the syngas.

Neither of the two process configurations described has any control over the quality of the product syngas or the carbonization rate. The carbonization reaction simply proceeds at a rate depending upon geometry of the equipment and the characteristics of the biomass material such as heat content, particle size, thermal conductivity, etc.

The process of choice, for me, separates the heat requirement for carbonization completely from the heat released by combustion of the syngas. I use an electrically heated reactor to accomplish the carbonization reaction. My tests with this kind of process indicate that carbonization can be accomplished with an energy input on the order of 2% of the heat released by combustion of the syngas. This makes the cost of the electricity minor compared to the heat released by the process.

This choice of process configuration also isolates the carbonizing biomass from all external gas flows, eliminating the requirement for process heat to elevate inlet air to process temperatures. Since inlet air is roughly 80% nitrogen which has no function in the carbonization reaction, it is a big drain on process heat. Carbonization without air throughput therefore produces a big boost in process efficiency. The insulated reactor with a short stack/secondary combustion chamber is shown in Figure 64.

Figure 64
Electrically Heated
Reactor

Also, externally heated carbonization appears to become exothermic in that it utilizes some of the oxygen content of the biomass molecules to produce carbon monoxide and carbon dioxide that are higher oxidation states. This process releases a lot of energy that drives the carbonization reaction. My experiments show that in the range of 250-400° C the carbonization reaction becomes self-sustaining, requiring no additional energy input. The electrical energy input is only required to provide thermal start-up conditions, after which the process proceeds without any supply of outside energy or oxygen. The operating carbonizer, spewing flame from the stack is shown in Figure 65.

Figure 65
Electrically Heated
Reactor in Operation

Finally, the quality of the biomass supplied to the carbonization reactor is not always easy to control. Moisture levels may vary from less than 10% to more than 50%. The higher moisture levels are detrimental to the carbonization process because they negatively affect heat balances, process kinetics and reaction temperatures. Supplementing process conditions by adding electrical energy when needed smooths out operational fluctuations and improves process continuity. Still, for process efficiency sake, it is important to use only the driest high quality biomass to feed the carbonization reactor.

The carbonization reaction simply proceeds at a rate depending upon geometry of the equipment and the characteristics of the biomass material such as heat and moisture content, particle size, thermal conductivity, etc.

Process Equipment

The reactor I use is a heavily insulated, electrically heated, temperature controlled batch reactor. The unit will hold about a gallon of wood chips or other biomass. The heating element is an 8 inch diameter ceramic fiber cylinder with built in high temperature electrical heating elements. The apparatus is capable of operating at temperatures of up to 1200° C.

My reactor fits into the cylindrical heating unit with about ½ inch to spare all around. Radiative heat transfer drives the process energy from the coils to the reaction vessel.

Temperature control is provided by a K-type thermocouple in the reactor discharge that transmits a signal to an on-off (fuzzy logic) temperature controller on the power supply to the coils. Input voltage to the reactor coils is controlled manually by an auto-transformer.

Process Cycle

A typical batch is started by activating the voltage control power supply, usually set at 60-to-80 volts. The temperature starts to rise immediately, and reaches 100° C in about 15 minutes. By half an hour into the batch smoke is beginning to come out of the secondary combustion chamber. Sometime in the next 10 minutes or so the smoke is becoming thick enough to burn. A propane lighter stuck into the smoke plume will light it off, and soon it will burn with a smokeless flame.

This all happens before the reactor discharge temperature reaches 200° C, but because the temperature sensor is placed in the reactor discharge, points closer to the coils are probably experiencing higher temperatures. The electrical temperature controller is now turning off the power input regularly and frequently and for more and more extended periods of time. When the reactor reaches about 275-300° C, the power supply can be shut down manually, and the temperature continues to rise to somewhere in the 400-450° C range. At this point the process enters a period of stable operation for 30-45 minutes with no external energy input.

Eventually, the flame emerging from the secondary combustion chamber begins to diminish. The color changes from yellow to more bluish. Finally, the flame goes out, and the reactor begins to cool.

As the reactor cools, the power controller kicks in again keeping the char hot. I like to soak the char at 400° C for an hour or so, to assure that the carbonization reaction is complete. This may be especially important if large chunks of biomass are being carbonized. Finally, the power is shut off and the reactor is allowed to cool.

Quenching

Even as the reactor continues to cool, the biochar continues to glow, indicating that a combustion reaction is continuing as oxygen leaks into the system. At some point, I quench the reaction with water to stop any further combustion and cool the reactor and its contents to the point where it is safe to remove it from the heating furnace and to discharge its contents.

The quenching process stabilizes an actively oxidizing batch of biochar. The same could be done by blanketing the reactor with inert gas such as nitrogen or by simply sealing off the reactor from its oxygen source, the air. This will stop the reaction and, over time allow the reactor to cool. I prefer the water-quench process because it dissipates the temperature of the reacting material immediately to well below 100° C.

Chapter Thirty Four
Making Biochar

The Product

This process gives me a gallon of clean, dull black biochar, each piece shaped exactly like the wood chip, branch, or compacted pellet it came from including the details of the grain of the original wood. In addition I have released about 40,000 BTU of heat into the atmosphere, heat that could be recovered to heat living space or hot water or to drive an energy consuming process.

Storage and Handling

The adsorptive capacity of dry char is such that it will adsorb oxygen from the air, releasing heat and becoming warm as it does so. The adsorption sites are activated by the adsorbed oxygen and may become more reactive with other materials as well. Dry biochar should be kept away from flammable materials such as solvents, fuels, etc.

In some cases, the adsorbed oxygen and the heat of adsorption combined may be enough to re-ignite the char, causing a fire hazard. Even if the carbon is not re-ignited, the storage space can become depleted in oxygen and can present a health hazard to those entering bulk storage areas. Storage in plastic bags is a preferred method of reducing oxygen uptake and the related fire and health hazards.

Dry char is dusty and can cause damage to lung tissues. A water quench reduces the hazards associated with dust including the potential for lung damage and/or dust explosions. It also reduces loss of carbon from wind at the time of application.

A water quench can also be a carrier of dissolved mineral nutrients which can charge up the adsorption sites in the biochar and prepare it to act as a source of nutrients for plants. If the biochar is to be used as a soil additive, this precharging can be an essential practice to enhance its function.

Due to the adsorptive and dusting properties of biochar, the best way to store it is in a wetted condition in a covered, but open – or well ventilated storage area. Bagging is helpful because it prevents oxygen from getting to the biochar and prevents it from drying out. Sometimes it is stored in bulk in an open pile, an acceptable means of storage, but causing minor losses in effectiveness because of leaching of nutrients from the product.

In its wetted state, biochar can be successfully handled in equipment intended for application of similar soil amending materials.

Choosing a Fuel. The properties of the biochar produced by the carbonization system depend very heavily on the type of fuel chosen. Since it is our premise that our planet is already suffering from a shortage of biomass, the ideal feed material would be recycled waste biomass. However, it is important to use only biomass that has not been contaminated by contact with toxic materials. In addition, since structure is such an important part of the functioning of biochar, it is important to use biomass that retains the maximum amount of its original structure.

Processed wood products such as paper and compressed products such as wood pellets in which the macrostructure has been destroyed are not expected to produce the same high quality biochar as virgin wood products will. My testing of biochar in small scale agricultural test plots seems to confirm this observation. More testing work in this area is needed in order to determine the general trend.

Processed wood products in which the macrostructure has been destroyed are not expected to produce the same high quality biochar as virgin wood products will.

Compacted lingo-cellulosic fuels are often stabilized by adhesion from their own lignin content. When these fuels are heated, the lignin bonding agent may soften allowing the product to re-expand, drastically reducing the ability of air and syngas to flow through the equipment. This property can be disastrous to process parameters, and it must be accounted for in the design of biochar reaction equipment.

My preferred feed material is wood chips that have been prepared for use as fuel in biomass energy systems. Ideally they should have been dried to 10 to 15% moisture content.

Chapter Thirty Four
Making Biochar

An emerging product that may be appropriate for biochar making is grass biomass. Grass biomass pellets work very well in our test apparatus. Care must be taken to allow for expansion of the pellets or plugs in the biochar reactor. The resulting biochar appears to be well suited for use in agriculture. It remains to be seen whether it is effective at stimulating plant growth in the field. [4]

Chapter Thirty Four References

Young, Daniel A.: "Entropy vs. Structure in Biochar" Proceedings of the National Biochar Initiative at the University of Massachusetts at Amherst (2013)

Taylor, Paul:and Hugh McLaughlin "The Biochar Revolution, Transforming Agriculture & Environment" Global Publishing Group, Copyright 2010

Ok, Yong Sik and Uchimiya, Sophie: "Biochar Production, Characterization and Applications (Urbanization, Industrialization and the Environment)":CRC Press, Boca Raton, FL; Copyright 2016

Bates, Albert: "The Biochar Solution, Carbon Farming and Climate Change": New Society Publishers, Gabriola Island, B.C., Canada; Copyright 2010

Chapter Thirty Five

How Does Biochar Work?

Chapter Summary

Biochar is a highly structured material derived from the biological structures in biomass. Carbonizing these structures makes them rigid and resistant to decay giving permanence and resilience to the functioning structures.

Biochar is able to function in many of the same ways that biomass does, but passively. Living systems surrounding biochar and supplying critical components that biochar doesn't have, such as ATP, the key to active energy transport in biological systems, can achieve a certain combination of functioning and longevity that neither could achieve by itself.

This chapter elaborates on the way these processes work.

Biochar is a breakdown product of the sugar polymers that make up plant tissues. The most abundant of these sugar polymers, cellulose, makes up the rigid portions of woody biomass stems. The chemical formula for cellulose is:

$$(C_6H_{12}O_6)_n$$

Where $C_6H_{12}O_6$ is a sugar group and n is the number of groups in a large polymer molecule, often in the 1000's.

Other types of sugar polymers such as lignin and hemicellulose are less fibrous and make up the adhesive matrix that holds cellulose strands together. All of these substances are sugar polymers made up of the same chemical elements, carbon (44%), hydrogen (6%) and Oxygen (50%).

There is more oxygen in wood than there is carbon. There are an identical number of carbon atoms as oxygen atoms, but the oxygen atoms are heavier.

Sugar molecules like the one shown in Figure 66 are the result of photosynthesis. Carbon dioxide from the air combines with water brought up from the roots to make sugar molecules. The photosynthesis reaction is:

$$6CO_2 + 6H_2O \longrightarrow \quad + 6O_2$$

Sugar molecules can bond to each other, releasing water and creating molecules that contain multiple sugar groups. Such a reaction is shown in Figure 67

Fischer Projection

Haworth Formula

| **Figure 66**

Sugar Molecule | A sugar is a 6 carbon chain that has an oxygen molecule connecting the second carbon and the last carbon.

Each Carbon has an alcohol (OH) group attached to it.

Sometimes the alcohol group is on the same side as the neighboring alcohol group: sometimes the opposite side. This leads to many different kinds of sugars.

Chemists name the sugar with names ending in "ose." Glucose is a single sugar unit. Sucrose (table sugar) is a dimer consisting of two sub-units. Cellulose is a very large sugar polymer consisting of many sub-units aligned into a very long molecule.

The sugar molecule is represented by the Fischer Projection (left). In actuality, the carbon-oxygen bond is short, like the other bonds, and forces the carbon chain to bend into a ring configuration more like the Haworth Formula (right). |

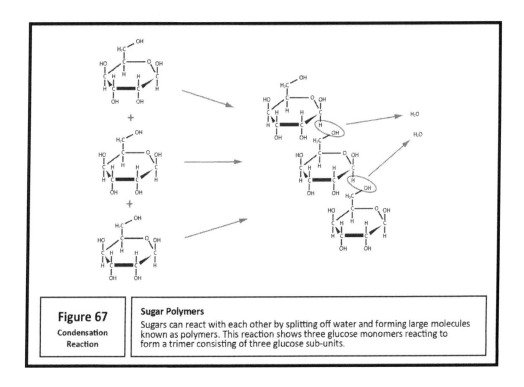

| **Figure 67**

Condensation Reaction | **Sugar Polymers**
Sugars can react with each other by splitting off water and forming large molecules known as polymers. This reaction shows three glucose monomers reacting to form a trimer consisting of three glucose sub-units. |

Two sugar groups create a dimer, three, a trimer, and many, a polymer. Polymers of sugar groups are called polysaccharides. Cellulose consists of long fibers of thousands of sugar molecules strung together in long straight chains of thousands of units. Such a molecule is shown in Figure 68.

When these mixtures of sugar polymers are subjected to high temperatures, they begin to vibrate through thermal agitation. The vibration becomes more intense as the temperature escalates until it reaches an energy intensity great enough to break molecular bonds. When this occurs, smaller groupings of atoms

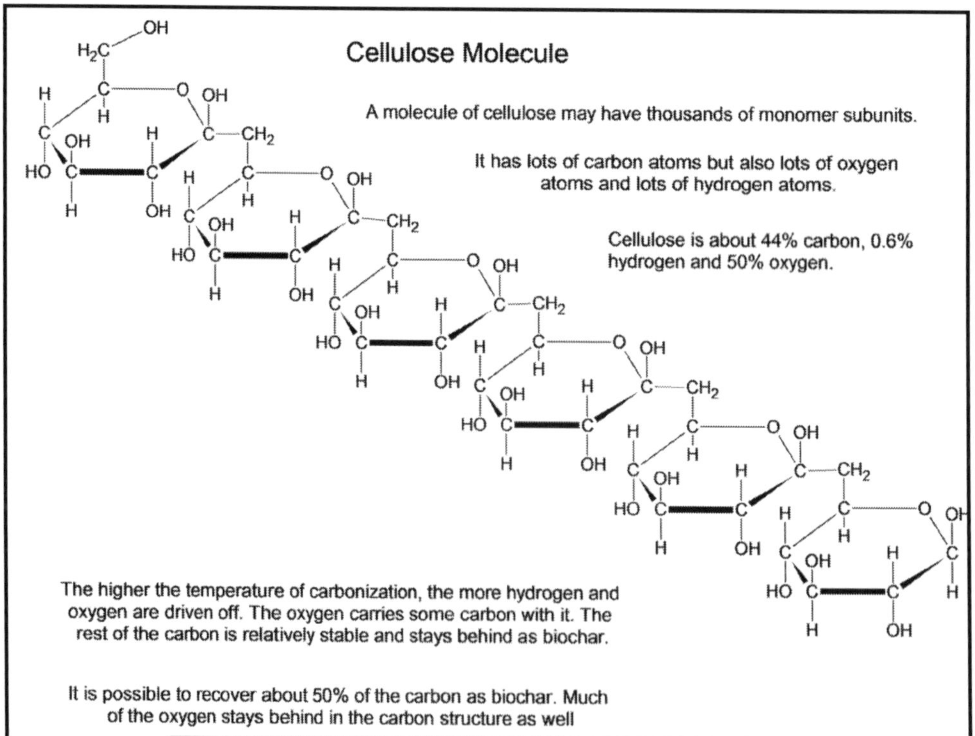

Cellulose Molecule

A molecule of cellulose may have thousands of monomer subunits.

It has lots of carbon atoms but also lots of oxygen atoms and lots of hydrogen atoms.

Cellulose is about 44% carbon, 0.6% hydrogen and 50% oxygen.

The higher the temperature of carbonization, the more hydrogen and oxygen are driven off. The oxygen carries some carbon with it. The rest of the carbon is relatively stable and stays behind as biochar.

It is possible to recover about 50% of the carbon as biochar. Much of the oxygen stays behind in the carbon structure as well

Figure 68
Long Chain Cellulose Molecule

break off from the polymer chain and dissipate in the surroundings as syngas.

The first bonds to break are hydrogen bonds that hold long cellulose strands to each other. Next to break are the covalent bonds that link the sugar groups together in the chains. And finally, the bonds that hold the carbon atoms into their ring formations may be broken or rearranged.

The result of this thermal rearrangement is a carbon-rich structure consisting of rings containing six carbon atoms that bond together in sheets one atom thick. The sheets are very stable and tough, but the bonds between the sheets are very delicate and easily broken. This structure is called graphite.

Biochar tends to relax its structure toward the graphite form when it is heated to very high temperatures. The high temperatures drive off the oxygen atoms that are in the mixture leaving a carbon that is ever purer and denser. But even biochar that has been heated to $600 - 800°$ C retains some of its oxygen content. The oxygen atoms are not the same size as the carbon atoms, and so they tend to destroy the regularity of the crystal formation of the carbon matrix. Wherever there is an oxygen atom the crystal in the structure, the chemical bonds are deformed creating defects in the structure. It is these defects in the structure that act as adsorption sites for biological nutrients.

> Wherever there is an oxygen atom the crystal structure, the chemical bonds are deformed creating defects in the structure. It is these defects in the structure that act as adsorption sites for biological nutrients.

Oxygen atoms differ from carbon atoms in ways other than size. They have an ability to polarize their bonds with carbon, a property known as electronegativity. The nucleus of an oxygen atom contains more protons than the nucleus of a carbon atom. This fact gives the oxygen end of a carbon-oxygen bond more power to attract electrons to its end of the bond. The oxygen atoms, therefore, are centers of negative charge throughout the carbon matrix. These sites become a point of attraction for positively charged ions (cations).

> The oxygen atoms are sites of negative charge throughout the carbon matrix. These sites become a point of attraction for positively charged ions (cations).

Cations include many of the mineral macronutrients that green plants need for their metabolism, such as ammonium (NH_4^+), Potassium (K^+), calcium (Ca^{++}), Magnesium (Mg^{++}), Iron (Fe^{++}) and manganese (Mn^{++}).

> Cations include many of the mineral macronutrients that green plants need for their metabolism, such as ammonium (NH_4^+), Potassium (K^+), calcium (Ca^{++}), Magnesium (Mg^{++}), Iron (Fe^{++}) and Manganese (Mn^{++}).

On the opposite end of the carbon-oxygen bond is a site of positive charge that becomes an active site that attracts negatively charged ions (anions). Some examples include: phosphorous (PO_4^{---}), Sulphur (SO_4^{--}) and Boron

> On the opposite end of the carbon-oxygen bond is a site of positive charge that becomes a an active site that attracts negatively charged ions (anions). Some examples include: phosphorous (PO_4^{---}), Sulphur (SO_4^{--}) and Boron (BO_3^{---}), all essential plant nutrients.

(BO_3^{---}), all essential plant nutrients.

Plant nutrient ions are fairly small groups that can access the micropores of the biochar structure, and so they have access to a very large activated surface area.

The carbon structure that is left after pyrolysis is laced with active sites caused by the oxygen atoms that are left within the carbon crystal structure. Each of

> The carbon structure that is left after pyrolysis is laced with active sites that form a reservoir of nutrition available to serve nearby plants when the nutrients are released.

the sites is polarized due to the electronegativity of the oxygen atoms, and due to the polarity of the bonds dissolved mineral nutrients are attracted to the active sites where they are held by electrostatic attraction forming a reservoir of nutrition available to serve nearby plants when the nutrients are released.

The capacity of biochar to adsorb plant nutrients is one measure of its value as a soil amendment. Biochar picks up nutrients from the surrounding soil and retains them, preventing their dispersion and loss into the environment.

However, when the weather warms in the spring the biochar absorbs an amount of energy greater than the heat of adsorption of the mineral nutrients, thus releasing the nutrients into the soil. When plants become active in the growing season they draw on the reserves in the soil, which depresses those reserves drawing even more nutrients out of the biochar. This event complements the release of nutrients from the biochar. At the end of the season, when plants stop growing or die back, they release their nutrient load to the soil. At the same time the weather is cooling, drawing energy from the biochar, which stimulates the biochar to adsorb the nutrients all over again.

Biochar treated soil contains an active, localized nutrient recirculation loop that exchanges the nutrients between two stable phases, the charged biochar and the growing plants, using the soil as an unstable intermediary phase. In the soil phase the

> Biochar treated soil contains an active, localized nutrient recirculation loop that exchanges the nutrients between two stable phases where the nutrients are retained and prevented from washing away to become pollutants in the environment.

nutrients are susceptible to depletion, but in the biochar and in the plants the nutrients are retained and prevented from washing away to become pollutants in the environment. Plants take up nutrients at warmer temperatures in the spring, when biochar releases them. They use them in their metabolism as they grow. Later on in the fall when the weather cools the plants release nutrients and the biochar adsorbs them due to the lower temperatures keeping their concentration in the soil low enough to minimize losses to the environment.

The localized nutrient recirculation loop prevents loss of nutrients and pollution of the groundwater while relieving the grower from the need to keep periodically adding nutrients to the soil.

Water Retention

The porous nature of the biochar carbon structure allows it to absorb (not adsorb) large quantities of water. Absorption is a function of structural properties and the surface tension of the water. Water is drawn into the pores of biochar in inverse proportion to the size of the pores. Smaller pores draw in water more strongly and hold it more tightly than larger pores do. Large pores draw in water when it is plentiful, relieving flooding conditions and saturation. Smaller pores draw in water, hold it more tightly, and release it more stringently in dryer periods when plants need it most.

As the soil dries after a rain event water empties from macropores by percolation into the soil keeping the soil from drying out. As drought stress increases during rainless days in the summer, water that has been more strongly held in the mesopores is progressively extracted. After the water in the mesopores is gone, the water in the micropores is finally removed.

This sequential removal of water from the pores of the char supplies moisture continuously over a prolonged period. Once the water in the macropores and in the interstices between the biochar particles is replaced with air the biochar becomes a source of air to the roots of the plants that reduces the effects of waterlogging.

> The sequential removal of water from the pores of the char supplies moisture continuously over a prolonged period.

Biochar Pretreatment

Freshly made char has no reservoir of adsorbed nutrients with which to enhance the growth of plants. Nutrients must be acquired through contact with the soil. But most soils are lacking in certain nutrients needed for optimum plant health, and so while the biochar is acquiring a reservoir of nutrients it is likely to be competing with already deprived plants for the same nutrients. This effect has been observed in tests where adding biochar to the soil led to reduced growth rates and diminished productivity. The effect of adding biochar usually improves with time as the biochar comes into equilibrium with the soil and acquires a reservoir of plant nutrients.

One way to minimize the competitive effect for nutrients is to apply the biochar to the land surface in the fall, after the harvest season. This allows the productivity of the plants to be completed before the biochar is added, avoiding the competitive conflict. In the fall, when the growing season is over and the plants begin to decay, the nutrients from decaying plant residues will be captured by the biochar to be stored through the winter and made available for new crop growth in the spring.

Another approach to the biochar competition problem is to treat the biochar with fertilizer solutions before spreading it on the soil. The active sites on the biochar matrix will adsorb the available nutrients from the fertilizer solution to the point of saturation, and the nutrient reservoir will be established before it is applied to the soil.

biochar may be treated with fertilizer solutions before spreading it on the soil. The active sites on the biochar matrix will adsorb the available nutrients from the fertilizer solution to the point of saturation, and the nutrient reservoir will be established before it is applied to the soil.

Pretreatment of the biochar in this way offers the opportunity to customize it for specific applications. One such possible application might alleviate a problem discussed by Dr. Edward O. Wilson in his book, "Half the Earth – Our Planet's Fight for Life"[1]. Wilson describes the scrublands of Southwestern Australia as one of the "Best places in the Biosphere", but he describes a problem in these words:

> *From Esperance, on the southwestern coast east to the edge of the Nullarbor Plain lies one of the earth's richest endemic floras. Possessing a mild Mediterranean climate and molybdenum deficient soil that excludes species other than those adapted to the deficiency, the scrublands have evolved much like the flora of an oceanic island. Unfortunately for the biodiversity of Australia and that of the world generally, molybdenum added to the soil makes it arable, and a large fraction of the scrubland has been converted to farm and cattle ranches accompanied by incursions of invasive weeds.*

Situations like this might be resolved by treatment with biochar pretreated with molybdenum. It would keep the molybdenum adsorbed on its surface , reducing contamination of adjacent lands, and it would minimize the amount of molybdenum that would have to be used to make the soils of the area arable.

Pretreatment of biochar is a practice that has implications far beyond adsorption of plant nutrients. The macropores of the biochar can be charged with bacteria and spores of symbiotic fungi to establish a community of soil microorganisms ready to establish itself when the biochar is spread across the surface of the soil. Mesopores might be induced to contain amino acids, polypeptides, and even whole enzymes that can mediate reactions between adsorbed nutrients and live biota in the macropores and in the soil.

Pretreatment of biochar is a practice that has implications far beyond adsorption of plant nutrients. The macropores of the biochar can be charged with bacteria and spores of symbiotic fungi to establish a community of soil microorganisms ready to establish itself when the biochar is spread across the surface of the soil.

A tremendous amount of testing and research is being done to determine the optimal use for biochar in all such agricultural and environmental applications.

Sanitation Applications

Biochar is useful in controlling odors, improving handling characteristics, absorbing liquids, sanitizing surfaces and controlling bacteria, fungi and insect infestations in agricultural environments. Treatment of manure with biochar removes odors and improves handling characteristics in dairy and animal farms. Biochar added to animal bedding removes moisture, absorbs odors, and improves handling characteristics.

Added to animal feed, biochar improves digestive health and function. Animals that have eaten biochar digest their food better and produce less methane emissions during the digestive process. There are implications that they utilize the nutrients and calories in their food better as well.

In general, manures from animals fed with biochar are dryer, less odorous, and easier to handle, and contain more stable carbon per pound than manures from other animals. Biochar has been fed to cattle, sheep, goats, birds, and even humans with positive health effects.

The carbon from biochar is fully charged with nutrients and microbiota during its passage through the gut of an animal. If the animal is then pastured or ranged on the farm, the biochar is effectively spread over the farm surface increasing the carbon composition and function of the soil.

Biochar has been mixed with waste biomass to make an optimal mix for composting. The structure of biochar aids in maintaining moisture levels and air ratios to assure rapid aerobic breakdown of the compost. Nutrient and microbial content can be maintained by biochar loading. Oxidation rate and temperature are both increased by utilization of biochar, and the product has a higher proportion of stabilized, functional carbon.

Biochar has also been used in the treatment of wastewaters. It is particularly useful in the polishing of effluents from sewage treatment plants. Residual ionic species like nitrogen and phosphorous can be further reduced by adsorption onto biochar. The biochar can then be applied to agricultural soils to recycle the nutrient materials and to enhance the structure and cation exchange capacity of the soil.

Addition of biochar to activated sludge systems has the potential to stabilize operations and to improve the treatment efficiency of the process while improving the utility of the sludge produced.

The physical adsorption characteristics of biochar coupled with the interactions with biological components of the soil create micro-ecosystems within the soil matrix that store and manage nutrient supplies and environmental conditions. These properties of biochar tend to optimize conditions for biomass production and for stabilization and ordering of climate conditions.[2]

Chapter Thirty Five References

[1] Edward O. Wilson: "The Future of Life": Vintage Books, A Division of Random House, Inc., NY

[2] Simons, Charles A.: "Biochar: Chemical Composition, Soil Applications and Ecological Impacts": Nova Science Publishers, Inc. ; Copyright 2017

Chapter Thirty-Six

Photosynthesis and Evolution

Chapter Summary

Evolution is a constant attempt by living organisms to self-assemble in ways that are more advantageous in their environment. It is very expensive in terms of energy requirements. Except for this constant need to readjust to environmental constraints, an organism could be much more productive. The whole science of agriculture is an attempt to provide the maximally productive environment so that an organism can put the largest portion of its energy into production and the least energy into adjusting to its environment. This chapter will explore some of these ideas.

Chapter Thirty Six
Photosynthesis and Evolution

Photosynthetic plants have many needs that must be satisfied by conditions in their environment.[1] Each species grows best in a given temperature range, at a given light level and a given water potential. There are other requirements for nutrient levels, carbon dioxide levels, etc. In his book "Physiochemical and Environmental Plant Physiology"[2] Dr. Park S. Nobel discusses the use of an "environmental productivity index" to evaluate the growth rate (productivity) that can be expected under a given set of environmental conditions. He begins his discussion by referring to the three soil conditions above, water potential, light level and temperature. and he evaluates the effect of each condition independently of the others. This he does by measuring the growth rate of several plants growing in identical soils while holding the other two conditions constant.

By this technique a range of independent productivity indices can be established for each environmental factor. The index is given a value of 0 for the level at which no growth occurs, and a value of 1 for the level at which optimal growth is observed. Proportional values are given to growth rates at intermediate levels. Once the indices have been measured for all three environmental factors, water, temperature and light; it is found that an overall environmental productivity index can be calculated by multiplying the three factor indices together.

$$EPI = I(water) \times I(temperature) \times I(light)$$

Notice that if any of the individual indices falls to zero the whole EPI drops to zero, which is consistent with expectations. The EPI represents a percentage of the optimal growth that would occur under optimal conditions (when all indices have a value of 1.0).

This system of growth indices can be expanded to include nutrient indices, a CO_2 index, or any other type of environmental growth factor. It is a valuable predictor of productivity under varying environmental conditions. For instance, it can predict how much irrigation is needed to increase productivity by a given amount, or how warm a crop must be kept, or how much shade a species can tolerate, or what the effect of fertilizer addition will be on productivity and what nutrients the fertilizer should contain.

Natural field conditions are seldom optimal for photosynthetic productivity. An astute farmer may be able to double his production by irrigating and fertilizing his crops at the right time, protecting them from frost or shading them from harmful solar radiation. All of these practices have been very successful in boosting productivity in agricultural operations.

Other means of control of environmental variables are also used to successfully manage productivity of growing crops. Removal of competitive plant species by soil preparation and monocropping optimizes production of specific crops from a given land area. Removal of pests and predators by application of chemical; pesticides will keep crops from being consumed or contracting disease.

In each case productivity of one crop is improved at the sacrifice of biosystem function. Monocropping tends to be optimized by the elimination of competition. Natural biosystems become resilient because of competition. A mixture of competitive species is resilient because it adjusts its species mix to changes in the environmental conditions.

As the species mix changes in response to environmental conditions, mutations and other evolutionary modifications emerge. Some modifications are removed by natural selection while others are favored. New species emerge in response to competition in a changing environment.

A dichotomy is emerging in this discussion. Total biomass productivity, diversity, resiliency and evolution are encouraged by competition from many species, while agricultural mono-cropping productivity and profits are stimulated by removal of competition. As competing species are removed, the ecology becomes unproductive, unstable and static while agricultural productivity is being enhanced. A well-tuned agricultural system requires so much human input that a farmer has to work hard all day just to keep the cycle going. Still, it is highly productive of the specific crop being grown.

Chapter Thirty Six
Photosynthesis and Evolution

Because of the Second Law of thermodynamics, the conditions that have been modified for optimization of agricultural crops diffuse into the environment and cause unhealthy changes in the surrounding ecosystem. Crop enhancing activities and materials have to be redone over and over again as they diffuse away from the application area contaminating the surroundings and allowing the treated area to revert to natural conditions.

High total biomass productivity is necessary to provide ecological services. Diversity is required for evolutionary progress and resilience. Evolution and resiliency are essential to keeping the biosphere working. But they are very expensive conditions, requiring a large fraction of the plant's energy to maintain. These conditions can be eliminated in order to maximize the production of any one species. But a biosystem so abused declines in quality and productivity unless human input can be applied to maintain the services normally provided by the ecosystem. Human input is energy consuming and causes environmental degradation, both on site (on the farm) and at remote locations where the input materials are obtained.

High productivity of desirable species is always purchased at the expense of total biomass productivity and ecosystem diversity. Environmental diversity and total biomass productivity are required for ecosystem resiliency and stability.

As the human species dominates and then over-populates the earth, the production of food stresses natural biosystems more and more and total biomass declines. With the decline of productivity, biomass density, resilience and stability suffer. Climate patterns that have co-evolved with biomass for billions of years are unable to continue their ecological services.

Under conditions such as these, cycles of disorder emerge. Ordered ecosystems, ordered climate systems and thermal stability begin to mix together into homogeneity. This is the beginning of a period of high entropy or disorder in which temperatures across the surface of the earth equilibrate, tropical temperatures spread poleward and reservoirs of low entropy fresh water in the liquid and solid states are pushed back and diminished.

The equilibration of the earth also has grave consequences for the diversity of species. Species diversification is a result of diverse climates and diverse niches into which to evolve. If climate diversification is diminished, then species diversification is diminished along with it.

As climates equilibrate there is less and less imperative for divergence of species. When this happens, evolution is driven toward a more uniform climate system, and the spread of similar characteristics in successful species over wider areas becomes more of an imperative than adaptation to different climate conditions.

An important step in the development of agricultural productivity is the separation of crop production from natural ecosystems. There is a natural progression from gathering food entirely within natural ecosystems through modifying ecosystems to foster food production to producing food entirely independently of ecosystems. Currently normal practice is to modify natural ecosystems to optimize food production. Practices like plowing, fertilizing and irrigation convert whole ecosystems to food production.

A more recent development is to abandon ecosystems altogether and create the perfect environment for biomass production in an enclosed space. Practices like greenhouse production and hydroponics dispense with the ecosystem and establish an environment completely isolated from the natural surroundings and completely tailored to meet the needs of specific plants. Delivery systems for light, water, nutrients, carbon dioxide and all other needs are engineered into the modular growing system.

One such system, made by Williamson Greenhouses, reports growing the equivalent of an acre of greens in a 320 square foot box, an area yield enhancement of 136 times as much production per square foot as is attained in natural ecosystems. This represents a tremendous yield increase attributable to growing under carefully controlled conditions.

Chapter Thirty Six
Photosynthesis and Evolution

This tremendous increase in area yield is due to detaching the biomass production from the ecological services/evolution function. Plants that are thus relieved can produce vastly greater amounts of food biomass because they are not required to further evolve or to perform any ecosystem management services while maintaining food production of the farm.

If 100 such boxes were set up on two acres of a 100-acre farm, they could produce all the food the farm can produce on the hundred acres and allow 98 acres to remain in natural ecosystems to provide ecosystem services.

Much work remains to be done in this area. The point is that it is not necessary to damage the environment and deprive the planet of its biomass and its climate to produce food.

Chapter Thirty Six References

[1] Burger, William C.: "Complexity: The Evolution of the Earth's Biodiversity and the Future of Humanity": Promethius Books, Amherst, NY; Copyright 2016

[2] Nobel, Park S.: "Physicochemical and Environmental Plant Physiology": Academic Press, Inc., San Diego, CA.; Copyright 1991

Part Ten

Conclusions

Chapter Thirty-Seven

Order, its Origins and Accumulation

Chapter Summary

Energy flowing through a thermodynamic system produces order, not chaos. Entropy generated in the process is rejected from the system along with waste heat. The process that rejects entropy leaves an ordered system behind. Entropy is more mobile than order is. It disperses more rapidly, and when it does it leaves ordered systems in its wake.

It is not enough to know that entropy always increases in any thermodynamic process. It is necessary to understand that entropy, like any fluid medium, flows along a potential gradient. As it does so it produces all the ripples, eddies, waves, troughs and patterns of any flow system in steady state.

In such a state a system seeks to maximize entropy production rate, not entropy content. This is done by ejecting more entropy than the system creates, a state of affairs that can lead to very ordered systems. This chapter will review some of these ideas.

Chapter Thirty Seven
Order, its Origins and Accumulation

This final part of the book reviews some of the most important discoveries that I have made in doing my research. These are personal discoveries, not scientific breakthroughs, but they are important because they argue the reverse of certain long-standing scientific tenants from the past. People whose education is more than 20 to 30 years old may be surprised to find the arguments they learned in physics and thermodynamics being used to support conclusions that are nearly the reverse of what they learned in school.

Maybe even more important is the willingness of commercial scientists to jump to simplistic explanations for the natural phenomena being observed today. Warming and cooling cycles of our earth's climate are often attributed to cycles of incoming solar radiation or outgoing thermal radiation from earth to outer space. Without discrediting the importance of these "energy balance" interpretations, it is my intention to point out that modern research has emerged showing that it is important to include an understanding of how energy is utilized by ecosystems on earth, including how it is received, transferred, distributed and returned, in order to fully understand the mechanics of global warming.[1]

The Biomass Reservoir: In particular the production of biomass on earth has significant effects on the thermodynamic condition of the surface of the planet. Biomass modifies surface convection, which is the major means of heat transfer and distribution on earth.

While a thermodynamic heat balance based on the First Law is essential, the kinetic mechanisms that transfer heat are totally unaddressed by such a heat balance. These mechanisms are based on the Second Law, and they determine the distribution of thermal energy everywhere. In the case of biomass, the biosphere and the climate co-evolve toward an ordered state driven and maintained by the flow of energy across natural resistances and constraints, some of which are generated by the growth of biomass itself.

On a small scale these relationships are not apparent. A farmer never dreams that his contribution to biomass destruction is contributing to the temperature rise of the planet. But on a global scale, and over geologic time, relationships like those in Figure 2 emerge.

The fact that biomass production is autocatalytic, that is, the creation of new biomass is dependent upon the presence of pre-existing biomass, means that the more biomass is removed, the slower it is to replace itself. This flies in the face of the present day wisdom that says that biomass is a renewable resource. The people that denuded Easter Island ignored this fact as they coveted the last bits of biomass available, and the island has never recovered. Biomass removal for energy production not only takes away the resource, it damages the potential for recovery as well.

It is important to maintain a reservoir of healthy biomass, fully adapted to the climate so that an ecology can recover without having to re-evolve. As the biomass reservoir declines, climate instability creeps into the ecosystem, further restricting the ability of the biosphere to recover.

An understanding of how this interdependent, self-sustaining system arose has been largely absent from the annals of science until physicists and chemists got together with biologists in the latter part of the twentieth century. The basic interpretations of the laws of thermodynamics have been rearranged to account for energy flows and the natural ordering of systems that result. We will briefly reiterate the findings that lead to these ideas and the conclusions that they lead us to in this final chapter.

Origin of Variability: Variety in materials and differentials in energy potential are all due to energy flows[2]. All such differences cease when energy flow stops. In the absence of energy flows, all matter and energy differences diffuse into uniformity. But that's not the most surprising part. In order to cause differences the energy flow must be resisted. Without resistance no differentials would occur with or without energy flow.

There is a fundamental distribution of resistances in the universe that causes system variability to precipitate when energy flows through. Some of these resistances are associated with solid structures, some are associated with fluid matter and some seem to be fundamental properties

Chapter Thirty Seven
Order, its Origins and Accumulation

of matter and of space itself. Some have been in existence since the very moment of the Big bang itself, and some have precipitated into existence, emerged, if you will, as the universal system cooled and became more ordered.

These ideas argue that space itself is not uniform, but it is variegated with undulating patterns of resistances that are, to some degree, ordered. This order limits the maximum amount of disorder or entropy that space can contain. There is an underlying order associated with space that prevents it from being entirely uniform or random. Space, even without energy or mass contains the rudiments of structure even though its intensity has been diminishing for 13.8 billion years.

Were it entirely random, or uniform, space would be entirely dysfunctional. There is no purpose without order. And there is no predictability in a completely random system. The reason why intelligent people can argue that the universe is too improbable to be the result of random interactions of energy and matter is because it is true. Random interactions don't function. Any functional system is not random. So the argument of improbability simply demonstrates that the system is not random. Ordered systems are predictable, random ones are not. The fact that science can predict the behavior of systems demonstrates that they are not random, but ordered.

Space reveals its ordered nature through organization from energy flow. Organization in the form of radiation, light, and eventually, matter precipitate from energy flowing through organized space. Ordering constrains space, limiting the disordered configurations it can occupy and increasing the probability of its functionality. Order, complexity and functionality emerge as energy flows through the inherent resistances contained in space.

The Second Law of Thermodynamics: The Second Law of thermodynamics says that any process occurring in a thermodynamic system increases the entropy of the universe. Entropy is considered to be an inverse measure of the usefulness of the system. Usefulness is defined as the ability of the system to do work. A low entropy condition is considered useful (able to function or to do work) while a high entropy condition is considered not useful (unable to function or to do work). As the entropy content of the universe increases, the usefulness of its energy content decreases, the energy content stays the same, but it becomes less useful.

Any process that increases the entropy of the universe decreases the usefulness. The Second Law has been used to assure us that the universe is running down, that any process in a thermodynamic system increases its entropy and decreases its usefulness or ability to do work.

But more recent analysis visualizes the opposite mechanism taking place in systems that are not isolated from mass and energy flows originating elsewhere in the universe. When energy flows out of a system, it carries away entropy as well, and this tends to decrease the entropy content of the system. Since energy flows from a condition of high temperature to one of lower temperature, it always has more entropy with it when it leaves the system than it had when it entered the system. Energy flow through a system always depletes the system of entropy. As energy flows through a system, order is increased within the system and entropy is discharged to the outside universe.

Some systems, it seems, accumulate order as energy flow depletes their entropy content. The greater the temperature differential between incoming energy and outgoing energy, the more strongly the system is induced to produce order.

Energy enters the earth system with an entropy content equivalent to the temperature at the surface of the sun – a very low entropy level indeed. The earth radiates this energy back out into outer space at an entropy level equivalent to the temperature at the surface of the earth – a very high entropy level. The difference between these two entropy levels is a measure of the tendency of the earth to build order on its surface. It is because of this huge entropy difference that the surface of the earth becomes ordered. It develops an ordered climate system, it drives ocean currents, and it causes continents to drift. But most of all it causes biomass to organize and grow.

Chapter Thirty Seven
Order, its Origins and Accumulation

The amount of organizational complexity on earth is greater than other planets because of the entropy balance – not the energy balance. Heat leaving the earth is extracted into outer space by negative energy potential. As it is radiated away it carries a huge amount of entropy compared to the minimal amounts of entropy in the incoming solar radiation. This vast entropy imbalance leaves the earth with a strong tendency to generate order on its surface.

In accordance with the principals of radiative heat transfer, warmer areas radiate more heat into space than cooler areas leading to greater accumulations of order at the surface in warmer climates. This results in greater biomass production in warmer areas like the tropical rain forests.

Clearly in order for complexity to occur, the raw materials, most notably water and carbon dioxide, must be present. Desert areas are prime regions for biomass growth if they only had water present to participate in photosynthetic reactions. In the absence of water the surface accumulates incoming entropy in the form of increased temperature until the surface temperature becomes high enough to reject it either radiatively, into space, or convectively through the warming of the atmosphere and the resulting flow to a different place.

As the surface rejects entropy, either by radiation or by convection it produces order either by cooling, or by a phase change from vapor to liquid to solid (in order of decreasing entropy) or by condensation reactions like turning carbon dioxide and water into cellulose, or linking amino acids to form proteins, or by linking nucleotides to form a DNA molecule. or by adsorption processes. . These reactions are all means of rejecting entropy by increasingly ordering the surroundings.

Complexity is the means by which order is expressed and compounded by imposing a new level of order on a system that is already saturated by order at a lower level. The extraction of energy will drive these entropy rejection reactions, enhancing complexity until the organization becomes unstable to destructive mechanisms such as thermal agitation or diffusion.

It should be clear from this that as a planet cools, the destructive mechanisms such as thermal agitation diminish increasing the opportunity for ever-more elegant, sensitive, complexity and lower physical entropy levels. Conversely, the warming of a planet increases the destructive mechanisms of thermal agitation, a situation that diminishes the probability of survival of elegant sensitive, complex systems that may have evolved.

Biomass has a tendency to resist its own destruction through the production of structurally resilient solid materials. The Principle of Maximum Entropy Production Rate states that *"Entropy will be maximized as rapidly as allowed by system constraints"*. Biomass constrains the rate of production of entropy, creating a quasi-stable ecosystem that has an inherent tendency to resist its own destruction.

Once an ecosystem is destroyed it cannot restore itself except through a prolonged process of evolution or, at least, rebuilding through ecological succession leading to a climax community. But a residue of order, a matrix, is capable of retaining enough information and stabilizing conditions so that ecosystems are empowered to recover and expand more quickly.

Chapter Thirty Seven References

[1] Swenson, Rod: "The Fourth Law of Thermodynamics or the Law of Maximum Entropy Production (LMEP)": Chemistry, Vol 18, Issue 5 2009

[2] Matsuno, Koichiro and Swenson, Rod: "Thermodynamics in the Present Progressive mode and its Role in the Context of the Origin of Life": Biosystems, 51 (1999) PP. 53-61

Chapter Thirty-Eight

The Carbon Cycle and the Climate

Chapter Summary

Biomass is an important reservoir of ordered carbon in the circulating cycles that recirculate over, under, around and through the earth. It is also critical to the thermodynamic functioning of energy distribution processes on the surface of the earth. Its depletion disorganizes heat transfer processes, destabilizes the climate and prevents ecosystem recovery. With the biomass reserve reduced to nearly half of its original level, it is no longer justified to consider biomass a "renewable resource". Every effort must now be made to facilitate the recovery of our biomass resource.

This chapter will reiterate the importance of this conclusion.

Chapter Thirty Eight
The Carbon Cycle and the Climate

In Chapter Thirty Six we discussed the importance of maintaining a reservoir of healthy biomass on earth so that the ecology can sustain itself. The above ground biomass reservoir presently contains 610 gigatons of biomass carbon, which is supported by another 1560 gigatons of subterranean biomass carbon. The total terrestrial biomass, 2170 gigatons, provides organized structure to maintain order, organize the climate and maintain ecosystem services. When this structure is destroyed, order degenerates and climate systems become more uniform (warmer in northern latitudes) and more erratic. If the biosphere expands the climate system becomes more organized (cooler in northern latitudes) and stable.

In the illustration provided in Figure 2 it is aptly demonstrated that the biomass level of the earth's ecosystems has been devastatingly depleted in recent centuries. The figure also implies that the climate tends to warm, or equilibrate, whenever this is the case regardless of the causal mechanism or the prevailing temperature at the time.

In pursuit of an appropriate carbon balance a recommended practice has emerged to obtain energy from current carbon sources (biomass) rather than fossil fuels. This recommendation is based on the assertion that biomass is a "renewable" resource since it removes carbon dioxide from the atmosphere and replaces biomass as it regrows.

But this distinction, while quantitatively attractive, is qualitatively false. Fossil fuels replace themselves just as current carbon sources do. While the replacement rate is several orders of magnitude slower, it is not distinctly different in nature.

The real difference between the two types of fuels is that fossil fuels have been relieved of their structural complexity long ago through the process of fossilization and therefore have no ability to function in the biological world. Biomass has the property of still being functional (actively or passively) in the biological world. Combustion of biomass removes this important functionality from the bio system. Combustion of fossil fuels does not.

This is one of the reasons fossil fuels were so attractive in the first place. They could be removed and destroyed without interfering with the function of the biosphere. The switch was made for environmental reasons as well as economic reasons. It's an example of Robert Costanza's "Empty World" – "Full World" dichotomy. It's not OK when the world is starved for biomass, restricted in its rate of regeneration, and suffering the effects of reduced complexity and emergent thermodynamic equilibration, to seek to further deplete this resource for additional energy supply which will quickly degrade into ever greater entropy levels in the environment.

Figure 2 shows that the rate of surface biomass removal in recent centuries has greatly exceeded the rate of biomass replacement, resulting in a drastic biomass depletion rate in the earth's ecosystems.[1] This results in a dramatic decrease in ecosystem services, one of which is cooling the surface of the earth, and another is organization of the climate.

If biomass continues to be categorized as a "renewable" resource it will be catastrophic for the earth's ecosystems and for climate stability. At present removal rates our existing biomass supply has only a few centuries to go before it and its ecosystem services will be completely used up and relegated to history.

The atmosphere contains about 750 gigatons of carbon as gaseous carbon dioxide, a very high entropy state. Each year green plants in the biosphere (both aquatic and terrestrial) soak up about 213 gigatons of carbon from the atmosphere and convert it to biomass, a very low entropy state. This is made possible by the flow of energy through the biosphere, stripping the entropy from carbon dioxide and discharging it into outer space while ordering the carbon into low entropy biomass.

Recall that the high entropy state means that carbon dioxide is capable of doing very little work, if any at all. It is well to understand that carbon dioxide still has great value by virtue of the fact that, given the right conditions of energy throughput and constraints, it can be organized, that is, it is the raw material for making biomass, but let's keep our attention on the entropy state of the carbon at the moment.

471

Chapter Thirty Eight
The Carbon Cycle and the Climate

By virtue of the fact that biomass is in a low entropy state it is very useful, having a very high energy content and a great deal of order and functionality. Combustion of the biomass can create about 8,000 BTU of heat energy per pound at a very high temperature (up to 1900° C at stoichiometric air ratios, but usually much lower since control of air supply to, and combustion conditions in, gas/solid reactions is difficult). The heat content of biomass is a measure of the amount of work it can do when it is combusted. Combustion of the biomass liberates its heat of combustion at the sacrifice of its structure, its complexity, its solid state and its functionality, in short the sacrifice of its low entropy condition.

Biomass is useful in many other ways beyond its energy content. Its material strength and workability allow it to be used to make tools and weaponry of all description. It can be used for construction. Its softer, fleshy parts become food. It provides shade, shelter, water, temperature modulation and a host of other ecosystem services that make the surface of our planet habitable. Its low entropy content reduces the uniformity and adds to the orderliness of the climate, the structure and the energy distribution on the surface of the earth.

Unfortunately, biomass is, for the most part, a single use material. Once its use has been decided upon it is not normally useable for anything else. If it is used for fuel, it cannot be used for food, if it is used for food, it cannot be used for construction, if it is used for construction it cannot be used for tools, etc. If it is used for fuel, tools, construction or any other anthropologic purpose, it is no longer available for ecosystem services. Its decay rate is such that once it has finished one service life it is usually not in good enough condition to be reused in another application. It is dispensed to the ecological waste bin from which the inevitable increase in entropy returns it to its original high entropy state, carbon dioxide in the atmosphere. About 210 gigatons of carbon are returned to the atmosphere as CO_2 in this way each year.

Notice that the entire atmospheric reservoir of carbon dioxide turns over through the biomass cycle in about 3.5 years. The terrestrial biomass reservoir, about 2,170 gigatons as carbon, stores circulating carbon for about 19.5 years, almost 6 times as long as the atmosphere does.

The top layers of the ocean, those that interact with the atmosphere, contain 1020 gigatons of carbon, about 1.4 times as much as the atmosphere. The depths of the ocean contain about 51 times more, and the geologic cycle contains about 133,000 times as much.

An atom of carbon circulating in the atmosphere stays there about for an average of only 3.5 years. A carbon atom entering the terrestrial biosphere stays there for an average of 19.5 years. The residence time for carbon in the surface layers of the ocean is about 20 years; in the deep ocean about 382 years. A carbon atom entering the geosphere can look forward to being there, barring an unforeseen incident, such as a volcanic eruption, about 500,000,000 (500 million) years.

The question is, "How can we manipulate this maze of circulating streams and interacting carbon reservoirs to maximize the utility and functionality of biomass structures and to minimize the heat and entropy trapping effect of carbon dioxide in the atmosphere"? If we pull the carbon dioxide directly out of the atmosphere and inject it directly into the geosphere, we may relieve the earth of its inability to pass energy and entropy through the atmosphere, but we are eliminating the raw material needed to replace the missing biomass, which is needed to stabilize the climate.

If we return to Figure 2, we can see that we presently have about 600 gigatons of carbon in the surface biomass on earth. We also know that our climate is presently warming. In addition, we know from Figure 2 that the earth was beginning to warm from the Wisconsin Ice Sheet Episode when the biomass reached about 500 gigatons.

As the climate warmed, the biomass spread again to about 1000 gigatons. At that level of biomass, the climate was warming more slowly, if at all.. It was stabilizing and starting a new cycle. Global thermal transfer activity passed through a minimum at this point

Since the glacial minimum humankind has removed more biomass faster than any other force on earth. At 600 gigatons we are experiencing a warming trend just like what happened at the 500-gigaton level at the end of the Wisconsin Ice Sheet Episode.

Chapter Thirty Eight
The Carbon Cycle and the Climate

Today's biomass is about 400 gigatons short of the point where it brought about a stabilizing trend to the warming that occurred after the Wisconsin Glaciation. It would seem to make sense that boosting the biomass to 1000 gigatons again, by adding 400 gigatons of biomass, would stabilize the climate and bring about an end to the warming just as it did at the glacial minimum.

From pre-industrial times when the atmospheric carbon concentration was about 287 parts per million, to the present time when atmospheric carbon is 400 parts per million, the atmospheric carbon concentration has increased by 39%. That means that the pre-industrial atmosphere had 538 gigatons of carbon in it – 212 gigatons less than it has now.

Dr. Robert Monroe, of the Scripps Institution of Oceanography,[2] has noted: *"Recent estimates have calculated that 26 percent of all the carbon released as CO_2 from fossil fuel burning, cement manufacturing and land use changes over the decade 2002-2011 was absorbed by the oceans (about 28% went to plants and roughly 46% went to the atmosphere).*

From this we can deduce that 54% of CO_2 released went to sinks other than the atmosphere. If these ratios have not been subjected to very much historical change , the actual amount of carbon released from anthropogenic activities was more like 460 gigatons, a figure that compares quite nicely with the 400 gigatons displayed in Figure 2.

It doesn't take much of a stretch of the imagination to conclude that global warming and climate instability could be corrected if we restored the lost biomass to areas of the world that have been depleted or denuded by human activities.

China's Loess Plateau covers 640,000 square kilometers (158 million acres). There they have restored the biomass by planting more than 60 billion trees with a potential biomass payoff of more than 15 gigatons. The results on the regional climate and biomass productivity have been impressive.

The African Sahel covers an area of 1.2 million square miles (768million acres). There is no shortage of biomass-depleted areas on which to restore the biomass.

For comparison, the Sahara Desert, which has had periods of biomass-covered ecosystems in its history, has an area of 3.63 million square miles (2.32 trillion acres). Restoration of an area the size of the Sahara to forested ecosystems might restore 45% of the missing biomass carbon. Combined with the work already done in the Loess Plateau, this accomplishment would replace 60% of the missing biomass. And there are other regions of the world, Tropical, Temperate and Polar that would readily respond to the right combination of ecosystem recovery efforts. The means to accomplish the ends is available if the will and the motivation can be found in our present society.

Chapter Thirty Eight
The Carbon Cycle and the Climate

[1] Smil, Vaclav: "The Earth's Biosphere: Evaluation, Dynamics and Change": MIT Press, Cambridge, MA; Copyright 2002

[2] Monroe, Robert: "Scripps Institution of Oceanography, The Keeling Curve, Measurement Notes, How Much CO_2 Can the Oceans Take up?" scripps.usd.edu/programs/keelingcurve/2013/07/03/how.much.co2 can the oceans take up

Chapter Thirty-Nine

Reducing Entropy – Rebuilding the Order of the Earth

Chapter Summary

To restore the lost biomass in the biosphere would require the creation of 400 gigatons of biological carbon. To restore the atmospheric carbon dioxide to pre-Industrial Revolution levels would require the creation of only 250 to 300 gigatons.

These options would stabilize the climate and restore the planetary energy balance and provide the necessary entropy rejection rate to sustain the delicate balance of order in its required steady state condition, to maintain the complexity of living systems on earth.

Chapter Thirty Nine
Rebuilding the Order of the Earth

Since the nineteenth century the biomass content of the earth has plummeted by nearly 400 gigatons, wiping out the gains that were made over the 10,000 year period that followed the maximum extent of the Wisconsin Ice Sheet. This loss of biomass has triggered a warming cycle just like the one that occurred 20,000 years ago. It is a natural reaction of the earth to diminishing energy extraction caused by sluggish permeability of the atmospheric boundary to energy and entropy contained in long wave radiation.

Energy and entropy that cannot penetrate the atmospheric boundary layer must distribute themselves over the surface of the earth. Energy that distributes itself warms the surface. Entropy that distributes itself destroys the order of the climate and of the biosphere.

The energy from the sun impinging on the earth is short wavelength, low entropy, energy. The energy leaving the surface of the earth is long wavelength, high entropy, energy. As discussed in Chapters Five and Six of this book, establishing an energy balance automatically creates an entropy deficit that creates and maintains ordered systems on earth.

This fact was recognized by Ilya Prigogine, a Belgian physical chemist and Nobel Laureate who also postulated that biological systems were *dissipative structures* generated by the rejection of entropy by the system.[1] Ecosystems, he proposed were products of non-equilibrium thermodynamics created by the extraction of entropy. Entropy removal has to take place across a system boundary, and biological systems develop extensive, convoluted boundaries in order to more effectively dissipate entropy. That's what living systems are, dissipative boundaries surrounding systems that become ordered by rejecting entropy.

Order is fragile and degenerates to form entropy unless it is prevented from doing so by barriers or constraints that maintain differentials. Even so, barriers and constraints are imperfect, and ordered systems degenerate into entropy. The only stability (other than an entropy heat death) is a quasi-stability dependent upon flow of energy and materials through a system to remain stable.

Incoming energy can do work on the system to combat the advance of entropy and create regional low entropy concentrations. Outgoing energy can carry away the entropy generated as order degrades. The persistent complex nature of biomass functions to stabilize and constrain energy and entropy flow, generating quasi-stable systems. The more biomass there is, the more dissipative surfaces are available to reject entropy, and the more structured and stable the system becomes.

This important fact was understood by Eric D. Schneider, an American marine biologist and thermodynamicist, at the National Oceanic and Atmospheric Administration and Director of the National Marine Water Quality Laboratory of the Environmental Protection Agency. Schneider teamed up with J. J. Kay, a Canadian ecological scientist to identify the ecological implications of non-equilibrium thermodynamic processes. The literature is rich with papers written by these two scientists, and the interested reader should read several of them to fully understand the impact of this rapidly expanding field of knowledge on the physical sciences.[2, 3, 4, 5]

In their paper called "Life as a Manifestation of the Second Law of Thermodynamics" Schneider and Kay cite the work of Luvall and Holbo,[6, 7][8] and Luvall et al[9] to emphasize the function of biomass ecosystems in cooling and stabilizing the earth's surface and its climate. They say the following about the work of these scientists:

> *Their technique allows assessments of energy budgets of terrestrial landscapes, integrating attributes of the ecosystems, including vegetation, leaf and canopy morphology, biomass, species composition and canopy water status. Luvall and his co-workers have documented ecosystem energy budgets, including tropical forests, mid-latitude varied ecosystems, and semi-arid ecosystems. Their data shows one unmistakable trend, that when other variables are constant, the more developed the ecosystem, the colder its surface temperature and the more degraded its reradiated energy.*

This paragraph makes it clear that degraded ecosystems are directly responsible for increased temperatures at the earth's surface and in its atmosphere. When more than half of the biosphere is operating at sub-climax conditions, warming of the climate is to be expected. Human degradation of the biosphere and its ecosystems leads to thermodynamic consequences that result in warming of the planet and its atmosphere.

Upon the death of J. J. Kay in 2004, Schneider teamed up with science writer Dorian Sagan to write a book, "*Into the Cool: Energy Flow, Thermodynamics and Life*", a wonderful read for the educated lay person describing how matter responds to energy flow.[10]

Biomass expansion is a self-generating, autocatalytic, process. The rate of expansion of biomass is a function of the amount of biomass in existence. In order to stabilize our out-of-control climate system it is necessary to increase the amount of biomass in our ecosystem with its biological barriers and constraints that promote quasi-stability and continuous energy flows.[11]

The generation of dissipative surfaces is recognized as part of the evolutionary process as discussed in a book by Daniel R. Brooks and E. O. Wiley.[12]

The task before us is to revegetate the planet with a healthy, stabilizing blanket of biomass. This will maintain the natural order of the climate system, isolating tropical warmth at the equator and polar cold at the poles.

The goal is to produce 400 gigatons of carbon in surface biomass to restore the climate. We have discussed the Three North Shelterbelt Project on the Loess Plateau in northern China where 60 billion trees have been planted, sequestering an estimated 15 gigatons of carbon from the atmosphere and converting it to biomass. It would take 28 shelterbelt programs to reach our goal.

Such projects would not only correct atmospheric instability and biomass shortage problems, they would also create ecosystem stability, biological diversity, life style quality, economic vitality and better living conditions for native peoples wherever such projects were undertaken.

Chapter Thirty Nine References

1 Prigogine, Ilya: "From Being to Becoming: Time and Complexity in the Physical Sciences": W H Freeman and Company, San Francisco; Copyright 1980

2 Schneider, Eric D. and Kay, J. J.: "Thermodynamics and Measures of Ecosystem Integrity": in Ecological Indicators, Volume 1, D. H. McKenzie, DD. E. Hyatt and V. J. MMc Donald (eds); *Proceedings of the International Symposium on Ecological Indicators, Fort Lauderdale, Fl; Elsivier, pp 159-182*

3 Schneider E.D. and Kay J. J.: "Complexity and Thermodynamics: Towards a New Ecology" *Futures* 24 (6) pp 626-647; 1994

4 Schneider E. D. and Kay J. J. :"Life as a Manifestation of the Second Law of Thermodynamics": *Mathematical and Computer Modeling, Volume 19, No. 6-8, pp25-48*

5 Schneider E. D. and Kay, J. J.: "Order From Disorder: The Thermodynamics of Complexity in Biology": in Michael P. Murphy, Luke A. J. O'Neill (ed), "What is Life: The Next Fifty Years: Reflections on the future of Biology", Cambridge University Press, pp161-172

6 J. C. Luvall and H. R. Holbo: "Measurements of Short Term Thermal Responses in Coniferous Forest Caonpies Using Thermal Scanner Data": 1989, *Remote Sense. Environ. 27*, (1-10)

7 J. C. Luvall and H. R. Holbo: "Thermal Remote Sensing Methods in Landscape Ecology": (1991), *Quantitative Methods in Landscape Ecology, (Eds: M. Turner and E. H. Gardner), Chapter 6, Springer-Verlag*

8 H. R. Holbo and J. C. Luvall: "Modeling Surface Temperature Distribution in Forest Landscapes": *Remote Sense. Environ. 27, (11-24)*

[9] J. C. Luvall, D. Lieberman, M. Lieberman, G. S. Hartshorn and R. Peralta: "Estimation of Tropical Forest Canopy Temperatures, Thermal Response Numbers and Evapotranspiration Using an Aircraft Based Thermal Sensor": (1990) *Photogrametric Engineering and Remote Sensing ,* **%^** (10) pp 1393-1410

[10] Schneider, E. D. and Sagan, Dorion: "Into the Cool: Energy Flow, Thermodynamics and Life": University of Chicago Press, Chicago, IL; Copyright 2005

[11] Sagan Dorion and Whiteside, Jessica H.: "Gradient Reduction Theory: Thermodynamics and the Purpose of Life": in "*Scientists Debate Gaia: The Next Century, p 173, MIT Press*

[12] Brooks, Daniel R. and Wiley, E. O. : "Evolution as Entropy: Toward a Unified Theory of Biology": University of Chicago Press, Chicago, IL; copyright 1986

About the Author

Dan Young is a graduate of the University of California at Berkeley with a Bachelor-of-Science degree in Chemical Engineering. He took a Master-of-Science degree in Environmental Science at New Jersey Institute of Technology in Newark, New Jersey.

Dan worked in chemical process design for pharmaceutical manufacturers in New York State and New Jersey before he developed his interest in water conservation and use. He pursued his interest with companies manufacturing water treatment equipment for municipal and industrial applications including chemical manufacturers, steel producers, nuclear power generators and food processors as well as developers and small municipalities. He set up a municipal water treatment facility in Egypt and wastewater facilities at oil rigs in Alaska.

Other areas of experience include waste treatment processes including liquid-solids separation, biological oxidation, multiple effect evaporation, drying and toxics removal (including precipitation, electrolytic plating, ion exchange and adsorption processes). He also has experience with the design, fabrication, installation and operation of solid waste combustion and energy recovery equipment. He has provided energy consumption assessment services for major corporations.

As a Professional Engineer, Dan established his own engineering company providing site assessment services, groundwater monitoring, underground storage tank removal, and hazardous waste management services.

Dan retired in1995 to work on carbon complexity and conservation studies. He no longer provides professional engineering services. He maintains an interest in carbon studies, groundwater protection, environmental quality, and sustainable living.

In 1997 Dan founded a research organization he called Carbon Resources Research based on the premise that carbon, the chemical basis of life, is a precious resource. It is not to be captured or sequestered and thrown away as a waste material. It needs to be carefully managed in order to maintain environmental conditions that are suitable to life as we know it.

Our research programs fall into three major areas:

- Basic understanding of environmental physics and chemistry
- Assessing the effects of elemental carbon on agricultural and ecological productivity
- Development of systems to recycle carbon with four major goals:
  - ❖ Retaining complexity
  - ❖ Optimizing energy efficiency
  - ❖ Maximizing agricultural and ecological productivity
  - ❖ Reducing atmospheric carbon dioxide concentrations

Made in the USA
Coppell, TX
28 September 2023

22157201R00275